D1635947

SPECULATION

SPECULATION

*A HISTORY OF THE FINE LINE
BETWEEN GAMBLING
AND INVESTING*

Stuart Banner

OXFORD
UNIVERSITY PRESS

OXFORD

UNIVERSITY PRESS

Oxford University Press is a department of the University of Oxford. It furthers
the University's objective of excellence in research, scholarship, and education
by publishing worldwide. Oxford is a registered trade mark of Oxford University
Press in the UK and certain other countries.

Published in the United States of America by Oxford University Press
198 Madison Avenue, New York, NY 10016, United States of America.

© Oxford University Press 2017

Library of Congress Cataloging-in-Publication Data
Names: Banner, Stuart, 1963– author.
Title: Speculation : a history of the fine line between gambling and investing / Stuart Banner.
Description: New York, NY : Oxford University Press, 2017. | Description based on print version
record and CIP data provided by publisher; resource not viewed.
Identifiers: LCCN 2016017786 (print) | LCCN 2016016710 (ebook) | ISBN 9780190623050
(E-book) | ISBN 9780190623067 (E-book) | ISBN 9780190623043 (hardcover : alk. paper)
Subjects: LCSH: Investments—Law and legislation—United States—History. |
Capital market—Law and legislation—United States—History. | Speculation—Law and
legislation—United States—History. | Speculation—United States—History.
Classification: LCC KF1070 (print) | LCC KF1070 .B365 2017 (ebook) |
DDC 346.73/0922—dc23 LC record available at https://lccn.loc.gov/2016017786

1 3 5 7 9 8 6 4 2
Printed by Sheridan Books, Inc., United States of America

CONTENTS

—⟫◆⟪—

ACKNOWLEDGMENTS

For advice on drafts of chapters, thanks to Iman Anabtawi, Steve Bainbridge, Steve Bank, James Park, and participants in workshops at the University of Minnesota, UNLV, and UCLA. For help with the research, thanks to the librarians at the UCLA School of Law and the archivists at the Franklin D. Roosevelt Presidential Library, the Harvard Law Library, the Herbert Hoover Presidential Library, the John F. Kennedy Presidential Library, the Library of Congress, the Morgan Library, the New York Stock Exchange, the University of Illinois at Chicago, the University of Virginia, the Wisconsin Historical Society, and Yale University.

ABBREVIATIONS

———⊰◆⊱———

AAB   Adolf A. Berle papers, Franklin D. Roosevelt Presidential
          Library, Hyde Park, New York
AS   Alexander Sachs papers, Franklin D. Roosevelt Presidential
          Library, Hyde Park, New York
CBT   Chicago Board of Trade records, Special Collections,
          University of Illinois at Chicago
CG   Carter Glass papers, Albert and Shirley Small Special
          Collections Library, University of Virginia
FDR   Franklin D. Roosevelt papers as president, Franklin
          D. Roosevelt Presidential Library, Hyde Park, New York
FF   Felix Frankfurter papers, Manuscript Division, Library of
          Congress, Washington, DC
GEA   George E. Akerson papers, Herbert Hoover Presidential
          Library, West Branch, Iowa
HHL   Hoover Presidential files, Herbert Hoover Presidential
          Library, West Branch, Iowa
HPPF   Hoover Post-Presidential files, Herbert Hoover Presidential
          Library, West Branch, Iowa
JML-HLS   James McCauley Landis papers, Harvard Law School
          Library, Cambridge, Massachusetts
JML-LC   James McCauley Landis papers, Manuscript Division,
          Library of Congress, Washington, DC

JNF   Jerome New Frank papers, Sterling Memorial Library, Yale University, New Haven, Connecticut

JPK   Joseph P. Kennedy personal papers, John F. Kennedy Presidential Library, Boston, Massachusetts

JPL   Joseph P. Lash papers, Franklin D. Roosevelt Presidential Library, Hyde Park, New York

JPM   J. P. Morgan Jr. papers, Morgan Library, New York

NYSE   New York Stock Exchange Archives, New York

WDS   Wisconsin Department of Securities: Investigation and Enforcement files, 1923–62, Wisconsin Historical Society, Madison, Wisconsin

WFV   William F. Vilas papers, Wisconsin Historical Society, Madison, Wisconsin

WOD   William O. Douglas papers, Manuscript Division, Library of Congress, Washington, DC

SPECULATION

Introduction

"WHEN AS A YOUNG and unknown man I started to be successful I was referred to as a gambler," the banker Ernest Cassel once said. "My operations increased in scope. Then I was a speculator. The sphere of my activities continued to expand and presently I was known as a banker. Actually I had been doing the same thing all the time."[1]

Cassel was retelling an old joke, but behind it lurked a dilemma that has troubled the legal system for a long time, a problem that is the subject of this book. For centuries there has been a consensus that *investment* is very useful and ought to be encouraged. There has also been a near consensus, one that has weakened recently but is still substantial, that *gambling* is dangerous and ought to be at least discouraged and maybe even prohibited. But what about *speculation*? Speculation lies somewhere between investment and gambling. It has attributes of both. Should speculation be legal? Should it be illegal? Should some kinds be legal and other kinds illegal? Which kinds? Throughout American history (and the history of other places too, but this book is just about the United States), speculation has presented a puzzle to the legal system. To figure out how to treat speculation, we have always needed to distinguish between two kinds of risky commerce: a good kind the law should promote and a bad kind the law should deter. We have always needed to draw a line between investment and gambling. This book is a history of our efforts to draw this line.

1 The quotation was attributed to Cassel by Bernard Baruch. Carter Field, *Bernard Baruch: Park Bench Statesman* (New York: McGraw-Hill, 1944), 76–77.

The issue is particularly salient today, when many argue that the recent financial crisis was caused by overspeculation, and that the way to prevent a recurrence is to prohibit certain risky transactions. Others respond by citing the benefits of robust markets and the dangers of overregulation. This book shows that this debate has been a perennial feature of our history, and that many of the same arguments have been made, on both sides, after every financial downturn since the 1790s.

Ambivalence about speculation can be found in the slipperiness of the word itself, which is notoriously hard to pin down.[2] Americans have offered competing definitions for two centuries, without coming any closer to agreement. Sometimes "speculation" is a pejorative term, implying that a speculator is someone engaging in unsavory conduct, as distinguished from an investor or a businessperson. Sometimes it is used in a morally neutral sense. And sometimes "speculation" is a term used with approval, often to distinguish the speculator from the gambler.

The difficulty in distinguishing the good risky transactions from the bad, and thus the difficulty in figuring out how to regulate speculators, has been caused by genuine substantive disagreement about the pros and cons of particular sorts of transactions. Should people be allowed to risk their fortunes and the welfare of their families by buying assets solely for the purpose of selling them later at a higher price? Should they be allowed to sell assets they don't yet own, in the hopes of profiting from a decline in the assets' value? Should they be allowed to buy and sell complex financial derivatives? Questions like these have constantly been asked throughout American history. The conflicting answers have been driven in part by differences in opinion about the economic consequences of particular transactions and in part by differences in moral views as to the propriety of particular forms of conduct.

---

2 Reuven Brenner with Gabrielle A. Brenner, *Gambling and Speculation: A Theory, a History, and a Future of Some Human Decisions* (Cambridge: Cambridge University Press, 1990), 90–112; Christine Hurt, "Regulating Public Morals and Private Markets: Online Securities Trading, Internet Gambling, and the Speculation Paradox," *Boston University Law Review* 86 (2006): 371–441; Thomas Lee Hazen, "Disparate Regulatory Schemes for Parallel Activities: Securities Regulation, Derivatives Regulation, Gambling, and Insurance," *Annual Review of Banking & Financial Law* 24 (2005): 375–441; Shaheen Borna and James Lowry, "Gambling and Speculation," *Journal of Business Ethics* 6 (1987): 219–24.

In economic terms, speculators have always presented the legal system with a dilemma, because the very things that make speculation useful can also make it dangerous. Sometimes speculators are like insurance companies: They make money by taking on risks others wish to shed. Sometimes speculators make markets more liquid, which makes markets more useful for people wishing to buy or sell. Sometimes speculators make markets more stable by selling when prices are high and buying when they are low. These benefits of speculation counsel in favor of not regulating speculators too strictly. On the other hand, speculators sometimes bankrupt themselves, and sometimes their financial distress hurts others, including their families and their creditors. Speculation can even imperil the entire financial system. These dangers counsel in favor of strict regulation. This is the dilemma. The more we give speculators free rein, the greater the risk that speculators will bring harm to others. But the more we constrain speculators, the smaller the benefits of speculation.

For two centuries, Americans have tried to come up with forms of regulation that will give us the good aspects of speculation without the bad. We have tried to prohibit certain transactions while allowing others. We have tried to keep particular speculators on a tight leash while giving more freedom to others. But no solution has ever been uncontroversial or permanent. The economic dilemma has never gone away, and probably never will, because it is a real tradeoff between positive and negative consequences of the same activity.

Speculation has presented the legal system with a moral dilemma as well, one that is also likely to be with us forever. Speculation has long been decried as immoral—a method of profiting by impoverishing others, a device for making money without performing any useful service, and a scheme rigged by crafty insiders to exploit the ordinary person. Speculation has been defended against such attacks for just as long. This moral debate is connected to the economic debate, because some of the moral critique of speculation has always rested on the belief that speculators are not providing value to society in the same way that producers are. But the debates are different and always have been. One can disapprove of speculators on moral grounds even if one accepts that speculators are sometimes useful, and one can refrain from moral disapproval even if one thinks that speculators help no one but themselves.

The moral dilemma, like the economic dilemma, is how to prohibit the bad without also prohibiting the good. The most ardent moral critics of speculation have never wanted to prohibit investment. The trouble is in distinguishing the two, because otherwise anything we do to reduce the quantity of one will reduce the quantity of the other. There is again a real tradeoff between the positive and negative attributes of a single activity.

Of course, attitudes toward speculation have been influenced as much by short-term contemporary events as by long-term basic beliefs. Regulation has followed a familiar pattern: New restrictions are virtually always imposed after market downturns, while existing restrictions tend to be relaxed, at least in practice, while the market is on the rise.[3] When people are making money, few elected officials are eager to stop the party, and when people who have lost money are looking around for someone to blame, speculators are always a tempting target. Debates about speculation tend to flare up at extremes, during booms and busts, when the benefits and perils of speculation are most visible. But the attitudes those debates elicit are never absent, and in some ways they have been remarkably consistent over two centuries.

Conventional thought on these questions has changed considerably over the past two centuries, in some respects. In the late eighteenth century, courts were reluctant to enforce commercial contracts that seemed too risky, but they nevertheless enforced bets on horse races. A half century later, the courts had switched positions on both. In other respects, however, conventional thought has scarcely changed at all. Consider these reactions to the financial crisis: The crisis was caused by overspeculation; the victims included small investors lured by unscrupulous speculators with promises of high returns; and the federal government should have intervened before prices rose too high. These are familiar sentiments, but these particular samples are reactions to the financial crisis of 1792, from Alexander Hamilton, Thomas Jefferson,

---

3 Erik F. Gerding, *Law, Bubbles, and Financial Regulation* (London: Routledge, 2014); Nolan McCarty, Keith T. Poole, and Howard Rosenthal, *Political Bubbles: Financial Crises and the Failure of American Democracy* (Princeton, N.J.: Princeton University Press, 2013).

and a correspondent to John Adams, respectively.[4] Similar views have been expressed after every market downturn up to the present.

Debates over speculation have always been closely related to many other issues, but because this book maintains a tight focus on the difficulty of drawing a line between good risks and bad, I want to be as clear as possible as to what the book is *not* about. It is not a history of all commercial regulation or all regulation of financial markets. A great deal of commercial and financial regulation concerns (and has always concerned) other matters, like preventing fraud, but this book has little to say about them. This is not a book that adds to the already-enormous literature about what causes financial crises or how to prevent them. Worries about financial crises have played a big role in forming attitudes toward speculation, but this book is about the attitudes, not the crises themselves. Nor is this book a history of speculation or of speculators. There are already many books about celebrated speculators and speculative episodes, and I am interested in them here only to the extent that they had some bearing on how the legal system has tried to distinguish investing from gambling.

So what *is* the difference between investing and gambling? Where exactly *is* the line that separates good speculation from bad speculation? The point of this book is that these are questions over which people have always disagreed, and are likely always to disagree, because at all times people have held different views about the moral and economic consequences of risky commerce. If you have an opinion on these questions, you're likely to find that many people expressed your opinion long before you were born, and that many of their contemporaries thought your opinion was nonsense. A good place to start is with one prominent critic of speculators, Abraham Lincoln.

---

4 Alexander Hamilton to William Seton, 4 Apr. 1792, Harold C. Syrett et al., eds., *The Papers of Alexander Hamilton* (New York: Columbia University Press, 1961–87), 11:225–26; Thomas Jefferson to David Humphreys, 9 Apr. 1792, Julian P. Boyd et al., eds., *The Papers of Thomas Jefferson* (Princeton, N.J.: Princeton University Press, 1950–), 23:386–87; Nathaniel Hazard to John Adams, 16 Apr. 1792, Founders Online, National Archives (founders.archives.gov/documents/Adams/99-02-02-1337).

I

The Land of Speculation

ABRAHAM LINCOLN BLAMED THE speculators.

In 1862, under the fiscal strain of the Civil War, the government had gone off the gold standard. The "greenback," the Union paper currency, had previously been fixed at one paper dollar per gold dollar, but once the greenback floated against gold, its value plummeted. By the summer of 1864, a dollar of gold was trading for nearly $2.50 in greenbacks. The Union currency had lost more than half its value. Because the government paid for the war in greenbacks, a weaker currency meant a weaker military. If speculators were intentionally driving down the greenback, that would be an act tantamount to sabotage.[1]

Andrew Curtin, the governor of Pennsylvania, happened to be visiting the White House on one of the greenback's better days, when it gained a few percent against gold. When Curtin mentioned this news, Lincoln's face knotted up in anger. "Curtin," he asked, "what do you think of those fellows in Wall Street, who are gambling in gold at such a time as this?" "They are a set of sharks," Curtin replied. Lincoln pounded his fist on the table. "For my part," he exclaimed, "I wish every one of them had his *devilish* head shot off!"[2]

1 Richard Franklin Bensel, *Yankee Leviathan: The Origins of Central State Authority in America, 1859–1877* (Cambridge: Cambridge University Press, 1990), 152; Gregor W. Smith and R. Todd Smith, "Greenback-Gold Returns and Expectations of Resumption, 1862–1879," *Journal of Economic History* 57 (1997): 698; *New York Times*, 23 June 1864, 3.
2 Francis Bicknell Carpenter, *Six Months at the White House with Abraham Lincoln* (New York: Hurd and Houghton, 1866), 84.

Lincoln was hardly alone in blaming speculators for the depreciation of the greenback. Salmon Chase, the secretary of the Treasury, sternly informed Congress that the dollar's decline against gold was attributable to "the efforts of speculators." Senator John Sherman, who had succeeded to Chase's seat in the Senate and who would himself become Treasury secretary a decade later, shared Lincoln's and Chase's certainty. "We are confident," he declared, that "speculative operations in gold at this time have an injurious effect on the public credit." Sherman accordingly introduced a bill to prohibit speculative transactions in gold.[3]

Lincoln, Chase, and Sherman were reacting to an immediate crisis, but behind their harsh judgment was a long and contradiction-filled history of thought regarding speculators and speculation. Americans were inveterate speculators—on that point there was little disagreement. But the consequences of all this speculation, and the moral character of the speculators, were matters of considerable debate.

THE GREATEST SHARPERS IN THE UNIVERSE

Foreign visitors to the United States often remarked on Americans' passion for speculation. "An American merchant is an enthusiast who seems to delight in enterprise in proportion as it is connected with danger," declared the German journalist Francis Grund. "He ventures his fortune with the same heroism with which the sailor risks his life; and is as ready to embark on a new speculation after the failure of a favorite project, as the mariner is to navigate a new ship, after his own has become a wreck." In Chicago, the English writer Harriet Martineau reported that "the streets were crowded with land speculators, hurrying from one sale to another," to the point where "it seemed as if some prevalent mania infected the whole people." The French economist Michel Chevalier found the same atmosphere in Pennsylvania. "Every body is speculating, and every thing has become an object of speculation," he observed. "The most daring enterprises find encouragement; all projects find subscribers." For an American, insisted the

3 *Congressional Globe*, 15 Apr. 1864, 1640.

English missionary Isaac Fidler, trading "upon speculation and credit" was simply "the custom of his country."[4]

Observers offered a variety of theories to explain why Americans were such ardent speculators. Tocqueville chalked it up to democracy. "Those who live amid democratic instability constantly have the image of chance before their eyes, and in the end they love all undertakings in which chance plays a role," he reasoned. "They are therefore all brought into commerce, not only because of the gain it promises them, but for love of the emotions that it gives them." Chevalier cited puritanical social norms, which left speculation the only available way to have fun. "Public opinion and the pulpit forbid sensual gratifications, wine, women, and the display of a princely luxury; cards and dice are equally prohibited," he mused. "The American therefore, has recourse to business for the strong emotions which he requires to make him feel life. He launches with delight into the ever-moving sea of speculation." The English naval officer Frederick Marryat, perhaps more plausibly, emphasized the fast-changing economic conditions in the United States. "If an American has money sufficient to build a two-story house, he will raise it up to four stories on speculation," Marryat remarked. "They speculate on the future, but the future with them is not distant as it is with us." But whatever the reason, foreign travelers had little doubt of Americans' propensity to speculate. "Were I to characterise the *United States,*" one English tourist concluded, "it should be by the appellation of the *land of speculation.*"[5]

4 Francis J. Grund, *The Americans, in Their Moral, Social, and Political Relations* (Boston: Marsh, Capen and Lyon, 1837), 240–41; Harriet Martineau, *Society in America* (London: Saunders and Otley, 1837), 1:350; Michel Chevalier, *Society, Manners and Politics in the United States* (Boston: Weeks, Jordan and Co., 1839), 305; Isaac Fidler, *Observations on Professions, Literature, Manners, and Emigration, in the United States and Canada* (New York: J. & J. Harper, 1833), 76.

5 Alexis de Tocqueville, *Democracy in America* (1835–40), ed. Harvey C. Mansfield and Delba Winthrop (Chicago: University of Chicago Press, 2000), 528; Chevalier, *Society, Manners and Politics,* 309; Frederick Marryat, *Diary in America* (1839), ed. Jules Zanger (Bloomington: Indiana University Press, 1960), 137; William Priest, *Travels in the United States of America* (London: J. Johnson, 1802), 132.

When Americans noticed the same trait in themselves, they tended to deplore it. "We know that there is a wild and daring spirit of mercantile speculation among us, and that there is such a thing as tempting this spirit, to a most disastrous extent," lamented the New Yorker Charles Glidden Haines. "The spirit of speculation beats high; extravagant and disastrous contracts are entered into, and golden dreams of wealth too often mislead, even the most cautious." A contemporary agreed that "speculation may perhaps be considered one of the foibles, to use no harsher name, of the American character." Another lamented "those peculiar characteristics of the American people which lead them rather to shine as jobbers and gamblers than to excel as merchants." As more and more businesses took the corporate form to sell shares to investors, some worried about all the new corporations for precisely this reason. "The people of these United States, are a race of men having few, if any equals in the world," declared one skeptic. "But they have their foibles. They cannot harden their hearts against the seductions of SPECULATION." As another put it, "there is not a nation on earth so vigilant to watch and so eager to catch at a prospect of speculation, as the citizens of the U. States."[6]

Were Americans more prone to speculation than Europeans? The economist John McVickar thought so. "We observe in our country," he reasoned, "the greater frequency of individual failures and of general commercial revolutions, than is exhibited in most of the older countries of Europe, where something like the slow pulse of age seems to render comparatively innoxious those seeds of disease, which in our own warmer temperament, run out into unsound and feverish speculation." The *Bankers' Magazine* thought so too. "The English might teach us Americans a wholesome lesson," it reflected. "It seldom happens that an English merchant, tradesman, or banker abandons his rightful trade or calling to engage in any thing like doubtful speculation." A missionary journal agreed that "in no other country has this rage for speculation

---

6 Charles G. Haines, *Substance of Mr. Haines' Remarks, Made at the City Hotel* (New York: William A. Mercein, 1823), 9; *Auctions Inconsistent with Regular Trade* (New York: Van Winkle, Wiley & Co., 1817), 4; "Merchants and Speculators," *The Round Table* 9 (1869): 294; *Letter on the Use and Abuse of Incorporations* (New York: G. & C. Carvill, 1827), 23; *New-Bedford Mercury*, 15 Apr. 1825, 3.

been more fully shown than in the United States." But this was hardly a universal view. James Kent, one of the leading judges of the early republic, recalled that there was no shortage of speculation in Europe either. "The dreams and the madness of speculation," he concluded, "is a disease which has prevailed on each side of the *Atlantic*."[7]

The primary commodity in which early Americans speculated was land. There was plenty of it; it came in all kinds, from small parcels of developed land in eastern cities to vast and scarcely populated western territories; and its prices fluctuated, sometimes quite sharply. As Charles Francis Adams complained, "the great object of domestic speculation in America is undoubtedly land." When lots were sold in the new capital city of Washington, according to Justice Hugh Henry Brackenridge of the Pennsylvania Supreme Court, most of the initial purchases "were on the speculation of an under sale to others, before the money was paid" by the ostensible buyer. Up in Maine, reported the promoter Moses Greenleaf, many of the landholders were nonresident speculators, who "purchased with a view of retaining the land for a time, in expectation of immense profits from the sale, when the country about them should become improved, and peopled by the exertions of others, without any trouble of their own." Affluent and prominent Americans pooled their capital to form land companies, some of the largest business enterprises of the era, to buy enormous swaths of land in the West in the hope that future settlement would make the land more valuable. Land was simply a smart investment, advised the French lawyer J. P. Brissot de Warville, who took a close look at the land market while touring the new nation in 1788. Rather than putting money in a bank to provide for one's children, Brissot suggested, "nothing appears to me better to answer this wise precaution, than to place such money on the cultivated soil of the United States."[8]

7 John McVickar, *Hints on Banking* (New York: Vanderpool & Cole, 1827), 4; "The Causes of Commercial Crisis," *Bankers' Magazine* 5 (1850): 1; "On the Fluctuations of Property, and the Increase of Speculation," *The Panoplist, and Missionary Herald* 16 (1820): 454; *Jackson v. Port*, 17 Johns. 479 (N.Y. Sup. 1820).
8 Malcolm J. Rohrbough, *The Land Office Business: The Settlement and Administration of American Public Lands, 1789–1837* (New York: Oxford University Press, 1968); Robert P. Swierenga, *Pioneers and Profits: Land Speculation on the Iowa Frontier* (Ames: Iowa State University Press, 1968); Elizabeth Blackmar, *Manhattan*

Contemporaries had little doubt that the United States was very different from Europe in this regard. "In Europe the value of real estate is in general comparatively stationary," explained the chemist Robert Hare, "but here it is always an article of speculation; and as a large portion, while unproductive, is still held with a view to its future value, the estimate put upon that value is liable to great changes." In Britain, noted Massachusetts Chief Justice Isaac Parker, no one owned sections of forest far away from their homes. "In this country, on the contrary," he observed, "there are many large tracts of uncultivated territory owned by individuals who have no intention of reducing them to a state of improvement, but consider them rather as subjects of speculation and sale." It was because of "the unrestrained spirit of speculation," agreed William Tilghman, the chief justice of Pennsylvania's Supreme Court, that "we see freehold estates pass in rapid circulation from owner to owner."[9]

Financial assets soon became a second big area of speculation, first with the issuance of state and national public debt securities to finance the American Revolution, then with the sale of US debt securities in the early 1790s, and finally with the steady expansion, all through the early republic, of the market for shares in banks and other business corporations. "Stockjobbing drowns every other subject," James Madison complained in 1791, shortly after shares of the Bank of the United States were first sold to the public. In New York, he reported, "the Coffee House is in an eternal buzz with the gamblers." Henry Lee traveled from Philadelphia to Alexandria, Virginia, around the same time and discovered that "my whole rout[e] presented to me one continued scene of stock gambling; agriculture commerce & even the fair sex relinquished,

for Rent, 1785–1850 (Ithaca, N.Y.: Cornell University Press, 1989), 183–212; Charles Francis Adams, *Reflections Upon the Present State of the Currency in the United States* (Boston: Ezra Lincoln, 1837), 21; *Stoddart v. Smith*, 5 Binn. 355 (Pa. 1812); Moses Greenleaf, *A Statistical View of the District of Maine* (Boston: Cummings and Hilliard, 1816), 92; Shaw Livermore, *Early American Land Companies: Their Influence on Corporate Development* (New York: Commonwealth Fund, 1939); J. P. Brissot de Warville, *New Travels in the United States of America* (Boston: Joseph Bumstead, 1797), 41.
9 Robert Hare, *An Effort to Refute the Opinion, That No Addition Is Made to the Capital of a Community by Banking* (s.l.: s.n., 1834); *Conner v. Shepherd*, 15 Mass. 164 (1818); *Jack v. Shoemaker*, 3 Binn. 280 (Pa. 1810).

to make way for unremitted exertion in this favourite pursuit." As shares of government debt and shares of business corporations became more widely traded, flurries of financial speculation would become regular features of American commercial life. By 1822, Chief Justice Tilghman could already deplore how quickly his fellow citizens threw their money into all these new corporations. "There has prevailed among us, to an unfortunate degree, a pestilent spirit of speculation, which has induced some, without means of payment, to subscribe to projects of all kinds, with a hope to selling out to advantage, as soon as the stock has risen," Tilghman lamented. "These speculative subscriptions have many bad consequences."[10]

Tilghman was hardly alone in worrying that Americans were speculating too much. As early as 1779, in the midst of the American Revolution, George Washington was already concerned. "Virtue and patriotism are almost extinct!" he declared. "Stockjobbing, speculating, engrossing, seem to be the great business of the day." (A decade earlier, Washington himself had been a major speculator in western land.) This sort of criticism never let up. "One most pernicious consequence of the unsettled state of commerce, is the prevalence of a spirit of speculation," insisted a committee of New York merchants in 1817. They deplored how speculation "corrupts the morals of the community, tarnishes its reputation, deranges its commerce, and more or less directly injures every portion of the state." "As fast as one bubble of speculation breaks another is blown up," one editorialist fretted. "We are in the high road of becoming the greatest sharpers in the universe."[11]

10 E. James Ferguson, *The Power of the Purse: A History of American Public Finance, 1776–1790* (Chapel Hill: University of North Carolina Press, 1961); Ronald E. Seavoy, *The Origins of the American Business Corporation, 1784–1855* (Westport, Conn.: Greenwood Press, 1982); James Madison to Thomas Jefferson, 10 July 1791, in William T. Hutchinson et al., eds., *The Papers of James Madison* (Chicago: University of Chicago Press, 1962–), 14:43; Henry Lee to James Madison, 24 Aug. 1791, in ibid., 14:73; *Bernia Turnpike Road v. Henderson*, 8 Serg. & Rawle 219 (Pa. 1822).

11 George Washington to Henry Laurens, 5 Nov. 1779, in Jared Sparks, ed., *The Writings of George Washington* (Boston: Russell, Odiorne, and Metcalf, 1834–37), 6:397; *Columbian* [New York], 11 Jan. 1817, 2; *General Advertiser* [Philadelphia], 20 Mar. 1792, 2.

Such expressions of concern often came near the top of a cycle, as a rise in prices drew newcomers to the market. For example, during the bubble of 1791–92, the first stock market boom and crash in American history, many observers were nervous even while things seemed to be going well. "They say the evil will cure itself," Thomas Jefferson brooded as the market kept heading up and up. "I wish it may. But I have rarely seen a gamester cured even by the disasters of his vocation." In 1835, the rising prices of land and corporate shares created what the political economist Thomas Dew called "a speculating mania," one he expected would cause ruin when prices came back down. "A gambling spirit is apt to prove epidemic," *Niles' Weekly Register* worried. "Verily, the people are mad!"[12]

And of course the bottom of a cycle drew even more criticism of speculation, from writers eager to explain what had gone wrong. After the crash of 1792, one gathering offered as a toast: "The Guillotine to all Tyrants, Plunderers, and *funding* Speculators." A committee of the Pennsylvania legislature blamed the panic of 1819 on "the inclination of a large portion of the community, created by past prosperity, to live by speculation and not by labor." Looking back at the recession of the late 1820s, the cartographer John Melish cited as a cause the fact that "speculation has been too often substituted for industry." The accountant Benjamin Foster offered the same explanation for the recession of the late 1830s. He recalled how in 1836 "the spirit of speculation and adventure pervaded the entire community. The gambling propensities of human nature were constantly solicited into action; and crowds of individuals of every description,—the credulous and the suspicious—the crafty and the bold—the raw and the experienced—the intelligent and the ignorant—politicians, lawyers, physicians and divines, hastened to venture some portion of their property in schemes of which scarcely any thing was known except the name." Sure enough, disaster ensued: "Suddenly, however, the bubble burst—unlimited confidence gave place to universal

---

12 Thomas Jefferson to Gouverneur Morris, 30 Aug. 1791, in Julian P. Boyd et al., eds., *The Papers of Thomas Jefferson* (Princeton, N.J.: Princeton University Press, 1950–), 22:105; Thomas R. Dew, "On Price," *Farmer's Register* 3 (1835): 65; *Niles' Weekly Register* 48 (1835): 167.

distrust—a reaction took place, and thousands found themselves involved in bankruptcy, misery and ruin."[13] No one seems to have worried that Americans were too timid with their money. The concern was all in the opposite direction.

SPECULATION'S NUMEROUS INTRIGUES

What exactly was wrong with speculation? Americans in the early republic addressed this question at great length. Most of their efforts, it seems fair to say, were instinctive expressions of suspicion rather than well-thought-out theories. Yet by the middle of the nineteenth century, so much had been written on the topic that we can piece together a few basic principles underlying what seems to have been a widespread antipathy toward speculation.

Perhaps the most common critique of speculation was that it was a form of gambling. At times speculation was merely analogized to gambling—critics charged that speculation "introduced a spirit of gaming," produced "all the pernicious effects of gaming," or was conducted "on common gambling principles." But others insisted that speculation *was* gambling, dressed up with a fancy name. "Gambling in business," insisted the printer James Ronaldson, "in our modern commercial technicality, is called 'speculation.'" The journalist William Leggett likewise condemned "this pervading spirit of speculation (or spirit of gambling, as it might with more propriety be called, for it is gambling, and gambling of the most desperate kind)." Henry Ward Beecher warned young men that "a Speculator on the exchange, and a Gambler at his table, follow one vocation, only with different instruments. One employs cards or dice, the other property." On Wall Street, agreed the satirist George Foster, "gambling is carried on as the chief business there; but it is

---

13 William Cobbett, *A Bone to Gnaw, for the Democrats* (Philadelphia: Thomas Bradford, 1795), 44; *Journal of the Thirtieth House of Representatives of the Commonwealth of Pennsylvania* (Harrisburg, Penn.: James Peacock, 1819–20), 422; John Melish, *The Traveller's Manual; and Description of the United States* (New York: A. T. Goodrich, 1831), 127; B. F. Foster, *The Merchant's Manual* (Boston: Perkins & Marvin, 1838), 32–33.

upon so gigantic, so systematic a scale, that it reaches the dignity of history."[14]

Speculation, on this view, was simply a euphemism employed to make gambling sound more respectable. "The words *speculate* and *speculation* have been substituted for *gamble* and *gambling*," the English writer William Cobbett argued in a book republished in New York. "The hatefulness of the pursuit is thus taken away." Indeed, until the late eighteenth century, *speculation* meant philosophical contemplation. The word's newer commercial meaning was only a few decades old in the early nineteenth century. Using it to refer to risky transactions thus carried a whiff of legitimization that it no longer does today. As the actor Leman Thomas Rede pointed out, "this species of gambling is called *speculation*, a philosophical word, dragged forcibly into the service of chicane and avarice."[15]

Critics who equated speculation with gambling were drawing upon a long tradition of antigambling thought in both Britain and the United States. Gambling "is an offence of the most alarming nature," lectured the English judge William Blackstone in his ubiquitous *Commentaries*, "tending by necessary consequence to promote public idleness, theft, and debauchery." And that was just among the poor. "Among persons of a superior rank," Blackstone continued, "it hath frequently been attended with the sudden ruin and desolation of antient and opulent families, an abandoned prostitution of every principle of honour and virtue, and too often hath ended in self-murder." The young lawyer (and

14 *Freeman's Journal* [Philadelphia], 27 July 1791, 3; *Facts Important to Be Known by the Manufacturers, Mechanics, and All Other Classes of the Community* (New York: s.n., 1831), 37; William M. Gouge, *A Short History of Paper Money and Banking in the United States* (Philadelphia: T. W. Ustick, 1833), 75; Laban Heath, *On Paper Money* (Philadelphia: s.n., 1825), 13; James Ronaldson, *Banks and a Paper Currency* (Philadelphia: s.n., 1832), 4; Theodore Sedgwick Jr., ed., *A Collection of the Political Writings of William Leggett* (New York: Taylor and Dodd, 1840), 2:87; Henry Ward Beecher, *Lectures to Young Men, on Various Important Subjects* (New York: M. H. Newman & Co., 1849), 76; George G. Foster, *New York in Slices* (New York: W. F. Burgess, 1849), 16.

15 William Cobbett, *Advice to Young Men* (New York: John Doyle, 1831), 17; Leman Thomas Rede, *The Art of Money Getting* (Boston: Richardson, Lord & Holbrook, 1832), 36.

future lord chancellor) Thomas Erskine agreed that gambling "is from the very beginning a sordid, ungenerous, dishonest passion." American ministers had long decried gambling as an especially grievous sin. "It is not easy to conceive any vice more hateful to God than Gambling," screamed the itinerant minister Mason Locke Weems in all upper-case letters, "BECAUSE NONE CAN BE CONCEIVED MORE DIAMETRICALLY OP-POSITE TO THE VERY END OF OUR CREATION!" Secular critics emphasized that gambling led inexorably to idleness and financial ruin, and often to madness and even suicide. Calling speculation a kind of gambling was a shorthand way of summoning up all these dire consequences. "Speculation and Gambling," mused one journalist—"on many occasions, these words are synonymous—and on some, there is another which has nearly the same meaning—to wit, *roguery*. Sometimes, perhaps also, *insanity* may convey nearly a similar idea."[16]

Like gambling, speculation was widely viewed as immoral and unchristian. This was a common theme in the religious press. "Speculation is contrary to the spirit of Christianity and a great hindrance to the spread of the gospel throughout the world," declared the *Religious Intelligencer*. The *Episcopal Recorder* maintained that "it is our duty not to sanction the pursuit of wealth through the medium of speculation,"

16 William Blackstone, *Commentaries on the Laws of England* (Oxford: Clarendon Press, 1765–69), 4:171; Thomas Erskine, *Reflections on Gaming, Annuities, and Usurious Contracts* (London: T. Davies, 1776), 6; William Stith, *The Sinfulness and Pernicious Nature of Gaming* (Williamsburg, Va.: William Hunter, 1752); *A Letter to a Gentleman on the Sin and Danger of Playing at Cards and Other Games* (Boston: D. Fowle and Z. Fowle, 1755); Eli Hyde, *A Sermon; in Which the Doctrine of the Lot, Is Stated, and Applied to Lotteries, Gambling, and Card-Playing, for Amusement* (Oxford, N.Y.: John B. Johnson, 1812); Mason Locke Weems, *God's Revenge Against Gambling* (Augusta, Ga.: Hobby & Bunce, 1810), 12; Jacob Rush, *Charges, and Extracts of Charges, on Moral and Religious Subjects* (New York: Jonathan Weeden, 1804), 120–21; Samuel Miller, *The Guilt, Folly, and Sources of Suicide* (New York: T. and J. Swords, 1805), 52–53; *Report of a Committee Appointed to Investigate the Evils of Lotteries* (Philadelphia: Daniel B. Shrieves, 1831), 11–12; George William Gordon, *A Lecture Before the Boston Young Men's Society* (Boston: Temperance Press, Ford & Damrell, 1833), 12; Job R. Tyson, *A Brief Survey of the Great Extent and Evil Tendencies of the Lottery System* (Philadelphia: William Brown, 1833), 27; "Speculation and Gambling," *Niles' Weekly Register*, 3 July 1819, 16.

while *Zion's Herald* warned that "a successful speculation is oftener an evil than a blessing; . . . it is a moral evil, because it violates the law of nature." A Quaker newspaper explained that "speculation in dealing, however common and popular," was nevertheless "wrong in principle," because "it is unjust for one man to seek to gain at the expense of another's loss." But assertions of the immorality of speculation pervaded the secular press as well. One newspaper called it a form of covetousness and idolatry. Another published a poem called *To Land Speculators*, which began:

> Of *you*, oh, ye land-sellers, will heaven demand
> An account of your buying and selling of *land*:
> By *you* is the arm of the murderer nerved;
> By *you* are the public with robbers well served:
> By *you* is the razor of suicide guided;
> By *you* is the christian religion derided.

One farmers' magazine adapted a quotation from the Book of Matthew. "When the demon of speculation has seized upon a man," the magazine pronounced, "he walketh through dry places, seeking rest but findeth none."[17]

Sometimes speculation was deplored because of its effects on the speculators themselves. Unless it was stopped, worried a New Jersey newspaper as the 1791 bubble began to inflate, "the rage for speculation . . . cannot fail of ruining many innocent and credulous persons, who are not proof against the temptations which are held out, nor capable of discerning the snares that are laid for them." Such amateur venturers were not the only victims, because their wives and children might be dragged down with them. "How many families enjoying a competence in quietude and peace," wondered one observer during the recession of the late 1820s, "have by such an unnatural state of things, been plunged

---

17 "Money Speculations Among Christians," *Religious Intelligencer* 21 (1836): 385; "Warning Against the Spirit of Pecuniary Speculation," *Episcopal Recorder* 14 (1836): 153; "Speculation," *Zion's Herald* 8 (1837): 112; "On Speculation," *Friends' Intelligencer* 15 (1858): 7; *New York Observer*, 17 July 1841, 1; *Young America*, 10 May 1845, 4; "The Spirit of Speculation," *Maine Farmer* 33 (1865): 2.

into distress and ruin[?]" Learned treatises and popular advice manuals alike advised the uninitiated to avoid speculating, lest they plunge themselves and their families into poverty. The French Duke de la Rochefoucault, traveling through the United States in the 1790s, worried that middling farmers were losing their farms—ironically, after an especially plentiful harvest—because they had been speculating in crop prices, which fell due to the increase in supply. Speculation was dangerous even for those who could afford to lose the most, warned John Bannister Gibson, Pennsylvania's long-serving chief justice. "We know from experience," he cautioned, "that when a spirit of speculation, or desire of inordinate gain, infects the rich, it terminates in scenes of ruin and devastation, as wide spread and deplorable in their consequences of misery and want, in the domestic relations of life, as if it had been confined to those who had comparatively little to lose."[18]

Other critics focused not on speculation's economic effects but on its moral and psychological implications. The problem was not that speculation made people poorer, but that it made them selfish and imprudent. By enabling one person to gain at the expense of another, one correspondent charged, speculation "tends to dissolve that natural tie, that binds man to man." As they grew accustomed to cheating, another alleged, "speculators have been generally strangers to mercantile habits, to mercantile accuracy and rectitude." The stereotype of the speculator was one who thought only of his own profit and would not hesitate to take advantage of others. As the poet Philip Freneau depicted him in the 1790s,

With soothing words the widow's mite he gain'd,
With piercing glance watch'd misery's dark abode,
Filch'd paper scraps while yet a scrap remain'd,
Bought where he must, and cheated where he cou'd.

---

18 *New Jersey Journal*, 10 Aug. 1791, 3; *A Peep Into the Banks* (New York: Vanderpool & Cole, 1828), 29; Francis Wayland, *The Elements of Political Economy* (New York: Leavitt, Lord & Co., 1837), 379; *Hints to Young Tradesmen* (Boston: Perkins & Marvin, 1838), 51; "Commercial Chronicle and Review," *Merchants' Magazine* 28 (1853): 466–67; Duke de la Rochefoucault Liancourt, *Travels Through the United States of North America*, 2nd ed. (London: R. Phillips, 1800), 1:242–43; *Seidenbender v. Charles's Administrators*, 4 Serg. & Rawle 151 (Pa. 1818).

The printer Asa Greene summed up this line of thought in his account of New York's commercial life, a book he subtitled *A Taste of the Dangers of Wall Street*. "The more a man engages in speculation," Greene argued, "the less tender his conscience grows on the subject of doing to others as he would have them do to him. So debasing are the arts and shifts which are too apt to prevail in a mercantile community."[19]

Speculation did not just make people meaner, on this view; it also made them turn to lives of luxury and vice. The young Clement Clarke Moore, who as an older man would become better known for the poem "A Visit from St. Nicholas," condemned "a spirit of speculation which tends, not to advance the permanent good of the society at large, but to the introduction of that luxury and dissipation which pervades our sea-ports." The scientist William Maclure agreed that speculation had the effect of "increasing luxury, dissipation and vice, by introducing an artificial anticipation of riches."[20]

Meanwhile, speculation made people unhappy and unpleasant. Speculative emotions in business "are transfused from the counting-house to the fire-side," one critic charged. "The visionary profits of one day stimulate extravagance, and the positive losses of another engender spleen, irritation, restlessness, a spirit of gambling and domestic inquietude." What is the "difference between speculation and honesty?" another asked. "Honesty is modest, humble, distant and reserved," while "speculation is forward, froward, bullying, hectoring and insinuating." The reason, according to one rural newspaper, was that "a *Speculator* appears surrounded by wants, when in fact he wants Nothing. He too frequently grasps at what he cannot get."[21]

19 *Dunlap's American Daily Advertiser* [Philadelphia], 28 Feb. 1793, 2; John M'Donald, *The Danger of America Delineated* (Cooperstown, N.Y.: Elihu Phinney, 1799), 17; Philip Freneau, "On Pest-eli-hali, the Travelling Speculator," in *Poems* (Monmouth, N.J.: Philip Freneau, 1795), 429; Asa Greene, *The Perils of Pearl Street* (New York: Betts & Anstice, 1834), 172.

20 Clement Clarke Moore, *An Inquiry Into the Effects of Our Foreign Carrying Trade* (New York: E. Sargeant, 1806), 41; William Maclure, *Opinions on Various Subjects* (New Harmony, Ind.: School Press, 1831), 1:329.

21 Ferris Pell, *Letter to Albert Gallatin, Esq. on the Doctrine of Gold and Silver* (New York: Gould and Van Pelt, 1815), 34; James Jackson, *The Letters of Sicilius, to the Citizens of the State of Georgia* (Augusta, Ga.: s.n., 1795), 54; *Kennebec Gazette*, 14 Nov. 1800, 1.

Worse, speculators were susceptible to illnesses brought on by the pressure of their vocation. "The gambling spirit as constantly haunts the Exchange and Corn-market as the play-table," one doctor cautioned, "and, by perplexing and distracting the mind, soon saps the basis of health, and anticipates old age." Benjamin Rush, the most prominent physician of the early republic, even cited speculation as a leading cause of mental illness. "In commercial countries, where large fortunes are suddenly acquired and lost, madness is a common disease," he noted. "It is most prevalent at those times when speculation is substituted to regular commerce." This was particularly noticeable in the United States, he continued. "The funding system, and speculations in bank scrip, and new lands, have been fruitful sources of madness in our country," Rush observed. "Sixteen persons perished from suicide in the city of New York, in the year 1804, in most of whom it was supposed to be the effect of madness, from the different and contrary events of speculation."[22]

Speculation was also widely criticized, not for its effect on the speculators, but for its effect on the economy as a whole. One common line of attack was that speculation was a nonproductive activity that sucked time and money away from productive labor. "Agriculture and manufactures, I consider as the sources and foundation of national wealth," declared Tench Coxe, who would soon become assistant secretary of the Treasury under Alexander Hamilton. Speculation, by contrast, was in Coxe's view "of no benefit to the nation, as the stock of national wealth receives no augmentation therefrom." (Coxe did not let this dim view of speculation prevent him from becoming one of the leading land speculators in the country, or from using information gained from his Treasury position to give investment tips to his friends.) Every hour spent speculating was an hour taken away from a more useful activity. "In my opinion nothing scarcely can be worse," explained the Philadelphia merchant Pelatiah Webster. Speculation just tended "to draw people from the honest and painful method of earning fortunes,

---

22 "Physical Effects of Mercantile Speculation," *Episcopal Recorder* 26 (1848): 88; Benjamin Rush, *Medical Inquiries and Observations, Upon the Diseases of the Mind* (Philadelphia: Kimber & Richardson, 1812), 66.

and to encourage them to pursue chimerical ways and means of obtaining wealth by sleight of hand." As one poet complained during the
1791–92 bubble,

> *Gambling, stock-jobbing,* form most powerful leagues
> With *Speculation's* numerous intrigues;
> Intrigues that add not to the nation's store,
> But for the rich defraud the helpless poor.

Or as Thomas Jefferson complained right around the same time, "ships
are lying idle at the wharfs, buildings are stopped, capitals withdrawn
from commerce, manufactures, arts and agriculture, to be employed in
gaming, and the tide of public prosperity almost unparalleled in any
country, is arrested in its course, and suppressed by the rage of getting
rich in a day."[23]

In later decades the point would be repeated by some of the early
American political economists, who likewise distinguished between
productive labor and nonproductive speculation. "Increasing the fortunes of individuals does not necessarily increase public wealth," Daniel
Raymond cautioned, "unless the gain is caused by an increase of industry; for what one gains by speculation, another must lose." John
McVickar agreed that speculation could "have no influence on national
prosperity," because "as the wealth of the country merely changes hands,
the profits are but the criterion of a rising market, since such accumu-
lation would have taken place had the commodity continued in the
hands of its original holders."[24] Early advocates for labor made the same

---

23 Tench Coxe, *Observations on the Agriculture, Manufactures and Commerce of
    the United States* (New York: Francis Childs and John Swaine, 1789), 85; Jacob
    E. Cooke, *Tench Coxe and the Early Republic* (Chapel Hill: University of North
    Carolina Press, 1978), 79–82, 311–33, 176–77; Pelatiah Webster, *A Seventh Essay
    on Free Trade and Finance* (Philadelphia: Eleazer Oswald, 1785), 23; *The Glass;
    or, Speculation: A Poem* (New York: s.n., 1791), 4; Thomas Jefferson to Edward
    Rutledge, 25 Aug. 1791, in *Papers of Thomas Jefferson,* 22:74 (spelling corrected).

24 Daniel Raymond, *Thoughts on Political Economy* (Baltimore: Fielding Lucas
    Jr., 1820), 306; Paul K. Conkin, *Prophets of Prosperity: America's First Political
    Economists* (Bloomington: Indiana University Press, 1980), 88–93; John Ramsay
    McCulloch, *Outlines of Political Economy,* ed. John McVickar (New York:
    Wilder & Campbell, 1825), 91 (the quoted material is from McVickar's editorial

argument: real wealth came from production, not from speculation. "What are speculators?" asked a farmers' magazine, which immediately supplied an answer: speculators were a class that "are a burthen upon society—that live off of it like leeches."[25] Speculation thus harmed the economy, by distracting people from doing more valuable things.

Speculation in land was especially vulnerable to this critique, because land speculators were not merely accused of wasting their own time and money; they were also open to the charge of wasting the productivity of the land itself, and in a particularly conspicuous way, when absentee-owned land lingered unexploited. Land speculators "traverse this fine country like a pestilent blight," Morris Birkbeck reported from Illinois. "When they see the promise of a thriving settlement, from a cluster of entries being made in any neighbourhood, they purchase large tracts of the best land, and lock it up in real *mortmain*, for it is death to all improvement." A Boston newspaper agreed that "the Land speculations in the United States are become a Pandora's box of evils to the people" and urged that public land should never be sold to speculators but only to actual settlers. When land was owned by speculators rather than farmers, concluded William Tilghman, "agriculture suffers—either the lands remain a desert, or they are occupied by poor intruders, who knowing the instability of their title, are afraid to attempt any valuable improvement."[26] Speculation, on this view, hindered the productivity of American land as much as American labor.

Many critics also cited a second reason speculation harmed the economy: it gave rise to a boom-and-bust cycle that destroyed even those who had not engaged in speculation themselves. "Of the panics and destruction of credit attendant on the re-action of all extensive

notes). On the range of early American economists' views of speculation, see Brian Harding, "Transatlantic Views of Speculation and Value, 1820–1860," *Historical Research* 66 (1993): 209–21.

25 Stephen Simpson, *The Working Man's Manual* (Philadelphia: Thomas L. Bonsal, 1831), 74; "Labor vs. Speculation," *Maine Farmer and Journal of the Useful Arts* 4 (1837): 394; "Speculators," *Prairie Farmer* 6 (1860): 147.

26 Morris Birkbeck, *Letters from Illinois* (Philadelphia: M. Carey and Son, 1818), 31; *Boston Gazette*, 21 Mar. 1796, 2; William Tilghman, *An Address Delivered Before the Philadelphia Society for Promoting Agriculture* (Philadelphia: William Fry, 1820), 7.

speculations," observed the lawyer William Beach Lawrence, "no one conversant with the transactions of our commercial emporium can be ignorant." This sort of criticism understandably tended to swell at the bottom of each cycle. As one correspondent put it, just after the crash of 1792, "the mad moment of Stock Jobbing—Land Jobbing—and wild Speculation is past—leaving us to rue the fatal effects." Timothy Dwight, the former president of Yale, was in nearby Middletown, Connecticut, not long after the Panic of 1819. The commerce of the town "has obviously declined within a few years past," he noted. "The first cause, both in time and efficiency, of this evil was, if I mistake not, what has been proverbially called in this country *Speculation*." In 1837, as banks were failing throughout the country, the New York socialite Philip Hone took real estate prices as a measure of his city's distress. Unimproved lots which had cost $480 just a year earlier were now selling for $50. "The immense fortunes which we heard so much about in the days of speculation have melted away like the snows before an April sun," Hone wrote in his diary. "No man can calculate to escape ruin but he who owes no money."[27]

Most such critics simply assumed a causal connection between speculation and economic cycles, but some tried to identify the mechanism linking the two. The economist Mathew Carey argued that speculators were the only beneficiaries of "those sudden vibrations of bank accommodation whereby money is rendered superabundant at one time, and immoderately scarce at another," an oscillation "pernicious to morals, industry, trade, and commerce." During the recession of 1834, a committee of the House of Representatives laid out the same mechanism in more detail. The committee identified the cause of recent economic conditions as the overwillingness of banks to lend to speculators during good times. "When business has been so successful for a time as to occasion an eager desire to speculate in merchandise and real estate," the committee reasoned, "extensive discounts and loans will be demanded,

27 William Beach Lawrence, *Two Lectures on Political Economy* (New York: G. & C. & H. Carvill, 1832), 63–64; *Federal Gazette* [Philadelphia], 25 Apr. 1792, 3; Timothy Dwight, *Travels; in New England and New York* (New Haven, Conn.: Timothy Dwight, 1821), 1:218; Bayard Tuckerman, ed., *The Diary of Philip Hone 1828–1851* (New York: Dodd, Mead and Co., 1889), 1:251.

which the banks cheerfully furnish to any extent, as it can be done without cost, and to their great profit." When things turned sour, and borrowers could not repay these loans, the result was "heavy and destructive losses, and much real suffering," to an extent "impeding, temporarily, the ordinary and salutary course of trade and industry." On this view, speculation was not a cause of the business cycle but an intensifier of it, a factor making the highs higher and the lows lower than they otherwise would be. But this distinction was not particularly relevant to most critics, because either way, speculation was at the root of the nation's troubles. "To what shall we ascribe this suspension of business which has thrown so many of the industrious out of employment and rendered it impossible for the poor mechanic to collect from his rich employer the wages of his labor?" asked one populist pamphlet. "I answer that the evil of the times may be comprehended in three words—OVERTRADING—OVERBANKING AND SPECULATION."[28]

Speculators were also widely accused of manipulating prices, to benefit themselves at the expense of the broader economy. They were often charged with making staple goods more expensive for consumers. "We every day hear loud complaints against the avarice of speculators," reported a Boston newspaper, which explained that speculators had driven the price of corn so high "that it is scarcely possible for a poor man to procure a bushel of indian corn to make jonny-cakes for his half-starved children." A New York paper reported that within the past two years, without any scarcity, "the *mania* of speculation" had caused the price of salt to rise from 42 cents to $1.75 per pound, and molasses from 45 cents to $1.50 per gallon. The *Maine Farmer* agreed that "the present *extra* high price of breadstuffs in this country is kept up by the mean tricks of the speculators." "Speculators are controlling the prices of sugar," another critic charged a few years later. "They buy up large quantities and withdraw most of it from the market, and then raise a hue and cry of scarcity." When food prices rose during the War of 1812, many placed the responsibility on speculators, who were alleged to have

28 Mathew Carey, *Essays on Banking* (Philadelphia: Mathew Carey, 1816), 89–90; *Report on Gold and Silver Coins, by a Select Committee of the House of Representatives of the United States* (Washington, D.C.: Gales & Seaton, 1834), 32; *The Times: or, The Pressure and Its Causes Examined* (Boston: s.n., 1837), 6.

created artificial shortages by buying up staples and keeping them off the market. The citizens of Wilmington, Delaware, held a public meeting to consider "the propriety of some measures with regard to the state of speculation and speculators," including whether to "withdraw all intercourse *commercial* and *social,* with those who are combining to raise the price of the necessaries of life."[29]

At other times, however, speculators were accused of *reducing* the prices received by farmers and ranchers. "The farmers of this state are annually, in the sale of their wheat crops, 'fleeced' to the tune of several hundred thousand dollars, which go into the pockets of chuckling, greedy speculators," despaired one correspondent to the *Michigan Farmer*. Another alleged a conspiracy among "speculators to keep the prices of wool down, until most of it has been purchased of those who produce it."[30]

Whether speculators were raising or lowering prices, critics were certain that a small wealthy cabal was exploiting the poor and middling classes. "It is speculation, in its endless diversities, which simultaneously augments the capital of the rich, the acute, the prosperous, and depresses the condition of the simple, the unfortunate, and the labouring poor," charged the *Southern Quarterly Review*. And when ordinary citizens tried to get in on the game by speculating for themselves, another magazine alleged, they would lose their all to "a minority of wealthier speculators" who could "absolutely control the course of the market for their own benefit."[31]

Finally, speculation was often criticized for causing political corruption. The major speculative assets in the early republic—land and public debt securities—were both initially brought onto the market through the decisions of government officials, and even business

---

29 *New-England Palladium,* 30 Nov. 1813, 1; *The Columbian,* 17 Dec. 1813, 2; "Tricks of Breadstuff Speculators," *Maine Farmer* 15 (1847): 2; "The Spirit of Speculation—How to Check It," *The Plough, the Loom and the Anvil* 8 (1856): 519; *New Hampshire Patriot,* 28 Dec. 1813, 2; *Petersburg Daily Courier,* 3 Oct. 1814, 2; *Enquirer* [Richmond], 28 Dec. 1813, 3.

30 "Farmers vs. Speculators," *Michigan Farmer* 6 (1848): 106; "The Wool Market," *Michigan Farmer* 11 (1853): 82.

31 "Speculation and Trade," *Southern Quarterly Review* 30 (1856): 1–2; "The Declension of Speculation," *Merchants' Magazine* 62 (1870): 103.

corporations were created one by one, through acts of the legislature. There was money to be made, by speculators and by public officers themselves, with foreknowledge of government decisions. In an era before government officials were prohibited from using that knowledge for their own gain, they were some of the leading investors in the public debt and the public lands, and they were known to share investment tips with their associates. "Our new Government is a Government of Stock-Jobbing and Favouritism," the elderly George Mason grumbled. William Findley, the Pennsylvania representative who was one of the leading opponents of Hamilton's financial program, agreed that the national debt "promoted a depravity of morals and a great decline of republican virtue." The point was made again and again: speculation in public assets like debt securities and land created an unholy alliance of legislators and gamblers powerful enough to transfer wealth "from those who earned it, to those who pilfered it," and "to concentrate it in a few hands." The result, as one newspaper editor put it, was "the subversion of our republican institutions."[32]

Speculation corrupted the nation's political culture in a second way, critics charged—by creating the conditions for European-style inequality. "In our rising manufacturing villages," a New Hampshire newspaper cautioned, "this speculating mania rages to a great extent, and is laying a foundation for that poverty, dependence and wretchedness which characterizes the population of similar places in Europe. The few are becoming immensely rich, the middling interest poor, and the poor abject." Unless speculation could be checked, "what the people affect so much to deprecate, a monied aristocracy, is in a great measure created by their own folly."[33]

32 *Public Speculation Unfolded* (New York: David Denniston, 1800), 3; George Mason to James Monroe, 9 Feb. 1792, in Robert A. Rutland, ed., *The Papers of George Mason, 1725–1792* (Chapel Hill: University of North Carolina Press, 1970), 3:1256; William Findley, *A Review of the Revenue System* (Philadelphia: T. Dobson, 1794), 52; John Taylor, *An Enquiry Into the Principles and Tendency of Certain Public Measures* (Philadelphia: Thomas Dobson, 1794), 42; James Cheetham, *Remarks on the "Merchants" Bank* (New York: Southwick & Hardcastle, 1804), 19.

33 *Farmer's Cabinet*, 8 May 1835, 3.

There were thus plenty of reasons in the early republic to be wary of speculation. Like other forms of gambling, it bankrupted the speculators themselves, it distracted people from engaging in more productive pursuits, and it made its practitioners selfish and sometimes even suicidal. And speculation posed other dangers that most kinds of gambling did not: it regularly plunged the country into economic crises, and it corrupted the new nation's political culture. By the middle of the nineteenth century, there was a considerable body of antispeculation thought. Most of it was neither systematic nor comprehensive, when taken one book or one article at a time. But when put together, it constituted a reservoir of ideas that could be drawn upon to criticize any particular speculator or instance of speculation. If the United States was a land of speculation, it was also a land of critics of speculation.

THE MADNESS OF A FEW FOR THE GAIN OF THE WORLD

But there was another side to the story. While Americans were elaborating reasons to dislike speculation, they were also building a set of justifications of the practice. This way of thinking was no more organized or complete than its antithesis, but it too could serve as a grab bag of debating points to rebut criticism of speculative transactions. By the middle of the nineteenth century, there was a body of thought defending speculation.

It began with the uncontroversial premise that the investment of capital in American enterprises was beneficial for the country. "It is a long time, since the reaping of interest from capital, has been set free from *an erroneous prejudice*," recalled one commentator. "Labor, without the assistance of capital, is very inefficient in the production of value," agreed the political economist Willard Phillips. Investors "hold in their hands the essential means, not only of future production, but of the very existence of the community." Speaking at the opening of the Auburn and Owasco Canal, the young politician William Seward gloried in the willingness of Auburnites to invest in exciting new ventures. If a traveler came to Auburn, Seward remarked, "we may call his attention to our market to which are appropriated 20,000 dollars, to this canal constituting an investment of 100,000 dollars, and to the Auburn and Syracuse Rail Road with its capital of 400,000 dollars, all of which funds, with inconsiderable exceptions, have been subscribed by our own citizens, since the first of January last, and ask what other population of five thousand have manifested within the year a more efficient spirit of enterprise?" Even when investment came from abroad, another future governor of New York suggested, Americans were the beneficiaries. "The interest of this capital goes to the foreign capital," John Dix conceded, "but the profits of the industry, which it puts in motion, comprehending the subsistence and compensation of the individuals employed, is obviously a gain to the country, in which the investment is made. The industry of New-York has been in some degree stimulated by contributions of this nature."[34] There was little doubt that investment was something to be welcomed and even encouraged.

Investment was necessary, but there was also no doubt that it was risky. "When a man loans his property to another, there is always a risk of his never being repaid," lectured Francis Wayland, the president of Brown University. "Now, the greater this risk, the greater will be the interest which the capitalist may justly demand." Few ways of employing capital were riskier than putting it into a new business venture. Looking at all the new manufacturing companies that had been started in Massachusetts over the past twenty years, one lawyer marveled at how many investors "were making this hazardous experiment, which if successful would prove a great public benefit." These new enterprises could scarcely exist unless people with money were willing to put it at risk. And what was speculation but putting money at risk? "Let us say what we may on the subject," one writer pointed out, "the establishment of any new branch of trade, or the setting on of a manufactory, partakes in no small degree of the character of a speculation; indeed commerce itself can be deemed little else." The same argument was made more enthusiastically by Ralph Waldo

34 *An Essay Upon the Principles of Political Economy* (New York: Theodore Foster, 1837), 31; Willard Phillips, *A Manual of Political Economy* (Boston: Hilliard, Gray, Little, and Wilkins, 1828), 63; *Address Delivered by William H. Seward, at the Commencement of the Auburn and Owasco Canal* (Auburn, N.Y.: H. Ivison & Co., 1835), 6; John A. Dix, *Sketch of the Resources of the City of New-York* (New York: G. & C. Carvill, 1827), 41.

Emerson. "How did our factories get built?" Emerson asked. "How did North America get netted with iron rails, except by the importunity of these orators who dragged all the prudent men in? Is party the madness of many for the gain of a few? This *speculative* genius is the madness of a few for the gain of the world. The projectors are sacrificed, but the public is the gainer."[35]

To encourage investment (which was universally acknowledged to be good) while discouraging speculation (which was often said to be bad), one would need to distinguish between the two. Contemporaries suggested several ways to draw the line separating investment and industry from speculation and gambling. One possibility was to draw a line between investors who had a long-term interest in the success of a venture and those who had no such interest but were merely hoping to sell after a short-term rise in the value of an asset. Alexander Hamilton seems to have been groping toward this distinction between two types of holders of the national debt in its early bubbly days. "'Tis time there should be a line of separation," he insisted, "between respectable stockholders and dealers in the funds, and mere unprincipled Gamblers."[36] Hamilton's meaning was not entirely clear, but his separation of "stockholders" from "Gamblers" suggests a difference between those who invested in the federal government out of patriotic motives, or at least an interest in the long-run welfare of the United States, and those who invested in the debt just to make money in the short run.

Another distinction that could be drawn was between people who bought an asset because they actually wanted to use the asset itself and those who bought the asset only because they hoped to be able to sell it later for a higher price. Congressman Gulian Verplanck drew this distinction in his treatise on the law of contracts. In his

---

35 Francis Wayland, *The Elements of Political Economy* (New York: Leavitt, Lord & Co., 1837), 357; "Manufacturing Corporations," *American Jurist* 2 (1829): 105; "The Joint-Stock Companies," *Museum of Foreign Literature, Science, and Art* 7 (1825): 154; Ralph Waldo Emerson, "Wealth" (published 1860, but written 1851–52), in *The Complete Essays and Other Writings of Ralph Waldo Emerson*, ed. Brooks Atkinson (New York: Modern Library, 1940), 698.

36 Alexander Hamilton to Philip Livingston, 2 Apr. 1792, in Harold C. Syrett, ed., *The Papers of Alexander Hamilton* (New York: Columbia University Press, 1961–81), 11:218–19.

view, speculation was "where purchases are made of lands peculiarly situated, or goods are bought, not with reference to present use or profit, but with relation to a future, and anticipated state of the market."[37] Someone who bought land and actually settled on it would not be a speculator, even if he hoped the land's value would rise; a speculator was someone who bought land solely in the hope of a rise in value.

A different strategy was to distinguish between different kinds of transactions, the necessary and the unnecessary. Usually, reasoned the former broker William Armstrong, "the business of buying and selling stocks is legitimate and necessary." That was because "in the ordinary course of events, causes too numerous to enumerate have an unavoidable tendency to make them change hands more or less, as different circumstances which influence men in making or withdrawing investments arise." But he felt very differently about "those transactions called time operations," or what today would be called futures, agreements to buy stock at a specific price at a specific time in the future. "They are essentially the same as so many bets upon what the future will bring forth," Armstrong argued, "for hardly one share out of fifty which is sold on time is actually transferred, the contract being 'settled' by one party paying to the other the 'difference' between the price specified at the time of the sale and the market price at the time the stock is to be delivered."[38]

Yet another way to draw the line was to consider the degree of risk: speculation was fine up to a point, but not when it became too hazardous. "In all trade there must be speculation to a certain extent; it is the very essence of commerce," acknowledged one writer, "but reckless gambling, in matters of trade, is as injurious, as in horse-racing, the hazard-table, or cards." Crèvecoeur's *American Farmer* praised the whalers of Nantucket for observing this distinction. "Many voyages do not repay the original cost of fitting out," he noted, but the whalers "bear such misfortunes like true merchants, and, as they

---

37 "The Downfall of Speculation," *New-Yorker* 8 (1839): 57; Gulian C. Verplanck, *An Essay on the Doctrine of Contracts* (New York: G. & C. Carvill, 1825), 109.

38 William Armstrong, *Stocks and Stock-Jobbing in Wall Street* (New York: New York Publishing Co., 1848), 11–12.

never venture their all like gamesters, they try their fortunes again; the latter hope to win by chance alone, the former by industry, well-judged speculation, and some hazard." The same line was drawn by the commercial moralist John Frost, who sought to confine the term *speculation* to "incurring extensive hazards of any kind in the hope of extensive emolument; in short, to whatever is foreign to the proper business of the individual."[39] On this view, there was nothing wrong with the inherent risks of a conventional business venture. It was only when the risk was larger than normal that it should be condemned as overly speculative.

A final possibility was to distinguish between positive-sum and zero-sum transactions, and to condemn only the latter. "There are two ways of acquiring wealth, not only essentially different, but as opposite to each other as east is opposite to west," the *Mechanics' Magazine* lectured its younger readers. "One of these ways may be properly denominated *enterprise*, the other *speculation*. The first of these ways creates the wealth it accumulates by bringing into existence the articles of which it is composed, or by increasing the value of articles which existed before; the other draws the wealth, generally, by some kind of deception or delusive practices, out of the possession of its right owner, without increasing its value, or adding anything to the public stock." The magazine had no doubt which was better. "The first of these modes is honest and highly laudable," readers were advised, but the second is "wholly dishonest, and subversive to the peace and happiness of mankind, because in the same ratio that it makes one richer it makes others poorer." The *Princeton Review* drew the same distinction, between "normal trade," in which the trader was compensated for performing some useful function like transporting a commodity from the producer to the consumer, and speculation, in which the trader performed no such function but merely hoped to profit from a change in the price. Even where they were equally risky, the risks of normal trade were inherent

39 "'Nothing Venture, Nothing Have,' the Maxim of the Speculator and the Merchant," *Merchants' Magazine* 30 (1854): 517; J. Hector St. John de Crèvecoeur, *Letters from an American Farmer* (1782), ed. Susan Manning (Oxford: Oxford University Press, 1997), 111; John Frost, *The Young Merchant* (Boston: George W. Light, 1840), 157.

in a commercial society, but speculation was "little else than simple unmitigated gambling."[40]

But many concluded that such definitional efforts were fruitless: there was just no way to distinguish useful investment from harmful speculation. "A *merchant* is in some sense a *gambler*," acknowledged a correspondent in Maine. "If his chance be unfortunate he will speculate again, hoping that his 'luck will turn'!" As the English economist Thomas Corbet put it, "trade and speculation seem to be, to a certain extent or in a certain manner, unavoidably connected." Risk was simply an inherent part of commercial life. "It is as difficult to tell at what point safe and laudable enterprise leaves off, and speculation begins, as it would be to mark off the precise line where delicate India ink shading begins to lighten," a Massachusetts writer observed.[41] All investment was a kind of speculation.

And who exactly were these oft-condemned speculators? "Gentlemen talk of these persons as if they were the veriest brokers and stockjobbers in the world," Representative Charles Ingersoll of Pennsylvania noted during the debates over the Bank of the United States. "But no misconception could be more unfounded." They were mostly ordinary people who had prudently invested their savings in the hope of a modest return. If one visited the bank on the day dividends were paid, Ingersoll argued, one would "find the widow and the orphan, the aged and the infirm, as well as the wealthy and the competent, waiting for their shares; some of them for small sums." There was no way to condemn speculators without also condemning the honest merchant and the frugal investor. "If, Sir, we forget the horrors that Envy and Ignorance have added to the sound of *Speculation*," thundered one letter writer to a Philadelphia newspaper, "we shall find childish Philosophers, and beardless Moralists, railing at *Contracts*, and

---

40 "Hints to Young Men, or Enterprise and Speculation Contrasted," *Mechanics' Magazine* 5 (1835): 5; "Ethics and Economics of Commercial Speculation," *Biblical Repertory and Princeton Review* 41 (1869): 237; for the same distinction, see "Trade and Speculation," *Independent*, 10 Feb. 1870, 8.

41 *Eastern Argus* [Portland, Me.], 5 Dec. 1815, 1; Thomas Corbet, *An Inquiry Into the Causes and Modes of the Wealth of Individuals* (London: Smith, Elder & Co., 1841), 159; *The Pressure and Its Causes* (Boston: Otis, Broaders & Co., 1837), 26.

execrating *Commerce*."[42] Speculation simply could not be separated from ordinary business.

John Sergeant, the Philadelphia congressman and diplomat, spoke at length on this theme in 1819, when the House was yet again debating the bank issue. "Speculation and speculators, sir, are terms of very vague import, and of very extensive application," he pointed out. "There are speculators of many kinds—there are speculators in lands—there are speculators in merchandise—there are speculators in manufactures—there are speculators in stocks; the variety is infinite, and in no country upon earth greater than in this. Every thing about us invites to speculation." How could one praise some people who took commercial risks and condemn others? "I should like, then, to know," Sergeant continued, "in what the discrimination consists, which makes one kind of speculation offensive, and another innocent, if both are permitted by law, and neither unfairly or fraudulently conducted. What is the difference between speculating in land, and speculating in merchandise, or the stocks?"[43]

Indeed, mused one anonymous writer, if one took the broad view, life was full of speculation, because life was full of risk. "The wife *speculates* with her husband when she constrains him by persuasion and tenderness, to convey her all his estate," he reasoned, "and when the husband in like circumstances, gains a like object, he *speculates* upon his wife." And that was not all. "The girl who, from 16 to 25, devotes herself to the acquisition of a good husband with a fortune, and finally obtains him, *speculates* well." "Some seem to suppose that it is peculiar to Wall-street," agreed the Cincinnati *Merchants' Magazine*, but the magazine insisted "that those seeking the gain of money are not the only speculators: but that men, women, and children, are all endeavoring to acquire something of which they are not now possessed—in fact, that we are *all speculators*." When life itself was a gamble, how could one distinguish the good risks from the bad? "As well might you attempt to stop the

---

42 *Legislative and Documentary History of the Bank of the United States* (Washington, D.C.: Gales and Seaton, 1832), 519; *General Advertiser* [Philadelphia], 23 Mar. 1792, 2.

43 *Selected Speeches of John Sergeant, of Pennsylvania* (Philadelphia: E. L. Carey & A. Hart, 1832), 164.

flow of the sea, or direct the course of the whirlwind," despaired the playwright and journalist Mordecai Noah, "as to say who shall, or who shall not speculate."[44]

The difficulty of distinguishing gambling from commerce was not necessarily a reason to refrain from regulating speculation. "If there be a want of precision in defining the thing condemned, it arises from the very nature of the case," one editorialist reasoned. "It is one which admits of no precise and infallible rules. There are instances where the evil is so palpable, that every eye can see it; but between this point and the point of departure from legitimate business, there is an infinite variety of abuses." "Let us not," another agreed, "confound reckless speculation and commercial pursuits in the same category." While there might be a blurry line between them, "they are in truth 'wide as the poles asunder.'" If "it would perhaps be difficult, in some cases," to distinguish legitimate from illegitimate speculation, a third insisted, "there are nevertheless certain broad distinctions between the two classes of operations."[45]

But others concluded that even if some speculation should, in principle, be prohibited, it would be impossible for the law to ban the bad without also sweeping away the good. "Speculation in paper hath been a kind of gambling," one observer lamented, but there was nothing the law could do about it. "It is not possible," he explained, for the government to inspect "all the private bargains of jockies, speculators and dunces—No rule of right can be ascertained" for separating the permissible from the impermissible. And even if it could be done, he continued, the cost would far exceed the benefits: "The expence of attempting it would bring a new debt on the country, ten fold greater than all the savings which can be made." Speculators would have to be left to their own devices. "One quarter of the bargains made are detrimental to one, and some of them to both parties," he concluded. "They

---

44 *Weekly Museum*, 19 May 1792, 1; "Speculation," *Merchants' Magazine and Commercial Review* 24 (1851): 781; M. M. Noah, "Speculation," *New-York Mirror* 17 (1839): 186.

45 *National Era*, 29 July 1847, 2; "Speculation and Commerce," *Flag of Our Union* 12 (1857): 133; "Speculation—Legitimate and Illegitimate," *Merchants' Magazine* 58 (1868): 297.

were made in folly, but for national policy particularly to inspect them would be greater folly, and a most unmanageable and endless business." People entered into all kinds of transactions in all kinds of commodities at all kinds of prices, another agreed. How could one ever figure out which transactions were too speculative? "Even at this time there is an extensive speculation all over the country in the article of bread stuffs, and advantage is taken of the necessities of consumers to demand exorbitant prices," he pointed out. "Does the law afford any relief? And what relief could it afford? Would you annul contracts between landlord and tenant, because the rents were excessive?"[46] If the law could not draw a line between the speculation that should be allowed and the speculation that should be prohibited, the wisest course was to refrain from limiting speculation at all.

Some took the argument a step further. Not only was speculation inseparable from ordinary commercial life, they contended, but speculation was also a positive good in its own right. One early proponent of this view was Alexander Hamilton, who had to justify speculation while responding to criticism of his financial program, a key part of which was the issuance of debt securities that were the primary speculative assets in the bubble and crash of 1791–92. Just after the crash, Thomas Jefferson wrote a long letter to George Washington summing up his complaints about Hamilton's policies. One of Jefferson's critiques was his characteristically negative view of the buying and selling of securities. "All the capital employed in paper speculation is barren and useless, producing, like that on a gaming table, no accession to itself," Jefferson argued. The capital spent on speculation "is withdrawn from commerce and agriculture where it would have produced addition to the common mass," he continued. Instead, "it nourishes in our citizens habits of vice and idleness instead of industry and morality." Washington promptly wrote to Hamilton to hear his response. (Although Washington did not specify whose critique he was quoting—he referred only to his efforts "to learn from sensible & moderate men . . . the sentiments which are

---

46 *Connecticut Courant*, 28 Jan. 1790, 4; *A Familiar View, of the Operation and Tendency of Usury Laws* (New York: John Gray, 1837), 53.

entertained of public measures"—Hamilton might well have guessed the source of the criticism.)[47]

Hamilton responded with one of the earliest sustained defenses of speculation in the United States. The buying and selling of paper did not remove capital from the productive economy, he argued. Rather, it *added* capital to the economy. "It is true that the Capital, that is the *specie*, which is employed in paper speculation, while so employed, is barren and useless," Hamilton began. "But the paper itself constitutes a *new Capital*, which being saleable and transferrable at any moment, enables the proprietor to undertake any piece of business as well as an equal sum in Coin. And as the amount of the Debt circulated is much greater than the amount of the *specie* which circulates it, the new Capital put in motion by it considerably exceeds the old one which is *suspended*." Paper securities made investment much easier, Hamilton added, because they allowed people to convert assets that were not easily invested into assets that were. "Every thing that has value is Capital—an acre of ground a horse a cow or a public or a private obligation; which may with different degrees of convenience be applied to industrious enterprise," Hamilton advised Washington. "That which, like public Stock, can at any instant be turned into money is of equal utility with money as Capital." If Jefferson's zero-sum view of the economy were correct, Hamilton continued, money would be scarcest in the societies with the most securities trading. In fact, the opposite was true. "Let it be examined whether at those places where there is most debt afloat and most money employed in its circulation, there is not at the same time a greater plenty of money for every other purpose," Hamilton noted. "It will be found that there is." He conceded that the limited number of people who spent significant portions of their time engaged in speculation might be diverting their hours from more productive pursuits, but that loss was swamped, he argued, by the gain to the economy from the capital they injected into it. "Jobbing in the funds has some bad effects among those engaged in it," he concluded. "But if the proposition be

---

47 Thomas Jefferson to George Washington, 23 May 1792, in *Papers of Thomas Jefferson*, 23:537; George Washington to Alexander Hamilton, 29 July 1792, in *Papers of Alexander Hamilton*, 12:129–31.

true, that Stock operates as Capital, the effect upon the Citizens at large is different. It promotes among them industry by furnishing a larger field of employment."[48]

Hamilton was defending a broad financial program, of which providing the material for speculation was just a part, but others made the same point while offering more specific defenses of speculation in its own right. Speculation did not reduce the amount of capital in the productive economy, one correspondent insisted, but rather *increased* that amount. "Speculators neither bury nor export their money," he pointed out. "On the contrary, they continually circulate it." To be sure, speculation was liable to abuse, but so was anything. "Honor and religion—everything that is useful, noble or virtuous, may be abused. Ought they therefore to be condemned or avoided? No, certainly." And while speculators might harm themselves, argued the Reverend Cyrus Mason of New York University, by spurring economic activity, they indirectly helped others. Mason was speaking just after the bursting of the mulberry tree bubble of the 1830s. (Silkworms live in mulberry trees, and the prospect of a domestic silk industry gave rise to overinvestment in mulberry trees.) "When the fever of speculation has gone by, and the laughers at speculation have had their turn, the mulberry trees will be found growing in vast numbers all over the face of this country," Mason affirmed. "And when there has been time to mature their growth, the business will be found attractive and profitable." He looked back at the Merino sheep bubble of a few years earlier, when the collapse of wool prices had left farmers throughout the northern states with a glut of sheep. "The fever had its course, and the laughers their fun," Mason recalled, "but the improved breed of sheep remains, the public revenue from imported fine wool and cloth has been reduced, and a rich blessing to our country has been the result."[49]

A second common defense of speculation was that it provided the useful service of deepening markets. It was widely recognized in the

---

48 Alexander Hamilton to George Washington, 18 Aug. 1792, in *Papers of Alexander Hamilton*, 12:246–47.

49 *General Advertiser* [Philadelphia] 29 Mar. 1792, 2; Cyrus Mason, *The Oration on the Thirteenth Anniversary of the American Institute* (New York: Hopkins & Jennings, 1840), 23.

late eighteenth century that speculators in any kind of asset made non-speculators more willing to hold that asset, and thus made the asset more valuable, because the speculators stood ready to buy and sell at any time. "As to Stock-jobbers he saw no reason for the censures thrown upon them," Elbridge Gerry remarked at the Constitutional Convention. "They keep up the value of the paper. Without them there would be no market." Robert Morris, one of the leading speculators of the era, agreed that "even if it were possible to prevent Speculation, it is precisely the Thing which ought not to be prevented; because he who wants Money to commence, pursue or extend his Business, is more benefited by selling Stock of any kind (even at a considerable Discount) than he could be by the Rise of it at a future Period."[50] On this view, speculators reduced the risk of investment, because an investor could have some confidence that someone would step up to buy in the event he needed to sell.

Another justification of speculation became common in the first half of the nineteenth century. Speculators, some argued, stabilized prices, by buying when the market was low and selling when it was high. "When the price has very much declined," Willard Phillips reasoned, "those who suppose it to be verging on its lowest point, and about to seek again its natural level, the mean cost, naturally use their funds and credit in purchasing, to take advantage of the change." By boosting demand, speculators reversed the decline in prices. "Speculations may have the effect of limiting the vibrations of price within narrower extremes," Phillips continued, "for if a great quantity be withdrawn from a declining market, it may cause a rise, and the same quantity being thrown onto a rising market may accelerate the change to a decline of the price." Speculators thus helped their fellow participants in the economy. "As far as speculation has these effects it is useful," Phillips concluded, "since extremes and irregular fluctuations of price, are followed by embarrassments and bankruptcies, by which the community at large suffers." By the same mechanism, others suggested, speculators

---

50 *Notes of Debates in the Federal Convention of 1787 Reported by James Madison* (New York: Norton, 1987), 529; Robert Morris to John Hanson, 29 July 1782, in E. James Ferguson et al., *The Papers of Robert Morris, 1781–1784* (Pittsburgh, Pa.: University of Pittsburgh Press, 1973–99), 6:70.

smoothed out fluctuations in supply, by bringing commodities to market when they were scarce and withholding them when they were plentiful. Without speculators, argued Alonzo Potter of Union College, the supply of grain and other goods "would be necessarily so irregular as to occasion profusion and waste at one period, and dearth and famine, as their consequence, at another."[51]

In any event, others contended, speculators were merely responding to public demand for their services. "When a financial crisis overtakes the community," the *Atlantic* observed, "we hear much and sharp censure of all *speculation*. Speculators, one and all, are forthwith consigned to an abyss of obloquy." But why were speculators buying and selling in the first place? Because of "that same public who denounce speculation in one breath, and in the next clamor for goods at low prices, and force the jobber into large stores and large sales at small profits as the indispensable condition of his very existence. Those who thus rail at speculation are generally quite unaware that their own inexorable demand for goods at low prices is one of the principal efficient causes of that of which they complain."[52]

On this view, speculation was quite different from gambling. Like any other business, it was simply a matter of giving customers what they wanted. As one defender of the "fluctuations of mercantile speculation" put it, "trade has all the fascination of gambling, without its moral guilt." Speculators did not force anyone to buy or to sell, and they could not raise or lower prices at will; like anyone else, they had to accept whatever prices the market produced. "There is a palpable mistake in the assumption" that speculators inflated prices, one observer insisted. "The real cause is an actual scarcity." And when speculators profited from scarcity, why should they be attacked? "The individual who bought one thousand barrels of flour last August at eight or nine dollars per barrel, and now sells it or refuses to sell it for thirteen, has

51 Willard Phillips, *A Manual of Political Economy* (Boston: Hilliard, Gray, Little, and Wilkins, 1828), 50–51; Henry Vethake, *The Principles of Political Economy* (Philadelphia: Nicklin & Johnson, 1838), 233; Alonzo Potter, *Political Economy* (New York: Harper & Brothers, 1840), 163.
52 "A Dry-Goods Jobber in 1861," *Atlantic Monthly* 7 (1861): 204–5.

violated no law of society, trade, or government, and may have acted uprightly throughout."[53]

Defenders of speculation attributed critiques of the practice to the ignorance of their fellow citizens. "Speculation," suggested the journalist Richard Hildreth, was simply one "of those verbal reasons by which practical men account for things they do not understand." Another proponent concluded that "when judicious minds condemn, *en masse,* speculators and speculation, I imagine that it is always for want of sufficient examination and reflection on the subject." On the other side, critics of speculation interpreted justifications of the practice as self-interested sophistry. It was hardly a coincidence that someone like Robert Morris would defend speculators, an anonymous opponent sneered. He was "engaged in those deep speculations" himself. By the middle of the nineteenth century, Americans had engaged in decades of debate over the merits of speculation. Both sides had ample arguments to draw upon.[54]

A PRACTICABLE LINE OF DISCRIMINATION

Of course, this was rarely a debate about speculation in the abstract. Arguments for and against speculation were almost always put forward in the context of individual speculative episodes, specific regulatory proposals, or particular legal questions. Should the legislature prohibit the most speculative kinds of transactions? Should speculative contracts be enforceable in court? Questions like these came up regularly in the early republic. There was always an occasion to think about the pros and cons of speculation.

The most fundamental of these issues involved the legality of gambling. English law had allowed most forms of gambling, with ad hoc exceptions. "All wagers are legal," explained the barrister John Disney

---

53 *Village Register and Norfolk County Advertiser,* 27 Apr. 1821, 1; "High Prices—Speculation," *New-Yorker* 2 (1837): 345.

54 Richard Hildreth, *The History of Banks* (Boston: Hilliard, Gray & Co., 1837), 77; *National Era,* 29 July 1847, 4; "Lucius" to Robert Morris, 12 Mar. 1783, in *Papers of Robert Morris,* 7:561; Scott A. Sandage, *Born Losers: A History of Failure in America* (Cambridge, Mass.: Harvard University Press, 2005).

in his treatise on the law of gaming, "excepting those which tend to a breach of the peace;—or are *contra bonos mores*;—or tend to hurt the character of, or expose to ridicule, a third person;—or are against the rules of sound policy and morality;—or are contrary to a positive enactment of the law." The United States inherited this rule at independence. In several early reported cases, American courts enforced contracts for wagers on the outcome of horse races. When the federal government tried to prosecute the proprietor of a gaming house in the District of Columbia, the court stopped the prosecution. Gambling, the judges told the prosecutor, was simply not illegal. On the other hand, courts refused to enforce wagers they deemed contrary to public policy. As New York's chief judge James Kent put it, "a wager contract is void, if it be against the principles of public policy, equally as if it contravened a positive law." For example, when two residents of Kent County, Maryland, bet on an election for sheriff, Maryland's General Court refused to order the loser to pay the winner. "The election of a sheriff is of great importance to the community," the court explained, "and ought to be free from corrupt and undue influence." A New York court took an equally dim view of a suit brought by the winner of a wager on the state's 1807 gubernatorial election. On the other hand, the Illinois Supreme Court was willing to enforce a wager between two Illinois residents on how many votes William Henry Harrison would receive in Kentucky in the 1840 presidential election, on the theory that the bet could not corrupt the election, because Illinoisans would be unable to influence events in Kentucky. As the New York lawyer George Caines summed up the early American law of gambling, it was "a system in which wagers are merely tolerated but not favoured."[55]

The law's toleration for gambling diminished over time. Virtually from the beginning, states passed statutes banning particular kinds of

---

55 John Disney, *The Law of Gaming, Wagers, Horse-Racing, and Gaming-Houses* (London: J. Butterworth, 1806), 2; *Williams v. Cabarrus*, 1 N.C. 54 (1793); *Barret v. Hampton*, 2 Brev. 226 (S.C. 1807); *United States v. Willis*, 28 F. Cas. 698 (C.C.D.C. 1808); *Mount & Wardell v. Waite*, 7 Johns. 434 (N.Y. Sup. 1811); *Wroth v. Johnson*, 4 H. & McH. 284 (Md. 1799); *Bunn v. Riker*, 4 Johns. 426 (N.Y. Sup. 1809); *Morgan v. Pettit*, 4 Ill. 529 (1842); *Davy v. Hallett*, 3 Cai. R. 16 (N.Y. Sup. 1805).

gambling. For instance, Delaware prohibited wagers on horse racing in 1786, and Virginia banned the card game of faro not long after. Within a few decades these narrow prohibitions had become so numerous and broad that they coalesced into a new general rule. Gambling had once been lawful except where specifically banned, but by the second half of the nineteenth century it tended to be unlawful except where specifically allowed (for example, some states had lotteries, and others allowed horse racing). Gambling hardly disappeared, but without the benefit of the formal legal system, nineteenth-century gamblers were increasingly left to norms of honor and the use of violence for the enforcement of their contracts.[56]

The law governing commercial speculation took the opposite trajectory—from ambivalence in the late eighteenth century to approval, with certain exceptions, by the early nineteenth. In 1778, for example, Nathan Wright agreed to sell 1,800 acres of land straddling the Maryland–Delaware border to Isaac Perkins. The contract specified that Wright would only convey the land once Perkins had made three annual payments in continental currency. The currency depreciated sharply over the next two years, so although Perkins diligently made all three payments, they turned out to be worth much less than Wright had expected. Wright refused to convey the land to Perkins, because in his view he had not been fully paid. As he testified, "he is willing to convey the said land upon receiving the real value thereof, agreeably to the true meaning of the contract." Perkins's suit came before Maryland Chancellor Alexander Hanson, who explained that the case raised a difficult question. On the one hand, he acknowledged, any contract involving payment in the future could be said to involve speculation, because the medium of payment might fluctuate in value between the contract date and the payment date. On the other hand, some contracts

---

56 *State v. Blackiston*, 2 Del Cas. 229 (1786); *Commonwealth v. M'Guire*, 3 Va. 119 (1798); *The Development of the Law of Gambling: 1776–1976* (Washington, D.C.: National Institute of Law Enforcement and Criminal Justice, 1977), 65–74, 142–56, 246–63; Ann Fabian, *Card Sharps, Dream Books, & Bucket Shops: Gambling in 19th-Century America* (Ithaca, N.Y.: Cornell University Press, 1990); John M. Findlay, *People of Chance: Gambling in American Society from Jamestown to Las Vegas* (New York: Oxford University Press, 1986).

were simply too speculative to be enforced, and he decided that this was one of them. Hanson concluded that a "court ought not to give its aid towards enforcing the specific performance of any speculating engagements." Rather than ordering Wright to convey the land to Perkins, he ordered Wright to give Perkins his money back. "A speculating contract for continental money," Hanson explained in a case involving a similar transaction, "is such a contract as this court has again and again said it will not enforce."[57]

Other early American judges, however, took a more benign view of speculative transactions. In November 1791, John Wilkes agreed to buy US "stock" (what we would today call bonds) from Robert Gilchreest ten months later, in September 1792. The stock's value dropped in the interim, a period encompassing the crash of 1792, so when Gilchreest delivered it to Wilkes in September, Wilkes refused to pay. The Pennsylvania Supreme Court had little trouble finding the contract enforceable. "The sale of stock is neither unlawful nor immoral," the court declared. "It is confessed, that an inordinate spirit of speculation approaches to gaming, and tends to corrupt the morals of the people. When the public mind is thus affected, it becomes the legislature to interpose. But we have no such law at present." The risk that prices might rise or fall was inherent in virtually all transactions, the court noted. "Call the 6 per cent. stock so many bushels of wheat," the court asked: "if it had fallen in price on the day of delivery, and the vendor was then ready and willing, and offered to perform his contract in all parts, ought not the principal or his surety to make him full compensation? If the wheat had risen in price, would not the adverse party be enabled to get like compensation, in case the vendor had receded from his bargain?"[58] If risk was a normal part of commercial life, judges had no basis for distinguishing lawful transactions from those too speculative to enforce.

This became the prevailing view in the early nineteenth century. In 1803, for example, Virginia's Supreme Court of Appeals considered the

---

57 *Perkins v. Wright*, 3 H. & McH. 324 (Md. Ct. App. 1793); *Hopkins v. Stump*, 2 H. & J. 301 (Md. Ct. App. 1808) (Hanson decided this case in 1804 and died in 1806; the Court of Appeals affirmed his decision in 1808).

58 *Gilchreest v. Pollock*, 2 Yeates 18 (Pa. 1795).

enforceability of what one of its members called "a mere speculation upon the paper currency of the country." Willis (the parties are identified only by their last names) had agreed to pay Griffin £25,000 in paper money in 1780 and 1781, in exchange for Griffin's promise to pay Willis £2,500 in specie ten years later, in 1790. "The contract in this case, was founded upon speculation on both sides," one of the judges acknowledged. "*Griffin* thought, the present use of the money would be advantageous to him; and *Willis*, that it would be more beneficial to receive the specie at a distant day." Yet the judges all agreed that the contract was nevertheless enforceable. The Maryland Court of Appeals reached a similar decision in a case involving a complex contract to speculate in US bonds, an arrangement that required one party to pay the other a sum that depended on the difference in the bonds' value on two dates. The defendant contended that the contract was unenforceable, because it was merely a wager. The court disagreed. It accepted the plaintiff's argument that "almost every contract depends on a contingency; and if this is considered a wager, it will put an end to all contracts."[59]

The Virginia judge Dabney Carr, Thomas Jefferson's nephew, summed up this way of thinking in an 1819 case that was just one tiny part of the litigation arising from the bankruptcy of Robert Morris two decades before. ("Morris was known to every one, as a man of great talents, particularly for speculation," Carr observed. "One of those Giants in speculation never falls alone; all connected with him feel the shock:—and those within his immediate vortex are generally drawn down along with him.") The transaction at issue involved the sale of notes signed by Morris. Both the seller and the buyer learned only after the purchase that Morris was bankrupt and that the notes were thus worth very little. "It is said," as Carr described the buyer's argument for why the contract was unenforceable, "that this was a *speculating* contract, with which this Court ought not to interfere." But Carr dismissed this contention. "I can not see how a practicable line of discrimination can be drawn between this sort of commerce, and that which we see every day carried on in Bonds, Bills and Notes," he reasoned. "A man

59 *Brachan v. Griffin*, 7 Va. 433 (1803); *Ridgely v. Riggs*, 4 H. & J. 358 (Md. Ct. App. 1818).

wanting to raise money, takes these evidences of debt, as he would any other species of property, to the market, and sells them for what they will bring; sometimes more, sometimes less."[60] If the value of any asset could rise or fall, all commercial transactions were speculative. There was no principled way for judges to distinguish between the good and the bad.

In certain contexts, however, legislatures stepped in to ban prospectively categories of transactions the judges would not annul in retrospect. The most important of these statutes was New York's 1792 "Act to prevent the pernicious Practice of Stock-Jobbing." After the crash of 1792, when concern about speculative stock trading was at its peak, New York declared void all contracts for the sale of securities that the ostensible seller did not own at the time of contract. This provision was copied from a 1734 English statute that had likewise been intended to curb speculative trading. The idea was to put a stop to a common form of speculation, in which two parties would agree to sell stock at a particular price on a particular date in the future. When that date arrived, the seller would not in fact transfer the stock to the buyer. Rather, one party would simply pay to the other the difference between the contract price and the stock's actual price. New York's statute remained in force until 1858. Massachusetts had a similar law from 1836 to 1910. Neither statute had much effect. Traders could no longer use the courts to enforce these transactions, but the transactions remained common nevertheless, enforced by the Stock Exchange and more diffusely by the loss of reputation that would be suffered by a trader known to breach his contracts.[61]

Legislatures sporadically considered, and occasionally enacted, other limits on speculation. In 1793 and again in 1794, Congress debated whether to tax securities transactions, in part to raise revenue and in part to dampen speculation. The idea was well received in Congress, to the dismay of Fisher Ames of Massachusetts. "This distresses Hamilton exceedingly, and well it may," Ames remarked. "To

60 *Armstrong v. Hickman*, 20 Va. 287 (1819).
61 *Laws of the State of New-York* (New York: Francis Childs and John Swaine, 1792), 66; Stuart Banner, *Anglo-American Securities Regulation: Cultural and Political Roots, 1690–1860* (Cambridge: Cambridge University Press, 1998), 171–75.

begin to tax the public debt, when we are afraid to tax snuff, is a bad omen." This proposed tax was approved by a committee of the whole House, but it was then added to a long list of other taxes that were rejected as a package. In 1834, a committee of the New York Assembly condemned "the great and palpable evils attendant upon the existing system of buying and selling stocks in the city of New-York," a system that in the committee's view "gives rise to a spirit of gambling which is carried out to an alarming extent." Nothing came of this report. But other states imposed limits on speculative transactions. Pennsylvania and Maryland voided all futures contracts for the sale of securities where the delivery date would be more than five days after the contract date. Several states required shareholders to own stock for a certain minimum period before selling it, to encourage long-term investment while discouraging short-term speculation. Some states restricted the amount of shares that could be purchased in a single day, to make it harder for one person to buy large quantities. The federal government repeatedly tried to discourage speculation in public land, through such methods as limiting the amount a single person could purchase and requiring grantees to reside on the land.[62] These were all efforts to ban a narrow range of the most speculative transactions without tramping too heavily on commercial activity considered more legitimate.

American law governing risky transactions thus distinguished, at an early date, between gambling and speculation. Transactions classified as wagers were presumed unenforceable, with certain exceptions. Transactions classified as speculation, by contrast, were presumed enforceable, again with certain exceptions. As historians have pointed out, the difference between the two categories was never completely stable, and it drew in part on a class distinction between the socially acceptable risks taken by respectable members of society and the less polite

62 Seth Ames, ed., *Works of Fisher Ames* (Boston: Little, Brown and Co., 1854), 1:141; *Documents of the Assembly of the State of New-York, Fifty-Seventh Session* (Albany, N.Y.: E. Croswell, 1834), No. 339; Banner, *Anglo-American Securities Regulation*, 222–26; Paul W. Gates, *History of Public Land Law Development* (Washington, D.C.: Government Printing Office, 1968).

risks taken by those on the margins.[63] But the difference between gambling and speculation was not entirely a matter of class, and it was not entirely void of substance. It was based on a perception, apparently widely shared among the managers of the legal system, that risk was tolerable as a means to some greater end, but that it was not a worthwhile end in itself. In the transactions proscribed as "wagers"—bets on horse races, card games, and the like—there was no purpose beyond the participants' enjoyment of the risk itself. The transactions called "speculation," on the other hand, involved some other useful societal end, even if the risks associated with speculation were indistinguishable from the risks associated with gambling. Speculation in trade made society richer, even if it made half the speculators poorer. Speculation in shares gave rise to valuable new enterprises, even if it beggared some of the shareholders. The line between speculation and gambling was often difficult to draw with precision, but this seems to have been the intuition behind the view that some such line had to be drawn.

Insurance provides the clearest early example. Marine insurance was already common by the late eighteenth century. It looked a lot like gambling: the insured would pay a small sum, and if the ship went down, he would receive a large payoff from the insurer. As Judge Jacob Peck of the Tennessee Supreme Court wondered, gaming "depends upon hazard and chance; so do all insurances depend upon hazard and chance. What is the difference?" Yet insurance also served a useful purpose. Insurance was "much for the benefit and extension of trade," William Blackstone explained in his commentaries on English law, "by distributing the loss or gain among a number of adventurers."[64]

English law accordingly adopted the concept of the "insurable interest," which permitted people to buy insurance only if they themselves

63 Karen Halttunen, *Confidence Men and Painted Women: A Study of Middle-Class Culture in America, 1830–1870* (New Haven, Conn.: Yale University Press, 1982), 16–20; Fabian, *Card Sharps*, 1–11.

64 Hannah Atlee Farber, *Underwritten States: Marine Insurance and the Making of Bodies Politic in America, 1622–1815* (Ph.D. dissertation, University of California, Berkeley, 2014); Edwin J. Perkins, *American Public Finance and Financial Services 1700–1815* (Columbus: Ohio State University Press, 1994), 282–92; *State v. Smith*, 10 Tenn. 272 (1829); William Blackstone, *Commentaries on the Laws of England* (Oxford: Clarendon Press, 1765–69), 2:461.

would bear a loss if the ship failed to arrive. Insurance policies on other people's voyages were unenforceable, because they "were very justly considered as mere gaming or wager-policies," declared the barrister James Park in his treatise on insurance. American law followed suit. "Wager policies ... though dressed up in the garb of insurance, are in fact nothing more than gambling contracts," huffed George Caines of New York. A wager policy was one in which "the party insured has not any interest in the thing underwritten." When the question came before the Massachusetts Supreme Court for the first time in 1806, the court found it an easy one. Thomas Amory had purchased two different insurance policies, from two different companies, on the same cargo aboard a ship that was to sail from the Canary Islands to the United States. On the way, the ship and its cargo were captured by the British and taken to Jamaica. Armory recovered on his first policy. When he tried to recover on the second, the second insurance company defended on the ground that Armory had already been fully compensated, and that his second policy was nothing but a wager that the ship would never reach its destination. The court agreed. "It would seem a disgraceful occupation of the courts of any country, to sit in judgment between two gamblers, in order to decide which was the best calculator of chances, or which had the most cunning of the two," sniffed Justice Isaac Parker. "There could be but one step of degradation below this—which is, that the judges should be the stake-holders of the parties." Chief Justice Francis Dana took the same view. "Wager policies are injurious to the morals of the citizens," he reasoned, and "tend to encourage an extravagant and particularly hazardous species of gaming." Insurance "ought to be reserved for the benefit of real commerce."[65]

By allowing merchants to insure their own losses but not the losses of others, judges were able to draw a line between commerce and gambling. "An insurance amongst us, is a contract of *indemnity*," reasoned Judge Jasper Yeates of Pennsylvania. "Its object is, not to make a *positive gain*, but to avert a *possible loss....* A policy therefore made without

---

65 James Allan Park, *A System of the Law of Marine Insurances*, 2nd American ed. (Boston: Thomas and Andrews, 1800), 262; George Caines, *Enquiry Into the Law Merchant of the United States* (New York: Abraham and Arthur Stansbury, 1802), 1:313; *Amory v. Gilman*, 2 Mass. 1 (1806).

interest, is a wager policy, and has nothing in common with insurance, but name and form." James Kent of New York put it rather more grumpily. "Wager policies ought not to be encouraged," he snorted, "and it is not pleasant that the time of the court should be occupied in discussing them."[66] Insuring one's own losses was like ordinary commercial speculation; it was a method of shifting risk from one party to another, for the benefit of all. One side might be the loser in any given transaction, but all those transactions would net out positive for the broader economy. Insuring other people's losses was understood as gambling. Some would win and some would lose, but no broader purpose would be achieved.

Insurers' desire to distinguish wagers from legitimate commerce was especially strong regarding life insurance, because of the unsettling aspect of betting that someone would die, and because of the distinct possibility that the holder of a policy on someone else's life might take steps to make his death come sooner. When life insurance first came on the American market in the early nineteenth century, promoters were thus careful to distinguish it from gambling. "It is very commonly imagined, that Life Insurance is of a nature purely speculative," conceded one insurance company—"that it is a mere gambling contract between the assurer and the assured." But nothing could be further from the truth, declared another. Life insurance "does not rest upon uncertain theories or vague speculations, as is by many supposed," the company explained; "nor is it founded upon calculations whether death *will* or *will not* happen; for that event is certain; but is based upon the law of the *average duration of life*, and secures the benefits of a mean duration of years, by rules and tables approximating so *nearly* to a certainty, that they may be depended upon, in all calculations." Life insurance "has been supposed to have some affinity to gambling," acknowledged another promoter. "But the analogy is shallow. It may more justly be considered a method of delivering human life from the tyranny of chance." When the president of a Utica bank declared in the pages of the *Merchants' Magazine* that "life insurance possesses many of the elements of gambling," he drew immediate

66 *Pritchet v. Insurance Company of North America*, 3 Yeates 458 (Pa. 1803); *Clendining v. Church*, 3 Cai. R. 141 (N.Y. Sup. 1805).

rejoinders from correspondents who pointed out that banking re-
sembled gambling more than life insurance did. Life insurance "is,
or ought to be, if rightly managed, *a science*," one insisted. The
"tables of the duration of life, are, to say the least, more reliable
than the chances of Banking in the United States." The president of
the Mutual Life Insurance Company of New York assured readers
that "the application of the law of average, so far from giving it the
character of a gambling transaction, in reality goes far to equalize
among all connected with it, a participation in all the chances of
life."[67]

Like older forms of insurance, life insurance took the form of a
wager, but it was a wager that served useful purposes. "It might be
the means of preventing many families of industrious tradesmen and
others, from becoming chargeable on the public charity and provide
the means of education to their orphan children," a committee of the
Pennsylvania legislature recognized in 1812, when asked to charter the
state's first life insurance company. Life insurance "might also assist
the aged infirm not blessed with an abundance of wealth to pass the
downward path of life with ease and comfort," the committee added.
A Rhode Island newspaper concluded that "life insurance companies
are in fact nothing more, when well conducted, than Savings Banks.
A man pays year after year his premium, and when he dies, whether
it be soon or late, his family has the benefit in such form as not to be
accessible to creditors." One minister advised that life insurance was "a

67 Geoffrey Clark, *Betting on Lives: The Culture of Life Insurance in England,*
    1695–1795 (Manchester: Manchester University Press, 1999), 40–59; Sharon
    Ann Murphy, *Investing in Life: Insurance in Antebellum America* (Baltimore:
    Johns Hopkins University Press, 2010), 81–85; *Prospectus of the Union*
    Insurance Company (New York: J. Seymour, 1818), 3; *Life Insurance: Its*
    Principles, Operations and Benefits, as Presented by the Connecticut Mutual
    Life Insurance Company (Hartford, Conn.: Case, Tiffany & Burnham,
    1846), 3; "The Regulation of Life Insurance," *Merchants' Magazine and*
    Commercial Review 27 (1852): 541; A. B. Johnson, "The Relative Merits of
    Life Insurance and Savings Banks," *Merchants' Magazine and Commercial*
    Review 25 (1851): 670; "Life Insurance," *New York Daily Times*, 26 Dec. 1851,
    1; Joseph B. Collins, "Life Insurance," *Merchants' Magazine and Commercial*
    Review 26 (1852): 196.

laudable, honorable and safe way, of preventing a very large amount of human wretchedness."[68]

Courts accordingly used the concept of an insurable interest to distinguish genuine life insurance from wagers that others would die sooner than expected. "In order to prevent individuals from gambling in life-insurance," one writer explained, the law "has declared that A shall not insure the life of B, unless he have what is called an *insurable interest* in that life; that is, unless A have some pecuniary interest in B's continuing to live." As early as 1815, when the life insurance business was still in its infancy, the Massachusetts Supreme Court considered the case of Nancy Lord, an unmarried woman who had insured the life of her brother, a seaman who died off the coast of Africa. Lord could not recover from the insurance company unless she had an insurable interest in her brother's life, the court reasoned, "for, otherwise, it would be a mere wager-policy, which we think would be contrary to the general policy of our laws, and therefore void." The court found that Lord did have an insurable interest in her brother, because she was "a young female without property," who "had been for several years, supported and educated at the expense of her brother, who stood towards her *in loco parentis*."[69] As Lord stood to suffer economic loss from her brother's death, she was understood not as betting that he would die, but rather as investing in a possible future after his death.

By the early nineteenth century, the law thus reflected the tension in American thought concerning risk. The law distinguished between gambling, the assumption of risk for its own sake, which was generally (although not always) proscribed, and speculation, the assumption of risk in a way that served some societal purpose, which was generally (although not always) permitted. This distinction was never a perfectly clean one.

68 *Journal of the Twenty-Second House of Representatives of the Commonwealth of Pennsylvania* (Lancaster: Benjamin Grimler, 1811 [*sic*]), 157 (although this publication bears an 1811 publication date, the committee report quoted is dated 6 Jan. 1812); *Rhode Island Republican*, 30 Apr. 1839, 3; "Life Insurance," *Bankers' Magazine and Statistical Register* 4 (1849): 371.

69 *Rates and Proposals of the New-York Life Insurance and Trust Company* (New York: Clayton & Van Norden, 1830), 11; Augustus de Morgan, *An Essay on Probabilities and on Their Application to Life Contingencies and Insurance Offices* (London: Longman, Orme, Brown, Green & Longmans, 1838), 102; *Lord v. Dall*, 12 Mass. 115 (1815).

There would always be debate over precisely where to draw the line, and over whether particular kinds of transactions should be placed on one side or the other. But there was little controversy over whether some such line had to be drawn. Speculation was something to be tolerated in general, but specific instances of speculation might be too harmful to be allowed.

GAMBLERS IN GOLD

The controversy over gold speculation during the Civil War was just one more installment in this recurring debate, but it was one with an especially sharp edge. Speculators were blamed, not merely for bringing ruin on themselves or for harming the wider economy, but for subverting the war effort. Abraham Lincoln was but one of many observers who held speculators responsible for the dollar's decline against gold. "Two-thirds of the public have been until now, and a very large proportion of them are still thoroughly satisfied that the rise in gold has been solely due to the efforts of speculators to break down the Government," reported the *New York Times*. One critic charged that fluctuations in gold prices were caused by "the reckless and gambling maneouvres of speculators, through fictitious sales, long and short, 'cornering' operations, and false rumours in regard to the war, and everything else that can further their nefarious schemes, by producing public distrust." Another New York paper declared that "partisans of the Rebellion quartered in our city have systematically and by concert striven and employed their means to increase the premium on Gold." The paper was certain that "they did this on behalf of their master, Jeff. Davis, and in the conviction that they were aiding the Rebellion as truly and palpably as though they were wielding muskets in the front rank of Lee's army." A judge in Washington, DC, went so far as to instruct a jury that the common law prohibited speculation in gold, which he deemed "contrary to public policy, and calculated to depreciate the value of the Treasury notes of the United States."[70]

In response to this widespread belief that gold speculators were weakening the Union Army, Senator John Sherman of Ohio introduced

---

70 *New York Times*, 20 Apr. 1864, 4; "The War and National Wealth," *Princeton Review* 36 (1864): 470–71; *New-York Daily Tribune*, 15 June 1864, 4; "The Legal Character of Gold Speculations," *Bankers' Magazine and Statistical Register* 14 (1864): 33.

legislation to prohibit speculative transactions in gold. The bill prohibited gold futures—that is, contracts for the sale of gold to be delivered at a later date. "The purpose of this bill is simply to prevent people from selling gold who have none to sell," Sherman declared on the Senate floor, "in such a way as to depreciate the price of our paper money."[71]

But if many blamed speculators for the fall of the dollar, there seemed to be just as many who thought it absurd to blame the speculators. Gold "is merchandise," the *Railway Times* observed, "and its price rises and falls for precisely the same reasons which govern the prices of other merchandise." It was "the fluctuating relation of demand and supply" that pushed gold prices up or down, not the machinations of speculators. "It is so with gold, as with everything else." A correspondent to another paper acknowledged that "gamblers in gold have caused it to rise and fall considerably at times," but insisted that speculators had no power to keep gold rising permanently. "There must be a permanent cause for a permanent effect," he reasoned. "In the case of gold there is no mystery about it at all. It rises because *its demand is constantly pressing on the limits of supply.*" The political economist Simon Newcomb deplored the common tendency to blame price movements on "good and evil spirits . . . who are waging a perpetual war, or playing an endless game of Stygian ten-pins, using government stocks for the pins. . . . Bull and bear are in fact equally powerless to effect any great or permanent change in the price of so universal and easily transportable an article as gold. At best they can only foresee the change. The stock market registers the price of gold, but does not fix it. It is governed entirely by the relation between the supply and demand."[72]

This view was well represented in Congress too. "Does any sane man in the world pretend to believe that the efforts of these people in thus betting can influence in the slightest the price of gold in the world's market?" asked an incredulous Edgar Cowan of Pennsylvania. The price of gold was determined "not by what the speculators or gamblers of

71 *Congressional Globe*, 15 Apr. 1864, 1640.
72 "Gold—Real Causes of Its Fluctuations," *Railway Times*, 14 May 1864, 154; *New York Times*, 4 July 1864, 2; Simon Newcomb, *A Critical Examination of Our Financial Policy During the Southern Rebellion* (New York: D. Appleton and Co., 1865), 16–17, 31.

New York may choose to do in the premises, but what the world at large does," Cowan continued. "The operation of this bill is not worth anything." Even some of the supporters of Sherman's bill admitted that it was very unlikely to stop the dollar from falling against gold. "Although we may not believe or feel that a bill of this kind will necessarily produce the effect," explained Senator William Fessenden of Maine, "it is nevertheless a duty in the present condition of things in this country to leave nothing untried." If Congress could do nothing about the fall of the dollar, at least it could make a show of trying to do something. Sherman's bill was enacted into law in June 1864, shortly after the Confederacy defeated the Union at the Battle of Cold Harbor.[73]

The ban on gold futures did nothing to halt the dollar's slide. Its only effect was to shut down the Gold Exchange, which made it more difficult even for lawful buyers and sellers of gold to find one another. "The passage of the gold act will long be remembered as the acme of folly at Washington," the *Bankers' Magazine* lamented. "Thus far every attempt made by the Secretary of the Treasury and Congress to stop the rise in gold has only accelerated the downward course of currency," despaired the *Commercial Advertiser*. "The veriest tyro in political science might have foreseen this." A hastily assembled group of New York bankers and merchants appointed a committee to travel to Washington to urge Congress and the Lincoln administration to repeal the gold law. At a meeting with Treasury Secretary Salmon Chase—which Chase found "good tempered on both sides & to me instructive"—the bankers argued that restricting the gold trade would only drive the greenback lower against gold. Chase replied that he "could not see that licence to gambling was essential to freedom of trade," and that the bankers' arguments were in any event better directed at Congress. Congress proved to be more receptive than Chase. The prohibition of gold futures, in effect since June 17, was repealed on July 2.[74] The speculators were back in business.

73 *Congressional Globe*, 15 Apr. 1864, 1641, 1640; 13 Stat. 132 (1864).
74 Kinahan Cornwallis, *The Gold Room and the New York Stock Exchange and Clearing House* (New York: A. S. Barnes & Co., 1879), 9–10; "The Financial Policy of the Government," *Bankers' Magazine and Statistical Register* 14 (1864): 1 (quoting the *Commercial Advertiser*); *New York Times*, 23 June 1864, 2; John Niven, ed., *The Salmon P. Chase Papers* (Kent, Ohio: Kent State University Press, 1983–88), 1:461–62; 13 Stat. 344 (1864).

In its details, the controversy over gold futures grew out of the unique crisis of the Civil War, but the controversy shared a structure with many other debates that took place in the early republic, and many more that would arise in later years. It required drawing a line between transactions thought to be harmful and those thought to be beneficial, a line between gambling and legitimate commerce. Everyone agreed that gambling was bad and that commerce was necessary. The difficulty was in telling the two apart.

2

Betting on Prices

IRA FOOTE AND STEPHEN HOOKER were carpenters from Peru, Illinois. They both moved to Chicago in 1854, within a few months of each other. Chicago was booming: the city's population nearly quadrupled in the 1850s, so there was plenty of work in the building trades. Foote was already thirty-eight years old when he arrived in Chicago. He would remain a carpenter for the rest of his working life. Hooker was a younger man. When he got to the big city he did not stay a carpenter for long. There was an exciting new kind of business underway in Chicago, and Hooker got in early. He became a broker on the Chicago Board of Trade.[1]

Foote kept his distance from the board of trade for many years. As the Chicago judge William McAllister would later put it, Foote was "rather ignorant and inexperienced in matters outside of his own proper business." It was not until 1874, when Foote was in his late fifties, that he was tempted to try his hand at speculating. McAllister said Foote was suddenly "seized with the desire to make money fast and easy," but that seems an uncharitable view.[2] After all, fortunes were being made at the board of trade, including by Hooker, Foote's former colleague in carpentry. For two decades Foote had been on the outside looking

1 Information in this and the following several paragraphs is from Transcript of Record, 73–97, *Pearce v. Rice*, 142 U.S. 28 (1891).
2 *Tenney v. Foote*, 4 Ill App. 594, 597 (1879) (affirming on the basis of McAllister's opinion in the trial court).

in. Now he finally ventured inside. Through a broker named George Adams, Foote purchased some oats.

Oat prices were rising, and within a short time Foote was $3,000 ahead. He asked Adams to sell the oats, but Adams persuaded Foote not to sell for a while—"I have got an inside track on the oats business," Adams claimed, with an air of mystery. By the time Adams finally sold the oats for Foote, most of Foote's gains had evaporated. To make matters worse, when Adams sent Foote a check for his much-reduced profits, he had deducted fees for storing and handling the oats. Foote resolved never to have anything to do with the board of trade again.

Soon after, however, he ran into his old friend Stephen Hooker. Foote recalled: "Mr. Hooker says, I am dealing pretty largely on the board of trade and I will speculate for you. Well, I said, I don't know. I thought I wouldn't do it any more. I had enough with Mr. Adams." Hooker would not give in easily. "He said, I can make you some money. Well, I said, of course I would like to make money. We all want to make money, but I don't want any more trading as I traded with Mr. Adams." Hooker offered Foote a deal too good to refuse: Hooker would trade on Foote's behalf without requiring Foote to put up any margin—that is, Foote would not have to deposit any money with Hooker to cover potential losses. Even better, Hooker offered to let Foote front-run his bigger clients. "I have large deals," Hooker declared, "have some people in Canada, some in Troy, some in Buffalo, and sometimes they give me large orders to buy." Hooker told Foote: "If the market is right I will buy for you first, then go on these large orders and raise the market, . . . and I can sell them right out for you and make you some money." Foote accepted the offer, but he was still upset that Adams had charged him for handling and storing oats, so he insisted on one condition. Under no circumstances was Hooker to buy any physical grain for him. "I told him I wouldn't have any grain," Foote recalled. Instead, Foote instructed Hooker to "speculate in what they call options, from one month to the other." The understanding between the two men was that Foote would neither accept nor deliver any physical commodity. His profit or loss would be the difference between the value of an option when he purchased it and its price when he sold it. As Foote explained it, "I was to pay the difference or they me."

Foote's second venture in commodity trading did not go as well as his first. Within a year he was down $22,000, a colossal sum at a time when the average annual wage for nonfarm employees was only around $400. In a normal brokerage relationship, a man of limited means like Foote could never have racked up such a large debt, because once his losses exceeded the margin he had deposited with his broker, the broker would have kept the margin and closed Foote's account. Special treatment from his old friend Hooker was what put him so far in the hole. Foote gave up his sideline as a speculator. "I said, I don't want any more; I must quit; I have no money for this thing." Hooker was left to pay Foote's debts and seek reimbursement from Foote, but Foote could not pay Hooker anything close to $22,000. All he could do was give Hooker notes (that is, promises to pay), which Hooker passed on to a variety of other people, doubtless at prices much lower than their face value to reflect the unlikelihood of payment. The holders of those notes would hound Foote for the rest of his life.

Foote spent his last years renting a room in a Chicago boarding-house, unable to work after suffering a stroke, accumulating more debts, and issuing more notes. Some of the notes were to James Rice, who paid Foote's rent and medical bills. One was to the boardinghouse keeper, Sarah Reed. Foote had promised to marry Reed, but when he changed his mind after his stroke, Reed insisted on a note as the price of releasing him from his marriage commitment.[3]

Most of Foote's outstanding notes were the result of his misadventure on the board of trade. They gave rise to two lawsuits against Foote to recover the amounts he had promised to pay. His lawyer raised the same defense in both: he argued that Foote had no obligation to pay, because the transactions Hooker had undertaken for him on the board of trade had been illegal. They had not been genuine purchases or sales, the lawyer contended. Rather, they had been wagers. Because Foote and Hooker had been betting on prices, he argued, the notes were nothing but gambling debts, and gambling debts were unenforceable.

These two cases came before two different Chicago judges within a span of three years. They posed the identical question: were Foote's

3 *Pearce v. Rice*, 142 U.S. 28, 31–32 (1891); *Chicago Daily Tribune*, 29 Dec. 1892, 14.

speculative trades unenforceable wagers? The law applicable to the cases was the same: it was the law of Illinois, which did not change in any relevant respect between the first case and the second. But the two judges reached opposite results.

In the first case, Judge William McAllister agreed that Foote's transactions were unlawful wagers. McAllister emphasized the fact that Foote and Hooker had explicitly agreed not to buy or sell any actual commodities; Foote intended neither to deliver nor receive any physical grain. McAllister reasoned: "It was, therefore, a mere engagement on the part of Hooker & Co. to gamble for Foote." He could perceive no reason "why this species of gambling, though wearing the respectable aspect of business, should be looked upon with any less disfavor by the courts than any other species." Because Foote had given his notes as payment for the debts he incurred in these transactions, he had no obligation to pay them off.[4]

The second case came before Judge Henry Blodgett, the former president of the Chicago and Northwestern Railway and thus a man more comfortable than McAllister with the ways of commercial life. Foote's transactions seemed perfectly ordinary to Blodgett. Hooker "did not contemplate or intend to make any different transactions for the defendant [Foote] than for his other customers," Blodgett explained. As brokers on the board of trade normally did, Hooker "could so manage the defendant's deals that he need not take any commodity bought, but could settle simply the difference between the purchase price and the market price." Because these trades were not illegal, Blodgett concluded, Foote could not evade his obligation to pay his debts.[5]

These particular events were of little significance to anyone besides Ira Foote and his creditors, but this disagreement between the two

4 *Tenney*, 597–601.
5 *Jackson v. Foote*, 12 F. 37, 39–41 (N.D. Ill. 1882). Strictly speaking, Blodgett conceded that the trades might have been unenforceable at common law as wagers, had the suit been brought by Hooker against Foote, but he held that this would not bar the notes' enforcement by a bona fide holder, and that the transactions did not violate the Illinois anti-option statute, which would have made the notes unenforceable by a third party. In the other case, McAllister held that the transactions did violate the Illinois statute. This statute and the common law will be discussed later.

judges was representative of a broader legal question that became quite important in the second half of the nineteenth century. The debate was over the legality of a very common type of transaction, one that was fundamental to the American economy. On the Chicago Board of Trade, or the New York Stock Exchange, or any of the many other commercial exchanges in cities all over the country, most of what was bought and sold lacked any physical existence. Contracts on the board of trade were denominated in bushels of grain, but few of the buyers and sellers ever saw any actual grain. Members of the stock exchange traded what were nominally shares of the ownership of large corporations, but in many, perhaps most, of these transactions neither party ever saw any physical share certificates. Contracts were settled not by the conveyance of items from one party to another but rather by the payment of money, representing the difference in the prices of those items at two different times. If one person expected the price of wheat or the value of a railroad company to rise, while another thought that the price of wheat or railroad shares would decline, the exchanges facilitated a deal between the two in which neither party needed to possess any wheat or any railroad shares. Whoever turned out wrong would simply compensate whoever turned out right.

Was this a smoothly functioning marketplace, in which investments could be made without the frictions of having to transfer and store the goods being bought and sold? Or was it a casino, in which the ostensible buyers and sellers were merely betting on whether prices would rise or fall? People were clearly speculating on the exchanges, but how were the winners earning money? Were they being compensated for making shrewd economic judgments and assuming risks others wished to shed? Or were they merely getting lucky on wild gambles on events they had no power to control? These questions preoccupied the American legal system throughout the second half of the nineteenth century.[6] The

6 For a wide range of perspectives on this set of questions, see Urs Stäheli, *Spectacular Speculation: Thrills, the Economy, and Popular Discourse,* trans. Eric Savoth (Stanford, Calif.: Stanford University Press, 2013), 43–92; Jonathan Levy, *Freaks of Fortune: The Emerging World of Capitalism and Risk in America* (Cambridge, Mass.: Harvard University Press, 2012), 231–63; Roy Kreitner, *Calculating Promises: The Emergence of Modern American Contract Doctrine* (Stanford, Calif.: Stanford University Press, 2007), 105–25; Joshua C. Tate,

answers that were worked out would help shape much of the economy for a long time to come.

THE INTENT TO DELIVER

Under the English common law inherited by the United States, there was nothing illegal about betting on prices. Stock speculators in London were trading options and futures as early as the late seventeenth century. It was widely recognized that many such sellers, perhaps most, did not actually own any of the shares they were nominally committing to sell, and that many such buyers, again perhaps most, had no intention of receiving any of the shares they were promising to buy. Transactions were settled, not by the transfer of shares, but by the payment of money, in the amount of the difference between the contract price and the market price on the settlement date. By this method, one observer of the London market pointed out in 1712, "a very beneficial Trade was daily driven with imaginary Stocks, and many Thousands bought and sold, to great Advantage, by those who were not worth a Groat." John Barnard, the mid-eighteenth-century member of Parliament who took the greatest interest in suppressing these transactions, complained that the market was nothing but "a Lottery, or rather a Gaming-House, publickly set up in the Middle of the City of London." Traders were wagering on stock prices, but wagers were enforceable under the common law as long as they weren't contrary to public policy, and English judges found that they were not. As one English judge, rebuffing a challenge to the legality of a difference contract on the price of Spanish bonds, put it, "we have no right to say that a wager on the price of foreign stock is void at common law."[7]

"Gambling, Commodity Speculation, and the 'Victorian Compromise,'" *Yale Journal of Law & the Humanities* 19 (2007): 97–114; Pat O'Malley, "Moral Uncertainties: Contract Law and Distinctions Between Speculation, Gambling, and Insurance," in *Risk and Morality*, ed. Richard V. Ericson and Aaron Doyle (Toronto: University of Toronto Press, 2003), 231–57.

7 *A New Way of Selling Places at Court* (London: John Morphew, 1712), 4; *The History and Proceedings of the House of Commons* (London: Richard Chandler, 1742–44), 7:381; *Morgan v. Perrer*, 132 Eng. Rep. 486, 490 (C.P. 1837).

English critics of these speculative transactions repeatedly urged Parliament to enact statutes prohibiting them. One critic was Daniel Defoe, who proposed that all sales of stock should be illegal unless the seller immediately transferred the stock to the buyer. The English stock market crash of 1720—the famous South Sea Bubble—brought forth a wave of similar calls for regulation. The Scottish essayist Thomas Gordon, for example, proposed "declaring all fictitious Contracts hereafter Illegal and Void, which shall not be immediately comply'd with, and punctually fulfill'd; and by inflicting a proper Punishment on all Persons assuming a false Power, and pretending to sell and buy Stock for themselves, or others, who have neither Money to Purchase, nor Stock to Deliver." Parliament eventually responded. Sir John Barnard's Act of 1734 banned stock options, prohibited parties from settling stock contracts by paying price differentials, and voided all contracts for the sale of stock that the seller did not actually own at the time the contract was entered into. This statute would remain in force until it was repealed in 1860. On paper, the law made it impossible to wager on stock prices, except by simply buying stock and holding it in the hope that the price would rise. In practice, options and futures remained common, as did the settlement of contracts by the payment of price differentials. Such contracts were no longer enforceable in court, but they could still be enforced by exclusion from the informal community of brokers, and later, with the creation of a formal stock exchange, by expulsion from the exchange.[8]

The United States inherited English common law but not most English statutes, so there was nothing illegal about betting on prices in the early United States either. As a Philadelphia speculator suggested to a colleague in Boston in 1789, "a sum of Continental Debt . . . might be sold to be *delivered* in any given time: that is to fix the price at present, and agree upon a mode of fixing it at the end of the Time,—and then without transferring, or delivering any Certificate to *pay* or receive the

8 Daniel Defoe, *The Villainy of Stock-Jobbers Detected* (London: s.n., 1701), 24; Thomas Gordon, *An Essay on the Practice of Stock-Jobbing* (London: J. Peele, 1724), 18; 7 Geo. III c. 8 (1734); Stuart Banner, *Anglo-American Securities Regulation: Cultural and Political Roots, 1690–1860* (Cambridge: Cambridge University Press, 1998), 106–7.

BETTING ON PRICES   63

difference of price. This is the Common practice in England." It soon became a common practice in the United States as well, as evidenced by the published court decisions of the 1790s enforcing such transactions. A few states responded by enacting statutes voiding certain speculative contracts for the sale of securities, as explained in the previous chapter. The most important of these statutes, New York's ban on the sale of securities the seller did not own at the time of the contract, was repealed in 1858, after a few decades of exerting little practical effect on the market. As one New York judge explained in 1844, "it is a well known fact that shares of stock are constantly sold at the board of brokers, which shares exist only in the imagination of the nominal buyers and sellers." One guide to the New York market noted that "the practice of betting upon the future rise and fall of prices is too well understood to need any particular explanation."[9]

These statutes were narrowly targeted at the stock market. They did not proscribe similarly speculative transactions in other commodities, which soon began to grow common. There was nothing new about speculating in commodity prices. Merchants who expected prices to rise had long been able to purchase items with the aim of reselling them, and those who expected prices to decline could agree to sell items in the future that one did not yet possess, in the hope of buying them at lower prices later. As the English judge William Blackstone observed in his widely used eighteenth-century treatise, "property may also in some cases be transferred by sale, though the vendor *hath none at all* in the goods." And there had long been futures markets in other countries. What was new to the United States in the early nineteenth century was the development of organized markets for commodity speculation along the lines of the stock markets that were already familiar. As early as 1819, the New York commercial press was reporting on the speculative market in tallow futures. (Tallow, or rendered animal fat, was used

9 Joseph Stancliffe Davis, *Essays in the Earlier History of American Corporations* (Cambridge, Mass.: Harvard University Press, 1917), 1:196; *Groves v. Graves*, 1 Va. 1 (1790); *Livingston v. Swanwick*, 2 U.S. 300 (C.C.D. Pa. 1793); *Graham v. Bickham*, 4 U.S. 149 (Pa. 1796); *Dykers v. Allen*, 7 Hill 497, 500 (N.Y. Sup. Ct. 1844); William Armstrong, *Stocks and Stock-Jobbing in Wall Street* (New York: New-York Publishing Co., 1848), 11.

to make candles.) Those who expected the price of tallow to rise "purchased on speculation, never intending to take or pay for them [that is, shipments of tallow], but to receive the difference between the contract prices and the market rates." Such merchants were not in the candle business; they were placing bets on the price of tallow. By the 1840s, New York and Buffalo had markets for trading grain futures, markets likewise organized to permit the "purchase" of future rights to receive agricultural commodities by people with no intention of ever receiving them, and the "sale" of such rights by people who would never possess them.[10] There was not yet any law prohibiting these transactions. Nor was there any in England, where the analogous statutes did not restrict trading in anything other than securities.

Speculating on commodity prices was nevertheless troubling to some judges, who looked for ways of interpreting the law so as to limit these transactions. In an English case from 1822, Chief Justice Charles Abbott allowed a buyer to rescind a contract for the future purchase of wheat when the seller admitted that he could not show samples of the wheat to the buyer because he did not yet have any wheat. If such a contract were enforceable, Abbott reasoned, "a man might bargain to deliver corn not then in his possession, and rely upon making a future purchase in time to fulfil his undertaking; but that is a mode of dealing not to be encouraged." A few years later Abbott refused to enforce a similar contract for the sale of nutmeg. In February, the seller had agreed to deliver nutmeg in May, but he did not acquire any nutmeg until March. The seller was speculating that nutmeg prices would decline between February and March. "Such a contract amounts, on the part of the vendor, to a wager on the price of the commodity," Abbott lectured, "and is attended with the most mischievous consequences." When the seller's lawyer informed him that such contracts were common, and that his decision would "introduce a most material change in the proceedings of the Royal Exchange," Abbott retorted that any such

---

10 William Blackstone, *Commentaries on the Laws of England* (Oxford: Clarendon Press, 1765–69), 2:449; Mark West, "Private Ordering at the World's First Futures Exchange," *Michigan Law Review* 98 (2000): 2574–615; *Commercial Advertiser*, 4 Mar. 1819, 2; Jeffrey C. Williams, "The Origin of Futures Markets," *Agricultural History* 56 (1982): 306–16.

change would be for the better. "If it had been acted upon during the last twelve months," he declared, "much of that distress which now presses upon the community would have been avoided."[11]

In the United States, Supreme Court Justice Joseph Story shared Abbott's concern about the ability of merchants to wager on prices by selling things they did not yet own. Story tried to influence the law as much through his legal treatises as through his judicial opinions. In his *Commentaries on the Law of Agency*, first published in 1839, he quoted Abbott at length in urging the adoption of a similar rule in the United States. "Such a contract amounts, on the part of the vendor, to a wager on the price of the commodity, and is attended with such mischievous consequences as to be prohibited by public policy," Story insisted. "There can be little doubt, that it is a gaming speculation, which no court ought to enforce or encourage."[12] Story, like Abbott, proposed to curb speculation with a simple rule: one could not contract to sell what one did not own.

The difficulty with the rule Abbott and Story sought to introduce was that such contracts had long been common. Farmers, for example, sold crops before the harvest, while manufacturers sold products before they were made. In such circumstances, the seller could not avoid selling something he did not yet own. It was hard to argue that such contracts posed dangers to trade, and even harder to claim that all along they had been contrary to the common law. In England, Abbott's holdings lasted only a bit more than a decade before being overruled. "I cannot see what principle of law is at all affected by a man's being allowed to contract for the sale of goods, of which he has not possession at the time of the bargain," declared Judge James Parke. "Such a contract does not amount to a wager ... and even if it were a wager, it is not illegal, because it has no necessary tendency to injure third parties." Judge William Henry Maule agreed that Abbott's rule was "contrary to law, and most inconvenient in practice: and I have often heard it spoken of with great suspicion, both by lawyers and mercantile men upon both

11 *Lorymer v. Smith*, 107 Eng. Rep. 1, 2 (K.B. 1822); *Bryan v. Lewis*, 171 Eng. Rep. 1058, 1059 (K.B. 1826).
12 Joseph Story, *Commentaries on the Law of Agency* (Boston: Little, Brown and Co., 1839), 233–34.

grounds,—as against law, and against all mercantile convenience." In the United States, Story's proposal never caught on. Courts had already declined to invalidate contracts to sell items the seller did not own, and they continued to do so afterward. "Many moralists doubt the policy of permitting a party to contract for the sale of goods which he does not own at the time of making the contract, because it partakes of the nature of a gambling transaction," one New York judge acknowledged, "but it is now well established" that such contracts were lawful. They were simply too useful to be proscribed. "The mercantile business of the present day could no longer be successfully carried on, if merchants and dealers were unable to purchase or sell that which as to them had no actual or potential existence," explained the Michigan Supreme Court, in upholding a contract for the sale of corn futures by a seller who possessed no corn on the contract date. "A dealer has a clear right to sell and agree to deliver at some future time that which he then has not, but expects to go into the market and buy."[13] By the middle of the nineteenth century, judges in England and the United States had decisively rejected the idea that the common law prohibited selling what one did not own.

Meanwhile, however, two developments were putting increasing pressure on the courts to find some alternative way to forbid betting on prices. One was the continued growth of organized markets in options and futures. The Chicago Board of Trade, which would become the leading American commodity exchange, was formed in the 1840s, followed by similar boards of trade in many other cities. A combination of technological changes in the 1850s—the construction of railroads, grain elevators, and telegraph lines, along with the implementation of a grading system for dividing grain into standardized quality classes—provided an infrastructure for the trading of options and futures in grain.[14] There were soon comparable infrastructures for speculative

---

13 *Hibblewhite v. M'Morine*, 151 Eng. Rep. 195, 197 (Exch. 1839); *Frost v. Clarkson*, 7 Cow. 24 (N.Y. Sup. Ct. 1827); *Eastman v. Fiske*, 9 N.H. 182 (1838); *Noyes v. Spaulding*, 27 Vt. 429 (1855); *Stanton v. Small*, 3 Sandf. 230, 237–38 (N.Y. Super. Ct. 1849); *Gregory v. Wendell*, 39 Mich. 337, 340 (1878).

14 Jonathan Lurie, *The Chicago Board of Trade 1859–1905: The Dynamics of Self-Regulation* (Urbana: University of Illinois Press, 1979), 25; William Cronon,

transactions in timber and livestock. The New York Stock Exchange continued to grow, as did stock exchanges in other cities, all of which permitted brokers to trade options and futures.

The second development was the gradual shift in the common law's treatment of gambling, discussed in the previous chapter. In the early nineteenth century, wagers had been enforceable contracts, except where they were contrary to public policy. By the middle decades of the century, gambling contracts were generally unenforceable. This change in the legal background had important consequences for speculative transactions. In 1800, if one classified a speculative purchase as a wager, that meant, with certain narrow exceptions, that it was an enforceable contract. In 1860, by contrast, to classify a speculative transaction as a wager meant that it was *not* an enforceable contract.

These factors contributed to the state-by-state emergence, between the 1850s and the 1870s, of a new common-law rule prohibiting the enforcement of "difference contracts"—that is, contracts in which the seller had no intention of delivering the item ostensibly being sold, and the buyer had no intention of receiving it, but both parties intended the contract to be settled by the payment of an amount of money representing the difference in the item's price between the contract date and the settlement date. The first step in this direction was an English case from 1851 called *Grizewood v. Blane*. On August 3, Blane had agreed to deliver stock to Grizewood on September 13 at an agreed-upon price. But on September 11, two days before the nominal delivery date, Grizewood agreed to deliver to Blane the same amount of the same stock, at the price then in effect. When the two agreements netted out, all that was left was a contract to pay the difference in the stock price between the two dates. Was it enforceable? Or was it a wager, and thus unenforceable? The court determined that the answer turned on the intentions of the parties. "If neither party intended to buy or to sell" any shares, reasoned one judge, and if "the whole thing was to be settled by the payment of differences," then "it was no bargain, but a mere gambling transaction." A second judge agreed that if the parties had never

Nature's Metropolis: Chicago and the Great West (New York: W. W. Norton, 1991), 97–147.

intended to deliver or receive any stock, "the transaction was clearly gambling, and a practice which every one must condemn."[15]

The new rule jumped to New York a few years later. In May 1856, Elisha Hinmann agreed to sell five hundred barrels of pork to George Cassard at $17 per barrel, to be delivered in September. Cassard was in the meatpacking business—he bought pork and beef; preserved the meat in brine, which was necessary for long-term storage in the era before refrigeration; and then sold it.[16] By purchasing meat several months in advance, Cassard assured himself of a supply and protected himself against future price increases. When September came, however, Hinmann refused to deliver the pork. Pork prices had risen from $17 to $23 per barrel, so Hinmann, who would have to buy pork at the current market price before he could deliver any to Cassard, stood to lose money on the transaction.[17] Cassard sued, and Hinmann defended on the ground that the contract was illegal because it was nothing more than a wager on the price of pork. He was not a dealer in pork, Hinmann declared, nor did he ever possess any pork. He never intended to deliver any pork to Cassard, and Cassard never expected to receive any. Rather, Hinmann argued, both men intended the contract to be settled by the payment of money in the amount of the difference between the value of the pork in May and its value in September. As wager contracts were unenforceable under New York law, Hinmann concluded, Cassard had no right to collect any money or any pork from him. This defense was probably wrong as a factual matter, because Cassard most likely expected to receive pork from Hinmann. Cassard genuinely needed pork for his business. But the litigation did not progress far enough to find out, because at the pleading stage Cassard argued that Hinmann's defense was not a good one—that is, Cassard contended that even if all the facts alleged by Hinmann

---

15 *Grizewood v. Blane*, 138 Eng. Rep. 578, 584 (C.P. 1851).

16 Cassard described his business as a witness testifying in *Adams v. Capron*, 21 Md. 186, 194–95 (1864). A price quotation for Cassard's hams in brine can be found in *New York Daily Times*, 3 May 1855, 1.

17 I am inferring that pork prices rose $6 per barrel, because the order was for five hundred barrels and Cassard alleged a loss of $3,000. See *Cassard v. Hinman*, 14 N.Y. Super. 207 (1857).

were true, the contract would still be valid. As a result, Justice Murray Hoffman of New York's Superior Court confronted a pure question of law: if neither a buyer nor a seller expects delivery of the item being sold, but both merely intend to bet on whether its price rises or falls, is their contract void as a wager?[18]

Hoffman decided that the contract was indeed void as a wager. After quoting extensively from *Grizewood v. Blane*, the English case from a few years before, he made no secret of his distaste for "the unbridled and defiant spirit of speculation." Hoffman was a prominent layman in the Episcopal Church. He had recently authored a lengthy treatise on Episcopal canon law, and he would later write books about ecclesiastical law more broadly. His opinion suggests that his religious convictions played a role in forming his view of speculation. Hoffman declared: "I rejoice that a court of justice is able to do this at least—to condemn the offence—to annul the contract; and to clear the law from the stain of enduring a practice teeming with temptation and disgrace to those engaged in it, and with baneful influences upon the efforts of the honest and just." The decision was affirmed on appeal, by judges who likewise quoted *Grizewood* at length.[19] In New York, a contract was now an unlawful wager on prices if neither party expected the delivery of the item supposedly being sold.

This new rule would eventually spread throughout the United States, but for several years New York was the only state to adopt it, because the new rule was not easy to reconcile with two well-accepted legal principles. One principle was that a party to a contract was normally not allowed to claim the existence of an oral understanding at variance with the written terms of the contract. If a contract said it was for the sale of pork, then it was for the sale of pork, and a person who had signed the contract could not evade his obligation by asserting that the contract was really about something else. The second principle was that

---

18 *Cassard v. Hinmann*, 14 How. Pr. 84 (N.Y. Super. Ct. 1856).

19 Murray Hoffman, *A Treatise on the Law of the Protestant Episcopal Church in the United States* (New York: Stanford and Swords, 1850); Murray Hoffman, *Ecclesiastical Law in the State of New York* (New York: Pott and Amercy, 1868); Murray Hoffman, *The Ritual Law of the Church* (New York: Pott, Young & Co., 1872); *Cassard*, 14 How. Pr. at 91; *Cassard*, 14 N.Y. Super. at 211.

the normal remedy for a breach of contract was the payment of money from the breaching party to the innocent party, in an amount equal to the difference between the contract price and the market price at the time of the breach, precisely the outcome that the New York rule condemned as a wager. When a pork seller failed to deliver pork to the buyer, a court normally would not order him to deliver the missing pork; rather, it would order him to compensate the buyer with enough money to enable the buyer to obtain equivalent pork from another vendor.[20] New York's new rule appeared to contravene both of these principles. The new rule allowed parties to wriggle out of contracts that were lawful as written by claiming that the written contract was merely a cover for what was truly a wager. And the new rule seemed to prohibit contracting parties from settling their differences by the method that judges routinely employed in contract cases—the payment of money from the breaching party to the nonbreaching party.

For these reasons, the first American court outside of New York to consider the question rejected New York's new rule. The case before Judge Thomas Drummond of Chicago involved an April contract to sell fifteen thousand bushels of corn in June at 48 cents a bushel. By June, corn was at 63 cents a bushel, and the seller had lost interest in delivering it for 48 cents. When the buyer sued for breach of contract, the seller tried the defense that had worked in New York: he argued that neither he nor the buyer had any expectation of possessing any corn, but that the contract had been a pure wager on the price of corn and was thus unenforceable. Judge Drummond would have none of it. The contract was for the purchase of corn, he observed, and "the rule is well settled that when two men make a contract, and reduce it to writing, and sign it that it is the contract between them. It cannot be shown verbally that something different was intended at the time from what appears in the writing." Drummond conceded that the outcome of the case—a judgment requiring the seller to compensate the buyer for the difference in the price of corn between April and June—would be identical to the outcome of a wager on prices. "So it is in any case of

---

20 Theodore Sedgwick, *A Treatise on the Measure of Damages* (New York: John S. Voorhis, 1847), 260.

this kind, when a party does not perform his contract," he noted. "But that circumstance does not make the contract the same" as a wager.[21]

The new rule nevertheless spread from state to state in the 1860s and 1870s. The reason is not hard to find. Judges often laid their cards on the table: they straightforwardly declared their moral opposition to speculation. Pennsylvania became the second state to adopt the rule in 1867, when the Pennsylvania Supreme Court heard a case involving a short sale of two hundred shares of Harlem Railroad stock. "It is said the form in which this contract appears enters largely into the business of stock brokerage," observed Chief Justice James Thompson. But he meant to put a stop to it. "The fewer licenses that are issued for such a business the better," Thompson continued. "Anything which induces men to risk their money or property without any other hope of return other than to get for nothing any given amount from another, is gambling, and demoralizing to the community, no matter by what name it may be called. It is the same whether the promise be to pay on the color of a card, or the fleetness of a horse." Thompson concluded with a summary of the dire consequences of speculation: "I apprehend that the losses incident to the practice disclosed in this very case, within the past five years, have contributed more to the failures and embezzlements by public officers, clerks, agents and others acting in fiduciary relations, public and private, than any other known, or perhaps all other causes; and the worst of it is, that in the train of its evils, there is a vast amount of misery and suffering by persons entirely guiltless of any partition in the cause of it." Thompson was careful to distinguish "bona fide time contracts about subjects of actual purchase" from mere wagers on prices. The former, he reluctantly acknowledged, "seem from custom necessary in our country." But he had no doubt that the parties before him were gamblers through and through. Their contract took the form of a sale of stock, but, as in famous historical episodes like the South Sea Bubble and the tulip mania in Holland, "the form served only as a thin covering of the most frightful systems of gambling ever known."[22]

21 *Porter v. Viets*, 19 F. Cas. 1077, 1078 (C.C.N.D. Ill. 1857).
22 *Bruas Appeal*, 55 Pa. 294, 298–99 (1867).

The same sort of moralizing can be found among many judges of the period. Oat options sold on the Chicago Board of Trade "are essentially nothing but bets upon the price of oats," insisted one of the city's federal judges, "and as it is obvious that the effect of such transactions is to beget wild speculations, to derange prices, to make prices artificially high or low, as the interests, strength and skill of the manipulators shall dictate, thereby tending to destroy healthy business and unsettle legitimate commerce, there can be no doubt of the injurious tendency of such contracts, and that they should be held void as against public policy." In the District of Columbia, a court refused to enforce a promissory note signed by General George Custer just a few months before he was killed at the Battle of Little Bighorn. Custer had been speculating on the New York Stock Exchange, and the promissory note had paid for futures transactions in which neither Custer nor his counterparties had ever transferred any stock. The court held that these transactions were illegal, and that Custer's note was accordingly void. "All observers agree that the inevitable effect of such dealings is to encourage wild speculations; to derange prices to the detriment of the community; to discourage the disposition to engage in steady business or labor, where the gains though sure, are too slow to satisfy the thirst for gaming when once aroused; and to fill the cities with the bankrupt victims of such disasters as any 'Black Friday' may develop," declared Justice Alexander Burton Hagner. "The extent of this form of speculation now rife in our country is unprecedented." Such transactions were "immoral and illegal," sniffed the Nebraska Supreme Court. "Betting on a game of faro, brag, or poker, cannot be more hazardous, dangerous or uncertain," agreed the Georgia Supreme Court. "Indeed, it may be said that these animals are tame, gentle and submissive, compared to this monster. The law has caged them, and driven them to their dens; they have been outlawed, while this ferocious beast has been allowed to stalk about in open mid-day, with gilded signs and flaming advertisements, to lure the unhappy victim to its embrace of death and destruction."[23] In state

---

23 *Ex parte Young*, 30 F. Cas. 828, 832–33 (N.D. Ill. 1874); *Justh v. Holliday*, 13 D.C. 346, 348–49 (1883); *Rudolf v. Winters*, 7 Neb. 125, 130 (1878); *Cunningham v. National Bank of Augusta*, 71 Ga. 400, 403 (1883).

after state, judges clearly took great satisfaction in adopting a rule that promised to limit practices they viewed as grave dangers.

This judicial attitude was almost certainly reflective of wider public opinion. There does not appear to have been any significant effort, in any state, to enact a statute to undo what the judges had done and allow transactions in which neither party had the intent to deliver. The prevailing view seems rather to have been that of the *Bankers' Magazine*, which declared that "in this evil time, when no power seems able to stay the spirit of speculation, it is cheerful to note how strongly and uniformly the Courts have set their faces against sustaining speculative transactions." In summarizing the decided cases, a pair of lawyers approvingly remarked of the line the judges had drawn, a "distinction between *gambling* with a commodity, and dealing there in by way of *legitimate speculation*."[24]

Occasional judges went so far as to declare that *all* options were illegal wagers. The transaction "called an 'option sale,'" averred Judge Thomas Gantt of St. Louis, was in fact "a wager respecting the rise and fall in the market of mess pork." Missouri law did not prohibit options, he acknowledged, but "it is altogether inadmissible to infer that everything is moral which the penal law does not forbid." Gambling was illegal and options were a form of gambling. A commentator agreed that "options" were lawful so long as the only choice open to the seller was the precise time of delivery, but that options were illegal where the seller had the option not to deliver the goods at all. But this was an extreme view. As the New York lawyer John Dos Passos (the novelist's father) explained, "options frequently represent real transactions." Where the owner of stock desired to sell if the price rose high enough, or to buy more if the price dropped low enough, it would be possible to wait for the market to change and act accordingly, but one could achieve the same result with more certainty simply by entering into option contracts to buy or sell stock at the appropriate prices. In such a case, Dos Passos observed, the stock owner was not wagering; he was

---

24 "Speculation and the Abuse of Trusts," *Bankers' Magazine and Statistical Register* 38 (1884): 653; Lewis H. Bisbee and John C. Simonds, *The Board of Trade and Produce Exchange* (Chicago: Callaghan & Co., 1884), 287.

genuinely committing to buy or sell stock if prices moved in a certain way.[25] A rule classifying all options as wagers was simply too broad.

Most judges accordingly drew a more accommodating line between permissible speculation and impermissible gambling. In one Pennsylvania case, for instance, the lawyer for one party argued that "all purchases of stocks, with a view to re-sell and make profit on their rise, or contracts to furnish stocks on time, should be declared gambling transactions and illegal." This argument, the court observed, "would make a great inroad into what has, for an indefinite period been regarded as a legitimate business." The true distinction, the court concluded, "is between a real transaction, where stock is actually bought and purchased and delivered, and a transaction in which that is not contemplated at all, and where the parties agree, from the beginning, that the stock is not to be delivered, but that they are to settle their mutual wagers upon the price of stock by paying the difference between the sales at the different times." A real transaction, involving the actual purchase of something, could be as speculative as the parties desired without thereby becoming illegal. "It is the business of all people who engage in trade to speculate," the court concluded; "all trade is based upon speculation, and no contracts are obnoxious to legal objection merely because they are speculations." But if the supposed buyer and seller never intended any delivery of stock, the transaction would be an unlawful wager.[26]

Court opinions of the 1870s are replete with lengthy discussions of this issue. Nearly all of them drew the same distinction, between speculative real transactions (which were lawful) and mere wagers on prices (which were not). "We must not confound gambling, whether it be in corporation stocks or merchandise, with what is commonly termed speculation," the Pennsylvania Supreme Court explained in

---

25 *Waterman v. Buckland,* 1 Mo. App. 45, 46–48 (1876); C.H.W., note appended to *Sawyer v. Taggart, American Law Register* 27 (1879): 229–30; John R. Dos Passos, *A Treatise on the Law of Stock-Brokers and Stock-Exchanges* (New York: Harper & Brothers, 1882), 445–46.

26 *Smith v. Bouvier,* 70 Pa. 325, 331, 328 (1872) (the latter two quotations are from the jury charge of the trial judge, which was approved by the Pennsylvania Supreme Court).

1872. "Merchants speculate upon the future prices of that in which they deal, and buy and sell accordingly.... But when ventures are made upon the turn of prices alone, with no bona fide intent to deal in the article, but merely to risk the difference between the rise and fall of the price at a given time, the case is changed." "The law does not undertake to prevent speculation," agreed a federal judge in Wisconsin. "The truth is, men are speculative creatures as certainly as they are eating and sleeping ones. And, although it is undoubtedly true that much harm comes to the community from over-speculation, it is more than doubtful if the world would be better off without speculators; or, if it would be, that the law can do much in the way of abolishing them." The important thing was not whether a contract was speculative, or whether it included an option. What was important was whether the contract was for a real sale. As New York's highest court concluded, if "there is no intention on the one side to sell or deliver the property, or on the other to buy or take it, but merely that the difference should be paid according to the fluctuation in market values, the contract would be a wager."[27]

By the 1880s, the intent-to-deliver rule was firmly established in American law. "The generally accepted doctrine in this country," the US Supreme Court declared in 1884, was that "a contract is only valid when the parties really intend and agree that the goods are to be delivered by the seller and the price to be paid by the buyer; and if, under guise of such a contract, the real intent be merely to speculate in the rise and fall of prices, and the goods are not to be delivered, but one party is to pay the other the difference between the contract price and the market price of the goods at the date fixed for executing the contract, then the whole transaction constitutes nothing more than a wager, and is null and void."[28] Over the preceding three decades, case by case, state by state, judges had crafted a new limitation on speculative transactions.

As a doctrinal matter, the judges were reconciling two developments that pulled in opposite directions—on one side, the rise of a blanket common-law disapproval of gambling; on the other, the growth

27 *Kirkpatrick & Lyons v. Bonsall*, 72 Pa. 155, 158 (1872); *Clarke v. Foss*, 5 F. Cas. 955, 960 (W.D. Wisc. 1878); *Bigelow v. Benedict*, 70 N.Y. 202, 206 (1877).
28 *Irwin v. Williar*, 110 U.S. 499, 508–9 (1884).

of organized futures and options trading, which facilitated forms of speculative trading that looked an awful lot like gambling. As a policy matter, the judges were drawing a line between two kinds of risky transactions—on one side, those they considered customary and useful, and on the other, those they deemed novel and dangerous. "Two conflicting tendencies exist" in the court opinions on the subject, observed the prolific legal writer Francis Wharton. One was "laissez faire," the view that "business should be left free" as much as possible. The other "starts from an ethical or police basis," Wharton noted, according to which certain contracts were immoral by their nature and deserved censure even if businesspeople found them useful.[29] The intent-to-deliver rule was the judges' way of mediating between these two goals.

But why exactly did judges consider transactions more dangerous when parties intended to settle their contracts through the payment of differences? What was it about the intended delivery of an item that made judges more willing to classify transactions in that item as acceptable business practice? The answers to these questions shed some light on why the rule was adopted so quickly and with so little recorded dissent.

In the summer of 1880, a man named Melchert in Davenport, Iowa, sold fifteen thousand bushels of rye on the Chicago Board of Trade, to be delivered any time in September, at prices ranging from 65½ to 68½ cents per bushel. When September came, rye was at 80 cents per bushel and rising. Melchert frantically telegraphed his broker, Erick Gerstenberg, to "cover immediately"—that is, to limit his losses by buying fifteen thousand bushels of rye at the current market price, before rye became even more expensive. But the direct telegraph line between Davenport and Chicago was not working. The telegraph company had to reroute the telegram through Omaha and St. Louis, which added a few hours to the time it took for Gerstenberg to receive it. In those few hours, rye jumped from 80 cents to 85 cents per bushel. Because of the faulty telegraph line, Melchert had lost an additional $750. He sued the telegraph company to get it back. One of the telegraph company's

---

29 Francis Wharton, note appended to *Melchert v. American Union Telegraph Co.*, 11 F. 193, 201, 203 (C.C.D. Iowa 1882).

defenses was that Melchert had not in fact lost anything, because his rye contracts were unenforceable wagers. Melchert did not have to buy any rye, the telegraph company argued, because neither he nor his counter-parties ever intended that any rye would be transferred between them. They were merely betting on rye prices.[30]

The law was clear by 1880: if no one involved in these contracts con-templated the delivery of any rye, the contracts were unenforceable, and Melchert would lose his suit against the telegraph company. Judge James Love accordingly focused his attention on what was in Melchert's mind when he entered into the contracts. Did Melchert actually own any rye in the summer, when he agreed to sell fifteen thousand bushels of it? No, he hadn't owned any rye whatsoever. When Melchert in-structed Gerstenberg to "cover immediately," was it likely that Melchert actually meant for Gerstenberg to go out and purchase fifteen thousand bushels of physical rye? To purchase fifteen thousand bushels of rye at 80 cents per bushel would have cost $12,000, but Melchert did not send any money to Gerstenberg, and it was not likely that Gerstenberg would have lent so much money to Melchert. In fact, Gerstenberg did not buy any physical rye. Rather, he entered into a contract to purchase fifteen thousand bushels of rye from a firm called A. M. Wright & Co., which turned out to be the very same firm to which Melchert had sold the fifteen thousand bushels back in the summer. And did A. M. Wright & Co. actually own any rye? No. Like Melchert himself, the firm owned no rye at all. Melchert's "purchase" from A. M. Wright served merely to cancel out his "sale" to A. M. Wright from two months before. Neither side ever had any rye, and neither ever intended to de-liver rye to the other.[31]

These facts prompted Judge Love to consider why such an arrange-ment should be illegal, when the very same transactions would have been lawful had Melchert and A. M. Wright simply intended to trans-fer ownership of some real rye. The answer, Love suggested, was that re-quiring the intent to transfer property was a way of limiting speculation to those who could best afford it. Someone who actually owned fifteen thousand bushels of rye would have to be a person of some means. At 80 cents a bushel, that much rye was worth $12,000, about thirty times the average annual wage. But Melchert's trades "required no capital, except the small sums demanded to put up margins and pay differences." His mode of dealing was open to "any impecunious gambler," Love reasoned. "It enables mere adventurers, at small risk, to agitate the markets." Love contrasted "the unscrupulous speculator, with little or no capital," with "the honest and legitimate trader," a person *with* capital, who could afford to buy and sell real commodities. The intent-to-deliver rule was not just a way of barring certain kinds of speculation; it was also a way of barring certain kinds of *speculators* from the market. The danger of letting the nonaffluent speculate was not just that they might bankrupt themselves, but that they would harm the respectable, by causing "sudden fluctuations in values" that could not be foreseen even by the steady merchant.[32]

The intent-to-deliver rule thus had a sociological as well as an economic significance. "The theory upon which these cases proceed," explained the New York lawyer T. Henry Dewey, is "that a man of small means would not undertake to perform contracts requiring large amounts of money to buy the commodities which he had sold short, or to pay for those which he had purchased, but that he would make a bet on the price, as he would then have to pay only differences if he lost." Respectable men of business "exhibit high mental grasp, and great knowledge of business, and of the affairs of the world," explained Justice Daniel Agnew of the Pennsylvania Supreme Court. "Their speculations display talent and forecast. . . . Such speculation cannot be denounced." But when actual commodities were not being bought and sold, speculation assumed a darker character. "No money or capital is invested in the purchase, but so much only is required as will cover the difference—a margin, as it is figuratively termed," Agnew observed. "The difference requires the ownership of only a few hundreds or thousands of dollars, while the capital required to complete an actual purchase or sale may be hundreds of thousands or millions. Hence ventures upon prices invite men of small means to enter into transactions far beyond their capital."

32 *Id.* at 195.

Such a man happened to be in Agnew's court. He was a Pittsburgh resident named Sterling Bonsall, who had options to buy forty thousand barrels of oil for $168,000. But what would Bonsall do with so much oil? As he admitted at trial, he was not a refiner of oil. He had no plans to consume any oil. He had no prospect of selling the oil to someone else. And even if he had some purpose for the oil, he had no chance of coming up with a sum anywhere near $168,000. "What intent would reasonably be inferred from these circumstances?" Agnew asked. "Certainly the belief induced that there was not an intent to bargain for oil for a real business purpose." Bonsall was a man of small means. One purpose of the intent-to-deliver rule was to shut such a man out of the market.[33]

Because the enforceability of transactions depended entirely on the intent of the parties, the rule required courts to make some difficult factual determinations. By the time of trial, the party who wanted to enforce the contract had every incentive to claim that he intended to deliver or accept some real commodity, while the party who wanted to get out of the contract had every incentive to claim the opposite, that it had been a wager all along. "It is by no means an easy matter," one commentator lamented, to figure out who was telling the truth. The problem was that speculators typically did not wager on prices explicitly, in contracts spelling out that the loser of the bet would pay the difference in prices to the winner. Contracts were normally worded as if the parties contemplated that a seller would transfer something to a buyer; the parties' intent to pay differences was merely implicit. "Undisguised gambling can easily be proven," a Chicago lawyer observed, "but disguised gambling is more difficult of proof." Such proof was necessarily circumstantial. One treatise explained: "it becomes necessary, to distinguish the real character of a contract, to look not merely at its terms, but to the action of the parties to it, in fulfilling it; that is, to regard not merely the agreement, but the transaction." Judges could not read contracts literally; they had to look behind the words, to guess at what was in the minds of the signatories. What made this

---

33 T. Henry Dewey, *A Treatise on Contracts for Future Delivery and Commercial Wagers* (New York: Baker, Voorhis & Co., 1886), 120; *Kirkpatrick & Lyons v. Bonsall*, 72 Pa. 155, 158–59 (1872).

task so difficult was that there was nothing illegal about paying price differences to settle a contract, so long as the parties had originally intended to transfer some item at the time they signed the contract. "If a contract for future delivery be made in good faith," explained the New Orleans lawyer Julius Aroni, "its validity cannot be affected by the fact that *afterwards* the parties may agree to settle it by waiving delivery and settling differences."[34] The fact that one party paid money to the other, rather than delivering or accepting the item being sold, was thus not enough to establish that the contract was unlawful. The payment of money was relevant only if it revealed what the intent of the parties had been back when they signed the contract.

One clue to someone's intent was his past conduct. If the person purporting to buy grain were a grain dealer, who had received shipments of grain in the past, one might take his grain contracts at face value, whereas if he had engaged in a series of gambling transactions in the past, one might suppose that his contracts were mere vehicles for wagering on prices. But "it would be very dangerous to permit the previous illegal conduct of one party" to invalidate a contract, cautioned the Michigan judge Thomas Cooley. A contract was only void if *both* parties intended to wager. And even an experienced bettor might genuinely buy grain, Cooley acknowledged, "for gamblers may make lawful contracts as well as others."[35] Past conduct was a clue, but that's all it was. There was no easy way for judges to figure out what was in the minds of people who entered into speculative contracts.

Further complicating matters was the circumstance that in all these cases, someone was trying to wriggle out of a contract by claiming that it had been illegal all along. Strictly speaking, the law paid no regard to whether a person's conduct was consistent with norms of appropriate

---

34 Francis A. Lewis, *Law Relating to Stocks, Bonds, and Other Securities, in the United States* (Philadelphia: Rees Welsh & Co., 1881), 95; James C. McMath, "Investment, Speculation and Gambling on the Fluctuations of the Market Prices of Corporate Stocks and Other Commodities," *Central Law Journal* 93 (1921): 225; Arthur Biddle and George Biddle, *A Treatise on the Law of Stock Brokers* (Philadelphia: J. B. Lippincott & Co., 1882), 313; Julius Aroni, *Futures* (New Orleans, La.: James A. Gresham, 1882), 10.

35 *Gregory v. Wendell*, 40 Mich. 432, 438 (1879).

commercial behavior; if a contract was an unenforceable wager, the loser did not have to pay off the winner. But this was often an intuitively uncomfortable outcome. To let a party off the hook, when one suspected that the same party would have earnestly tried to enforce the contract had the market gone in the opposite direction, seemed to reward the most devious litigants. Because intent was so hard to discern, and because a strict application of the law often favored the unethical, judges tended to strain to find an intent to deliver. "Frequently a court has failed to enforce the rule, for the avowed reason that in the case at bar the wagering feature of the transaction was not clear to the court," one lawyer complained. "It must be confessed that some of the cases in which this conclusion is reached are painfully unsatisfactory."[36]

A case that arose in Maine provides a good example of the dilemma. In 1872, Nicholas Berry of Bangor traveled to Chicago and visited the board of trade, where he met a broker named Israel Rumsey. Berry ordered Rumsey to sell ten thousand bushels of wheat, to be delivered the following month. Berry was not in the wheat business and had no wheat to deliver. Brokers on the board of trade, as on other exchanges, protected themselves against loss by requiring clients to deposit a "margin," or a sum of money the broker could draw upon if the client lost from the transaction. Berry left a margin with Rumsey, and when wheat prices began to rise, Rumsey called upon Berry for an additional margin, which Berry provided. Wheat prices continued to rise, but when Rumsey demanded a further margin, Berry refused. Rumsey then followed the normal practice at the board of trade. He repurchased the wheat at the current price, at a loss of around $3,000. Berry's margin was only $700, so Rumsey sued Berry to recover the difference. Berry defended on the ground that his supposed sale of wheat could not be the basis for Rumsey's suit, because it was an unenforceable wager.[37]

The Maine Supreme Court, by a vote of four to three, held that Berry's wheat sale was a valid contract. Justice Charles Danforth, writing for the majority, admitted that "it may indeed appear a little singular and even suspicious that a man residing in Bangor, having no wheat

36 "Option Sales," *Central Law Journal* 10 (1880): 221.
37 *Rumsey v. Berry*, 65 Me. 570, 571 (1876).

of his own, should undertake to sell and deliver wheat in Chicago." Nevertheless, Danforth concluded, "we cannot assume that anyone has violated the law and been guilty of immoral and corrupting practices in his business transactions, without proof, even though he may ask it himself"—and here Danforth likely revealed the true reason for the decision—"for the purpose of being relieved from the obligation of a losing contract." In choosing whether to place the loss on Berry, who had stiffed his broker, or Rumsey, who had done nothing wrong, it was hard not to sympathize with Rumsey, even if that meant squinting a bit to find an intent to deliver wheat.[38]

Of course, the difficulty of discerning intent also allowed judges the same leeway to invalidate transactions when their instincts pointed in that direction. A few years after the Maine court held Nicholas Berry to his contracts, an Illinois court considered the seemingly similar case of a young Chicago office clerk named McCurdy, who got in over his head speculating at the board of trade. The Illinois court showed considerable sympathy for McCurdy, who the court described as "a young man . . . who was not, and never had been, engaged in buying or selling wheat, corn, pork, lard, or other like commodities" until a three-month binge at the board of trade left him owing his brokers $840, nearly a year's salary. The court held that his brokers must have known that McCurdy had no intent to deliver or accept any commodities. "It matters not how nicely the forms adopted may be adjusted to legal requirements," the court lectured, "if the transaction, when stripped of its covering, discloses what is in substance a bet or wager on the future price of grain." The brokers thus could not collect on the debt.[39]

In cases like these, which presented common fact settings, courts could plausibly impute to the parties either the intent to deliver or the intent to gamble on prices. One suspects that the outcome often turned on the judges' sympathies for the particular parties before them, or—as in Ira Foote's two cases discussed at the beginning of this chapter—on the judges' unarticulated policy views as to the value of speculation more broadly.

38 *Id.* at 573.
39 *Beveridge v. Hewitt*, 8 Ill. App. 467, 479, 482 (1881).

THE WICKEDNESS OF THE CHICAGO BOARD OF TRADE

Despite the difficulty of applying the intent-to-deliver rule, it was well entrenched as a matter of common law by the late 1870s. In later years, many states enacted statutes codifying the rule. Some of these laws strengthened the rule by invalidating contracts even where only one party had no intent to deliver. A few states restricted speculation even more. The first was Illinois, which in 1874 banned the sale of options. California's constitution of 1879 prohibited stock futures. Georgia prohibited short sales. Arkansas and Mississippi enacted statutes banning all futures.[40] To get a sense of the political forces motivating these provisions, it is worth taking a close look at the two that were the most significant, the Illinois statute barring options (significant because options were staple fare at the Chicago Board of Trade) and the California constitution's ban on stock futures (likewise for the San Francisco Mining Exchange). Both were enacted in response to local concerns, but both were early appearances of issues that would become nationally salient in later years.

The Illinois statute was enacted during a period of agrarian discontent with the intermediaries between the farmer and the consumer—primarily railroads and grain warehouses, which farmers believed charged far too much. During this period, farmers in several states, including Illinois, successfully lobbied for state regulation of railroad and warehouse prices. Dealers were intermediaries in the grain trade as well, and they too were viewed with suspicion by many farmers. "We often hear the Boards of Trade, or what is known as dealing on 'Change,' denounced as a system inimical to the interests of farmers," declared M. L. Dunlap at the 1873 convention of the Illinois State Farmers' Association. Dunlap, a farmer from Savoy, in the central part of the state, was expressing the common view among farmers that trading in futures and options, especially short selling, had the effect of depressing commodity prices. Dunlap himself was skeptical about this. Nevertheless, he contended, "trading in options is no doubt a species of gambling highly reprehensible, and with which the farmer has nothing

---

40 T. Henry Dewey, *Legislation Against Speculation and Gambling in the Forms of Trade* (New York: Baker, Voorhis & Co., 1905), 15–50.

to do." As Dunlap saw it, "it is a practice that should not be permitted among a class of men whose integrity is a large part of their capital."[41]

In 1874, when the Illinois legislature convened to revise the state's statutes, agrarian pressure produced a bill to prohibit contracts for the sale of any commodity that the seller did not own and actually have in his possession at the time of the contract. This was the same rule first suggested in the United States by Joseph Story thirty-five years earlier, when it had been roundly rejected. The proposal was directly targeted at short selling on the Chicago Board of Trade, the single most vivid circumstance in which a trader necessarily contracted to sell something he did not yet own.

The bill was promptly criticized, for the same reason that Story's proposal had been criticized—it banned good transactions, as well as bad. "So far as such a law could be made to prevent wild speculations, 'scalping' options and their resultant 'corners,' it would prove beneficial," the *Chicago Tribune* argued, "but, unfortunately, the law is so sweeping." Farmers could not survive without making contracts to sell grain before the harvest, the *Tribune* pointed out. "With such a law in operation, it would require an amount of capital to transact business which would simply be unattainable, and the farmers would soon find themselves ruined." And the law would yield even more absurd results in other industries. A meat packer could not contract to deliver meat in advance. An opera manager could not sell tickets in advance, because the singers were not yet in the theater. A newspaper could not sell a year's subscription, because the publisher did not yet possess the entire year's news. "Such a law," the *Tribune* lamented, "would put a complete embargo on all business."[42]

The bill was especially unpopular at the board of trade. Many of the contracts made at the board were for large quantities, like a thousand hogs or ten thousand bushels of grain. The board's president wondered how sellers could fit so many hogs or so much grain into their offices to satisfy the "possession" requirement. The broker John Bensley thought

41 Lurie, *The Chicago Board of Trade*, 52–56; *Proceedings of the Illinois Farmers' State Convention, Held at Bloomington, Ills., Jan. 15 & 16, 1873* (Chicago: Inter-Ocean Print, 1873), 22–23.
42 *Chicago Daily Tribune*, 15 Jan. 1874, 4.

the bill would only hurt farmers by reducing prices. "If the grain was shipped in here, and left for sale to only those men who would come forward and buy it for shipment, they would only buy when it had accumulated here to such extent as to be sold cheap," he argued. "As it is now, there is a constant market, and if they are not ready to take it, speculators are, and they keep it up to a price higher than the country shippers would be able to get for it."[43]

These concerns sparked extended debate in the Illinois legislature. On one side were rural members who, as the *Tribune* put it, "expatiated on the wickedness of the Chicago Board of Trade, and the way in which country innocents were fleeced." On the other were urban legislators who could see value in the board's activities. The resulting compromise yielded a weaker bill, one that prohibited options but preserved futures trading in commodities one did not yet own or possess. This was the bill that became law in 1874. It made the sale of options a crime punishable by fine or prison sentence up to a year, and declared that options "shall be considered gambling contracts, and shall be void." As the Illinois Supreme Court explained several years later, the purpose of the law was "to break down the pernicious practice of gambling on the market prices of grain and other commodities." There was "nothing illegal or even immoral in an option contract within itself," the court noted. "The evil aimed at nevertheless grew out of such contracts," and for that reason Illinois abolished them.[44]

In California at approximately the same time, a different political issue yielded a different prohibition. The Nevada mining boom of the 1870s was financed in large part by the sale of mining company stock in California, especially in San Francisco, which was the tenth-biggest city in the country and home to the region's only stock exchange. "Californians, as a class, gamble in mining stocks," the *San Francisco Chronicle* observed in 1875. "From the lady leader of fashion to the poorest seamstress, from the dignified bishop and the august Judge, down to the boy who blacked their boots, each and all owned shares."

43 *Chicago Daily Tribune*, 16 Jan. 1874, 2.
44 *Chicago Daily Tribune*, 21 Jan. 1874, 5; 23 Jan. 1874, 5; *The Revised Statutes of the State of Illinois* (Springfield: Illinois Journal Co., 1874), 372; *Schneider v. Turner*, 22 N.E. 497, 499 (Ill. 1889).

As on other exchanges, people of modest means could speculate with little capital, either by buying stock on margin or by entering into futures contracts to be settled on price differences, and as a result some were ruined. "Mining is a legitimate business, while dealing in stocks is gambling," the *Chronicle* lectured. "Twenty thousand people have lost where twenty have made money." Worse, with all these sales came ample opportunities for fraud. Sometimes promoters simply claimed a mine was more productive than it really was, to induce purchasers to overpay for stock. The *Chronicle* warned its readers not to believe hucksters. "If the mine is worth more than its selling price in stock," the paper pointed out, "they would keep it" rather than selling. But the operators of a mine had a more insidious way of fleecing shareholders, one that shareholders had scarcely any way of preventing. A mine could deliberately be made less valuable. "It has very frequently happened," the *Chronicle* charged, "that the managers of a mine, knowing very well that good ore was easily obtainable, would so direct the work to lead away from the direction of the valuable deposits and into the worthless rock. Sometimes the mine has been allowed to become flooded." Before doing such things, the mine operators would sell the stock short, so when news of the mine's failure reached the market, the share price would plummet and the operators would profit at shareholders' expense.[45]

Fraud in the sale of corporate shares was thus an important issue during the California Constitutional Convention of 1878–79. Among the hundreds of clauses stuffed into California's lengthy Constitution of 1879 was one that voided "all contracts for the sale of shares of the capital stock of any corporation or association, on margin or to be delivered at a future day." This was the "one provision in the instrument which will commend it as a whole to the mass of the people," a Los Angeles newspaper declared, because "it will do away with stock gambling." "For this alone," the *Chronicle* agreed, the new constitution "will deserve the

45 Charles A. Fracchia, "The Founding of the San Francisco Mining Exchange," *California Historical Society Quarterly* 48 (1969): 3–18; *San Francisco Chronicle*, 15 Sept. 1875, 2; 14 May 1873, 2; 10 May 1873, 2; 3 Mar. 1872, 1.

support of every good citizen who wishes to see confidence restored among businessmen."[46] For many years, California would be the only state to prohibit futures and margin contracts in corporate stock.

These Illinois and California provisions had little effect in practice. Illinois's ban on options must have been frequently flouted at the Chicago Board of Trade, because there were perennial complaints, both from within the board and outside, about how often options were being bought and sold. In 1886, for example, approximately one hundred members of the board found it necessary to petition their board of directors to disallow options. The trading of options was "dangerous and hurtful to our legitimate business, and prejudicial to our good name as a commercial organization," they declared. They urged the board of directors to "use every possible means to suppress this business." A few years later, the *Chicago Tribune* likewise deplored the prevalence of options at the board of trade. "The put and call business is about on a level with the so-called 'trading' in a bucket-shop," the paper charged. Options were defended as a form of hedging, but the *Tribune* was skeptical. "It is a notorious fact that the great majority of those who buy privileges [that is, options] have nothing to insure," the *Tribune* observed. "The men who pay out their money for either puts or calls do so merely as bets on the course of prices." In California, speculators continued to buy stock on margin despite the constitutional ban on such purchases. The main effect of the constitutional provision, recalled the broker John Percy, was to put every broker "absolutely at the mercy of his client, who, if he lost, could simply turn on the broker and recover all margins put up in the transaction." The situation was so "intolerable from the broker's standpoint" that the brokers pressed for an amendment to the state constitution, one they finally procured in 1907. The amendment replaced the ban on margins and futures with a new provision that simply restated the common-law intent-to-deliver rule.[47]

---

46 California Constitution of 1879, art. IV, sec. 26; *Los Angeles Express* quoted in *San Francisco Chronicle*, 25 Mar. 1879, 1; *San Francisco Chronicle*, 29 Apr. 1879, 2.

47 Petition, June 1886, CBT, box 13, folder 29; *Chicago Tribune*, 11 Feb. 1892, 4; John Percy to A. M. Clement, 25 June 1910, CBT, box 353, folder 8.

The propriety of betting on prices was not just a legal question. The experience of Illinois and California showed that under the right circumstances, it could be a significant political question as well. Before long, as we will see in chapter 3, it would assume a large role in national politics.

THE POOR MAN'S STOCK EXCHANGE

From the 1870s on, contracts were unenforceable—because they were classified as wagers on price changes—when neither party intended that the item ostensibly being purchased would actually be delivered. Such was the rule on paper, but in a great many of the transactions on the nation's leading exchanges, and probably in most of them, neither party had the slightest intention of delivering anything.

To be sure, contracts were carefully written to appear to comply with the law. One member of the Chicago Board of Trade declared that his grain contracts "all provide for delivery in Chicago." When the Illinois Supreme Court castigated the board of trade for selling "imaginary wheat" that neither buyer nor seller ever intended to have delivered, the board immediately protested. The court's decision "grossly reflects upon its members by characterizing contracts between them as gambling contracts," the board resolved at its next meeting. "The decision appears to be based upon the erroneous inference" that board members did not intend to fulfill contracts by delivery, the resolution insisted, "when the contrary is the case." In practice, however, delivery was a rare event. William Warren, the president of the board of trade, estimated that in the previous year he had bought or sold, on behalf of his clients, five million bushels of wheat, two or three million bushels of corn, and more than a million bushels of oats. He could not recall any of it having been delivered. Walter Haugh, who was a member of the board of trade for twenty-five years, reported that in his experience "there wouldn't be one per cent of the stuff delivered."[48]

Most of the people buying and selling at the board of trade did not actually want to deliver or receive the commodities in which they were

48 CBT, box 351, folder 1, page 3; *J.B. Lyon & Co. v. Culbertson, Blair & Co.*, 83 Ill. 33, 40 (1876); CBT, box 3, folder 6; box 352, pages 935–36; box 352, page 182.

transacting. Some were speculators, who wanted to receive (or pay, if on the losing end) the difference between the price of the commodity at the contract date and its price at the nominal delivery date. They had no grain to deliver and no desire to acquire any.

Many of the others transacting on the board of trade were *hedging*, or insuring against losses from price fluctuations. John Bradenbaugh, for instance, was a grain merchant in Kansas City. His business consisted of buying grain from farmers and then selling it at a profit to shippers. Sometimes Bradenbaugh had to hold grain for several months before selling it. If grain prices declined during that period, he would lose money. When he bought grain, therefore, Bradenbaugh would simultaneously sell grain futures on the Chicago Board of Trade—that is, he would enter into a contract in which he nominally promised to deliver grain at a future date for a stated price. That way, if grain prices fell, any losses he suffered in his business of selling real grain would be offset by his gains on the grain futures. (He would have gains on the grain futures because if grain prices fell, he would have the right to acquire grain at the now-lower market price, and the right to receive the older higher price when he delivered it.) Of course, by insuring against losses from a fall in grain prices, Bradenbaugh was giving up the possibility of gains from a rise in grain prices, because any gain he stood to make from a rise in the price of grain would be similarly offset by losses on the grain futures. But that was precisely the purpose of hedging. Bradenbaugh did not want to speculate in grain prices. He wanted to conduct his business without having to worry about price movements. "It simply means protection," Bradenbaugh explained, "against ups and downs of the market. If you are short you buy and if you are long you sell." Hedging was thus useful to anyone in the chain of agricultural distribution who had to hold a commodity for a period of time or who had to make commitments to deliver a commodity in the future. "I never saw a firm that didn't," Bradenbaugh observed. "They would be doing a very dangerous business and treading on very dangerous ground if they didn't."[49] Hedging was the very opposite of speculating. Speculators sought to bear the risk of price changes, while hedgers sought to avoid that risk.

49 CBT, box 351, folder 3, pages 3–4, 13.

Farmers also confronted the risk of price changes, so they too could benefit from hedging. A farmer had to decide whether to plant seed long before there would be any crops to sell. A sensible decision at planting season could turn disastrous by the harvest if grain prices fell in the interim. One way a farmer could avoid this risk was by finding a customer who was willing to lock in a price and buy his crop far in advance. But another method was to hedge. Like a grain dealer, the farmer could simply sell futures in the planting season that would come due at the harvest. By doing so, the farmer was, in effect, insuring against the risk of price changes.

Hedgers, like speculators, normally did not intend to settle their futures contracts by delivering or receiving any grain. The grain futures that Bradenbaugh sold at the board of trade nominally obligated him to deliver a certain quantity of grain on a given day for a stated price. Once Bradenbaugh no longer needed to hedge, however, he simply returned to the board of trade and closed the transaction by purchasing grain futures in the same amount as he had previously sold. When commodities were sold as hedges, Walter Haugh recalled, they were never actually delivered, and when they were bought as hedges they were never actually received. Such contracts were settled the way Bradenbaugh settled his, by a second transaction that was a mirror image of the first.[50] The second transaction did not have to be with the same counterparty as the first. When Bradenbaugh closed out his position by purchasing grain futures, he could buy them from someone other than the person to whom he had sold grain futures months before. At the end of each day, when all the transactions on the board of trade were tallied up, long and short positions would mostly cancel out, and all that would be left was a list of who owed money to whom.

The board of trade's rules explicitly permitted parties to settle their contracts by the payment of money rather than the transfer of the commodities nominally purchased.[51] The rules could hardly have stated

---

50 CBT, box 351, folder 3, page 6; box 352, page 201.

51 See, e.g., *Act of Incorporation, Rules, Regulations and By-Laws, of the Board of Trade, Chicago, Ill.* (Chicago: Dunlop, Sewell & Spalding, 1865), 14–15, CBT, box 43, folder 1; *Act of Incorporation, Rules, By-Laws and Regulations of the Board of Trade of the City of Chicago* (s.l.: s.n., 1896), 38, CBT, box 44, folder 1.

otherwise without making speculation and hedging extraordinarily cumbersome. The board of trade, along with the nation's other commercial exchanges, thus occupied a curious legal position. Most of the transactions that took place there were unenforceable in court, because in most, neither the buyer nor the seller contemplated delivery of the commodity being sold.

One consequence was that members of the exchanges had to enforce contracts themselves rather than relying on the courts to do it. This was nothing new. The New York Stock Exchange had long operated a miniature legal system of its own to enforce all the contracts that could not be enforced in the New York courts under the New York stockjobbing statute of 1792, which voided contracts for the sale of stock the seller did not own. When stock exchange members breached their contracts, the exchange punished them by suspending or expelling them. Exclusion from the exchange was a significant penalty, one that was at least as capable of deterring breaches as anything a court could have ordered. The stock exchange was able to thrive despite the fact that most of the promises made within its walls were not recognized as binding by the legal system. Even after New York repealed the stockjobbing statute, the exchange continued to operate its own enforcement system, which was probably faster and cheaper than resorting to the courts, and which was staffed by fellow exchange members with expertise in the ways of buying and selling stock.[52]

The Chicago Board of Trade adopted a similar system. The board created an arbitration committee, made up of members elected for two-year terms, with the power to resolve contract disputes. Members who disregarded the arbitration committee's orders were subject to suspension or expulsion. As in New York, disputes could be resolved much more quickly by the committee than in the courts, in part because committee members knew the board of trade's business much better than any judge could. "It is not now, nor has it ever been the policy of our firm to litigate in the courts," declared one member of the board of trade, "but on the contrary to submit our differences to" arbitration within the board, where members could have their cases

---

52 Banner, *Anglo-American Securities Regulation*, 270–80; *Constitution and By-Laws of the New-York Stock Exchange* (1865), 21, NYSE.

decided by "less annoying and expensive tribunals." For example, in one 1877 case, a dispute between R. M. Weaver and the firm of Talbot & Eckley, the arbitration committee heard all the evidence and issued its order within a single day. The committee ordered Weaver to pay Talbot & Eckley $178.75 in damages and an additional $10 in costs. Much of the work of the board of trade's board of directors consisted of ruling upon such disputes. In May 1873, one typical month, three members wrote letters to the board of directors complaining of contract breaches on the part of other members, all of which most likely involved contracts that were unenforceable in the court system.[53] The intent-to-deliver rule thus did not prevent the emergence and growth of the board of trade and similar exchanges in other cities, organizations facilitating transactions in which scarcely anyone had any intent to deliver anything.

The primary difficulty the intent-to-deliver rule created for the exchanges was not that it curtailed their ability to trade, but rather that it greatly complicated their decades-long battle with their primary competitors, the bucket shops.[54] A bucket shop was a simulated brokerage, where customers could go to "buy" or "sell" stocks or commodities. The invention of the stock ticker in 1867 allowed anyone with a telegraph connection to receive price information nearly in real time. A bucket shop operator would buy a stock ticker and allow customers to place wagers on price movements. Unlike a real broker, who acted as the customer's agent in transacting with a third party, the operator of a bucket shop was on the other side of the customer's trade; the bucket shop stood in the same relation to its clients as a casino to gamblers. "A legitimate broker actually buys or sells for his customers," explained *Munsey's Magazine*, a popular monthly. "The

53 Lurie, *The Chicago Board of Trade*, 29; CBT, box 13, folder 31; box 4, folder 34; Letters to Board of Directors from Howard Priestley (8 May 1873), J. K. Fisher & Co. (24 May 1873), and Dupee & Hammond (29 May 1873), all in CBT, box 1, folder 16.

54 The best account of bucket shops is David Hochfelder, "'Where the Common People Could Speculate': The Ticker, Bucket Shops, and the Origins of Popular Participation in Financial Markets," *Journal of American History* 93 (2006): 335–58.

bucket shop, on the contrary, simply bets its patrons that stocks, grain, cotton, provisions, or any other speculative commodity will go up or down."[55] Brokerage houses earned commissions on their clients' trades, whether the clients made or lost money. Bucket shops took commissions too, but they profited mainly by winning whatever their clients lost.

By the later decades of the nineteenth century, there were bucket shops in towns all over the country. Some offered honest gambles on prices without any pretense of doing anything else. Some falsely claimed to be real brokers with membership in an established exchange. Some were pure swindles, with concocted prices that always seemed to move against the customer. All of them hurt the exchanges. The honest bucket shops took legitimate clients away from the exchanges, while the dishonest ones brought the entire enterprise of speculation into disrepute.

Dishonest bucket shops used a variety of tricks. Prices came by telegraph from the cities where the exchanges were located. In small towns, customers without telegraph connections of their own had no way of knowing whether the prices posted by the bucket shop were the real ones, so a bucket shop could make its prices rise or fall nearly at will. "The city trader can compare bucket-shop prices with the regular Board of Trade figures, and thus to a degree protect himself against wholesale extortion," the *Chicago Tribune* cautioned—under the large headline "How Bucket Shop Men Fatten on Dupe Speculators"—"but the countryman is entirely at the mercy of the firm with which he deals." Or a bucket shop could "hold the market"—that is, post prices only after a delay, so the bucket shop operator would know the market's direction before his clients did. A bucket shop could even fleece its customers with real prices. Customers typically purchased on very small margins, putting down as little as 1 percent of the value of the stock or commodity nominally being purchased, so a price movement of 1 percent in the wrong direction was enough to wipe out a customer's account. A bucket shop operator seeking to make prices move by 1 percent

55 Patton Thomas, "The Bucket Shop in Speculation," *Munsey's Magazine* 24 (1900): 68.

could buy from a confederate on the real exchange at the desired price, which would be duly reported by telegraph. Once the customers' accounts had been emptied, the confederate would buy back at the same price from the bucket shop operator. As the financial journalist Edwin Lefèvre recalled in his thinly fictionalized biography of the speculator Jesse Livermore, on the New York Stock Exchange "they had what were frankly referred to as 'bucket-shop drives,' when a stock was offered down two or three points in a jiffy just to establish the decline on the tape and wipe up the myriad shoe-string traders who were long of the stock in the bucket shops." And if all else failed, and the market turned in favor of the customers, the bucket shop operator "simply locks his door at night and disappears from the town before morning," one critic charged, "leaving the traders who have taken profits, to bewail their losses and their cupidity."[56]

It was commonly observed that dishonest bucket shops harmed the reputation of the established exchanges, because many customers could not tell the difference between the two. As a special committee of the New York Stock Exchange lamented, "the ignorant people who have been robbed by the bucket-shop feel that they have been robbed by the Stock Exchange." This was one reason the exchanges tried for decades to stamp out the bucket shops. Dishonest bucket shops also harmed the reputation of honest bucket shops, who thus had an interest in supporting the exchanges' efforts, so long as those efforts could be narrowly targeted. An agent of the board of trade reported that the proprietor of a Cincinnati bucket shop "says that he would be glad if the B. of T. would go after several b[ucket] s[hop] houses who are doing business on the bunco plan, as they are [the] kind who are giving houses who do business on strictly business principles a black eye, and he would like to see them all put out of business."[57] The dishonest bucket shops

56 *Chicago Daily Tribune*, 19 Sept. 1897, 37; Deposition of A. H. Sheldon, 1 June 1907, CBT, box 331, folder 6; Merrill A. Teague, "Bucket-Shop Sharks," *Everybody's Magazine* 15 (1906): 34; Edwin Lefèvre, *Reminiscences of a Stock Operator* (1923) (Cutchogue, N.Y.: Buccaneer Books, 1976), 192–93; "Bucket Shops," *The Ticker* 2 (1908): 22.
57 "The Doom of the Bucket Shop," *Independent* 79 (1914): 452; "Bucket-Shops: Attacked by the Stock Exchange," *Outlook*, 6 Oct. 1915, 298; "The

had no defenders. Everyone agreed that fraud was wrong and should be stopped.

The exchanges had a harder time fighting off the honest bucket shops, which took customers away by offering similar services at lower prices. Bucket shops normally allowed trading in smaller lots than the exchanges did. They required smaller margins. They typically took a lower rate of commission. Bucket shops could thus be an attractive alternative to speculators and hedgers alike. John Bradenbaugh, the Kansas City grain merchant, often hedged on the Chicago Board of Trade, but he also often used a Kansas City bucket shop for that purpose. "So far as we are concerned it was identically the same," Bradenbaugh explained. "Exactly the same in every particular." From his point of view, "the whole Chicago Board of Trade has been a bucket shop for the last ten years."[58]

Attitudes like Bradenbaugh's were of great concern to the exchanges. "The idea is assiduously cultivated by the proprietors of these places that the bucket-shop is the poor man's stock exchange," the New York Stock Exchange complained. People who might otherwise have been its own customers "feel that the bucket-shop performs a useful function in no way different from that of the great central Exchange."[59] The exchanges accordingly went to great lengths to suppress this competition. They sponsored state legislation to outlaw bucket shops. They helped prosecutors prepare cases against bucket shops. They took to the press with public relations campaigns aimed at dissuading customers from resorting to bucket shops. In all of these efforts, the first step was to establish that the exchanges were fundamentally different from bucket shops. The exchanges were sites of legitimate commerce, the argument went, while the bucket shops were not, because the business of bucket shops was betting on prices.

Bucket Shop Failures," *Bankers' Magazine* 104 (1922): 623; Special Committee on Bucket Shops, "Digest of the Preliminary Work of the Special Committee of June 25, 1913," 7, NYSE; "Tom" to "Owen," 17 July 1908, CBT, box 324, folder 13.

58 *New York Times*, 2 Mar. 1878, 8; CBT, box 351, folder 3, pages 12–13.
59 Special Committee on Bucket Shops, 7.

The Chicago Board of Trade hammered this point home in a series of pamphlets about bucket shops that it distributed to journalists and legislators. "They are gambling houses, pure and simple," the board insisted. "Under the guise of a contract to buy or sell," the board declared, "the proprietor of the 'shop' will wager any comer that the price will advance before it declines, or will decline before it advances." On a real exchange, the board argued, "mind meets mind, a contract is made, enforceable under the law, just as bona fide a transaction as buying a carload of lumber." But in a bucket shop, "no transaction is made. It is simply a bet." An enforceable contract required at least one of the parties to intend the delivery of the item ostensibly being sold, but that could never be possible in a bucket shop. "Bucket shopping," the board concluded, was nothing but "gambling in prices."[60]

This was a distinction that could hardly hold up to scrutiny, because the participants in most of the transactions on the established exchanges likewise had no intention of delivering the items that were nominally being sold. If betting on prices was the distinguishing feature of a bucket shop, then the exchanges were in large part bucket shops too. "If the bucket-shop man, or independent, violates the law of Illinois, the Chicago Board-of-Trade member is equally guilty," responded the bucket shop proprietor C. C. Christie. "The members of that institution who climb upon a pedestal and assume a 'holier-than-thou' expression at the mention of bucket-shops or independents, are confirmed lawbreakers." In Christie's view, the board of trade was "the biggest bucket-shop on earth." The humor magazine *Puck* acknowledged that the operators of bucket shops "simply bet on quotations" but observed that the same was true on the exchanges, "for nineteenth-twentieths of Stock and Produce Exchange transactions are pure and simple betting and gambling." So long as a bucket shop dealt honestly with its customers, agreed the *Wall Street Journal*, "we confess ourselves unable to distinguish any difference in the moral standing of such concerns and that of an exchange." The *Journal* concluded that it could not

---

60 *What Is the Bucket Shop?*, CBT, box 326, folder 8, page 3; *The Grain Exchanges Versus Bucket Shops*, CBT, box 326, folder 8, page 3; *Evils of the Bucket Shop System*, CBT, box 326, folder 8, page 3; *Why Bucket Shops Should Be Outlawed*, CBT, box 326, folder 8, n.p.

"see what indictment can be sustained in the matter of principle against the 'bucket shop' without it being likewise sustained as against the stock exchange." The exchanges emphasized gambling in their attacks on the bucket shops because gambling was what made bucket shop transactions unlawful, but by emphasizing gambling, the exchanges were only inviting this sort of criticism, which hit them at their weakest point. As the former broker Frederick Dickson pointed out, the pot was calling the kettle black. "The bucket-shop man makes money, much money, out of the vanity and folly of fellows," Dickson chortled, "and herein is the vital point of difference between the two; for the stock-exchange man deems it quite irregular for any one to do this save a member of an accredited exchange." Indeed, the congruence between the two kinds of organizations was close enough that some bucket shops were also members of the board of trade, while many of the men who worked at the New York Stock Exchange frequented bucket shops after hours.[61]

There *were* real differences between the exchanges and the bucket shops, but betting on prices was not one of them. *Some* of the traders on an exchange intended to deliver what they were selling or to receive what they were buying, unlike in a bucket shop, where no one did. Bucket shop operators had a greater incentive to cheat their customers than did brokers on an exchange, because bucket shop operators gained whatever their customers lost, dollar for dollar. Perhaps most important for the broader economy, trades made on an exchange influenced the prices of stock and commodities and in the long run could be expected to cause their prices to reflect their true values, while trades made in a bucket shop did not affect prices at all. But these distinctions were too subtle for the exchanges to use in their campaign against the bucket shops. The exchanges argued instead that the bucket shops should be outlawed because they were gambling.

61 Ann Fabian, *Card Sharps, Dream Books, & Bucket Shops: Gambling in 19th-Century America* (Ithaca, N.Y.: Cornell University Press, 1990), 198; C. C. Christie, "Bucket-Shop vs. Board of Trade," *Everybody's Magazine* 15 (1906): 707, 708; "A Plea for Bucket-Shops," *Puck*, 10 Sept. 1884, 23; *Wall Street Journal*, 10 Aug. 1904, 1; Frederick S. Dickson, "The Poison of the Street," *Everybody's Magazine* 20 (1909): 230; *Chicago Daily Tribune*, 31 Oct. 1895, 6; *New York Times*, 7 Oct. 1878, 2.

Whenever the board of trade sued a bucket shop, this strategy left the board's leaders stammering under cross-examination as they struggled to articulate why bucket shops were any different from the board of trade. "What is a bucket shop?" one lawyer asked William Warren, the board's president. Warren replied, "It is a place where dealings are had upon the fluctuations of the market without any bona fide transaction." The lawyer continued: "Would it be a bona fide transaction if the parties did not intend to receive or deliver?" Warren said it would not. And here the lawyer moved in for the kill. He and Warren both knew that the transactions he was describing were common on bucket shops and the board of trade alike. "But if they did intend to receive or deliver," the lawyer asked, "and did then settle on the difference in market prices, that would be a bona fide transaction?" All Warren could do was feebly reply: "Not in a bucket shop." The lawyer: "Would that transaction have to be conducted on the Board of Trade in order to make it bona fide?" Warren: "I think it would." The president of the board of trade had been forced to concede that there was no real difference between the business of his organization and that of a bucket shop. In the board's view, the very same transaction was lawful on the board and illegal anywhere else.[62]

When the Chicago Board of Trade and the New York Stock Exchange tried to help prosecutors go after bucket shops for violating the laws against gambling, they faced the same problem of distinguishing the bucket shop business from their own. The board of trade sent George Burmeister all over the country to explain to district attorneys and grand juries why bucket shops were different from exchanges. "I take pleasure in telling you that I done my little stunt before the Grand Jury today," Burmeister reported from Detroit. "I was first and had to give them a wide-scope outline of a legitimate house and a bucket-shop, the way we execute orders and the way they are filled in a bucket-shop. Several very inquisitive fellows on it but I gave a most satisfactory explanation; the two assistant prosecutors both complimented me after we all got out saying they both learned a heap." From Cleveland, Burmeister reported: "I have spent all my

62 CBT, box 352, pages 926–29.

time in the District Attys office here while they are writing indict-
ments." He lamented that "this case is entirely strange to all of them,
the Dist Atty, Asst Dist Attys and the Inspector have never made a
trade or even been in a Brokerage office or Bucketshop and practically
had to learn the entire business."[63]

The same problem arose when the exchanges lobbied state legislatures for statutes banning bucket shops. "I went to Sacramento for
the purpose of securing the introduction of a bill to put the bucket-
shops out of business," John Percy reported to the board of trade. "I
was personally acquainted with a large number of the members of
both houses, and interviewed them on this subject." But Percy had no
success, because he could not persuade legislators that bucket shops
were any different from the board. "In practically every instance," he
despaired, "I found that the members were entirely ignorant as to
the difference between bucket-shops and legitimate brokerage houses,
and all seemed to have the idea that a marginal trade through a legitimate broker was, to all intents and purposes, as fictitious as the
so-called 'purchases' and 'sales' in the bucket-shops. The general impression seemed to be that the legislation I was urging was simply
an attempt on the part of the big fellows to squeeze out the little
ones." The grain dealer Harry Kress was a board of trade member who
lived in Piqua, Ohio. He tried to persuade his state legislature to ban
bucket shops as gambling houses, but he was not optimistic, because
most people thought the board's transactions were gambles too. "The
average individual having no connection with the Grain Trade, does
not understand the necessity of trading in futures," Kress complained,
"and right here is where we may expect trouble." The proponent of
an Indiana bill to prohibit bucket shops acknowledged that "the first
question that will naturally arise in the minds of my colleagues is,
what is the difference between a bucket shop and a legitimate board
of trade[?]" The bucket shops themselves did much to promote the
impression that bucket shops and exchanges were identical. As one
Illinois legislator observed, the bucket shops' standard argument

63 George Burmeister to H. A. Foss, 16 Dec. 1912, CBT, box 329, folder 1;
George Burmeister to J. C. F. Merrill, 13 Oct. 1914, CBT, box 329, folder
6. Burmeister's reports fill several folders in CBT, box 329.

against this sort of legislation was "We are bad of course, rotten in fact, but no worse than the board of trade."[64]

The exchanges were walking a very thin line. They were trying to stamp out a business that was not very different from their own, based on the one attribute that exchanges and bucket shops shared in abundance. Despite this obstacle, several states did enact statutes prohibiting bucket shops in the late nineteenth and early twentieth centuries. But this only converted the problem into one of legislative drafting, because any such statute had to distinguish bucket shops from exchanges. Some of these laws did not even try to define the term *bucket shop*. In Iowa, for example, the legislature simply declared that its purpose was to prohibit "places commonly known and designated as bucket-shops." The statutes that defined the term did so by restating the familiar common-law ban on transactions where neither party intended delivery. Wisconsin, for instance, declared that "a bucket-shop, within the meaning of this act, is defined to be an office, store or other place" in which transactions were made "for the purchase or sale of any such commodity wherein the parties do not contemplate the actual or *bona fide* receipt or delivery of such property, but do contemplate a settlement thereof based upon differences in the prices at which said property is, or is claimed to be, bought and sold." The statutes added new penalties to bucket shopping, but they did not make anything unlawful that was not already unlawful. They merely replicated the problem of how to distinguish bucket shops from legitimate exchanges, because by this definition, the exchanges were bucket shops too. "We do not see how any legal distinction can be made between the two operations," the *New York Times* noted shortly after New York enacted its statute. Was the business of a bucket shop "betting on future prices? In form it is not, and in substance it is no more so than the 'regular' speculation" on the New York Stock Exchange. After more than a decade of ineffective enforcement, the *Times* concluded that no law could be drafted to ban bucket shops without also banning the exchanges. "Bucket shops in a

64 John A. Percy to A. M. Clement, 25 June 1910, CBT, box 353, folder 8; Harry W. Kress to A. H. Schuyler, 19 Feb. 1908, CBT, box 331, folder 7; CBT, box 353, folder 3; "Anti-Bucket Shop Bill," CBT, box 353, folder 9.

financial community are something like sorrel in one's front lawn," the paper mused. "No general methods can be taken to exterminate them without danger to the legitimate growth surrounding them." Even the New York Stock Exchange lost faith in the ability of the legal system to stamp out bucket shops. A stock exchange committee appointed to recommend some course of action regarding bucket shops concluded that "these laws are not enforced and never can be enforced." The bucket shops were too popular, and they were popular because they provided the same service as the stock exchange itself. New York and Pennsylvania had enacted statutes prohibiting bucket shops, largely at the stock exchange's behest, but "there are more bucket-shops in New York State and Pennsylvania today than there ever were before."[65]

The exchanges eventually won the war against the bucket shops, not by persuading anyone that they were fundamentally different, but by cutting off the bucket shops' access to the exchanges' price quotations. A bucket shop could not exist without timely price information, so if the exchanges could prevent the bucket shops from receiving price quotations, they could put the bucket shops out of business. But that was easier said than done. The exchanges repeatedly tried to persuade the telegraph companies to deny service to nonmembers, without much success, because the bucket shop business was simply too lucrative for the telegraph companies. In 1890, the board of trade took the extreme step of stopping the telegraphic distribution of price quotations, an extraordinary inconvenience to the board's many out-of-town members who were accustomed to receiving prices by telegraph. But the board quickly discovered that the bucket shops were getting the quotations anyway, apparently because someone inside the board was flashing signals out the window. The next day the board tried soaping the windows, but even that desperate measure only delayed the bucket shops by about fifteen minutes. The board resumed telegraphing its prices. In 1898, when the board suspected that someone was using the new telephones

65 Morris J. Cashel, "Bucket Shops," *American Political Science Review* 2 (1907): 48–50; T. Henry Dewey, *Legislation Against Speculation and Gambling in the Forms of Trade* (New York: Baker, Voorhis & Co., 1905), 51–65, 54, 63; *New York Times*, 13 June 1889, 4; 22 May 1904, FS3; Special Committee on Bucket Shops, 154, 157.

on the exchange floor to leak price quotes to bucket shops, there was a proposal to remove them, which drew complaints from board members all over the country that without telephone contact they could not compete with the bucket shops, because the telephone was the only way they could get prices faster than the bucket shops did.[66]

Toward the end of the century, the exchanges turned to a different tactic. They began filing suits against bucket shops, alleging that the price quotations were their property and that the bucket shops had stolen it. These suits had a mixed record at first, but in 1905 the exchanges scored a final victory in the US Supreme Court, which affirmed that the prices resulting from transactions on an exchange were property belonging to the exchange. The case was brought by the Chicago Board of Trade against the Christie Grain & Stock Company, a Kansas City bucket shop that was presumably obtaining board price quotations by telegraph, despite a provision in the board's contracts with the telegraph companies not to furnish price information to any bucket shop. The board's "collection of quotations is entitled to the protection of the law," Justice Oliver Wendell Holmes wrote for the court. "It stands like a trade secret. The plaintiff has the right to keep the work which it had done, or paid for doing, to itself." By sending prices over the telegraph wires to members throughout the country, Holmes continued, the board had not given up this privilege of secrecy. "The plaintiff does not lose its rights by communicating the result to persons, even if many, in confidential relations to itself, under a contract not to make it public," the court held. "Strangers to the trust"—that is, the bucket shops—"will be restrained from getting at the knowledge by inducing a breach of trust, and using knowledge obtained by such a breach."[67] The exchanges had established their right to control their price quotations.

The Christie Grain & Stock Company's primary defense was that the board of trade "itself keeps the greatest of bucket shops," that its

66 *Chicago Daily Tribune*, 18 Nov. 1890, 6; CBT, box 37, folder 25.

67 *Kiernan v. Manhattan Quotation Telegraph Co.*, 50 How. Pr. 194 (N.Y. Sup. Ct. 1876); *New York & Chicago Grain & Stock Exchange v. Board of Trade*, 19 N.E. 855 (Ill. 1889); *National Telegraph News Co. v. Western Union Telegraph Co.*, 119 F. 294 (7th Cir. 1902); *Chicago Board of Trade v. Christie Grain & Stock Co.*, 198 U.S. 236, 250–51 (1905).

price quotations were thus the product of illegal conduct, and that even if prices were property when created lawfully, the board should not be allowed to profit from its own illegality. In the course of rebuffing this defense, Holmes launched into an extended discussion of the legitimacy and importance of speculative trading on organized exchanges, using words that would be quoted liberally by the exchanges in the years to come whenever the opportunity arose. "In a modern market, contracts are not confined to sales for immediate delivery," Holmes began. "People will endeavor to forecast the future, and to make agreements according to their prophecy. Speculation of this kind by competent men is the self-adjustment of society to the probable. Its value is well known." Even if some of the contracts on the board of trade were unenforceable wagers, he continued, "there is no doubt that a large part of those contracts is made for serious business purposes." The idea that the board's transactions were mere wagers "seems to us hardly consistent with the admitted fact that the quotations of prices from the market are of the utmost importance to the business world."[68] Of course, many bucket shop transactions were made for business purposes that were just as serious, but unlike transactions on the board of trade, they did not set prices for the country.

Holmes's opinion in the *Chicago Board of Trade* case was a strong endorsement of the exchanges, but it did not change the law. Most of the transactions on the exchanges were still unlawful, just as they had been since state courts began adopting the intent-to-deliver rule a few decades before. The Supreme Court had ratified the prevailing view among the lower courts that price quotations were the exchanges' property, but that did not stop the bucket shops from continuing to use every means at their disposal to get the quotations anyway. It would be another decade before the exchanges finally won the war. The key to victory was probably not the spate of anti–bucket shop statutes or the Supreme Court's formal recognition of a property right in price quotations, but rather the increasing size and thus clout of the exchanges, which eventually enabled them to force the telegraph companies to restrict the distribution of price information. When the bucket shops were starved for prices, most of them died.

68 *Chicago Board of Trade v. Christie*, 246, 247–49.

"Time was when the bucket shop was almost as the locust in a seventh year," the *Saturday Evening Post* recalled in 1916. "Every considerable town had from one to forty concerns where the inexperienced and credulous could bet away their money on variations in the price of grain, cotton, stocks." But not any longer. "Our impression is that the species has been pretty nearly exterminated. Certainly it persists only sporadically and in a meager fashion."[69] Bucket shops never disappeared completely, but they ceased to be serious competition for the exchanges.

The intent-to-deliver rule had not disappeared, however. It was still a part of the common law throughout the country, and it had been enacted into statute in many states as well. The rule drew a line—a very fine line, as many saw it—between legitimate and illegitimate speculation, between speculation considered as business and speculation considered as gambling. Meanwhile, even before the bucket shop war ended, the exchanges had to confront another challenge, in the form of a concerted national effort to redraw the line so as to prohibit even more forms of speculation.

69 "A Scientific Reform," *Saturday Evening Post*, 13 May 1916, in CBT, box 353, folder 10.

3

The Anti-Option Era

SPECULATION IN AGRICULTURAL COMMODITIES was a major national political issue from the early 1890s through the early 1920s. Year after year, Congress considered—and sometimes nearly passed—bills that would have drastically curtailed speculation. These were popularly known as "anti-option" bills, but they addressed more than options. Their real targets were the commodity exchanges in cities throughout the country, which would likely have had to shut down had any of the bills before the 1920s become law. The controversy did not subside until 1921, when Congress established a new federal regulatory framework for commodity trading, the basic features of which remain in place today.

The political support for these measures came primarily from farmers, many of whom were suffering from sharp drops in the prices they received for their crops. Between 1888 and 1894, wheat fell from 93 cents a bushel to 49 cents, and cotton from 8.5 cents a pound to 4.6 cents. Corn declined from 50 cents a bushel in 1890 to 21 cents in 1896, while oats dropped from 42 cents a bushel to 18 cents. The resulting agrarian discontent took various forms, including most famously the creation of a new political party, the People's (or Populist) Party, which achieved considerable success in congressional elections during the 1890s.[1]

---

1 Susan B. Carter et al., eds., *Historical Statistics of the United States*, Millennial Edition On Line (Cambridge University Press, 2006), tables Da719, Da757, Da697, Da672; Lawrence Goodwin, *Democratic Promise: The Populist Movement in America* (New York: Oxford University Press, 1976).

One of the farmers' grievances involved commodity speculation. Crops had once been sold locally, and thus prices had been determined in a local market, but by the late nineteenth century crops were shipped around the world, and prices were determined in a global market, mediated through the commodity exchanges newly established in the nation's major cities. Commodities were traded at the Chicago Board of Trade, at the New York Produce Exchange, and at similar exchanges in Minneapolis, Duluth, Milwaukee, St. Louis, Kansas City, Toledo, Philadelphia, and other cities. "Exchanges have sprung up in many places," the *Bankers' Magazine* marveled in the 1880s. "Within a few years speculation has spread out enormously in many directions."[2] When farmers sought to understand why they had been impoverished by falling prices, these exchanges were natural institutions to blame. Farmers and their supporters could draw upon the long tradition of thought critical of speculation.

The result was a three-decade national debate about speculation. The arguments on both sides scarcely changed from one year to the next. In 1921, John Hill observed that "the subject of future trading has been almost constantly before Congress since 1890 and hearings such as those had in recent months are mere repetition." Hill had been defending the Chicago Board of Trade for years, and he was tired of it. "There is no variation in the charges, no variation in the arguments of the defense," he complained. "All the claims of both sides can be found in the hearings of 1892." In 1908, when the New York Cotton Exchange mounted a public relations campaign against proposed legislation, it merely had to reprint the open letters it had published in the early 1890s. By the end of this period, these recurring rural calls to restrict speculation were a source of some amusement, and no small amount of condescension, on the part of urbane defenders of the status quo. "There breaks forth periodically from prudish but well-meaning people a protest against all forms of speculation," noted the editor of the New York *Financial World*. "The word 'speculation,' to the impassioned social reformer, is

2 Jerry W. Markham, *The History of Commodity Futures Trading and Its Regulation* (New York: Praeger, 1987), 7–8; "Speculation and Money," *Bankers' Magazine and Statistical Register* 37 (1883): 811.

like red to a bull," agreed the philosopher Robert Hutcheon. "All his latent belligerency against things as they are is roused into strenuous action when he hears the word or reflects on the crazy mentality and the reckless activities it stands for."[3]

But there was much more than ignorance behind the farmers' call to prohibit speculation in their products. The anti-option movement was part of a broader battle over the organization of agriculture, fought by an occupational group who could see their relative numbers dwindling and their influence in the market slipping away. Many of the farmers' arguments against speculation may have been wrong as a matter of economics, but there was nothing irrational about them as a matter of politics.

HAYSEED LEGISLATION

William Vilas served only a single term as a senator from Wisconsin, but it lasted from 1891 to 1897, when the agitation for restricting commodity speculation was at its peak, so he found himself bombarded with appeals from both sides of the struggle. Political considerations pulled Vilas in both directions. There were many farmers in Wisconsin, but Milwaukee was already a big city, and the Milwaukee Grain Exchange was a center of grain speculation, so any position Vilas took would be sure to alienate a substantial fraction of voters and a good number of the state legislators who still had the power to select Wisconsin's senators. Vilas was a Democrat, in an era when the Democratic Party, especially in the West, was identified with the small farmer, but Vilas himself was about as far from the farm as a Wisconsinite could be. He had been a lawyer, a law professor at the state university in Madison, and then postmaster general and secretary of the interior during the first Grover Cleveland administration. He had much more in common with the bankers and brokers of Milwaukee than with the state's farmers.

3 John Hill Jr. to E. F. Ladd, 17 June 1921, CBT, box 328, folder 3; *Bills in Congress Affecting Cotton Contracts for Future Delivery* (New York: Latham, Alexander & Co., 1908); Louis Guenther, *Investment and Speculation* (Chicago: La Salle Extension University, 1921), 157; Robert J. Hutcheon, "Speculation, Legitimate and Illegitimate," *International Journal of Ethics* 32 (1922): 289.

Throughout 1892 and early 1893, Vilas received a steady stream of letters in support of the pending bills to curtail speculation. All were from farmers or their representatives. George Stowe, the vice president of the Wisconsin Farmers' Alliance, urged Vilas to "stop the gambling in grain & provisions." Stowe reported that the state's farmers "feel that the gamblers on the Boards of trade have no right to sell produce they do not have nor ever expect to have and by selling so many millions of bushels of grain more than is in the whole world it is a very great wrong." The publisher of the *Western Rural and American Stockman* declared that although the cities opposed the bills, "the country is practically a unit in favor of anti option legislation," which was supported by "the farm organizations of the northern states, five in number, representing a membership of upwards of one million members, practically all voters." As another rural correspondent pointed out, "it is quite noticeable that the chief opposition to these bills comes almost wholly from money centers and capitalists, and from organizations of grain and produce or stock speculators."[4]

Vilas received an equally large set of letters from opponents of the legislation. Many came from the Milwaukee Chamber of Commerce, whose more than six hundred members voted unanimously to oppose the bills. Vilas heard arguments against restricting speculation from grain traders, from bankers, from the Chicago Board of Trade, and from the Toledo Produce Exchange. "I do not wonder," he confessed to the president of the Milwaukee Chamber of Commerce, "that there is a rising feeling on the part of farmers and producers that something ought to be done in their interest." But he thought the legislation would do little to help farmers, so he opposed it, after trying to mollify rural voters by declaring on the Senate floor that his opposition was based not on the bill's merits but on his view that it was unconstitutional.[5]

4 G. E. Stowe to Vilas, 9 May 1892, box 14, folder 1; Milton George to Vilas, 6 July 1892, box 14, folder 1; N. F. Fox to Vilas, 29 Feb. 1892, box 13, folder 1, all in WFV.

5 E. P. Bacon to Vilas, 5 Mar. 1892, 29 Apr. 1892, and 3 Dec. 1892, and "A Protest" (27 Apr. 1892), all in WFV, box 14, folder 1; Robert Eliot to Vilas, 15 Jan. 1892, WFV, box 13, folder 1; John Johnston to Vilas, 17 Feb. 1892, WFV, box 13, folder 1; George Stone to Vilas, 30 Dec. 1892, WFV, box 15, folder 1; Denison B. Smith

The rural–urban divide that Vilas encountered was representative of the nation as a whole. The urban northeast, from Massachusetts down to Maryland, was the only part of the country from which a majority of members of Congress voted against restricting speculation in the early 1890s. The idea was popular everywhere else. In 1890, the House of Representatives first considered a bill to impose a prohibitive tax on people who sold agricultural products they did not own, a bill that would have put an end to commodity trading on all the boards of trade and produce exchanges. Petitions of support poured in from farmers' alliances in Iowa; from a group of farmers in Indiana who castigated "the gigantic gambling devices known as short selling"; from the citizens of Wyandotte County, Kansas, and Buffalo County, Wisconsin; from the farmers of Spokane County and Lincoln County in Washington; and from a group of Indianans who declared that "the so-called business of dealing in options as it is commonly practiced on boards of trade is as clearly a mere gambling device as a 'wheel of fortune' or faro lay-out." The primary opposition came from the New York Produce Exchange, the New York Cotton Exchange, the Chicago Board of Trade, and the New Orleans Cotton Exchange.[6]

House opponents of the 1890 bill were able to keep it from coming to a vote, but the legislation returned in the next session of Congress, in the summer of 1892, with the same configuration of supporters and opponents. The farmers were in favor, while the commodity exchanges, joined by many banks, were against. This time, bills were passed by both the House and the Senate. An election was looming, and both parties were anxious not to lose votes to the Populists, who nominated their own presidential candidate, as well as candidates in many congressional districts. "The passage of the Hatch Anti-Option bill in the House is simply a Democratic bid for the favor of the Farmers' Alliance," charged the *St. Louis Globe-Democrat*. "It does not mean that the men who spoke and

to Vilas, 11 Mar. 1892, WFV, box 13, folder 2; Vilas to E. P. Bacon, 7 Mar. 1892, WFV, box 14, folder 1; *New York Times*, 6 Jan. 1893, 3.

6 Cedric B. Cowing, *Populists, Plungers, and Progressives: A Social History of Stock and Commodity Speculation, 1890–1936* (Princeton, N.J.: Princeton University Press, 1965), 22; *Journal of the House of Representatives of the United States*, 51st Cong., 2nd Sess. (1890), 69, 118, 114, 169; *New York Times*, 12 Apr. 1890, 3.

voted for it are anxious to promote the interests of the agricultural class, but only that they think to help their party by humoring a silly prejudice against a certain form of trading." The *Pittsburg Dispatch* sarcastically referred to the bills' House and Senate sponsors as "Farmer Hatch" and "Farmer Washburn," despite the fact that neither William Hatch of Missouri nor William Washburn of Minnesota was a farmer; Hatch was a lawyer and Washburn engaged in a variety of businesses. The bill was "hayseed legislation," cracked one member of the New York Produce Exchange. "The farmer, as a rule, imagines everyone in the city is his enemy, and there are just enough demagogues lying around loose to encourage him in this opinion."[7]

The Senate's version of the bill was slightly different from the House's, so it had to return to the House, but by then the 1892 election had already taken place, so there was less need to make a conspicuous show of supporting the farmers. Opponents of the bill were able to stall until the session expired. "By persistently postponing a vote on the bill to prohibit dealings in options and futures, the minority of the members of the House accomplished its defeat," a relieved *New York Times* reported.[8]

Proponents of a national ban on commodity speculation would never come so close again. Hatch returned with a similar bill in 1894; it passed the House but never came to a vote in the Senate. Another bill in 1895 could not get through the House. Commodity prices leveled off and even rose a bit over the next few years, so there would be no more antispeculation bills until 1903, but then they started appearing in increasing numbers. The Panic of 1907 elicited no fewer than twenty bills to prohibit futures trading, followed by thirteen more in 1909 and another eight in 1911. In 1912, the Democratic Party platform

---

7 *Journal of the House of Representatives of the United States*, 52nd Cong., 1st Sess. (1892), part II, 251, 255, 267, 270, 275, 277, 278, 282; *Dealings in "Options" and "Futures": Protests, Memorials and Arguments Against Bills Introduced in the Fifty-Second Congress* (s.l.: New York Cotton Exchange et al., 1892); *Globe-Democrat* quoted in *Chicago Daily Tribune*, 13 June 1892, 4; *Pittsburg Dispatch*, 20 Feb. 1892, 1; *New York Times*, 18 July 1892, 10.
8 *New York Times*, 2 Mar. 1893, 5.

even included a pledge to "suppress the pernicious practice of gambling in agricultural products by organized exchanges."[9]

Low prices were the immediate cause of the farmers' anger, so many of their complaints about commodity speculation focused on its effects on prices. Critics made a variety of claims about the relationship between speculation and prices, not all of which were consistent, but all of which proposed mechanisms by which speculation harmed producers in the end.

One common contention was that speculators had the power to manipulate prices to their own advantage. "Prices are almost entirely artificial and are controlled by powerful cliques of speculators," one critic charged when cotton and wheat prices began to fall. When prices rose, the *Michigan Farmer* blamed "the power of speculators to force the market of a great staple commodity up." Speculators were alleged to manipulate prices by conspiring to buy and sell at prices that varied from the true value of a commodity, and by securing the publication of false crop reports in the newspapers. Some critics contended that speculators' goal was to depress the prices paid to the producers of commodities. "There can be no doubt that the price of our food products is fixed by the sales of futures or options," insisted Representative Edward Funston of Kansas, who was a farmer himself. "The bull and the bear work together to keep prices down for unless they are down, there is no profit to the buyers and sellers." Other critics claimed that speculators' real interest was to engineer fluctuations in prices, because that is how they made their profits. "Whether it was up or down, it was always to the detriment of the farmer," lamented Representative Jasper Tincher, another Kansas farmer in Congress. "If it was up it was to the detriment of the farmer who sold his grain the day before, and if it was down it was to the detriment of the farmer who was going to sell some the next day." Whether speculators were depressing prices or making them fluctuate, critics were certain that

9 H.R. Rep. No. 845, 53rd Cong., 2nd Sess. (1894); H.R. Rep. No. 1999, 53rd Cong., 3rd Sess. (1895); Carl Parker, "Governmental Regulation of Speculation," *Annals of the American Academy of Political and Social Science* 38 (1911): 141–44; Democratic platform at http://www.presidency.ucsb.edu/ws/index.php?pid=29590.

speculation caused prices to diverge from the true values they would have had in a market free from manipulation. "We neither ask for our produce, and are unwilling to pay more than the actual value," declared T. J. Kimbrough, master of the Georgia State Grange. "Supply and demand should control."[10]

Opponents of legislation replied that while speculators might be able to manipulate prices for very short periods of time, they lacked the resources to do so for long. "With regard to the present price of cotton," argued the cotton speculator Daniel Sully, "no plan of manipulation, unless financed on a scale sufficient to take over a large portion of the crop," could keep prices higher or lower. "No clique of speculators could be found with money enough and daring enough to attempt such a thing." As the economist Richard Ely put it, "buying and selling in themselves cannot raise prices. . . . If it were possible thus to raise prices, there would be an easy road to fortune for everyone." Speculators thus could not be blamed for the long-term decline in commodity prices. Others repeated the familiar observation that the effect of speculation was not to increase fluctuations but to smooth them out, because speculators bought in a declining market and sold in a rising one. Without them, reasoned the journalist Harold Howland, "booms would tend to be wild and unrestrained, with inevitable disaster when the break finally came," while "declines would be sudden, rapid, and extensive, with equally disastrous consequences." The financial writer Charles Conant, anticipating a way of thinking that would become orthodoxy later in the twentieth century, provided a second method by which speculators smoothed price changes. "Every event in the world which affects price is felt upon the exchanges; and it comes to be said that future events, when they occur, have been already 'discounted,'"

10 "Speculation and Prices," *Independent* 34 (1882): 22; "The Fruit of Speculation," *Michigan Farmer* 45 (1904): 301; "When Speculation Is Immoral," *Current Literature* 44 (1908): 67; "Newspapers as Aids to Speculation," *Ohio Farmer* 64 (1883): 328; *Omaha Daily Bee*, 9 Apr. 1890, 1; J. R. Dodge, "The Discontent of the Farmer," *Century* 43 (1892): 454; Richard Wheatly, "The New York Produce Exchange," *Harper's New Monthly Magazine* 73 (1886): 217; *Future Trading: Hearings Before the Committee on Agriculture, House of Representatives*, 67th Cong., 1st Sess. (1921), 5–6; "Gambling in Futures," *Southern Cultivator* 48 (1890): 496.

he noted. "Many important events which would cause a sudden break or rise in prices, if they came like thunderbolts from a clear sky, are thus 'discounted' before they actually take place. This fact is the highest compliment to the organization of the exchanges, and the best proof of their usefulness. The mere suspicion in well-informed quarters that wheat is to be scarce six months hence leads to its gradual rise in price." The grain trader Egerton Williams concluded that without speculators to support the market, the fall in grain prices that took place in the early 1890s would have been even worse.[11]

A second line of criticism was that price declines were caused not by manipulation but by *short selling*, the practice of selling, for future delivery, a commodity one did not yet own. A short seller hoped that the price would drop between the contract date and the delivery date, so that he could purchase it on the delivery date at a price lower than the seller had agreed to receive. "The man who sells hundreds of thousands of bushels of wheat, although he does not possess a bushel, affects the market," argued Benjamin Butterworth, the Ohio representative who sponsored the 1890 bill that would have put an end to short selling. "For every bushel of grain grown a hundred are sold, and I maintain that the effect is to lower the market price. . . . When the market supply is 100 times greater than it really is you drive the price down." C. Wood Davis, the Kansas farmer turned activist who devoted years to the anti-option cause, offered an analogy. Davis asked the House Agriculture Committee, "If the offering of too many coats will reduce the price of coats, will not the offering of wheat or cotton or any other article in like excess of requirements, reduce the price of wheat or cotton, or other articles?" Such sellers of fictitious crops were competing with farmers selling real crops, Davis explained, and so long as "the broker's lung power is good, they can continue to offer 10,000 bushels every minute in competition with the 10,000 bushels of wheat which we produce."

11 Daniel J. Sully, "Is the High Price of Cotton the Result of Manipulation?," *North American Review* 178 (1904): 194; Richard T. Ely, "Land Speculation," *Journal of Farm Economics* 2 (1920): 130; Harold J. Howland, "Gambling Joint or Market Place?," *Outlook* 104 (1913): 437; Charles A. Conant, "The Uses of Speculation," *Forum* 31 (1901): 701; Egerton R. Williams, "Thirty Years in the Grain Trade," *North American Review* 161 (1895): 33.

John Whittaker, a commodity merchant in St. Louis, testified that in New York in January 1892 alone, three million bushels of physical wheat were sold in the spot market, while eighty-three million bushels of theoretical wheat were sold in the futures market. "I do not think it will occur to any reasonable man that the selling of that 83,000,000 bushels did not depress the value of the actual wheat that was sent to the market for sale," Whittaker concluded. "Unqualifiedly I call that the greatest outrage committed on the American people."[12]

The idea that short selling depressed prices was widely believed but simply mistaken, as representatives of the exchanges pointed out year after year. Every short seller had to be a buyer eventually, so sellers and buyers would cancel each other out. "The moment a man sells property he has not got he is a buyer from necessity," explained Charles Hamill, the president of the Chicago Board of Trade. "They are the most anxious of buyers." And of course all those bushels of wheat *sold* on the futures market were simultaneously being *purchased* on the futures market by the person on the other side of the transaction, so the downward pressure from the sales had to be exactly counterbalanced by the upward pressure from the purchases. "The bear is seen offering to sell a commodity," one defender of speculation noted, "but the speculative buyer is not seen, as he bids for even greater quantities of 'wind.'" The *New York Times* offered a simple demonstration that the supposed link between short selling and price declines was "of the *post hoc ergo propter hoc* kind." Prices had dropped for commodities like wheat and cotton that were sold short on the exchanges, but they had dropped just as much for commodities that were not traded on exchanges, like wool, pig iron, and the animal hides used for leather. The *Times* concluded: "Trading in 'futures' has no more been the cause of depression in cotton, wheat, and hog products than its absence has been the cause of it in wool, hides, and pig iron."[13]

---

12   *Chicago Daily Tribune*, 17 Feb. 1890, 5; *Fictitious Dealing in Agricultural Products: Testimony Before the Committee on Agriculture* (Washington, D.C.: Government Printing Office, 1892), 12, 15, 47.

13   *Fictitious Dealing*, 169; Harrison H. Brace, *The Value of Organized Speculation* (Boston: Houghton Mifflin Co., 1913), 100; *New York Times*, 28 May 1892, 4.

Agrarian critics had a third reason for believing that speculation reduced the farmer's earnings, one that was not as easy to dismiss. Speculators were intermediaries between the producers and consumers of agricultural products. The ultimate price to the consumer was capped by what consumers were willing to pay, which meant that every dollar earned by a speculator was taken directly from the farmer's pocket. The idea that speculators were parasitic middlemen was a staple of the agricultural press. "We believe it necessary to have *some* middlemen to keep the wheels of trade moving properly," explained the *Ohio Farmer*, "but do not believe it necessary for farm products to go through three, four, five or six hands, each reaping a profit, before reaching the manufacturer or consumer, and causing the farmer to sell for less than cost of production." The *Indiana Farmer's Guide* agreed that "between the man who produces food today and the man who consumes the food, operates a long and complicated system of buying and selling which has nothing to do with real service to either of these primarily interested parties." The *Farmer's Guide* cited a local example: "a carload of Indiana eggs sold to a New York wholesaler at 24 ½ cents a dozen, was resold nine times without leaving the cold storage warehouse, until the St. Regis hotel paid 43 cents a dozen for the lot." While farmers were suffering, "a lot of fellows make millions of dollars every year by so-called business transactions in food-stuffs which contribute nothing at all toward bringing the food from the producer to the consumer." As the *Southern Cultivator* complained, "the farmer gets a small price, the manufacturer pays a good one, and the intervening speculator pockets the difference."[14]

From the farmers' perspective, all this speculation in agricultural commodities stood in conspicuous contrast with the lack of speculation in other goods, which consumers bought directly from producers. "No one who is about building a house or block goes into the option pit to make his contract," the *Wichita Daily Eagle* reasoned, while the Butterworth bill was before Congress in 1890. "He looks for the actual owners and laborers with whom to make his contract. Merchants who

14 "Wool," *Ohio Farmer* 59 (1881): 421; "Oust the Speculators," *Indiana Farmer's Guide* 31 (1919): 36; "The Panic," *Southern Cultivator* 31 (1873): 409.

wish to contract for the future supply of an article go to the manufacturer and engage with him to supply the article when needed in the future. He does not contract for it with people who do not have it. Why should farm products be on a different basis?"[15] If all these other industries could flourish without speculators to take a cut of the producer's profit, why couldn't agriculture?

Implicit in this question was the ancient view, still very much alive, that speculation was a nonproductive activity, one that added no value to the commodities being bought and sold. "If A goes to Chicago and buys wheat and transports it to New York and sells it, he is a producer," reasoned one critic. "But the speculator never enhances the value of anything." Merchants and speculators both took risks, another explained, but the difference between the two was that the merchant's profit "is sought as a fair equivalent for services rendered to the community in bringing some needed article to market," while the speculator's profit was simply taken from someone else's pocket.[16] The farmers' anger was not directed at all middlemen indiscriminately, but only at those, like the traders on the commodity exchanges, who seemed to be amply rewarded for no good reason.

Defenders of speculation had an answer: commodity speculation *did* add value to commodities, and farmers were accordingly gainers, not losers, from the chain of intermediaries who stood between them and the consumer. The difference between agriculture and other industries, they argued, was that agricultural products were harvested during only one season of the year but were consumed all year round. Someone had to hold commodities for the remainder of the year, which meant that someone had to bear the risk that commodity prices would decline before they could be sold to the consumer. That was the function served by speculators. The speculator "performed a distinct service to the agriculturalist," explained John Hill of the board of trade, "by providing a market for one million bushels of wheat at a time when the consumer was in no hurry to buy, and when the wheat was accumulating

15 *Wichita Daily Eagle*, 4 Sept. 1890, 4.
16 "The Bank as a Promoter of Speculation," *Bankers' Magazine and Statistical Register* 6 (1872): 657–58; "The Tragic Side of Commercial Speculation," *Zion's Herald* 52 (1875): 292.

in the warehouses." Speculators were often said to "carry" commodities throughout the year, a term that had two meanings. Sometimes speculators literally possessed commodities—they purchased commodities when farmers needed to sell but consumers were not yet ready to buy. Without them, one journalist pointed out, "the farmer could not sell except throughout the year as the demand arose." But speculators "carried" commodities in a metaphorical sense as well. They relieved the farmer of the risk that prices would fall between the harvest and the sale. Without speculators, suggested the *Chicago Tribune*, farmers would have to "borrow money with which to pay their way and take their chances of a falling market." The broker Alexander Hudnut pointed out that *someone* had to bear the risk that commodity prices would decline. If it wasn't a speculator it would be the farmer, and in that case the farmer would be speculating just as much as any trader on an exchange. If there were no speculators in the chain of distribution, farmers would have to become speculators themselves.[17]

Farmers were not the only ones who faced the risk that prices would fall while commodities were in their possession. The same risk confronted all the useful intermediaries between the farmer and the consumer—the miller, the shipper, and so on—who bought commodities at one time and sold them at another. These market participants used the commodity exchanges to hedge that risk; they sold futures to offset the risk of price declines. A Minneapolis trade journal explained that "there is no grain or milling concern in the northwest with capital enough to stand 'pat' on its share of purchases without some sort of assurance of the character supplied by future sales." W. C. Brown, a miller in Fostoria, Ohio, testified that each fall he took possession of approximately seven hundred thousand bushels of wheat. "As soon as we buy it we sell a future against it," he reported. "Then it makes no difference to us whether the price of wheat goes up or down, the mill is absolutely protected and we do not gamble in grain." Of course, it

---

17 John Hill Jr., *Gold Bricks of Speculation* (Chicago: Lincoln Book Concern, 1904), 420–21; "Business and Speculation," *Independent* 48 (1896): 21; *Chicago Daily Tribune*, 25 Dec. 1891, 4; Alexander M. Hudnut, "Dealing in Futures Is Not Gambling," *Town and Country*, 20 May 1905, 37; L. D. H. Weld, "High Food Prices, Middlemen, and Speculation," *North American Review* 206 (1917): 589.

would not be possible to sell futures unless someone stood ready to buy futures. One could not sell a risk without a counterparty willing to assume it. Speculators thus performed the same function for millers and other intermediaries that they performed for farmers. "This is where the speculator comes into play by being willing to take a chance that we will not take," explained E. A. Duff, who operated thirty grain elevators in Nebraska and Kansas. "It is mathematically true that hedging can not exist without some speculation," agreed George McDermott of the Kansas Grain Dealers' Association.[18]

Members of exchanges accordingly liked to analogize their role to that of an insurance underwriter: they were compensated for assuming risks others wished to shed. The grain trade was a "vast system of insurance," declared Walter Fitch, the former president of the Chicago Board of Trade. In its promotional material, the board described itself as "an insurance underwriter for all of these elements of the trade." F. B. Wells, the vice president of a grain warehousing firm and thus a frequent hedger, thought commodity exchanges the American equivalent of Lloyd's of London, the venerable English insurance market. "The only difference between those men and speculators in the grain exchange," Wells reasoned, "is that they received a fixed amount for assuming the risk, whereas the speculator in the grain pit backs his own opinion that he will receive something for assuming the risk. The principle involved is the same."[19]

Critics found the analogy absurd. Insurance companies "have no financial interest in the risks except in decreasing them," observed the Illinois Agricultural Association, an organization of farmers. "Fire insurance companies spend large sums of money in educating the public to prevent fires. They are certainly not benefited by any increase in the number of fires. Grain speculators, on the other hand—the men

---

18 *Daily Market Record*, 8 Jan. 1892, 1; *Fictitious Dealing*, 213; *Future Trading in Grain: Hearings Before the Committee on Agriculture and Forestry, United States Senate*, 67th Cong., 1st Sess. (1921), 109–10, 207.

19 *Hearings Before the Committee on Agriculture During the Second Session of the Sixty-First Congress, vol. II, Hearings on Bills for the Prevention of "Dealing in Futures" on Boards of Trade, Etc.* (1910), 438; Board of Directors Resolution, 28 Feb. 1921, CBT, box 334, folder 8; *Future Trading in Grain*, 393–94.

who provide this so-called grain insurance in the form of hedging—are interested in increasing the risk." There was no hedging, and no futures trading, in most markets. "There is none on hay, there is none on iron, there is none on coal, and there is none on an enormous amount of important products," noted T. J. Brooks, speaking on behalf of the Farmers' Educational and Cooperative Union. "There are no futures on farm machinery," he pointed out, and "a manufacturer may produce a machine five years before it is sold." Hedging, in his view, was no more necessary for cotton or for wheat than it was for anything else. After all, the price of any item could fall while someone was holding it; how could hedging be needed only for certain commodities? "The obvious answer" to the claim that speculators assumed risk, argued the Populist theologian John Ryan, was that "traders in produce should take the risks of fluctuating prices themselves." If traders bore their own risks, "many of them would doubtless go to the wall, but the community would be the gainer through the elimination of the unfit." Why should farmers pay for an elaborate infrastructure of speculation just to prop up the weakest grain traders?[20]

George Norris, the long-serving Nebraska senator, grew up on a farm in Ohio. At the hearings on the bill that would eventually become the Grain Futures Act of 1922, Norris summed up the farmers' skepticism about the insurance function supposedly served by speculators. "If I buy a piece of land because I think it is cheap, why should there not be some organization on which I could rely in that transaction?" Norris asked Rollin Smith, the Agriculture Department's supervisor of grain markets. There was no hedging in the real estate market, despite its evident risks. "Why should not the man who buys wheat be subject to the same rule of commerce that the farmer is, or the local dealer who buys hogs in a town lot?" Such people, like most Americans, bore their own risks. "Why should there be any difference; why does not the same rule of trade apply to all of them?" Smith recognized the implication of Norris's question. "That touches on a sort of nerve center of the whole system," he responded. "Why should a vast volume of speculation by

20 *Future Trading in Grain*, 176; *Hearings Before the Committee on Agriculture*, 7; John A. Ryan, "The Ethics of Speculation," *International Journal of Ethics* 12 (1902): 338.

the public, the professionals, the cash grain men, elevator companies and others, continue to go on just to create an insurance market for a few grain dealers? That is what it amounts to." Norris replied, "If you ask me, I say I do not know why." "Neither do I," admitted Smith, "but that is the situation."[21]

Norris and Smith were likely being disingenuous, because the exchanges and their supporters had been providing an answer to their question for three decades: if the intermediaries in the distribution system had to bear their own risks, they would have to be compensated for doing so, in the form of a bigger spread between the price they paid to farmers and the price they charged to consumers. Without speculators, the farmers' earnings would be even lower than they already were. Traders "would certainly be compelled to buy on a wider margin to protect themselves against declining markets while the grain is in transit," the grain merchant S. W. Tallmadge advised William Vilas, "and in so doing the producer receives less pay for his grain." "If the farmers succeed" in their efforts to ban the exchanges, the *Chicago Tribune* editorialized, "they will find themselves even worse off than now, the remedy being even more bad than the disease they seek to have cured." The broker S. V. White wondered: "Is there a man so blind as not to see that if the buyer had to take the risk of a two weeks' fluctuation in the grain market he could not pay within many cents per bushel of the advanced prices?" R. C. Clark, a member of the Chicago Board of Trade, agreed that "there isn't a farmer in the West who could get as much for his grain by two to five cents a bushel as he gets now if trading in futures were prohibited." "Before trading in grain for future delivery became a custom," recalled John Messmore of the St. Louis Grain Exchange, grain exporters "made from 10 to 20 cents per bushel on every bushel they exported." The exchanges had driven this margin sharply down. "The exporter of today works on a very small margin, frequently only 1 cent per bushel profit," Messmore explained. "The millers also work on a small margin. They are able to do this because they can protect their purchases or sales in the terminal or primary markets, by buying or selling the grain for future delivery." Speculation thus left more money for

21 *Future Trading in Grain*, 52–53.

farmers. Messmore concluded that "to pass a law abolishing the trading in grain for future delivery would be a calamity to the farmers."[22]

Even worse, exchange members suggested, an inability to hedge might make the grain trade too risky for all but the largest dealers, which would leave the farmer with a constricted market for his products. "The result of the bill," predicted Murry Nelson of the Chicago Board of Trade, "would be to crush out the small dealers and place the farmer at the mercy of the large capitalist, who can buy cash grain; but they will buy it at such a price that they can hold it until Gabriel blows his horn without sustaining loss."[23] Without competition among many potential purchasers for grain, farmers would be forced to sell at lower prices.

Of course, it would be possible for farmers to bypass the intermediaries altogether and sell grain directly to the consumer as in the old days, but this was yet another route to lower prices. "If the producer should sell direct to the consumer," board of trade member Charles Counselman expected, "the farmers of Kansas and Nebraska, instead of receiving 10 to 15 cents a bushel for corn this winter, which was little enough, would not have received five cents a bushel." Counselman's colleague J. H. Norton pointed out that "the speculator doesn't buy merely what he himself can consume, as does the farmer's neighbor, but he buys what a nation or part of a nation may need. In this way he gives the farmer the benefit of the world's prices instead of being limited to local demand." Benjamin Hutchinson, one of the leading grain speculators of the 1880s, posed the problem in more concrete terms. "If there were no speculation," he suggested, "the farmers could only sell their grain to local buyers, who would be liable to get full and stop buying, and then the farmer would be compelled to wait for customers; and in the meantime a mortgage might be foreclosed on his farm, even while the wheat in his bins would more than satisfy the mortgage, if converted into cash. But speculation, flashing its news over the wires from one side of the world to the other, keeps the market always open to him."

22 S. W. Tallmadge to William Vilas, 12 Mar. 1892, WFV, box 14, folder 1; *Chicago Daily Tribune*, 6 Mar. 1892, 12; 26 Aug. 1890, 5; Jan. 1891, 7; *Hearings Before the Committee on Agriculture*, 470.
23 *Chicago Daily Tribune*, 12 Apr. 1890, 5.

Hutchinson concluded that "if farmers are hostile to boards of trade and futures, in my opinion they are mistaken."[24]

On this view, the farmers were miscalculating their own interests and agitating for measures that would leave them worse off. "The destruction of the system, which is a perfectly legitimate development of trade, would produce immediate disaster" for farmers, the *New York Times* editorialized. "Their demand for its abolition comes from a lack of understanding of the function performed by the system and a misconception of its effects."[25] But how could millions of farmers have made such a big mistake about a matter so central to their own well-being?[26]

WHERE ARE ALL THESE HORSES?

William Vilas visited the Chicago Board of Trade in January 1893 for a meeting with the board's leaders. The Senate had already passed the Washburn anti-option bill, despite Vilas's opposition, and it was pending in the House. Board president Charles Hamill and his colleagues welcomed the opportunity to discuss legislative strategy with an ally, but Vilas had a more precise purpose in mind. "I was a little anxious," Vilas explained to Hamill, "to see if there was not something in the way of figures that we could obtain that would satisfy the farming community generally that the idea was an erroneous one that speculation in wheat necessarily depressed prices, or indeed at all." Vilas was getting

24 *Chicago Daily Tribune*, 10 Apr. 1890, 6; 21 Jan. 1890, 3; B. P. Hutchinson, "Speculation in Wheat," *North American Review* 153 (1891): 414, 416.

25 *New York Times*, 28 Apr. 1892, 4.

26 For answers to this question I find less plausible than the one offered here, due to the absence of evidence that anyone was thinking along these lines during the debates of the late nineteenth and early twentieth centuries, see B. Peter Pashigian, "Why Have Some Farmers Opposed Futures Markets?," *Journal of Political Economy* 96 (1988): 371–82 (arguing that farmers would have gained from abolishing futures if the owners of grain elevators were using futures prices to facilitate the formation of buying cartels); Roberta Romano, "The Political Dynamics of Derivative Securities Regulation," *Yale Journal on Regulation* 14 (1997): 307–11 (arguing that farmers would have gained from abolishing futures if farmers had been able to form selling cartels of their own).

ready to defend his vote back home in Wisconsin, where the farmers believed that the board of trade was responsible for their financial distress. "We want to say answer a fool according to his folly and pass him by. But you can't do it," Vilas lamented. "You have got to begin patiently at the bottom and build up this argument." As Vilas saw it, the farmers "have been in a certain sense hoodwinked into the support of something that was not to their interest." Vilas hoped to set the farmers straight, but he knew it would not be easy. "I should have no apprehension of meeting any farmers in this world," he explained, "but there is a class of men who make a very loud outcry—what I call the political farmers; they are presidents of alliances, and all sorts of agricultural organizations." These were "men who are continually making political headway for themselves," in Vilas's view, rather than looking out for the real interests of the farmer.[27]

On the exchanges there was little doubt that "the farmers have been misled on this subject," as a member of the Toledo Produce Exchange put it. "I do not wonder that the uninstructed person" could be convinced that speculation reduces prices, agreed Charles Hamill of the board of trade.[28] But who would take the trouble to deceive so many farmers about commodity trading? Who had an interest in making them believe it was harmful? On the exchanges and in the urban press, the answer seemed clear: the real backers of this legislation, the men pulling the strings behind the scenes, were the millers.

Millers bought grain from farmers, just like speculators did. If they could push the speculators out of the market, they would be the only buyers left. "The only competition the millers now have is in the exchanges in the buying of grain for future delivery," declared H. A. Foss of the board of trade. "Therefore, the abolition of time dealings would eliminate this competition and in the end surely would reduce the number of buyers of cash cereals from the farmer." The *Chicago Tribune* recognized that the bill "will benefit the millers more than any other class," because it would allow them "to beat down the farmer when he wants to sell his wheat." In Congress, the *New York Times* reported, the

27 "Minutes of Conference," 2 Jan. 1893, WFV, box 15, folder 2, 1, 8–9, 20, 49.
28 Denison B. Smith to Vilas, 15 Dec. 1892, WFV, box 15, folder 1; "Minutes of Conference," 1.

bill was known as "the millers' friend." The *Times* alleged that the petitions of support ostensibly streaming in from farmers' organizations throughout the country were in fact written in Washington and sent out for signatures, as part of a public relations campaign funded by the millers. "There isn't any question about it," William Vilas told the leaders of the board of trade. "They have worked up a fictitious, apparently agricultural sentiment to support their interests."[29]

Several of Vilas's correspondents likewise singled out the millers. "It is promoted by the millers," insisted the grain merchant Robert Eliot, "who seem to wish to get a monopoly of the trade, and rule out the speculator, who is a competitor and who aids in keeping up prices." E. C. Wall, writing on behalf of the Milwaukee Chamber of Commerce, called the legislation "an absurd bill" that "will do the farmers infinite harm," but one that "is a good thing for wealthy millers; for they can then buy the farmers' grain at their own price." Even some of Wisconsin's farmers recognized who stood to gain. "I am a farmer," declared E. H. Harris of Beloit, "and while I am opposed to the Chicago methods of playing wheat 'Poker,' still I prefer it rather than take the chances of being dumped bodily into the Mill Elevators at Minneapolis."[30]

Indeed, William Washburn, the Senate's leading proponent of legislation, was in the milling business himself, as the urban press missed no opportunity to point out. His family owned a large milling company in Minneapolis, the predecessor to the firm that would later be called General Mills. The *Tribune* accused him of "pushing this bill for mercenary and not philanthropic motives." Washburn provided only the lamest of defenses. "I know there has been a good deal of this talk running in the newspapers, assuming that this bill is in the interest of the millers," he acknowledged on the Senate floor. "I should like to understand under what provision of this bill the miller gets any advantage

---

29 Untitled typescript (1909), CBT, box 328, folder 2; *Chicago Daily Tribune*, 26 Aug. 1890, 5; *New York Times*, 31 Jan. 1893, 3; 25 June 1892, 5; 28 Feb. 1893, 4; "Minutes of Conference," 20.

30 Robert Eliot to Vilas, 15 Jan. 1892, box 13, folder 1; E. C. Wall to Vilas, 3 Mar. 1892, box 13, folder 2; E. H. Harris to Vilas, 3 Jan. 1893, box 15, folder 2, all in WFV.

over anybody else in the world; how he occupies any different position from anybody else who wants to buy wheat."[31] Of course, other than speculators, no one but a miller had any occasion to buy wheat straight from the farmer.

For opponents of the legislation, the millers' incentive to push the speculators aside provided the answer to the puzzle of how so many farmers could be so wrong. It was all a nefarious plot: the millers had tricked the farmers into believing that speculators were taking their money, when in fact the speculators were the very people who were protecting the farmers from the millers themselves, who would take even more of the farmers' money if speculation were prohibited.

In assessing the truth of this theory, it will be useful to separate the incentives of the millers from those of the farmers. The largest millers almost certainly did stand to gain from the abolition of commodity speculation. Smaller millers needed to hedge on the exchanges, but the bigger millers may well have been able to bear the risk of price declines themselves, if they could pay a low enough price to farmers. Prohibiting commodity speculation might have cleared the field, not just of the speculators, but of the smaller millers as well. At harvest time, the big millers would have had the farmers over a barrel. "Gentlemen, if you put the exchanges out of business, who would profit?" the cotton dealer Solomon Cone asked the House Agriculture Committee. "Do you see the representatives of the big mill interests of the South?" Cone was there to testify against the legislation, but, he explained, "I guarantee that my own brother, who buys for his different mills over 100,000 bales of cotton, if he could control me, would not have me here."[32] The millers would likely have been the main beneficiaries of prohibiting commodity speculation.

But the millers hardly invented the notion that speculation hurt farmers. As we saw in chapter 1, there was a long tradition of belief that speculators could manipulate prices to their advantage, and that speculators were nonproductive middlemen who took money out of the pockets of producers. These propositions would have been tenets

31 *Boston Evening Transcript*, 13 July 1892, 5; *New York Times*, 16 July 1892, 9; *Chicago Daily Tribune*, 23 July 1892, 4; *Congressional Record* 23 (1892): 6442.
32 *Hearings Before the Committee on Agriculture*, 95.

of late nineteenth-century agrarian populism even without the millers. The millers were opportunistically exploiting beliefs that were already widespread; they did not need to convince anyone of anything.

Farmers, meanwhile, had a few reasons to object to commodity speculation, regardless of whether it had any effect on prices. Commodity prices had once been determined in local markets, in which farmers participated themselves, but now prices were determined in a worldwide market by a host of other actors. Farmers were left feeling powerless, their livelihoods controlled by others. "It is the offering of these immense quantities of fictitious products that fixes the price," C. Wood Davis complained. "The farmer has nothing to do with fixing the price, he is the only man on earth that is not allowed to have anything to do with the fixing of the value of the property that he has produced." Farmers were forced to accept prices dictated by exchanges in big cities, where traders who had never worked the soil bought and sold crops, most of which did not even exist. The farmers "have found that before their crop is harvested, possibly before it is planted, that some one without authority from them had contracted to sell it; and they tell us that this is right and in the interest of the farmer," declared an indignant J. H. Brigham, the master of the National Grange. "We do not believe that any man has any right to sell our products before we have authorized their sale."[33]

Representative Albert Burleson of Texas, who counted many cotton farmers among his constituents, provided a useful parable to illustrate how the exchanges looked from the point of view of a farmer. "Suppose a man who had a horse to sell heard that there was a horse exchange in town and should carry his horse to the exchange to dispose of him," Burleson began.

> Arriving there he finds that on this exchange they are not selling horses but future contracts for the delivery of horses, and that these transactions were going to control the price he was to receive for his horse. Suppose he should see a future contract for the delivery of a horse sold for a given price, then another future contract for a

33 *Fictitious Dealing*, 14, 260.

horse at a lower price, and then another at a higher price, and somebody standing by, a member of the exchange, should say to him as
these contracts were being sold and bought: "Now, the price of your
horse has gone down, now it has gone up." And if you asked why,
should answer, "Because these sale contracts for the delivery of horses
that are taking place, actual contracts, where there is an expectation
that delivery will take place, indicate the market value of your horse,
in fact control the price you are to receive for him." When he saw
these transactions going on and on and on would it be surprising if
he finally asked, "Where are all these horses? I don't see any horses
that are being traded in under these contracts; where are the horses?
I have seen dozens of sales, I have seen hundreds of contracts for
horses sold, but I have not seen a horse." Would you blame him if
he reached the conclusion that they were phantom horses that were
being dealt in? Why, of course, you would not. Neither would you
blame him if he objected to having the market price of his horse
influenced or controlled by these transactions.

A Minneapolis trade magazine expressed the farmers' unhappiness more
sharply: Farmers "are heartily sick of the reign of the gamblers. Under
the tyrannical rule of the few who neither toil nor spin, the grower
and the manufacturer find themselves slaves. The natural servant has
become an unnatural master. The beggar is on horseback and is riding
roughshod over . . . the farmer." In such circumstances, banning speculation was a way to restore power to the farmers, regardless of whether
it increased prices. "A revolt is in order," the magazine concluded, and
a law terminating the commodity exchanges "is, perhaps, the first sign
of the coming warfare."[34]
   Believing their lives unfairly controlled by speculators, farmers had
little trouble summoning up all the traditional critiques of speculation.
Speculation still had a moral dimension. It was still widely seen as unchristian. The *Christian Observer* and the *Christian Union* both editorialized in favor of antispeculation bills in the 1890s, not because of

34 *Hearings Before the Committee on Agriculture*, 421; *Weekly Northwestern Miller*
   29 (1890): 477.

any economic effects the bills might have, but because, as the *Observer* put it, "the principle that controls in this matter is set forth by the Lord in the decalogue"—the commandment that prohibits stealing. The *Union* saw the bills as evidence of "the awakening moral sentiment of the Nation." The journalist George Muller pronounced commodity speculation "unworthy of nineteenth century progress. It is selfish and dehumanizing." He thought it should be abolished on moral grounds even "if in the process of reformation, the farmer temporarily gets less for his product." The minister George Hubbard agreed that "when weighed in the balances of eternal justice, speculation is found wanting. Its character will not stand the supreme test. It is a moral wrong."[35]

Speculation was still widely understood as a form of gambling, a practice moralists considered wrong regardless of whether it was profitable to any particular participant. Speculation on the board of trade "can hardly be justified in the light of the moral law," one critic charged. "With regard to the character of gambling there is no controversy. Every one admits its immorality." The *Massachusetts Ploughman* contrasted the gambler, who knows he is doing wrong, with the grain speculator, who erroneously "imagines he is doing a very respectable thing." In the late nineteenth century, the Louisiana State Lottery was a popular metaphor for all the evils associated with gambling, because it was the only legal state lottery in the country. "But, after all, what a small affair has the Louisiana lottery been," declared one magazine in 1892, "when compared with the 'bucket shop' and Board of Trade." When the lottery was abolished, a rural Minnesota newspaper declared that it was "time that the option room of the Chicago Board of Trade was catalogued with the Louisiana State Lottery and relegated to the shades of an ancient and barbarous method of appropriating the unearned increment from the pockets of the hardworking citizens of the great northwest. By the side of comparatively honest methods in gambling, trading in options will in the history of the near future take its place as the co-partner and twin fraud of bunco steering." In the Senate,

35 "Is Speculation Right?," *Christian Observer* 84 (1896): 1; "The Anti-Option Discussion," *Christian Union* 47 (1893): 60; *The Sunset Club* (Chicago: Sunset Club, 1892), 143; George H. Hubbard, "The Ethics of Speculation," *New Englander and Yale Review* 14 (1889): 44.

William Washburn shrewdly capitalized on the widespread belief that speculation was tantamount to gambling. His bill, he insisted, "is aimed at a system of gambling the most unique, insidious, the most pernicious, and bringing with it the most widespread and disastrous results of any scheme of gambling that the wit and skill of man has ever yet been able to devise." He concluded his speech with a biblically inflected call to "drive the gamblers from our temples and reinstate therein the genius of legitimate trade."[36]

Opponents of regulation responded by distinguishing between speculation and gambling. Speculation, they argued, was the rational application of intellectual effort to the estimation of future prices, while gambling was pure chance. "Speculation is a venture with calculation," one explained, "gambling a venture without calculation." But those who saw the board of trade as a gambling den were hardly convinced. "What shall we say about the Chicago grain speculators?" asked one proponent of regulation. "What do they know about next year's droughts, or next month's prairie fire, or next week's Charleston earthquake[?]" These supposed rational calculators "have no special 'revelations' in regard to what may happen in the 'future.'" Their enterprise was based on chance just as much as the gambler's.[37]

Speculators were still widely depicted as greedy, dishonest people who cared more about money than about their fellow man. "Speculation is the child of covetousness," declared the *Christian Observer*. "Its tendencies are grasping and selfish." The *Christian Advocate* warned its readers to "avoid speculation of every kind," because "the life of the speculator is one of consuming anxiety. He never knows where he is or what he is worth." Speculation "corrupts the speculator," cautioned the *Western Christian Advocate*. "It cannot be carried on in honor and honesty,

---

36 "Speculation in Business," *Chautauquan* 4 (1884): 282; "Agricultural Comment," *Massachusetts Ploughman and New England Journal of Agriculture* 43 (1884): 1; "The Progress of the World," *Review of Reviews* 6 (1892): 135; *New Ulm Review*, 5 Oct. 1892, 3; *Congressional Record* 23 (1892): 5980, 5993.

37 Thomas L. Greene, "Legitimate and Illegitimate Speculation," *Independent* 44 (1892): 7; "What Is Speculation?," *Outlook* 74 (1903): 1006; D. G. Watts, "Speculation as a Fine Art," *Cosmopolitan* 10 (1891): 592; "Speculating and Speculators," *Independent* 38 (1886): 24.

because it is essentially dishonest in its principles." Phrenologists even claimed that speculators were prone to baldness just above the right ear, because that was the location of "the organ of Acquisitiveness, or love of gain," which speculators would rub when they became excited.[38]

Farmers thus had several reasons to be suspicious of commodity speculators, even apart from whether speculation lowered prices. The fall in commodity prices was a catalyst that sharply increased the salience of these older noneconomic critiques of speculation, but these critiques would have had some force under any circumstances. As for whether speculation *caused* the drop in prices, the answer depends on how broadly the question was framed. The speculators were almost certainly correct that shutting the exchanges would not bring higher prices to the farmer, and indeed would probably bring lower ones. Commodities were traded, and prices were set, in an international market. Farmers had to sell their crops to *someone*; if it wasn't speculators, it would be millers, exporters, or other intermediaries, none of whom would pay higher prices than the speculators had. Expelling a class of buyers from the market was not a likely route to higher prices.

But we can get a sense of the farmers' perspective if we frame the question more broadly. The exchanges were just one component, and to the farmer the most visible component, of the international network of commodity distribution constructed in the nineteenth century. In 1800, most crops were sold locally. Prices probably varied considerably from region to region and even from town to town, reflecting local variations in supply and demand. By 1900, crops were traded in a worldwide market, and prices were much more uniform. When farmers lashed out at the board of trade and other exchanges, these were just the closest and most tangible symbols of a fundamental change in the organization of agricultural life.[39] If the exchanges had been abolished but the rest of the system left in place, the farmers would not have benefitted.

38 "Honest Speculation," *New York Evangelist* 53 (1882): 4; "What Is Speculation?," 528; "The Temptations of Speculation," *Christian Observer* 87 (1899): 2; "Letters to Young Men," *Christian Advocate* 59 (1884): 254; "Legitimate Business Better Than Speculation," *Western Christian Advocate* 25 (1874): 196; "How Stock Speculators Become Bald-Headed," *Phrenological Journal* 57 (1873): 313.

39 David S. Jacks, "Populists Versus Theorists: Futures Markets and the Volatility of Prices," *Explorations in Economic History* 44 (2007): 358.

But the agrarian critique of speculation was often something more than that. It was a critique of the entire system, a desire to return to earlier ways of moving food from the farm to the consumer. If the entire system could have been dismantled, commodity markets would have been local once again, and prices would have once again varied widely from one place to the next. The economic effect on farmers would have varied widely too. Some would have been better off some of the time, and some would have been worse off some of the time.

Of course, there was no possibility of dismantling the entire distribution network. The only parts of it available to attack were the exchanges. The farmers had to focus on the exchanges, but by linking speculation on the exchanges to the decline in commodity prices, the farmers were stuck with an implausible economic argument. And while lower commodity prices were bad for farmers, they were a great benefit to consumers, so in calling for legislation on the ostensible ground that it would raise food prices, the farmers were making it much less likely that nonfarmers would join their cause. That Congress nevertheless came so close to shutting down the exchanges is a testament to the political force of the agrarian movement in the 1890s.

JUSTIFIABLE GAMBLING

The argument that commodity speculation hurt farmers was even less plausible in 1920 than it had been in 1890. In the intervening years, the issue's political visibility had given rise to some thorough defenses of speculation's role in the economy. The American political economists of the first half of the nineteenth century had tended to classify speculation as a nonproductive activity, one that added no value to the goods being traded. In the later part of the century, however, American economists began to take a different view. Speculation, they asserted, was just as useful as manufacturing.

The leading voice in this school of thought was Henry Crosby Emery, who spent most of his career in the economics department at Yale. Emery's doctoral dissertation, *Speculation on the Stock and Produce Exchanges of the United States*, was published as a book in 1896, not long after the peak of antispeculation agitation. "The criticism directed against speculation is made from two somewhat conflicting points of view," he argued. "The first is that speculation is merely gambling and has no reference to actual trade, except that it consists in betting on the course of prices. The second is that speculation is all-powerful in trade, which has become completely demoralized by its subjection to fictitious speculative conditions." He contended that both lines of criticism were wrong. Speculators, he asserted, played a crucial role in absorbing the risks that would otherwise deter traders from efficiently moving products from the farmer to the consumer. "Speculative losses cannot be met by mutual insurance," he pointed out, "since they fall on all members of the class at once. These are risks that inhere in ownership, and they can be met only by a transfer of ownership." By transferring risk to those better able to bear it, the commodity exchanges allowed the distribution system to operate at a lower overall cost. "The only payment for the transfer of risk is the coincident transfer of the chance of gain," Emery argued. "To assume risks in this manner is the function of the speculator." The result, he concluded, was that speculation was essential: "It is difficult to see how a great world trade in such staples as grain and cotton would be possible without it."[40]

The economist Albert Stevens offered another defense of speculation with an equally modern ring. When prices fell as a result of speculation, he argued, the speculator "was not unduly depressing the price. He was putting quotations . . . *where they should have been.*" Speculators on the commodity exchanges performed a service, in Stevens's view, by causing the prices of commodities to reflect the commodities' true value, a service that no other institution could possibly perform. Speculators "put the price of wheat where it belonged, from the point of view of its statistical situation," Stevens suggested; "they did that which neither the national Agricultural Department, the Vienna Congress, *Bradstreet's*, the Cincinnati *Price Current*, Beerbohm's or Dornbusch's (London) *Lists*, or any other of the governmental and private statistical bureaus of the world had been able to do." Once these prices had been

40 Henry Crosby Emery, *Speculation on the Stock and Produce Exchanges of the United States* (New York: Columbia University, 1896), 98; Henry Crosby Emery, "Legislation Against Futures," *Political Science Quarterly* 10 (1895): 62–64; Henry Crosby Emery, "The Place of the Speculator in the Theory of Distribution," *American Economic Association Publications* 1 (1900): 103.

established, added the Chicago law professor Van Buren Denslow, they were telegraphed around the world, "so that every producer and purchaser gets his quotation with his morning paper and as often during the day as he wishes." The value of such timely and exact knowledge of prices, Denslow explained, could be seen by contrasting grain markets with markets in nonstandardized items like clothing, furniture, and jewelry, where participants had to spend substantial time simply trying to ascertain the true value of what they were buying and selling. With the commodities traded on exchanges, market participants "know that millions of dollars are staked in behalf of a rise in price, and an equal number of millions in favor of a fall, and that the actual price quoted is the precise point at which these millions balance. They know that the published quotation is not one fixed by the arbitrary determination of any one dealer, but by the aggregate verdict of them all." As the Cornell economist James Boyle concluded in his book-length defense of the board of trade, speculation's long-term benefits greatly exceeded whatever temporary dislocations it might cause.[41]

These new, sophisticated defenses of speculation joined the older, more intuitive defenses that had been circulating for a century. Opponents of regulation still argued that every merchant was in some sense a speculator. They still pointed out that speculation was the driving force behind the establishment of new enterprises. And they still contended that regulation would in any event be fruitless. "What a bewildering effect Washington air must have on the human brain!" exclaimed one commercial newspaper while Congress was considering the Hatch and Washburn bills in 1892. "So many men when they get there acquire so exaggerated an idea of the power of a statute as panacea for every commercial and financial irregularity." The *Chicago Tribune* agreed that "the amateur merchants who think they know it all suppose themselves able to legislate the community into a Utopia." In fact, the

---

41 Albert Clark Stevens, "The Utility of Speculation in Modern Commerce," *Political Science Quarterly* 7 (1892): 425; see also Albert C. Stevens, "'Futures' in the Wheat Market," *Quarterly Journal of Economics* 2 (1887): 37–63; Van Buren Denslow, "Board of Trade Morality," *North American Review* 137 (1883): 375–76; James E. Boyle, *Speculation and the Chicago Board of Trade* (New York: Macmillan, 1921).

Tribune concluded, "to legislate 'options' out of existence will be of no more avail than the effort of the old lady to sweep back the waves of the Atlantic with her broom." In the view of another proponent of the status quo, "prohibiting 'speculation' is babyish," because "so long as there is trade, there will be speculative trade."[42]

Perhaps as a result of such defenses, the congressional debate over speculation in commodities grew narrower. By the 1910s, rather than trying to shut down the exchanges entirely on the theory that all speculation harmed the farmer, critics tended to focus on particular speculative practices they found harmful. These specific attacks produced some significant federal regulation. The first clear example was the Cotton Futures Act of 1914. The Populists had once railed against cotton speculation. In the previous three decades, Congress had considered several bills that would have imposed prohibitive taxes on cotton speculators to drive the cotton exchanges out of business, and some of those bills had come close to passing. The Cotton Futures Act, by contrast, was directed at one specific practice, the rule on the New York and New Orleans Cotton Exchanges establishing what were called "fixed differences" between the prices of different grades of cotton. The rule was a bit arcane to anyone not in the cotton business, but its effect was to allow traders to exploit divergences between exchange prices and market prices outside the exchange, often to the detriment of farmers. The Cotton Futures Act required exchanges to allow the price of all grades of cotton to be determined by their actual market values.[43]

---

42 Joseph C. Ely, "Monopolies, Labor Unions, and Speculation," *Unitarian Review and Religious Magazine* 26 (1886): 537; "Speculation vs. Investment," *Christian Union* 14 (1876): 227; "Legitimate Speculation," *Christian Union* 27 (1883): 3; Morris H. Smith, "Morals of Speculation," *Christian Advocate* 62 (1887): 287; "The Financial Situation," *Commercial and Financial Chronicle* 55 (1892): 124; *Chicago Daily Tribune*, 21 Jan. 1890, 4; "The Offset to Speculation," *Independent* 37 (1885): 28.

43 Francis G. Caffey, "The United States Cotton Futures Act," in US Department of Agriculture, *Service and Regulatory Announcements No. 5* (1915), 54–55; S. Rep. No. 289, 63rd Cong., 2nd Sess. (1914); 38 Stat. 696 (1914); I. Newton Hoffman, "The Cotton Futures Act," *Journal of Political Economy* 23 (1915): 465–89; Luther Conant Jr., "The United States Cotton Futures Act," *American Economic Review*

Unlike in earlier installments of the debate over speculation, even the proponents of regulating the cotton exchanges acknowledged the utility of speculation. "Any legislation ... which eliminates from the cotton trade the element of legitimate speculation and legitimate speculators, must, in the opinion of the committee, result disastrously to the producer," the House Committee on Agriculture declared. "The legitimate speculator, operating through the exchanges, is the only buffer standing between the helpless producer and the powerful buyer of his product." The Cotton Futures Act "is constructive and regulatory, not destructive or oppressive," pronounced Secretary of Agriculture David Houston. "It recognizes that the exchanges, when they are properly conducted, may benefit both the purchaser of raw cotton and the manufacturer."[44] After decades of contention over speculation, the terms of the debate had narrowed.

Futures trading on the exchanges was suspended in 1917 due to World War I. When trading resumed in 1920, commodity prices, which had been high during the war, promptly plummeted. Corn dropped from $1.51 to 61 cents per bushel, wheat from $1.82 to $1.03 per bushel, and cotton from 35 cents to 16 cents per pound. Farmers once again called for regulating the exchanges, but in Congress, the climate was nothing like it had been in the 1890s. Even most of those who favored legislation acknowledged that futures trading was useful. "The only one absolutely in favor of entirely abolishing the legitimate hedge, I think, is a man who does not know what a legitimate hedge is," declared Representative Jasper Tincher of Kansas, one of the House sponsors of the bill. The farmers' organizations had once been the most outspoken critics of the commodity exchanges, but now T. C. Atkeson, the Washington representative of the National Grange, testified to the importance of preserving the ability to hedge. Speculators were necessary because they took the other side of hedging transactions, Atkeson explained. The

5 (1915): 1–11. The Cotton Futures Act was held unconstitutional in *Hubbard v. Lowe*, 226 F. 135 (S.D.N.Y. 1915), but was promptly re-enacted in constitutional form, 39 Stat. 476 (1916).

44 H.R. Rep. No. 765, 63rd Cong., 2nd Sess. (1914), 6; *Annual Reports of the Department of Agriculture* (Washington, D.C.: Government Printing Office, 1914), 23.

speculators were gambling, he concluded, but "it is perhaps justifiable gambling," because it served a useful purpose. Not everyone agreed. "It is not necessary for men to speculate in futures upon the boards of trade," declared James Strong of Kansas, who reported that the farmers in his congressional district still wanted to "stop gambling in the staple foodstuffs of the nation."[45] But this view seems to have been less widely held than it had been a generation before.

Legislators still declared that they wanted to prohibit a certain sort of gambling, the kind that had no useful purpose, but they had all but given up hope of being able to do it without curtailing the speculative transactions that most parties wanted to allow. "The point is how are we going to get at the bad features and prohibit them and still permit hedging," wondered George Norris, the chair of the Senate Agriculture Committee. "How can you tell the difference between a hedge and a gamble?" As a representative of the Minneapolis Chamber of Commerce admitted, "the difference between gambling and speculation or investment is a rather difficult thing to state." The Senate requested guidance from the Federal Trade Commission, which offered a few possible ways of drawing the line between speculation and gambling but concluded that "it is questionable whether any of these definitions is capable of practical administrative application in distinguishing the speculator from the gambler."[46]

If the good speculation could not be distinguished from the bad, commodity speculation could at least be required to take place in a small number of easily observable arenas. In the Future Trading Act of 1921, Congress accordingly imposed a prohibitive tax on futures trades conducted by anyone other than the actual physical owner of a commodity but exempted transactions on government-approved commodity exchanges. To qualify for approval, an exchange had to comply with several requirements: it had to report the terms of all transactions to the government, it had to prevent its members from disseminating false information that could affect prices, and it had to prohibit price

45 *Future Trading*, 7, 300–301, 64–65.
46 *Future Trading in Grain*, 123, 290; *Report of the Federal Trade Commission on Methods and Operations of Grain Exporters* (Washington, D.C.: Government Printing Office, 1922), I:xxii.

manipulation. The goal, explained the Senate Agriculture Committee, was "to correct some practices on the grain exchanges and to authorize supervision of the grain-futures markets, but not to disturb any of their legitimate and useful functions." Market participants would still be free to hedge and to speculate. The law would merely "eliminate from the market some of the undesirable practices of professional speculators."[47]

The Supreme Court found the Future Trading Act an unconstitutional exercise of the federal government's taxing power, on the ground that it was really a commercial regulation disguised as a tax, so Congress promptly re-enacted it as the Grain Futures Act of 1922, but this time as a regulation of interstate commerce rather than a tax. Congress blessed the new law the following year.[48] Ever since, commodity futures trading has been lawful on an approved exchange, but not otherwise.

In retrospect, the period from the early 1890s through the early 1920s saw the first sustained national debate over the propriety of particular forms of speculation. The debate forced both sides to articulate theories distinguishing legitimate business from illegitimate gambling. The result was a compromise: commodity speculation could go on, but only under the close supervision of the federal government. There would never again be so much argument over speculation in agricultural commodities. Speculation in financial assets, by contrast, would remain controversial throughout the twentieth century. Indeed, while the old debate over commodities was winding down, a new debate over the government's role in supervising the stock market was just getting underway.

47 42 Stat. 187 (1921); S. Rep. No. 212, 67th Cong., 1st Sess. (1921), 4.
48 *Hill v. Wallace*, 259 U.S. 44 (1922); 42 Stat. 998 (1922); *Board of Trade v. Olsen*, 262 U.S. 1 (1923).

4

Selling Blue Sky

IT STARTED MORE AS a hobby than an official government activity. But within a few years it turned into one of the fastest-spreading and farthest-reaching regulatory programs the country had ever seen.

"Why, I had been in the banking business here in Kansas a good many years before I became banking commissioner," Joseph Dolley recalled. "Every now and then I would hear of one of these swindles—that somebody had lost his money through buying stock in a fake mine, or in a Central America plantation that was nine parts imagination, or in some wonderful investment company that was going to pay forty per cent dividends." As chairman of the state Republican Party, Dolley had achieved a double victory in the 1908 election, when Walter Stubbs was elected governor and the state's electoral votes went to William Howard Taft. Stubbs rewarded Dolley by making him the state banking commissioner. "After I was appointed banking commissioner," Dolley continued, "I heard more reports and complaints of fake stock swindles than ever." Times were good for Kansas farmers, who were beneficiaries of high commodity prices and thus had money to invest. "So reports of these stock swindles drifted to me. I received complaints and inquiries direct from people who had been swindled, wanting me to look up the company and see if they couldn't get their money back—after they had parted with the money!" Dolley soon realized that stock sellers, mostly from out of state, were keeping an eye on real estate sales and probate courts, to identify inexperienced investors who were coming into money and would be easy marks.[1]

1 Will Payne, "How Kansas Drove Out a Set of Thieves," *Saturday Evening Post*, 2 Dec. 1911, 3–4.

So Dolley began providing free investment advice. He placed notices in the state's newspapers informing Kansans that if they were offered stock for sale, they were welcome to write to him with inquiries about the financial status of the company. The letters began streaming in. "In the case of every one of these companies I can give exact and authentic information about their financial standing and their investments and their general character," Dolley told the press. "We have access to financial and industrial information of all kinds and know just where to get in touch with any company that is promoting something." Soon Dolley was receiving telephone calls as well. One day in June, for example, a Topeka widow called Dolley for advice. She had just received the proceeds of her late husband's life insurance when she was visited by a stock salesman who promised a 30 percent annual dividend. Dolley told her to buy municipal bonds instead.[2]

After several months of such informal consultations, Dolley requested an appropriation from the state legislature to hire employees to carry on the work. He also requested the enactment of a state law that would require everyone wishing to sell stock in Kansas to get permission from his office, which would assess the merits of an offering before allowing it to be sold. The legislature gave him everything he asked for. In 1911, Kansas enacted the first of what would come to be called "blue sky laws." Before anyone could sell stock in Kansas, they would first have to persuade Joseph Dolley and his staff that the stock was a sound investment.[3]

The idea swept the country. Within two years, half the states had blue sky laws. Within two decades, nearly all did.[4] They were called

2 *Kansas City Journal*, 2 Apr. 1910; *Topeka Journal*, 8 Apr. 1910; *Kansas City Journal*, 4 June 1910. The citations in this chapter to Kansas newspapers are from the Kansas Historical Society's *Kansas Memory* website, at http://www.kansasmemory.org.

3 *Tenth Biennial Report of the Bank Commissioner of the State of Kansas* (Topeka: State Printing Office, 1910), xiii; Rick A. Fleming, "100 Years of Securities Law: Examining a Foundation Laid in the Kansas Blue Sky," *Washburn Law Journal* 50 (2011): 583–609.

4 The blue sky laws, with dates of adoption, are usefully summarized in Paul G. Mahoney, "The Origin of the Blue-Sky Laws: A Test of Competing Hypotheses," *Journal of Law & Economics* 46 (2003): 232. For details of the blue

blue sky laws because "blue sky" was a common metaphor for a worth-less investment. "When a promoter by artful persuasions succeeds in getting money for something which has no value except in the mind of the credulous purchaser," an 1895 newspaper explained, "he is said to have been selling 'blue sky.' " In a 1906 advertisement for shares in a Colorado mine, the promoter insisted, "I am not selling 'Blue Sky.' "[5] Selling blue sky was what the blue sky laws were supposed to prevent.

The blue sky laws responded to a very old concern with speculation—that speculators were likely to harm themselves and their families by taking on risks they lacked the ability to evaluate intelligently. But if the problem was an old one, the solution was something that had never been tried before: to have the government evaluate the risks and guide investors to safety. If the state could screen out the investments that were too speculative or were likely to be frauds, one of the primary dangers of speculation would be a thing of the past.

A FAIR RETURN

No one could have expected the blue sky law movement in 1910, when Joseph Dolley opened his informal investment advisory service in the office of the Kansas state bank commissioner. In retrospect, to be sure, one can see the blue sky laws as emblematic of a broader concern for consumer protection in the progressive era, the same concern that gave rise to pure food and drug laws, occupational licensing, and antitrust laws.[6] More broadly, one can see the blue sky laws as an example of the use of government to mitigate risk, like the establishment of work-ers' compensation and unemployment insurance, two other develop-ments that were then in progress.[7] But at the time it would have been

sky laws in effect as of 1919, see John M. Elliott, *The Annotated Blue Sky Laws of the United States* (Cincinnati: W. H. Anderson Co., 1919).

5 Lawrence R. Gelber, *The Gelberlaw Glossary*, http://www.gelberlaw.net/Glossary .html; *Chicago Tribune*, 25 Feb. 1906, 10.

6 Morton Keller, *Regulating a New Economy: Public Policy and Economic Change in America, 1900–1933* (Cambridge, Mass.: Harvard University Press, 1990). For contemporary recognition of this point, see William B. Shaw, "Progressive Law-Making in Many States," *Review of Reviews* 48 (1913): 84–93.

7 David A. Moss, *When All Else Fails: Government as the Ultimate Risk Manager* (Cambridge, Mass.: Harvard University Press, 2002).

very difficult, probably impossible, to predict that the first serious stock market regulation of the twentieth century would take the form of blue sky laws. In the preceding decades, while there had been calls to regulate securities sales in just about every other conceivable way, no one had proposed that government officials should decide, company by company, which investments would offer a fair return.

All the old worries about speculation were still very much alive. Speculation was still widely viewed as a form of gambling. "Of all the varied types of gambling doubtless the most colossal is that of the great stock exchanges," declared one minister in 1895, "and the success of every rich man's corner is apt to be followed by the dishonesty or suicide, or both, of some of his victims." As the humor magazine *Puck* described the successful speculator, "it is a common thing to see bestowed upon a man who began with nothing of his own and ended with a great deal of other people's property the flattering commendation that he was a self-made man." The press was still full of articles worrying that speculators would bankrupt themselves and their families, that speculation was a nonproductive activity, and that prices were controlled by a small cabal of insiders. "The editor who fails to have a fling at Wall Street as often as two or three times a week, especially if he live[s] in the South or West, must be unusually well supplied with prize fights and divorce cases," smirked Brayton Ives, the president of the New York Stock Exchange. "And what demagogue addressing his constituents omits in any speech to denounce it as the home of the monopolist and the hotbed of injustice?" The investment banker Henry Clews agreed that "it seems to be a genial pastime for men in various walks of life who know very little about financial affairs, and the methods of doing business in Wall Street, to denounce this great centre of the moneyed interests, as the sum of all villanies, a kind of Pandora's box, but without any hope at the bottom."[8]

8 "Gambling Speculations," *Bankers' Magazine* 14 (1879): 19; John F. Hume, "The Heart of Speculation," *Forum*, Oct. 1886, 130; Joseph Parker, "Gambling and Speculation," *Independent* 49 (1897): 6; C. H. Hamlin, "Gambling, or Theft by Indirection," *Arena* 2 (1895): 414; W. J. Henderson, "Speculators Not Appreciated," *Puck* 18 (1885): 227; "Money Matters," *New York Evangelist* 61 (1890): 4; "Speculation and Business," *Bankers' Magazine* 37 (1882): 88; "Stock Speculation," *Independent* 38 (1886): 24; "To Amateur Speculators," *Christian*

Such concerns brought forward a wide variety of proposals for regulation in the late nineteenth and early twentieth centuries. "The enterprising speculator rejoices and grows fat in that domain that lies just beyond the common law, and has not yet attracted the attention of statutory enactment," the *Bankers' Magazine* observed. "Here he can give himself full swing until the slow foot of legislation overtakes him."[9] Toward the turn of the century, as legislatures passed more and more statutes regulating various aspects of the economy, many suggested that it was high time to regulate the speculators as well.

These proposals tended to avoid outright bans on speculative transactions, because of the perennial problem of how to prohibit the bad without also forbidding the good. As the New York investment banker Adolph Lewisohn noted, "it is very difficult to draw the line between where investment ceases and speculation commences."[10] The regulatory proposals of the late nineteenth and early twentieth centuries were thus primarily directed at other targets.

Perhaps the most common complaint about the stock market was that corporate directors and officers had an unfair advantage, because they had more information about their own firms than anyone else did. "They know what is going to happen beforehand," one critic alleged. "There is no 'future' in the stock market to these men: they themselves make the future." The ordinary investor had to pit his "blank ignorance against billions of money and certain knowledge. He is guessing where they are certain sure." Worse, corporate insiders could deliberately spread false information about their own firm to profit when the true information was revealed and the stock price moved back to where it ought to have been all along. "Directors who are unscrupulous speculators start and circulate rumors of the badness of the business," complained one lawyer. They could make money by selling short as the

Union 21 (1880): 242; "Speculation," *Ohio Farmer* 69 (1886): 104; W. R. Givens, "Does Wall Street Speculation Pay?," *Independent* 59 (1905): 496; "The Spirit of Speculation," *National Police Gazette*, 12 Feb. 1881, 11; Brayton Ives, "Wall Street as an Economic Factor," *North American Review* 147 (1888): 555; Henry Clews, "Delusions About Wall Street," *North American Review* 145 (1887): 410.

9 "Agitation and Speculation," *Bankers' Magazine* 56 (1898): 808.

10 *New York Times*, 25 July 1909, 6.

stock price declined, and then make even more by buying as it went back up. "This is pure swindling," he concluded.[11]

To level the playing field, some proposed requiring corporations to disclose their financial status. "Make the seller of securities publish an accurate analysis of the values, equities, and earnings of which these securities are representative," one writer urged. "Such reports should be promptly published in order to permit investors to see exactly what the assets and liabilities are," agreed Charles Batchelder, a director of the Boston Lumber Company. If the law could require food to be honestly labeled, he suggested, it could do the same for securities. "Publicity," he concluded, was "the best safeguard [not only] for the investor, but also for the community." In the first decade of the twentieth century, a handful of states began to require such disclosures, but only for public utility companies and railroads, two kinds of firms the states already regulated more intensively than other forms of enterprise. The economist Earl Howard even proposed a similar disclosure requirement for brokers. If they had to reveal the name of the person for whom they were trading, he argued, the manipulation of prices by insiders would become impossible. "No manipulator would care to try the game with all the cards on the table," he concluded, "for the first essential of manipulation is secrecy."[12] But no state adopted this proposal.

11 "A Game of Speculation," *Albion* 51 (1873): 328; "Hydraulic Pressure in Wall Street," *North American Review* 135 (1882): 60; Samuel Untermyer, "Speculation on the Stock Exchanges and Public Regulation of the Exchanges," *American Economic Review Papers and Proceedings* 5 (1915): 47–48; "The Confessions of a Stock Speculator," *Independent* 62 (1907): 672; "Directors as Stock Speculators," *American Law Review* 3 (1882): 919.

12 Theodore H. Price, "Speculation: The Wisdom of Restricting It by Law or Otherwise," *Outlook*, 16 May 1914, 128; Charles C. Batchelder, "The Character and Powers of Governmental Regulation Machinery," *Journal of Political Economy* 20 (1912): 393, 386; Arthur U. Ayres, "Governmental Regulation of Securities Issues," *Political Science Quarterly* 28 (1913): 586–92; Leo Sharfman, "Commission Regulation of Public Utilities: A Survey of Legislation," *Annals of the American Academy of Political and Social Science* 53 (1914): 1–18; William Z. Ripley, "Public Regulation of Railroad Issues," *American Economic Review* 4 (1914): 541–64; Earl Dean Howard, "The Speculators and the Banks," *Bankers' Magazine* 77 (1908): 191.

Other proposed laws were meant to address other perceived problems with speculation. To deter overspeculation, how about prohibiting banks from lending money to speculators? To ensure that a speculator's distress did not spread to others, what about banning speculators from investing on behalf of others? After the bank failures of the Panic of 1907, some suggested that banks should no longer be allowed to speculate with their depositors' funds. The financial writer Charles Conant thought the most constructive thing the government could do was "not to hamper legitimate corporations by new laws, but to teach the public to judge investments with discrimination." If people could be taught "that high returns almost inevitably mean risk," Conant concluded, they would be much less tempted by uninformed speculation.[13] None of these ideas was put into practice at the time.

During this period, the most thorough review of possible methods of regulation was undertaken in the wake of the Panic of 1907 by a "Committee on Speculation in Securities and Commodities" appointed by New York governor Charles Evans Hughes. The committee was chaired by the financial journalist Horace White, and its members were praised by one magazine as "men of large knowledge both in practical affairs and in the theory of finance." They included Charles Schieren, a banker and the former mayor of Brooklyn; David Leventritt, who had recently retired as a judge; Clark Williams, the state's bank superintendent; and John Bates Clark, the Columbia economist. "It is unquestionable that only a small part of the transactions upon the Exchange is of an investment character; a substantial part may be determined as virtually gambling," the committee observed. "Yet we are unable to see how the State could distinguish by law between proper and improper transactions, since the forms and the mechanisms used are identical." The committee nevertheless offered several regulatory proposals, including a ban on misleading or unsupportable promises

---

13 "Banks and Speculation," *Bankers' Magazine* 36 (1882): 572; "The Credit System, and Speculation," *Oneida Circular* 12 (1875): 284; "Speculation With Bank Deposits," *Independent* 68 (1907): 1063; "Bank-Plundering by Speculators," *Outlook*, 23 Oct. 1909, 359; Charles A. Conant, *Wall Street and the Country* (New York: G. P. Putnam's Sons, 1904), 48–51.

in advertisements for stock.[14] The committee's proposals did not result in any legislation.

Yet for all these proposed limits on speculation during the late nineteenth and early twentieth centuries, the one thing that was *not* proposed—not until Joseph Dolley began putting it into practice in Kansas—was a government agency to evaluate whether a proposed sale of stock would be a good investment. The blue sky laws came from out of the blue.

Once the Kansas blue sky law went into effect in early 1911, stocks and bonds could not be sold in Kansas unless the seller could persuade Joseph Dolley that they promised "a fair return" on the investment. "A man came in here yesterday with a stock proposition that wasn't worth a continental," Dolley related a few days after the law took effect. The man "said he had been selling it in Kansas, but that he had read about the 'blue sky' bill and wanted to know what we were going to do about it." Dolley had his first request for permission to sell securities in Kansas. "I looked at his stock and found that we had already investigated it thoroughly," before the law had been enacted, when Dolley was conducting these investigations on his own at the request of potential purchasers. "I told him he couldn't sell another dollar's worth in Kansas."[15]

The volume of applications to sell stock quickly grew very high, but his office approved very few of them, at least according to the figures that Dolley regularly released to reporters. In October 1911, after only seven months under the blue sky law, Dolley reported that five hundred companies had applied to sell securities in Kansas, that his office had approved only forty-four of the applications, and that the office supposed that many more would-be fraudsters had been scared away by the prospect of filing an application. By March 1912, Dolley's numbers were up to more than seven hundred applications, of which only forty-eight had been approved. In his September 1912 report to the governor, Dolley claimed that between fourteen hundred and fifteen hundred

14 "Speculation and Gambling," *Outlook*, 26 June 1909, 422; *Report of the Committee on Speculation in Securities and Commodities* (Albany, N.Y.: J. B. Lyon Co., 1910), 8, 28–29.

15 Kansas Session Laws 1911, ch. 133, § 5; *Topeka Capital*, 18 Mar. 1911.

companies had been investigated by his office, and fewer than one hundred had been allowed to sell securities. Dolley also provided recurring but widely variant estimates of how much the people of Kansas had saved in investment losses by virtue of his guidance—amounts ranging from $2 million to $77 million in the first year alone. He often declared with pride that whatever the annual figure, it was more than the cost of running the entire state government for the year.[16]

How could an office consisting of only a few people conduct investigations of so many companies in such a short time? The task was perhaps not as monumental as it might seem. By Dolley's own account, most of the firms "never get farther than making the application. It was not necessary for us to turn them all down. As soon as they found out what information we were going to ask them for and what the nature of our investigation was going to be they suddenly changed their minds and withdrew their applications." When necessary, Dolley could also seek advice from other government officials and from experts at the University of Kansas. "For example," he explained, "a company recently came to the department with a new electric battery, which they claimed was going to revolutionize the electrical world." The firm had endorsements from prominent bankers. "We at once presented the matter to the electrical experts at our State University, and they advised us within thirty days that the battery was an absolute fake, and would not do what the company claimed for it." Dolley refused to allow the company to sell stock in Kansas.[17]

But even with many applications aborted, and even with the assistance of experts, Dolley's office still had to evaluate the merits of hundreds of securities offerings, many of which were based on assets located out of state. Dolley claimed to conduct thorough investigations of all of them. "If the financial statement does not satisfy him—and he is a trained banker—he sends an expert auditor to go over

16 *New York Times*, 13 Oct. 1911, 10; *Wall Street Journal*, 2 Mar. 1912, 6; *Eleventh Biennial Report of the Bank Commissioner of the State of Kansas* (Topeka: State Printing Office, 1912), 6; William Allen White, "Free Kansas: Where the People Rule the People," *Outlook*, 24 Feb. 1912, 412; "A Blue Sky Law," *Independent* 72 (1912): 375; *Topeka Capital*, 12 May 1912.
17 "The Kansas 'Blue Sky Law,'" *Central Law Journal* 75 (1912): 222.

the company's books," marveled one magazine, based on information supplied by Dolley. "If the applicant is a gold-mine, he sends a trained engineer to the spot to investigate; if it is an industrial concern, the best man available goes to look over the plant and its product."[18] This would have been an enormous expenditure of time and money, if Dolley's accounts were true.

But they were probably not true. Dolley's term as bank commissioner ended with the election of 1912, when George Hodges, a Democrat, became governor. Not long after, the Canadian lawyer and government official Thomas Mulvey read through the files in Dolley's old office, because Canada was considering adopting a blue sky law and wanted to learn from the experience of Kansas. According to Mulvey, from March 1911 through March 1913, permits to sell securities had been granted to forty-nine companies and denied to only sixty-two. Dolley had claimed to have resolved fourteen hundred to fifteen hundred cases in the first eighteen months of that period. Mulvey found no basis for any of Dolley's claims about how much money he had saved the people of Kansas. The office did not keep such statistics. Mulvey also discovered that Dolley had been granting temporary permits to firms that had not been investigated, a practice the blue sky law did not authorize. Some of these firms had committed serious frauds. The state's blue sky law was much less impressive than Dolley's enthusiastic public relations suggested.[19]

The Kansas blue sky law nevertheless attracted great interest all over the country, and indeed in much of the world. Governor Walter Stubbs received inquiries from Missouri to New York and many states in between, all asking for copies of the Kansas law. "Such a law is very much needed in our state for the protection of its citizens from the confidence sharks," declared E. T. Merritt of Minneapolis. Dolley even heard from the British and German consuls, who requested information they could send home to their governments. By the spring of 1913, Connecticut, Arizona, West Virginia, and Vermont had enacted blue sky laws. So had Manitoba and New South Wales, which copied the Kansas law almost

---

18 Isaac F. Marcosson, "Barring Out the Stock Thieves," *Munsey's Magazine* 46 (1912): 680.

19 Thomas Mulvey, "Blue Sky Law," *Canadian Law Times* 36 (1916): 39–40.

verbatim. By the end of 1913, twenty-four states had blue sky laws. Most of the remaining states would have blue sky laws by the end of the decade. Even the US-governed Philippines got one.[20]

Why were blue sky laws so popular? Some of their support no doubt came from prospective investors, who were genuinely fearful of being defrauded by fast-talking salesmen. Public participation in the securities markets increased dramatically in the early twentieth century.[21] Many people were buying stocks and bonds for the first time. They must have welcomed some guidance from the state. Stock promoters "are said to fleece Californians out of at least $20,000,000 a year," gasped the *San Francisco Chronicle* in an editorial urging California to give its citizens the protection Kansans already enjoyed. In the paper's view, the blue sky law was simply "a good idea, floated on a good phrase."[22]

But inexperienced investors were not the only supporters of blue sky laws. In Kansas, Joseph Dolley's scrutiny of securities sales had been welcomed by the state's business community, who recognized that the blue sky law would be a barrier to out-of-state competitors. One of Topeka's leading bond brokers praised Dolley for making it easier for in-state firms to sell bonds. The treasurer of the Atchison, Topeka & Santa Fe Railroad was just as happy with Dolley's work. "I believe the established corporations of the state . . . should receive the support of the people of the state," he explained. "A Kansan having

20 Letters to Walter Stubbs from John Sullivan, 7 Feb. 1912; W. C. Edson, 16 May 1912; H. J. Fitzgerald, 9 July 1912; Wade H. Barnes, 28 Aug. 1912; John Wright, 12 Oct. 1912; William Dinwiddie, 30 Dec. 1912; E. T. Merritt, 30 Dec. 1912, all from the Kansas Historical Society's *Kansas Memory* website, at http://www .kansasmemory.org; *Topeka Capital*, n.d.; C. A. Dykstra, "Blue Sky Legislation," *American Political Science Review* 7 (1913): 231–32; *Los Angeles Times*, 5 Feb. 1916, 12.

21 Julia C. Ott, *When Wall Street Met Main Street: The Quest for an Investors' Democracy* (Cambridge, Mass.: Harvard University Press, 2011); Mary O'Sullivan, "The Expansion of the U.S. Stock Market, 1885–1930: Historical Facts and Theoretical Fashions," *Enterprise and Society* 8 (2007): 489–542. For an argument that increased public participation in the stock market fundamentally changed the nature of speculation, an argument I find unpersuasive, see Lawrence E. Mitchell, *The Speculation Economy: How Finance Triumphed Over Industry* (San Francisco: Berrett-Koehler Publishers, 2007).

22 *San Francisco Chronicle*, 11 Sept. 1912, 6.

$100 or $500 to invest could buy preferred or common stock of the Atchison Topeka & Santa Fe Railway Company." Dolley himself felt the same way. "We are putting in a foundation for a great work," he declared, "and it means Kansas money for Kansas investments." Local businesses had local reputations and their managers had local contacts. If the officials administering a state's blue sky law scrutinized firms from other states more closely than they scrutinized local firms, a blue sky law could be an effective means of protectionism, benefitting in-state banks and securities issuers by hindering out-of-state competition.[23]

In state after state, local business groups were thus among the most vocal supporters of blue sky laws. In Illinois, the push for a blue sky law was led by the Illinois Bankers' Association. In Ohio it was the Ohio Bankers' Association. In California, a group called the Credit Men's Association played the same role. "The law has the support of the well-known and reputable bond houses" of California, the *San Francisco Chronicle* explained, because "although the law is general in its terms, such houses have no difficulty in establishing their standing with the Commissioner." At least in some cases, this expectation of in-state favoritism was well justified. Of the firms Joseph Dolley allowed to sell securities, most turned out to be from Kansas. In Nebraska, the state official responsible for blue sky matters frankly declared that his "Department is opposed to the sale of securities in this state by any eastern financial house" and would accordingly "interpose every available legal obstacle to their sale."[24]

The most significant opponents of blue sky laws were the elite urban investment bankers, who sold securities in multiple states and were thus the ones who lost out when states favored local firms. They broke

---

23 *Topeka Journal*, 25 Sept. 1910; *Kansas City Journal*, 30 Dec. 1910; Jonathan R. Macey and Geoffrey P. Miller, "Origin of the Blue Sky Laws," *Texas Law Review* 70 (1991): 347–97. For the view that protectionist concerns were a bigger influence on the *form* of blue sky laws than on whether blue sky laws were adopted, see Mahoney, "Origins of the Blue-Sky Laws," 229–51.

24 *Chicago Daily Tribune*, 18 Feb. 1912, 5; 22 Feb. 1912, 14; 26 Feb. 1912, 14; *Wall Street Journal*, 22 Nov. 1912, 6; *Los Angeles Times*, 17 Oct. 1912, II2; *San Francisco Chronicle*, 3 June 1915, 16; "The Kansas 'Blue Sky Law,'" *Central Law Journal* 75 (1912): 222; Lee Herdman to L. W. Berle, 6 Oct. 1932, AAB, box 20.

away from the American Bankers Association in 1912 to form their own group, the Investment Bankers Association of America, in large part to lobby against blue sky laws. At the IBA's first annual convention, held in New York in the fall of 1912, the Cleveland investment banker Warren Hayden spoke at length on the danger "that legislation may be brought forward by those who have no familiarity with the financial mechanism of the country, or with the investment business in particular, and that as a result of careless work, however well intended, we might find ourselves obliged to modify our business." He pointed out that an established investment bank might have a list of two hundred different securities for sale at any given time, adding perhaps five new ones every day, each of which would have to be individually approved by the Kansas banking commissioner before it could be sold in Kansas. If other states enacted similar laws, Hayden predicted, investment banks would be overwhelmed by the task of complying with all of them.[25]

The IBA's primary argument against the Kansas-style blue sky laws, and the argument that gained the most traction in the press, was that they vested in government officials a dangerous degree of power over the economy. "A state's commercial and industrial progress is in the hands of one man," worried the *Wall Street Journal.* "Human fallibility is not equal to the task. New companies must necessarily be constantly formed if the country's resources are to be developed. And to give to one individual (or any set of individuals) the arbitrary power of saying this company may sell its securities and that one may not, is dangerous in the extreme. The solid investments of today were the speculations of yesterday." When the New York Assembly passed a blue sky bill, the *New York Times* joked that state officials could not even manage their own affairs competently, much less supervise the investment decisions of all New Yorkers. The *Los Angeles Times* thought the state's blue sky law ought to be renamed a "black-sky law" or a "murky-sky

25 Vincent P. Carosso, *Investment Banking in America: A History* (Cambridge, Mass.: Harvard University Press, 1970), 165–73; *Proceedings of the Organization Meeting and of the First Annual Convention of the Investment Bankers' Association of America* (Chicago: Investment Bankers' Association of America, 1912), 140, 144–45.

law," because it made politicians "the judges of the solvency . . . and the honest intentions of corporations."[26]

The IBA pursued a two-part strategy. The first part was to propose a milder blue sky law for states to adopt, one that required sellers of securities to disclose information about the securities but did not empower a government official to determine whether they would be a sound investment. The IBA wished to avoid giving the "impression that the position of the Association is negative and opposed to the popular sentiment in favor of necessary legislation to prevent the promotion of fraudulent securities," explained Robert Reed, the IBA's lawyer. Instead, "we should try to work out an effective general law that will meet the situation," a law that "will settle the 'blue sky' frauds without further resort to 'blue sky' or imaginative remedies." Reputable sellers of securities had an interest in driving the disreputable out of business, so long as that could be accomplished without unduly burdening the reputable. The IBA accordingly drafted a model blue sky law, which it circulated to its members, who sought to have it introduced in their home state legislatures. The IBA's version of a blue sky law borrowed from the British Companies Act of 1908, which required a company selling securities to file a prospectus with the government, disclosing a wide range of information about the company.[27]

The second part of the IBA's strategy involved filing lawsuits seeking to have the existing blue sky laws declared unconstitutional. The IBA did not file the suits itself; rather, it organized them, by identifying plaintiffs, retaining local counsel, and formulating legal arguments. The plaintiffs were typically out-of-state investment banks and corporations.

26 "The 'Blue-Sky' Laws," *Bankers' Magazine* 84 (1912): 636; Henry C. Emery, "Speculation on the Stock Exchanges and Public Regulation of the Exchanges," *American Economic Review Papers and Proceedings* 5 (1915): 80; *Wall Street Journal*, 11 Apr. 1913, 1; *New York Times*, 27 Mar. 1913, 10; *Los Angeles Times*, 30 June 1913, II4; 1 Mar. 1913, II8.

27 "Report of General Counsel," *Investment Bankers' Association of America Bulletin* 2 (1914): 8–9; Robert R. Reed and Lester H. Washburn, *Blue Sky Laws: Analysis and Text* (New York: Clark Boardman Co., 1921), x–xi; "Pursuit of Swindlers," *Independent* 74 (1913): 486; *Wall Street Journal*, 21 Feb. 1913, 5; *Wall Street Journal*, 26 Nov. 1912, 1; 27 Mar. 1913, 1; "Blue Sky Laws," *Columbia Law Review* 24 (1924): 79–80.

These efforts bore fruit quickly. In 1914, courts invalidated the blue sky laws of Michigan, Iowa, and West Virginia. The Michigan judges seem to have been taken aback by the breadth of the state's law, which, as in Kansas, prohibited the sale of securities if a state commission concluded that investors were likely to lose their money. "It does not cover fraudulent securities merely, but reaches the sale of securities that are honest, valid, and safe," the court huffed. "It does not simply protect the unwary citizen against fraudulent misleading, but it prevents the experienced investor from deliberately assisting an enterprise which he thinks gives sufficient promise of gain to offset the risk of loss." The judges were equally alarmed by the commission's "uncontrolled discretion" to grant or deny approval based on its view as to the fairness of the company's business plan. "Broader and vaguer language could not be chosen," the court observed. That was enough for the court to find that Michigan's blue sky law unconstitutionally denied due process and interfered with interstate commerce. The Iowa and West Virginia judges had the same reaction. The Iowa court acknowledged that Iowa's blue sky law was enacted with a laudable purpose—"to protect the humble, honest citizens of the state, unlearned in the intricacy of business affairs as conducted at this day from being plundered and despoiled of their small earnings and property, acquired through years of patient toil, by the alluring machinations and the deceptive, misleading, and fraudulent devices which the unscrupulous, cunning, and deceitful 'Get-Rich-Quick-Wallingfords' of our day practice." But a praiseworthy goal did not allow the state "to punish the doing of such customary, everyday transactions" as the sale of securities, because the prohibition exceeded the state's limited power over interstate commerce.[28]

The IBA's winning streak continued in 1915 and 1916. Ohio's blue sky law met the same fate. After the Michigan legislature amended its blue sky law, the court struck it down once again. In light of all these decisions, concluded the lawyer Lee Perrin, while a state could prohibit

---

28 "Report of General Counsel," 6–7; *Topeka Journal*, 22 Oct. 1914; *New York Times*, 16 Aug. 1913, 1; *Wall Street Journal*, 27 Aug. 1913, 8; "Blue Sky Laws," *Independent* 77 (1914): 244; *Alabama and New Orleans Transp. Co. v. Doyle*, 210 F. 173, 175, 181 (E.D. Mich. 1914); *William R. Compton Co. v. Allen*, 216 F. 537, 545–46 (S.D. Iowa 1914); *Bracey v. Darst*, 218 F. 482 (N.D.W.Va. 1914).

fraud in the sale of securities, the state lacked the power to substitute its own judgment for that of the investor. "With the security and the material facts once fairly before him," Perrin advised, "he should be left to his own discretion."[29]

Meanwhile, in states with blue sky laws that were still in force, administrators were reconsidering the wisdom of evaluating the soundness of every security offered in the state. Even Joseph Dolley was having second thoughts as he neared the end of his term in office. It was simply impossible to investigate them all. He proposed a new law that would allow reputable investment bankers to obtain licenses that would entitle them to sell any security, without the state having to scrutinize each one. The Kansas legislature enacted this new law in 1913.[30]

As a result of these three developments—lobbying by the IBA, court decisions striking down several of the early statutes, and state officials' realization that a full merit review of all securities issues was impractical—the nature of blue sky laws changed in the mid-1910s. Most of the states in the first wave of blue sky laws, from 1911 to 1913, sought to prohibit the sale of securities that were unlikely to offer a fair return. But the second generation of blue sky laws, from 1915 on, by and large abandoned the effort to evaluate the soundness of investments. The new laws tended instead merely to prohibit fraud and to require sellers to disclose information. Even Kansas, which had pioneered merit review in 1911, gave it up in 1915. Kansas's new law, like its counterparts in other states, omitted any requirement that securities offer a fair return.[31] The IBA's campaign had been a success.

By the time the constitutionality of blue sky laws reached the United States Supreme Court, in three cases decided in 1917, all three of the laws at issue were of the second-wave type, prohibiting fraud but not otherwise empowering state officials to judge the merits of an investment. The court upheld all three. "It may be that there are better ways to meet the evils at which the statute is directed," Justice Joseph McKenna said

29 *Geiger-Jones Co. v. Turner*, 230 F. 233 (S.D. Ohio 1916); *N.W. Halsey & Co. v. Merrick*, 228 F. 805 (E.D. Mich. 1915); Lee J. Perrin, "The 'Blue Sky Laws,'" *Bench & Bar* 10 (1916): 496

30 *New York Times*, 18 Mar. 1913, 10; Fleming, "100 Years," 604–5.

31 Fleming, "100 Years," 606.

of Michigan's revised law. "We can only reply that it is not our function to decide between measures." In prohibiting fraud, the state was doing what it had always done. All that was new was that the state was policing fraudulent sales before the sales took place rather than after. "The policy of a state and its expression in laws must vary with circumstances," McKenna continued. "It burdens honest business, it is true, but burdens it only that, under its forms, dishonest business cannot be done."[32] Had one of the first-wave statutes reached the court, the result might well have been different.

Only seven years had passed since Joseph Dolley had begun offering investment advice to the citizens of Kansas. Blue sky laws had swept the country, but they had weakened. Many states had briefly experimented with a scheme in which government officials would serve as investment advisors to the public, separating the good investments from the bad, to ensure that state residents were not ruined by speculation. The experiment had been a failure. The plan exceeded both the states' authority under the constitutional law of the era and the limited institutional capacities of the officials charged with determining which investments would offer a fair return.

A RIDICULOUS SITUATION

Joseph Dolley's experiment had failed, but the nation was left with a body of law that had not existed before he began offering investment advice to Kansans. By the late 1910s and early 1920s, most of the state blue sky laws had a family resemblance. They required sellers of securities to disclose information, and most authorized government officials to scrutinize these filings for signs of fraud before granting permission to sell. But this similarity on paper concealed some very large differences among states in practice.

Wisconsin, for example, had a typical second-generation blue sky law. The law did not even apply to many classes of securities that were unlikely

---

32 *Merrick v. N.W. Halsey & Co.*, 242, U.S. 568, 589, 586–87 (1917). The other two cases were *Hall v. Geiger Jones Co.*, 242 U.S. 539 (1917) (concerning Ohio's law), and *Caldwell v. Sioux Falls Stock Yards Co.*, 242 U.S. 559 (1917) (concerning South Dakota's).

to be out and out frauds—government bonds, short-term commercial paper, securities of public utilities, securities listed on one of the major stock exchanges, and securities of banks and trust companies. Nor did it apply to the sale of securities by their owner, so long as the owner was not in the business of selling securities. It placed only very mild restrictions on the sale of stock in businesses that had operated at a profit for the preceding two years. Authorized brokers could sell such stock without requesting permission. Wisconsin's law had real teeth only for securities being sold by brand new companies or companies that were losing money. These were the transactions with the greatest potential for fraud. These companies had to file a detailed application with the Securities Division of the Wisconsin Railroad Commission. In the application, a company had to provide full information about the securities and how they would be sold, as well as financial statements detailing the company's income and expenses over the past two years. If the company was a new one, the application had to lay out its business plan in considerable detail. The Securities Division then determined whether, in the words of the statute, "the proposed plan of business . . . is not unlawful, unfair, unjust, or inequitable"; whether "the company intends to fairly and honestly transact its business"; and whether the sale of securities at the proposed prices "will work a fraud upon the purchaser thereof." If nothing seemed amiss, the Securities Division would approve the application.[33]

The Securities Division approved the large majority of applications. It approved 651 in 1920–21, for instance, while only 125 applications were denied or withdrawn, and those figures grew even more lopsided in succeeding years.[34] The division seems nevertheless to have been an aggressive enforcer of the law, at least in those instances for which records survive.

In 1925, for example, the Securities Division investigated a number of proposed bond issues intended to finance the construction of

33 Edwin L. Schujan, "Wisconsin Blue Sky Legislation," *University Journal of Business* 1 (1923): 393–405.

34 *Annual Report of Securities Division July 1, 1920, to June 30, 1921* (Madison: Railroad Commission of Wisconsin, 1921), 5; *Annual Report of Securities Division July 1, 1922, to June 30, 1923* (Madison: Railroad Commission of Wisconsin, 1923), 3; *Annual Report of Securities Division July 1, 1923, to June 30, 1924* (Madison: Railroad Commission of Wisconsin, 1924), 5.

buildings. In one case, John Hunholz, the builder of two Milwaukee apartment buildings, had inflated the building costs in his application, in an effort to sell more bonds than the building was actually worth. The division learned this by interviewing the contractors, who reported receiving less than Hunholz claimed to be paying them. The division denied Hunholz permission to sell the bonds and turned the case over to the state attorney general, to prosecute Hunholz for filing false information. In another case, the Civic Realty Company asked its contractors to sign contracts providing for payment greater than the amounts called for by their bids, with the understanding that the contractors would rebate the excess amount to the builder. The motive, again, was to make the building appear more valuable so as to sell more bonds, and once again the division discovered the fraud by interviewing the contractors. There were many more such cases in Milwaukee at the same time—so many that for a while the Securities Division was functioning as de facto auditor of construction costs, whenever construction was to be financed by a bond issue.[35]

The division also spent considerable time policing the sale of furry animals. In the 1920s, several promoters organized companies in Wisconsin to sell rabbits, muskrats, and mink. The plan was to sell customers "units" consisting of one male and two females, along with "ranching contracts" under which the company would care for the animals and share with the customers the profits from the sale of pelts. The division took the position that this plan involved the sale of a security and thus required compliance with the blue sky law. "We will not allow the sale of contracts of this sort at any more than a fair market value for the animals," the division informed the proprietor of one such scheme, called the Hillside Spring Fur Farm. "Your proposition, however, seems to us unfair on the face of it," because even on optimistic assumptions it "would leave the investor a net return of $15 on an investment of $350. The investor could do much better by investing that sum in a high grade bond."[36]

35 Arthur Snapper to L. E. Gettle, 16 Dec. 1925, WDS, box 1, folder 1.

36 G. B. Brubaker to Securities Division, 21 Apr. 1928; Railroad Commission of Wisconsin to William Speck, 31 Jan. 1929, both WDS, box 1, folder 2; H. W. Harriman to file, 2 Sept. 1930, WDS, box 1, folder 4; Railroad Commission of Wisconsin to Hillside Spring Fur Farm, 24 July 1930, WDS, box 1, folder 4.

Much of the division's work involved simply making sure that sellers of securities complied with the rules. Greenbaum Sons, a Chicago bond dealer, sold 182 different bond issues in Wisconsin before it bothered to apply for permission. The division informed Greenbaum Sons that it would be barred from doing business in Wisconsin unless it promptly qualified all those bonds. Nearly half of the issues had been under $1,000, and for those the division allowed Greenbaum Sons the alternative of repurchasing them from their holders for the sale price plus accrued interest. But the division made clear that its authority under the blue sky law concerned only the sale of securities, not the ongoing conduct of corporations once the securities had been sold. "It was not intended that stockholders should be freed from any necessity of protecting their rights when this law was passed," explained Garfield Canright, the division's director in the 1920s. "Our jurisdiction has to do rather with the right to start the enterprise. After it is started the stockholders must see that they elect proper directors and that the directors properly perform their duties." So far as one can tell today, the Wisconsin blue sky law seems to have succeeded in preventing at least some of the more egregious forms of fraud in the sale of securities. "It is, of course, impossible entirely to prevent violations of any law," Canright acknowledged. "We believe, however, that this situation is gradually improving."[37]

At the other end of the spectrum was Illinois, which had a blue sky law that was similar to Wisconsin's on paper but very different in practice. "The Illinois blue sky law is practically null and void in its operation," admitted Walter Flint, who ran the state's securities department. "There is no appropriation for its enforcement." Flint's office had allowed approximately seven hundred companies to sell securities without conducting much of an investigation. "The trouble is that we have no investigators," Flint explained. "Our method is simply this. We take the list of officers of the company applying for a license and ask for their references. We then correspond with the persons referred to.

37 Railroad Commission of Wisconsin to Greenbaum Sons Investment Co., 19 Sept. 1924, WDS, box 1, folder 19; Garfield E. Canright to Lewis E. Gettle, 15 Jan. 1924, WDS, box 1, folder 7; *Annual Report of the Securities Division July 1, 1920, to June 30, 1921*, 8.

The license is granted or withheld as a result of the correspondence."
This method's utter failure to prevent fraudulent stock sales came to
light in a 1919 lawsuit against the Consumers' Packing Company filed
on behalf of shareholders who had bought the company's worthless
stock. (The judge was Kenesaw Mountain Landis, who would leave the
bench a year later to become the first commissioner of baseball.) Flint
had granted a permit to the Consumers' Packing Company because the
company's officers and directors had adequate references, even though
Flint had reason to know that the company was a scam. One of the
references was a state politician who had been paid for his services. "We
have not a single investigator and the work of the office is handled by
a force of seven clerks," Flint despaired. "There have been nearly 400
applications this year."[38]

The Consumers' Packing scandal prompted the Illinois legislature
to make appropriations for investigators, but the episode highlighted
how difficult it could be for a state agency to figure out ahead of time
which ventures were likely to be fraudulent. Daniel Holt, who has conducted the closest study of the blue sky laws in operation, concludes
that many blue sky offices had only a handful of employees. Unable to
conduct thorough investigations of every proposed sale of securities,
they tended to adopt rules of thumb instead. They were extremely skeptical of mining companies, whose worth depended on the uncertain
value of what might be found underground. The Nebraska Bureau of
Securities, for instance, rejected 84 percent of the mining companies
that applied to sell stock, but only around 18 percent of the nonmining
companies. Aviation companies also met with high rejection rates. Blue
sky offices were likewise skeptical of corporate promoters who were not
sharing the risks with investors by putting their own money into the
business.[39] Such determinations were not written into any law; they
were the last resort of state employees overwhelmed with the job they
had been given. Even the watered-down second-generation blue sky
laws, which tasked state agencies with ferreting out fraud rather than

---

38 *Chicago Daily Tribune*, 15 Mar. 1919, 1; 17 Mar. 1919, 5.
39 Daniel Stephen Holt, *Acceptable Risk: Law, Regulation, and the Politics of
    American Financial Markets, 1878–1930* (Dissertation, University of Virginia,
    Department of History, 2008), 173–246.

assessing the wisdom of an investment, were often impossible for the states to enforce literally.

The young economist James Waterhouse Angell, writing in 1920, diagnosed two problems with this sort of haphazard enforcement. The first was that blue sky bureaus had no real way to separate the fraudsters from the people who genuinely wanted to raise money for new businesses that were speculative but honest. "If a fraudulent enterprise applies for qualification," Angell pointed out, "the evidence upon which its application is judged is, primarily, its own sworn statements, which it can falsify at pleasure." The second problem was that the blue sky bureaus, aware of their own ineffectiveness but wanting to show the public that they were enforcing the law vigorously, made the application process cumbersome, so they would be able to reject a respectable percentage of applications. As a result, Angell concluded, the blue sky law "exactly inverts its supposed purpose; it burdens the class that is honest with endless red tape, and guards it carefully from law-breaking; while it calmly permits the more dubious classes to operate almost without hindrance."[40]

The investment bankers felt the same way. "The amount of good accomplished by any or all of the so-called 'Blue Sky' acts," declared the IBA's committee on legislation in 1919, "is infinitesimal in comparison with the amount of expense and annoyance which they entail upon legitimate business." The laws were "worse than useless," the committee complained, "in that reputable people do not need to be controlled," while the disreputable had been "granted licenses which they have adroitly used to create the impression that what they were offering had in some measure received the approval of the legally constituted authorities."[41]

Because of such concerns, some of the later blue sky laws entirely gave up the effort to screen securities sales ahead of time. These laws simply prohibited fraud, without requiring a permit before one could sell securities. They were enacted primarily in the northeastern states,

40 James Waterhouse Angell, "The Illinois Blue Sky Law," *Journal of Political Economy* 28 (1920): 316, 314.

41 *Proceedings of the Eighth Annual Convention of the Investment Bankers Association of America* (Chicago: Investment Bankers Association of America, 1919), 122.

including the financial centers of New York and Pennsylvania, but also in New Jersey, Maryland, Delaware, and Connecticut. Keyes Winter, New York's deputy attorney general, called his state's law a "substitute for a blue sky law," because "it is not a license law." Five thousand corporations a month were organized in New York, and on some days three million shares of stock were traded on the New York Stock Exchange. "A license law restricting these transfers of securities in New York State preliminary to a thorough investigation would choke business, not only in the state, but in the entire United States," Winter explained. Instead of requiring a license, New York's law gave the state attorney general broad powers to subpoena witnesses and to compel the production of corporate records, when there was reason to suspect fraud.[42]

Dissatisfaction with state blue sky laws gave rise to considerable support for a national blue sky law. The idea was appealing to an unlikely coalition: on one side, proponents of regulation who hoped the federal government would be a stronger enforcer than the states could ever hope to be, and on the other, business interests who preferred a uniform national scheme of regulation over a hodgepodge of laws that varied from state to state, both on paper and in practice. In the 1912 presidential election, the Progressive Party platform called for a federal blue sky law. Theodore Roosevelt, the Progressive candidate, praised the recently enacted Kansas law and urged it as a model for the nation. Only a few months later, the *Bankers' Magazine* also declared its support for a federal blue sky law. "The sale of securities should, if practicable, be brought under Federal regulation rather than be committed to the numerous States with their varying standards of legislation and administration," the magazine insisted. "It would be comparatively simple to comply with a single Federal statute, but would prove irksome to comply with the requirements of the laws of every State in which it was desired to transact business." The *Bankers' Magazine* advocated a federal blue sky law repeatedly over the next several years. Soon the idea had received the support of virtually all the relevant regulatory

---

42 Keyes Winter, "State Regulation of Corporations by Policing Sales of Securities," *Annals of the American Academy of Political and Social Science* 129 (1927): 153, 152; Keyes Winter, "Parasites of Finance," *North American Review* 224 (1927): 520.

and banking organizations. The National Association of Supervisors of State Banks favored it. So did the Federal Trade Commission. The Investment Bankers Association of America supported it too. "We need a federal 'blue sky' law," the IBA's lawyer declared in 1920. "The solution of that problem lies with the federal government. Neither one nor forty-seven states can solve it and forty-eight states never will without federal compulsion."[43]

Federal financial regulation was very much in the air at the time. In the well-publicized "Money Trust" hearings of 1912–13, led by Louisiana congressman Arsène Pujo, a House subcommittee heard extensive testimony about the extent to which the nation's financial system was dominated by a small clique of bankers. The hearings were about banking rather than the stock market (they took place just before the establishment of the Federal Reserve System in 1913), but the underwriting of securities was one of the things that bankers did, so part of the Money Trust hearings involved the sale of speculative securities. The Pujo Committee's final report found that there was too much speculation on the New York Stock Exchange and that powerful traders sometimes manipulated prices by engaging in sham transactions. As a cure for both problems, the committee recommended requiring corporations listed on the stock exchange "to make a complete disclosure of their affairs," particularly any commissions they had paid to bankers out of the proceeds of the sale of securities.[44] But such matters were tangential to the thrust of the Money Trust investigation, and Congress did not act on these particular recommendations.

Once blue sky laws had been enacted in most states, and once the world war was over, Congress took the issue up in earnest. In 1919, the

43 *New York Times*, 3 Sept. 1912, 2; *Current Literature*, Dec. 1912, 34; "Regulation of the Sale of Securities," *Bankers' Magazine* 86 (1913): 418–19; " 'Blue Sky' Laws Obscured by a Judicial Cloud," *Bankers' Magazine* 88 (1914): 283; "Federal Blue-Sky Legislation," *Bankers' Magazine* 104 (1922): 979; *Los Angeles Times*, 9 July 1914, I5; *New York Times*, 8 Oct. 1919, 29; Robert R. Reed, " 'Blue Sky' Laws," *Annals of the American Academy of Political and Social Science* 88 (1920): 184, 183. See also "Finance & Investment," *Current Opinion*, 1 Nov. 1924, 652.

44 *Money Trust Investigation: Investigation of Financial and Monetary Conditions in the United States* (Washington, D.C.: Government Printing Office, 1913), part I, 6; H.R. Rep. No. 1593, 62nd Cong., 3rd Sess. (1913), 42–54, 162–63.

House Judiciary Committee held hearings on a bill that was generally referred to as a "federal blue sky law," although its official name was the Federal Stock Publicity Act. The bill, introduced by Representative Edward Taylor of Colorado, required all corporations engaged in interstate commerce to file financial statements with the Treasury Department before selling stock. Unlike most of the state blue sky laws, the bill did not empower government employees to screen proposed sales for fraud ahead of time. Rather, the financial statements filed by sellers of securities would be made available for public inspection (and mailed to anyone willing to pay the postage). If the statements included any false information, purchasers would be deemed to have relied on the statements, and the seller would have to give them their money back. "My earnest hope is to secure the enactment of some fair, sane, and workable Federal 'blue-sky' law," Taylor declared. He had the support of nearly all the state blue sky commissions, who had difficulty exercising authority over interstate transactions. But the IBA opposed the bill, despite the organization's professed support for a federal blue sky law, because of the provision making the seller responsible for incorrect information in the financial statements filed with the government. "We have no objection to being made responsible for fraud or any negligence," explained Paul Keyser, testifying on behalf of the IBA. "But we do not think it is fair to make us responsible for mere mistake or accident where all good faith exists."[45] The bill never made it out of the committee.

Congress considered several other federal blue sky bills over the next several years, none of which was enacted. The idea that got the most attention was embodied in bills repeatedly introduced by Representative Edward Denison of Illinois, who proposed a federal ban on the interstate sale of securities whenever the sale would violate the blue sky law of the state in which the purchaser was located. At the time, this was a familiar way of supplementing the states' limited power over interstate commerce. Before national Prohibition, Congress had enacted the same kind of statute to help dry states keep out alcohol shipped from

45 *Proposed Federal "Blue-Sky" Law: Hearing Before the Committee on the Judiciary, House of Representatives*, 66th Cong., 1st Sess. (1919), 3–10, 126.

wet states. But Denison's bills were consistently opposed by the IBA, who wanted federal legislation precisely so that state officials would not be able to exercise so much discretionary power over their business. "It would be a ridiculous situation," scoffed the New York investment banker George Hodges, "for the Federal Government to delegate its power to a blue-sky commission in Kansas or wherever it might be."[46]

By the late 1920s, despite the existence of blue sky laws in nearly every state, and despite the interest of both bankers and regulators in adopting a federal version, Congress's efforts to enact a federal blue sky law had foundered on disagreement over the details. Of course, the stock market was booming. Speculators were making money. It was not the best time to interest lawmakers or investors in imposing new limits on speculation.

That would change.

---

46 Joel Seligman, *The Transformation of Wall Street* (Boston: Houghton Mifflin, 1982), 49; *"Blue-Sky" Bill: Hearings Before the Committee on Interstate and Foreign Commerce of the House of Representatives*, 67th Cong., 2nd Sess. (1922), 53; *Regulating Sale of Securities: Hearings Before a Subcommittee of the Committee on Interstate Commerce, United States Senate*, 67th Cong., 4th Sess. (1923).

5

Aftershocks of the Crash

BETWEEN MARCH 1925 AND September 1929, the Dow Jones Industrial Average rose from 115 to 381. By the middle of 1932, it had plummeted to 41. The stocks listed on the New York Stock Exchange were worth nearly $90 million in the fall of 1929, but by the summer of 1932, their value was only $15.6 million.[1] Never before in the history of the United States had so many people lost so much money so quickly.

The stock market crash of 1929–32 gave rise to several far-reaching reforms. The Securities Act of 1933 required sellers of securities to disclose a wide range of information. The Securities Exchange Act of 1934 imposed a variety of restrictions on the buying and selling of stock.[2] The Glass-Steagall Act (a part of the Banking Act of 1933) separated commercial banks from investment banks. The two securities acts still govern the stock market today; the Glass-Steagall Act would continue to structure the banking industry, despite gradual weakening, until it was repealed in 1999.

1 *Stock Exchange Practices: Report of the Committee on Banking and Currency Pursuant to S. Res. 84* (Washington, D.C.: Government Printing Office, 1934), 7.
2 The best accounts of the drafting and enactment of the two securities acts are Joel Seligman, *The Transformation of Wall Street: A History of the Securities and Exchange Commission and Modern Corporate Finance* (Boston: Houghton Mifflin, 1982), 1–100, and Michael E. Parrish, *Securities Regulation and the New Deal* (New Haven, Conn.: Yale University Press, 1970). On the Glass-Steagall Act, see Edwin J. Perkins, "The Divorce of Commercial and Investment Banking: A History," *Banking Law Journal* 88 (1971): 483–528.

If one takes a long-term perspective on the regulation of speculation, the remarkable (and thus far underappreciated) thing about these New Deal reforms is not what they did but what they didn't do. Earlier market downturns had yielded regulation that was intended to restrict speculators in a much more serious way. After the crash of 1792, New York prohibited stock futures. When the dollar fell against gold during the Civil War, Congress banned gold futures. When agricultural prices fell in the late nineteenth century, Congress came within a whisker of shutting down the commodity exchanges, and some states imposed major limits on commodity trading. Yet after the biggest crash of all, the regulatory response was relatively mild. The crash was widely blamed on speculators, and there were many calls for placing serious limits on speculation to prevent such a thing from happening again, but the reforms that followed the crash curtailed speculation only very modestly. Why?

A MAMMOTH GAMBLING MACHINE

As the stock market reached new heights in the late 1920s, many worried that the rise was the product of speculation rather than genuine prosperity. "Rarely, if ever, has the stock market appeared to get so far out of touch with business conditions as it has in the last year or two," the economist Lewis Haney cautioned in early 1928. "Stocks have risen in value much more than twice as fast as our industrial activity." "It is ridiculous to term purchases of stocks at present prices investments," lectured the banker Alan Temple. "They are speculations." But such warnings could hardly deter investors from jumping into the market after they had seen their neighbors grow rich. "Increasing thousands of first-time speculators are watching their paper profits mount, and are concluding that anyone who works for a living is a boob," *Time* magazine reported. It became a commonplace in the press that the nation was in the midst of a speculative craze that, like similar episodes in the past, was sure to end badly. Carter Glass, the Virginia senator and former Treasury secretary, reported in early 1929 that "there is a firm determination in Congress to enact some legislation to abate this infernal menace of stock gambling."[3]

3 Lewis H. Haney, "The Stock Market and Business," *North American Review* 225 (1928): 175; Alan H. Temple, "The Financial Outlook," *North American*

Others were more optimistic. "Agitation against speculation in Wall Street is very largely a case of sour grapes," the *Wall Street Journal* insisted. "It is felt that some people are making money with apparent ease and it is known that they are making it in Wall Street, which is always an object of distrust to the demagogue." One booster concluded that stock prices were entirely justified in light of all the spectacular technological changes of the 1920s. "Indeed," he imagined, "who shall say what the future profits of such new industries as radio, television, electric power, chain store methods of merchandising, and so on will be?" In 1929, J. P. Morgan's partner Thomas Lamont assured the new president Herbert Hoover that even if stocks were overvalued they were only modestly so, and that the bull market was attributable instead to two positive developments. One was the new willingness of ordinary Americans to invest in stocks, which attracted capital that had formerly lain dormant in small towns throughout the country. The other cause was the genuine underlying prosperity of the United States. ("This document is fairly amazing in light of two years after," Hoover later scrawled across the top.) The investment advisor H. W. Moorhouse concluded that advanced stock prices were the product of "a new economic era" in which constantly growing demand for stock would yield constantly rising prices. If prices seemed higher than economic principles warranted, perhaps it was the principles that needed adjusting. In Moorhouse's view, the market was "vaulting easily over economic precepts formerly considered impregnable." As the Yale economist Irving Fisher famously put it in mid-October 1929, just a week before the market began to plummet, stock prices had reached "what looks like a permanently high plateau."[4]

Review 226 (1928): 641; "Stock Market Jamboree," *Time*, 28 May 1928, 32; A. M. Sakolski, "American Speculative Manias, Past and Present," *Current History* 30 (1929): 861; Carter Glass to G. H. Gray, 11 Feb. 1929, CG, box 311.

4 *Wall Street Journal*, 15 May 1928, 1; Donald Rea Hanson, "In Defense of Speculation," *Forum* 81 (1929): 57; Thomas W. Lamont to Herbert Hoover, 19 Oct. 1929, HHL, box 1049; H. W. Moorhouse, "What's Happening in Wall Street," *North American Review* 226 (1928): 678; *New York Times*, 16 Oct. 1929, 8.

Some were worried that stock speculation had spiraled out of control, others thought it entirely justified, and there was a third position in the middle, that even if there was too much speculation, nothing constructive could be done about it. George Roberts, the vice president of the National City Bank of New York, was willing to concede that "there is a vast amount of uninformed speculation" that served no economic purpose. But "it is impossible to require everybody to pass a civil service examination before engaging in any kind of speculation," Roberts observed, "and it is exceedingly difficult if not impossible to discriminate at least in law, between acts of the same kind which in one case represent perfectly legitimate operations and in another case may be of the undesirable class." Legislation curbing speculation might be a cure worse than the disease, because it risked driving off the good transactions, as well as the bad. Without speculation, "the conduct of railways and large-scale industry would probably be found a hard job," reckoned the *Bankers' Magazine*. "To carry on these enterprises requires a lot of money, which cannot be had from those who are investors of the purely conservative type."[5]

Previous booms had seen similar debates about the dangers of speculation, but the debate in the 1920s was more intense and more consequential than in earlier episodes, because the establishment of the Federal Reserve System in 1913 gave the government a new policy lever. By raising interest rates, the Federal Reserve could dampen speculation, by making it more difficult for speculators to earn a positive return with borrowed money. Throughout the second half of the decade, critics repeatedly called upon the Federal Reserve to do just that. "I have noted with growing anxiety the steady increase in speculation in the country, more particularly centered in the New York Stock Market, which has for some time been engaged in positive gambling in securities," Wisconsin senator Irvine Lenroot wrote in 1925, in an urgent plea to Federal Reserve Board governor Daniel Crissinger to raise interest rates. "Does not the present cheap money induced by the low discount rates indirectly stimulate speculation on the New York Stock

---

5 George E. Roberts, "Speculation and Its Influence Upon Business," *Bankers' Magazine* 117 (1928): 967; "Fresh Outburst of Speculation," *Bankers' Magazine* 116 (1928): 625.

Exchange[?]"[6] The *Bankers' Magazine* recalled that in earlier speculative booms, the rise in demand for money to invest would cause interest rates to rise sharply, which would check speculation. The Federal Reserve System had the beneficial effect of preventing disabling shortages of money, the magazine concluded, but at the cost of removing this former limit on speculation.[7]

In the Senate, the Michigan Republican James Couzens complained in the summer of 1929 that "the Federal Reserve Board has been dumb in not dealing with a situation that should have been dealt with months ago." If the board had only raised interest rates, he charged, "this great orgy of speculation would not have occurred." The Wisconsin Republican Robert La Follette proposed barring the Federal Reserve from lending any funds that would be put to speculative purposes. And these were the Senate's more temperate and urbane critics of the Federal Reserve's role regarding speculation. When the topic was debated in the Senate, the result was, as *Time* magazine put it, "a mingled outburst of oratory, ethics, provincialism and a little economics." The Alabama Democrat James Heflin thundered that Wall Street was a gambling monster that was destroying American homes. Smith Brookhart of Iowa suggested prohibiting all banks from lending to speculators. William King of Utah wanted to ban margin trading. Thaddeus Caraway of Arkansas suggested prison terms for dealing in grain and cotton futures.[8] If the Federal Reserve could cause the amount of speculation to come down from a dangerous level simply by raising interest rates, critics wondered, why would it hesitate?

The question was hotly debated both within and outside the Federal Reserve. The difficulty was that the interest rate was a blunt instrument. Raising interest rates would make borrowing more costly for everyone, not just for speculators, so it would dampen all business activity, not

---

6 Irvine Lenroot to D. R. Crissinger, 23 Nov. 1925, HPPF, box 122. Herbert Hoover claimed in his memoirs to have written this letter for Lenroot to sign, while Hoover was secretary of commerce. Herbert Hoover, *Memoirs* (New York: Macmillan, 1951–52), 3:9–11.

7 "Federal Reserve System and Speculation," *Bankers' Magazine* 115 (1927): 129.

8 *Washington Post*, 6 June 1929, 6; *New York Times*, 19 Jan. 1928, 10; "Federal Reserve v. Speculation," *Time*, 25 Feb. 1929, 49.

just speculation. Was it worth it? "The policy of raising the rediscount rate in order to stop speculation is . . . based on the theory that the millions of innocents should be punished for the sins of the few," argued the banker Edward C. Stokes, the former governor of New Jersey. "If a young inexperienced patron of my bank is branching out too much in the speculative field, I quietly call him to my desk and tell him that he has reached his limit, but I don't raise the rate of interest on every other borrower of our institution." The banker Russell Leffingwell cautioned that it would be impossible for the Federal Reserve to distinguish borrowers seeking to speculate from borrowers seeking to use money for ends that seemed more productive. "We are all, good and bad, sheep and goats, farmers and bankers and merchants and speculators and industrialists, engaged in one great joint venture," Leffingwell mused. "If the Federal Reserve authorities set out to ruin some, by denying credit to those they don't approve of, the speculators, they will most likely injure us all."[9]

Higher interest rates, moreover, would slow or even reverse the remarkable rise in stock prices, a result that was sure to be unpopular. Before taking such action, the Federal Reserve had to be confident that curtailing speculation justified harming so many people, but how could officials, or indeed anyone, be sure that prices were already too high? And as many suggested, any move by the government, even by the quasi-independent Federal Reserve, that was perceived to have ended the boom was likely to have disastrous consequences for the incumbent Republican Party. As one editorialist noted of Treasury Secretary and Federal Reserve Board member Andrew Mellon shortly after the 1928 presidential election, "it would be too much to expect of any incumbent of that distinguished office to take otherwise than a roseate view of the situation in the face of a national political campaign."[10]

9 Allan H. Meltzer, *A History of the Federal Reserve: Volume I, 1913–1951* (Chicago: University of Chicago Press, 2003), 224–57; William J. Barber, *From New Era to New Deal: Herbert Hoover, the Economists, and American Economic Policy, 1921–1933* (Cambridge: Cambridge University Press, 1985), 71–77; E. C. Stokes, "Control Speculation? No!," *Bankers' Magazine* 118 (1929): 714; Russell Leffingwell to Carter Glass, 29 Apr. 1919, CG, box 283.

10 *Wall Street Journal*, 24 Apr. 1928, 1; "Federal Reserve Policy and Speculation," *Bankers' Magazine* 118 (1929): 541.

As it turned out, the Federal Reserve did raise the discount rate three times in 1928, from 3.5 percent to 4 percent, then to 4.5 percent, and finally to 5 percent. These measures had no discernible effect on the amount of speculation or on stock prices. In the spring of 1929, as the market continued to rise, Hoover and Mellon urged the Federal Reserve Board to raise the rate yet again. The Federal Reserve Bank of New York asked the board several times to increase the rate to 6 percent. Each time, a majority of the board declined to do so.[11]

"The stock boom was blowing great guns when I came into the White House," Hoover recalled in his memoirs. "Being fully alive to the danger inherent in this South Sea Bubble and its inevitable reaction, my first interest was to get it under restraint." Hoover's memory was colored by hindsight. Before the crash he had told the banker Martin Egan that he was "dubious about doing anything for fear that more harm than good might result." And of course in his later years Hoover had an interest in defending himself against charges that as president he had done too little—he pointedly titled this chapter of his memoirs "We Attempt to Stop the Orgy of Speculation." Even so, Hoover was no doubt right that there was not much even a president could do apart from badgering the Federal Reserve to lower interest rates. "To ask Congress for powers to interfere in the stock market was futile," he recalled, "and, in any event, for the President to dictate the price of stocks was an expansion of Presidential power without any established constitutional basis." So Hoover did what he could to talk the market down. He asked the publishers of the major newspapers and magazines to run editorials warning readers of the dangers of speculation. He gave speeches to the same effect. He urged bankers to exercise restraint in lending, and he urged Richard Whitney, the president of the New York Stock Exchange, to do something to curb the manipulation of stock prices. None of these actions had any effect. In August 1929, the Federal Reserve Board finally did raise the discount rate to 6 percent. It made no difference. "The real trouble," Hoover lamented, "was that the bell-boys, the waiters, and the host of unknowing people, as well as the

---

11 David Cannadine, *Mellon: An American Life* (New York: Alfred A. Knopf, 2006), 359, 388–89.

financial community, had become so obsessed with the constant press reports of great winnings that the movement was uncontrollable."[12]

When the crash finally came, speculators took much of the blame. Alexander Noyes, the financial editor of the *New York Times*, castigated "professional speculators of large private means but utter recklessness," as well as amateur "outside speculators, large and small, most of whom were totally ignorant of intrinsic values and inspired by nothing but the gambling purpose of bidding on a market for an expected further rise." The financial journalist John T. Flynn complained that buying stock had become just like betting on racehorses. "Trading in stocks and bonds should be limited to buying and selling between persons who use stocks and bonds as media of investment," Flynn insisted. "Their use as counters in a gigantic game of gambling ought to be brought to an end." The *North American Review* scoffed at those who, before the crash, "incessantly preached that a new era had arrived," when the supposed new era turned out to be just another speculative bubble. Even the *Wall Street Journal*, which had defended investing in stocks on the way up, acknowledged after the crash that "many people all over the country have learned the essential difference between investment and speculation."[13]

In late 1929 and the early 1930s, as the market slid ever lower and the Depression deepened, there was considerable public demand for some form of retribution against "Wall Street," the shadowy force that had plunged the nation into distress. "Wall Street speculation has ruined hundreds of thousands of people in the United States," complained one correspondent to President Herbert Hoover. Another charged that "this 'Stock Market' is nothing more or less than a Mammoth Gambling Machine, out to rob any and every one." The mayor of Mobile, Alabama, advised Hoover that "the most important work you have to do in the

---

12 Martin Egan to Thomas Lamont, 23 Oct. 1929, HHL, box 1049; Hoover, *Memoirs*, 3:16–19.
13 Alexander D. Noyes, "The Stock Market Panic," *Current History* 31 (1929): 619; John T. Flynn, "Speculation and Gambling," *Harper's Magazine* 160 (1930): 201; John T. Flynn, "The Wall Street Debt Machine," *Harper's Magazine* 167 (1933): 138; Max Winkler, "Paying the Piper," *North American Review* 229 (1930): 50; *Wall Street Journal*, 5 Nov. 1929, 1.

interest of civilization is to abolish the gambling features in our stock exchanges," while a Minneapolis bond salesman shared his view that the New York Stock Exchange "is like a boil or fester, eating away at the vitality of the economic life of our country." The Ohio representative Charles Truax expressed this sentiment on the House floor, when he declared that "there are a lot of financial buzzards down on Wall Street who ought to be shot." Truax favored any legislation that "will do something to the bloodiest band of racketeers and vampires that ever sucked the blood of humanity, John 'Pirate' Morgan & Co." He urged the government to imprison "the bloody butchers of Wall Street who have lived in high style on the blood of the common people."[14]

Others contended that much of the blame belonged to the government, for failing to put a stop to the speculative excess while there was still a chance. "Who caused the Panic of 1929?" asked the economist H. Parker Willis in early 1930. It was the Federal Reserve Board, he contended, for keeping interest rates artificially low. "We had the control in 1925, in 1926, in 1927, in 1928, and in 1929, and we did not use it," lamented Percy Johnson, the chairman of the board of Chemical Bank. "We had the control in the power of the Federal Reserve Board, and if the board had not bent its policy to meet the wishes of the Treasury, which wanted to borrow cheap money for the government, but had raised these rates, as it should have done, we could have stopped this speculation in its incipiency in 1927 and 1928 and avoided this colossal crash that has come with such widespread disaster to every one." The columnist Walter Lippmann faulted Hoover for having been too weak to put pressure on the Federal Reserve. The Federal Reserve was even accused of having deliberately prolonged the boom for political reasons, to ensure Hoover's victory in the election of 1928.[15]

14 *Washington Post*, 27 Oct. 1930, 6; M. Rosenbaum to Herbert Hoover, 13 Nov. 1929, HHL, box 159, folder 5; L. I. Conrad to Herbert Hoover, 14 Nov. 1929, HHL, box 159, folder 5; Harry T. Hartwell to Herbert Hoover, 17 Feb. 1930, HHL, box 159, folder 6; Francis H. Gill to Walter H. Newton, 10 Apr. 1932, HHL, box 159A, folder 2; *Congressional Record* 78 (1934): 7939, 7941.

15 H. Parker Willis, "Who Caused the Panic of 1929?," *North American Review* 229 (1930): 174; *New York Times*, 18 Mar. 1934, E4; Walter Lippmann, "The Peculiar

Whether one faulted speculators or the government that had failed to control them, it was clear that something had to be done to prevent such a calamity from happening again. But what? "It was easy, after the Market had broken, to denounce speculators as fools and speculation as vicious," *Time* magazine observed. But "where could the line be drawn between farsightedness and folly?"[16] How could the country protect itself against the excesses of speculation without killing off investment?

THE RUIN OF THOUSANDS

Previous market downturns had yielded new regulatory proposals aimed at curbing speculation, so it was no surprise that the stock market crash of 1929–32 brought forth a wide range of calls to regulate the market. "If there ever was a time when a bill restricting speculation would be acclaimed with favor, it is at the present time," recognized the Cincinnati broker J. R. Edwards. At the Investment Bankers Association's 1932 convention, the IBA's Legislation Committee reported that it could barely keep up with all the bills that had been introduced in Congress.[17]

Some of these proposals were quite severe. Many people urged President Hoover to shut down the nation's stock exchanges until conditions had stabilized. The veteran Kansas senator Arthur Capper informed Hoover that "this feeling is wide spread." The Colorado representative John Martin thought that if the question were put to a referendum, most Americans would even vote in favor of abolishing the stock exchanges permanently. "The exchanges are lucky," Martin remarked, "that Congress and not the country is regulating them." Others, including the Kentucky legislator Herman Handmaker, suggested fixing stock prices so they could not fall. Henry Heimann, the executive manager of the National Association of Credit Men, reported "a very pronounced feeling" among the association's members that

Weakness of Mr. Hoover," *Harper's Magazine* 161 (1930): 1; J. M. Daiger, "Did the Federal Reserve Play Politics?," *Current History* 37 (1932): 25.

16 "Market 'Lesson,'" *Time*, 18 Nov. 1929, 51.

17 J. R. Edwards to Carter Glass, 9 Jan. 1932, CG, box 301; *Proceedings of the Twenty-First Annual Convention of the Investment Bankers Association of America* (Chicago: Investment Bankers Association of America, 1932), 163.

stock prices should be pegged at their values as of some date in the past and then not permitted to decline. The Boston banker Allan Forbes had the same idea, but his friend J. P. Morgan politely talked him out of it. If "people did not like the prices when they were fixed," Morgan told Forbes, "it would simply mean they would go and set up an outside market" and trade there instead of on the exchange.[18] It is a good indicator of the magnitude of the crisis that such desperate measures could have been proposed by such knowledgeable people.

Previous downturns had given rise to proposals to ban short selling, the practice of agreeing to sell in the future an item one did not yet own to profit from a decline in its price. There were many more such calls in the early 1930s. Letters poured into the White House decrying "the destructive practice of short selling," as one New Jersey entrepreneur put it. An engineering professor at the University of Michigan insisted in 1930 that "if there had not been avalanche after avalanche of short selling last fall we would have had an orderly recession of only about half the historic panic drop." As always, something seemed unsavory about a practice that made someone desire—and possibly even act to bring about—a crash. "A man who sells and destroys the value of your securities is no better than the man who burns down your house," insisted one of Herbert Hoover's many correspondents. One of Arthur Capper's constituents urged him to "tell the Banking Committee that if they have any doubt that short selling is the principal cause of the depression to put a ban on short sales for ninety days and watch the general market advance fifty percent." It seemed unfair that short sellers should profit from the despair of others. "How is it that a practice so contrary to public policy can be permitted in this country?" asked the oilman Joseph Pointer. "In whose possession are the twenty billions that disappeared from the pockets of the carpenter, the actor, the

18 George W. McPherson to Herbert Hoover, 29 Oct. 1929, HHL, box 159, folder 4; M. B. Friend to Lawrence Richey, 1 June 1932, HHL, box 159A, folder 3; Arthur Capper to Hebert Hoover, 27 Apr. 1932, HHL, box 159A, folder 2; *Congressional Record* 78 (1934): 8016; Herman H. Handmaker to Herbert Hoover, 13 Nov. 1929, HHL, box 159, folder 5; Henry H. Heimann to Herbert Hoover, 26 May 1932, HHL, box 159A, folder 3; J. P. Morgan Jr. to Allan Forbes, 19 Apr. 1932, JPM, box 25, letterpress book 43.

small executive, and the chorus girl?" Short sellers were "people who put profits before patriotism," reasoned William Buck, a Philadelphia salesman—or else they were "foreigners who wish no good to the United States." The Kansas Republican Charles Scott advised Hoover that "if you can succeed in suppressing short selling in stocks and bonds and food products it will win you the vote of every Republican farmer in the country." Democrats too, suggested the humorist Will Rogers. If the practice were banned, he predicted, "at least 115,000,000 out of the 120,000,000 would put on a celebration that would make Armistice Day look like a wake."[19]

Hoover himself was dubious about short selling. "Men are not justified in deliberately making a profit from the losses of other people," he wrote in early 1932. Hoover also shared the widespread suspicion that short sellers manipulated prices by "pounding down" the market. He worried that "these operations destroy public confidence and induce a slowing down of business." The Hoover administration accordingly took some modest steps to limit short selling. George Akerson, Hoover's press secretary, prepared a list of prominent New York "bears" who "organize short selling at certain hours of the day, thereby creating a real strain on the market." Hoover met with the leaders of the New York Stock Exchange and the Chicago Board of Trade, to urge them to adopt rules to curb short selling. He told Richard Whitney, the president of the stock exchange, that "whatever defense there may be for the practice of short selling during ordinary and normal times," it was "most injurious during periods of depression like the present." Hoover issued Whitney an ambiguous threat, that "unless the Stock Exchange itself would promptly take steps to stop such injurious practices he would feel it his duty to proceed along other lines." At Hoover's request, in January

---

19 Ansley H. Fox to Herbert Hoover, 17 Oct. 1930, HHL, box 159A, folder 7; William S. Hazelton to Herbert Hoover, 16 Oct. 1930, HHL, box 159A, folder 7; E. C. Stokes to Herbert Hoover, 27 Sept. 1930, HHL, box 159A, folder 7; H. L. Stout to Arthur Capper, 23 Apr. 1930, HHL, box 159A, folder 2; Joseph Pointer to Herbert Hoover, 20 Nov. 1929, HHL, box 159A, folder 6; W. L. Buck to Louis McHenry Howe, 23 Mar. 1933, FDR, POF 34, box 1; Charles F. Scott to Herbert Hoover, 24 Feb. 1932, HHL, box 159A, folder 5; Rogers quoted in Nathan T. Porter, "Business and Finance," *Overland Monthly and Out West Magazine* 90 (1932): 41.

1932, the stock exchange began sending reports of short-sale statistics to the White House, at first daily and then weekly, a regimen that lasted for the remainder of Hoover's term in office.[20]

There was also substantial sentiment in Congress against short selling. "In the fall of 1929 I started a crusade against short selling," the Chicago congressman Adolph Sabath declared. "I have done everything humanly possible to have the stock exchanges stop short selling." His Idaho colleague Compton White agreed that "businesses have been ruined and various enterprises have been destroyed by piratical attacks" by short sellers. "We know that something should be done to curb this practice." In early 1932, the House Judiciary Committee held four days of hearings on several bills that would have curbed short selling or even completely abolished it. The Senate issued subpoenas to nearly thirty brokerage firms "to find out whether a large short interest in the market does artificially depress the value of the securities," as Senator Frederic Walcott of Connecticut put it.[21]

Short selling had been defended against such attacks for more than a century, on the grounds that short selling does not in fact cause prices to decline (because there has to be a purchaser on the other side of every short sale, and because every short seller has to become a buyer at some later date), and indeed that short sellers benefit markets by steering them away from the highest peaks and the lowest valleys. But these arguments were not at their most plausible in the early 1930s, when the preceding few years had seen the highest peaks and the lowest valleys in living memory, and when hoping for lower prices seemed like cheering for disease. Short selling was "losing caste," the business writer J. George Frederick observed; "the classic economic defenses for the practice are all down." Louis Guenther, publisher of the magazine *Financial World*,

20 Herbert Hoover to Thomas W. Lamont, 2 Apr. 1932, HHL, box 1049; "Memorandum," 3 Oct. 1930, GEA, box 19; Silas H. Strawn to Lawrence Richey, 28 Oct. 1931, HHL, box 851; B. H. Meyer to Theodore Joslin, 19 Mar. 1932, HHL, box 159A, folder 10; short-sale reports in HHL, box 159A, folder 13.

21 *Congressional Record* 78 (1934): 8028, 8027; *Short Selling of Securities: Hearing Before the Committee on the Judiciary, House of Representatives* (Washington, D.C.: Government Printing Office, 1932); Frederic C. Walcott to Walter H. Newton, 20 Apr. 1932, HHL, box 159A, folder 2.

perceived that "short selling is coming into bad repute with the public," and he thought it a good development in a depression, because "it is in just such a time that everyone should endeavor to employ his abilities and resources towards the maintenance of public confidence."[22]

The leaders of the New York financial community nevertheless made the case for short selling, both in private and in public. "We are deathly afraid of Hoover," the New York broker Charles Chambers told Carter Glass. "The big men in the street do not know just what piece of economic quackery he is going to propose next. It is plain that he is a desperate man and is snatching at every little straw in order to attempt to stave off the bad beating that is surely coming to him in the next election." Chambers and his colleagues were particularly worried about a ban on short selling. "Hoover and the group of petty men who are running the government will stoop to anything, even to ruining an organized security market," Chambers despaired. "For centuries we have been striving for liquidity and now certain members of Congress propose to ruin the liquidity of securities by abolishing short selling. Senator, it would be a catastrophe." Thomas Lamont assured Hoover that the fall in the stock market was caused not by short sellers but by declining company earnings, and that banning short selling would only impede the recovery, because "bulls will not buy in a market where bears cannot sell, for today's bull wants to be able to change his foot and sell tomorrow." New York Stock Exchange president Richard Whitney defended short selling in speeches all over the country, some of which were broadcast live on the radio and printed as pamphlets for distribution. His 1931 speech before the Hartford Chamber of Commerce, entitled "Short Selling," was heard on sixty radio stations in over forty states and had a print run of more than 750,000 copies.[23]

22 J. George Frederick, "Short Selling Loses Caste," *North American Review* 234 (1932): 58; Louis Guenther, "Vicious Short Selling," *Financial World*, 22 Oct. 1930.

23 Charles W. Chambers to Carter Glass, 14 Dec. 1931, CG, box 301; Thomas W. Lamont to Herbert Hoover, 1 Apr. 1932, HHL, box 1049; Richard Whitney, "Short Selling" (16 Oct. 1931), HHL, box 160, folder 8; Richard Whitney to "All Members and Partners of Stock Exchange Firms," 4 Nov. 1931, HHL, box 159A, folder 12. Other examples of Whitney speeches defending short selling include "Speculation" (10 Oct. 1930), "Short Selling and Liquidation" (15 Dec.

The major exchanges also took small steps of their own to limit short selling, in the hope of fending off more serious legislative incursions. In 1931, the New York Stock Exchange asked its members not to accept orders for short sales except where customers were hedging against losses from securities they already owned. The following year the stock exchange prohibited members from lending customers' securities to other brokers (short sellers borrowed securities before selling them) without first obtaining the customers' written authorization. These measures were more cosmetic than substantive; the former carried no sanctions for violators, and the latter was easy to comply with. The New York lawyer W. R. Perkins shared what seemed to be the unanimous view of the local press that short selling would proceed unabated. The Chicago Board of Trade prohibited what the board called "harmful speculative short selling." This was likely just as cosmetic, as it was clear that the board of trade did not share the Hoover administration's view as to which kinds of transactions were harmful.[24] Despite such efforts, there was a real possibility in the years after the crash that the government would do something to curb short selling, certainly a greater possibility than at any time since the agrarian protests against commodity trading in the 1890s.

Another common regulatory proposal was a ban on margin trading. Stockbrokers and commodity brokers normally did not require their customers to pay the full price of whatever the brokers bought on their behalf. The customer merely had to deposit a "margin," or a percentage of the purchase price, and the broker would lend him the rest. If the customer's losses reached the margin, the broker would call upon the customer for more money, and if the customer did not deposit more, the broker would close out the customer's account. It

1931), and "The New York Stock Exchange" (27 Dec. 1932), all in HHL, box 160, folder 8.

24 A. S. Brown to Herbert Hoover, 25 Sept. 1931, HHL, box 159A, folder 8; New York Stock Exchange Circular, 18 Feb. 1932, HHL, box 159A, folder 10; W. R. Perkins to Herbert Hoover, 20 Feb. 1932, HHL, box 159A, folder 9; Chicago Board of Trade Circular, 26 Oct. 1932, HHL, box 159A, folder 5; Walter H. Newton to Arthur M. Hyde, 20 Oct. 1932, HHL, box 159A, folder 5; Chicago Board of Trade to Herbert Hoover, 2 Nov. 1931, HHL, box 159A, folder 4.

was widely understood that margin trading—trading with borrowed money—had caused prices to fall more steeply than they otherwise would have. When prices started to decline, investors had to sell some of their stocks to keep up their accounts in their other stocks, and this sell-off caused prices to decline even more, in a vicious circle. The brokers, in turn, often borrowed money from banks to cover their loans to customers, with the loans secured by the stock. When the value of this collateral dropped, banks would call in the loans, which likewise caused even more selling as brokers all scrambled for money at the same time. When the market fell by even a small amount, everyone had to sell simultaneously, which could turn a small drop into a big one. "The real major cause of the collapse," explained Michael Cahill, president of the Plaza Trust Company, "was not merely that securities were purchased at levels far beyond their sound investment values, . . . but it was this situation added to the fact that such purchases were made on borrowed capital."[25]

Many accordingly suggested that the real danger lay not in speculation but in speculation on margin. Arthur Capper, the Kansas senator, wanted to prohibit it outright. So did Adolf Berle, the Columbia law professor who advised Franklin Roosevelt on financial regulation during and after Roosevelt's 1932 presidential campaign. "Margin trading ought not to be permitted," Berle declared. "There is no real reason why credit should be involved in the stock market to the extent it is now." The problem was that "the free use of credit encourages the wild fluctuations." If speculators had to use their own money rather than borrowing it from their brokers, their losses might cause harm to themselves, but their losses would not set off a chain reaction of defaults and forced sales that harmed the broader public. "Gambling, as gambling, we shall never eradicate by any process of law," Berle concluded. It would be better instead, he advised, to "restrict the class of gamblers to a group which can afford to lose, and the total volume of gambling to a point where it will not involve the whole financial structure."[26]

25 Michael B. Cahill to Herbert Hoover, 3 May 1930, HHL, box 159, folder 6.
26 Arthur Capper to Herbert Hoover, 26 Jan. 1932, HHL, box 159A, folder 9; "Memorandum to the Committee on Stock Exchange Regulation" (24 Oct. 1933), AAB, box 22.

In the floor debates over the bills that would become the legislation of 1933 and 1934, several members of Congress urged the prohibition of margin trading. "Security speculation is practically the only gambling game which can be carried on on credit," argued Senator Robert Bulkley of Ohio. "You cannot go to a race track and make a bet on a horse race unless you have your money in your hand. There is no money desk in the betting ring where loans can be negotiated for betting purposes. And there ought not to be a money desk on the floor of the stock exchange." Margin trading, Bulkley declared, "is fundamentally wrong." Duncan Fletcher, who chaired the Senate Banking Committee, believed that "margin trading in this country has led to a great many abuses and to excessive speculation," because it allowed too many people to get in over their heads. "When a person is permitted to put up a few dollars on margin to buy stocks and take chances of winning or losing, he is tempted to do so," Fletcher worried. "Margin operation, in my judgment, is responsible for the ruin of thousands and thousands of people." In the House, Martin Smith of Washington State described margin trading as "evil," because it "acts as a snare or a trap, and a great many people buy more stocks than they can afford to buy, and when the call for additional margin comes their accounts are wiped out. Undoubtedly more money was lost by the American public because of marginal sales in the stock collapse of 1929 than on account of insufficiency of value in the securities when they were originally issued." This heartfelt statement moved Smith's colleagues to applause.[27]

Another proposal aimed at the same target was to ban banks from lending to brokers and speculators. The chain of credit from brokers to their customers had banks at its origin, so if the funds could be cut off at their source, speculators would be unable to buy stock with borrowed money. Behind the banks lay the Federal Reserve, which meant that the government was in effect the ultimate source of the loans. The Senate Banking Committee held hearings on the subject as early as 1928, when the market was still on the way up. "I do not object to a

27 *Congressional Record* 78 (1934): 8387, 8386, 8175; *Congressional Record* 77 (1933): 2941.

man throwing away his money," declared Earle Mayfield of Texas, "but what I object to is the Government lending about $3,000,000,000 to help him do it." A few months before the crash, William Henry King of Utah again proposed an investigation into the propriety of bank loans to brokers and speculators. The idea was revived after the crash. If his proposal had been acted upon promptly, King argued, it "would have prevented the debacle of 1929."[28]

There were also several proposals for a federal tax on securities transactions as a means of curbing speculation. The federal government already taxed stock transactions, as did New York, but these taxes were very small because they were intended to raise revenue rather than to deter trading. The new proposals were much more substantial. Representative Fiorello La Guardia of New York introduced a bill imposing a quarter of a percent tax on all securities sales and a 25 percent tax on short selling, the latter of which would have been tantamount to a prohibition. Herbert Claiborne Pell, the former congressman (and the father of Claiborne Pell, who would represent Rhode Island in the Senate for decades), repeatedly suggested a 1 percent tax on all sales of securities, to prevent speculative transactions without deterring genuine investment. "Such a tax would practically do away with all 'in and out' speculation as it would be too big a percentage for the gambler to face," Pell reasoned, but the tax would be small enough to "achieve this result without in any way interfering with legitimate purchase and sale." As Pell told his friend "Frank" Roosevelt, "a tax of one percent would so lessen the profits of those who have to rely on the maintenance of a quick market for their profits that the business would be wound up." Carter Glass favored a tax on sales of stock held by the seller for less than sixty days. "People do not ordinarily 'invest' their funds for an hour or day or week or month," Glass insisted. "Ninety per cent of such transactions constitute unadulterated gambling on the state of the market and the thing should be abated." Representative Jed Johnson of Oklahoma introduced legislation imposing a 1 percent tax

28 *Brokers' Loans: Hearings Before the Committee on Banking and Currency, United States Senate* (Washington, D.C.: Government Printing Office, 1928), 7; *New York Times*, 11 July 1929, 33; 25 Oct. 1929, 3; 15 May 1930, 21; *Congressional Record* 78 (1934): 1991.

on securities sales, or as Johnson referred to it on the House floor, a tax on "those white-collared parasites." Johnson explained that "I would go further if I had my way. I would make the tax so much that it would tax the damnable stock exchanges out of business."[29]

The most common and well-known laws governing stock transactions in the years before the crash were the state blue sky laws, so it is not surprising that after the crash, many suggested that Congress should enact a federal blue sky law. Some used the term "blue sky" in a general sense, to describe any laws that would govern the stock market. Adolf Berle, for example, discussed "the purpose of national blue sky regulation" without meaning that the federal government should actually copy what the states had done. But others hoped Congress would enact a law that would do exactly what the first generation of state blue sky laws had done back in the 1910s—set up a government body to evaluate the soundness of proposed stock issues and bar the unsound from ever being offered to the public. Representative Adolph Sabath introduced a federal blue sky bill that would have established a three-person commission to pass on the merits of all stock issues. The idea was supported by state blue sky officials, who were all too aware of their own impotence. Donald Pomeroy, who ran Minnesota's Securities Division and served as the president of the National Association of Securities Commissioners, thought that a federal blue sky agency would be "of invaluable assistance and benefit" to state regulators, because "the sale and distribution of securities generally is a national rather than a state problem." One former state blue sky official, James Mott, now represented Oregon in the House of Representatives. He thought the securities bills that eventually became law in 1933 and 1934 were "amateurish" because their drafters had no blue sky experience and had neglected to speak with anyone who did. "The State blue-sky laws of this country constitute the entire corpus juris of securities regulation in the United States," Mott declared. "The authors of this bill would have done well

29 *Pittsburgh Post-Gazette*, 8 Dec. 1931, 33; *Congressional Record* 78 (1934): 8097; Herbert Claiborne Pell, "A Cure for Speculation," *North American Review* 231 (1931): 313; Herbert Claiborne Pell to Franklin Roosevelt, 14 Apr. 1933, FDR, POF 34, box 1; Carter Glass to L. C. Soule, 1 Oct. 1931, CG, box 278; *Congressional Record* 78 (1934): 8102–3.

to consult some of them before trying to draft a Federal securities law." What was missing, Mott insisted, was a "securities commissioner with authority to make an investigation of every security proposed to be sold."[30]

But the state blue sky laws, especially the early ones that empowered government officials to judge the merits of stock offerings, also served as a negative model, a reminder of a regulatory approach that had proven unworkable. "Competition and the progress of invention make it inevitable that many enterprises will fail," explained the law professor William O. Douglas. "This is reason enough why the state should not pronounce investments sound or unsound." It was simply impossible to predict whether an investment would pay off. The Washington lawyer Huston Thompson, a former member of the Federal Trade Commission, recalled "some promotions started in the Southwest which looked perfectly ridiculous, as wildcat as they could be. Of course, they were advertised as great opportunities for investment and profit," so the FTC investigated to determine whether they were frauds. "In one of those wildcat schemes," Thompson continued, "they drilled wells and one of them brought in a 10,000-barrel well. Where would we have been if we had said, 'You cannot go ahead with that speculation'?" And when state officials had tried to separate the sound businesses from the unsound, their record had not been good. "I have worked with Blue Sky Commissions in the various states for some years and I have never found them anything but an annoyance," remarked the New York corporate lawyer Guido Pantaleoni. "I have never known them to stop a fraud." It was just too hard a job. As the lawyer William Breed concluded, "it is impossible for a body of men to determine how a business is going to come out." "Speculative risk . . . will be present in the future as it has been in the past," acknowledged Joseph Kennedy, the first chairman of the Securities and Exchange Commission, "for no body of men, no government, no nation, is sufficiently wise to define

30 "The Purpose of National Blue Sky Regulation," n.d., AAB, box 20; *New York Times*, 6 Feb. 1932, 25; Donald L. Pomeroy to A. A. Berle Jr., 28 Nov. 1932, AAB, box 20; *Congressional Record* 78 (1934): 8101; *Congressional Record* 77 (1933): 2947.

the perfect investment, or to guarantee it, or to eliminate the risks of speculation."[31]

Corporate officers and directors were especially criticized in the wake of the crash, for taking advantage of their inside knowledge to speculate at shareholders' expense. One such critic was the industrialist Alfred du Pont, who had sued his own brother over such matters during his days at the family chemical company. "How officers placed in positions of trust, as all the officers of corporations are, can betray those trusts by speculating on information which comes to them officially is beyond my understanding," du Pont despaired. For a cure, he favored "government control over the operation of stock exchanges to ... prohibit just this sort of thing." The ability of insiders to enrich themselves at the public's expense was the main topic of high-profile hearings in the Senate Banking Committee in 1933 and 1934, led by the committee's chief counsel, Ferdinand Pecora.[32]

The stock market crash and the Depression thus gave rise to a wide variety of proposals to curtail speculation. In the early 1930s, a well-informed observer might reasonably have expected Congress to prohibit short selling, to prohibit margin trading, to bar banks from lending to brokers and speculators, to impose a substantial tax on securities transactions, to ban insider trading, or perhaps even to enact a federal blue sky law modeled on the state laws of the preceding two decades. As it turned out, however, Congress did none of those things.

---

31 William O. Douglas and George E. Bates, "The Federal Securities Act of 1933," *Yale Law Journal* 43 (1933): 172; *Federal Securities Act: Hearing Before the Committee on Interstate and Foreign Commerce, House of Representatives* (Washington, D.C.: Government Printing Office, 1933), 58; Guido Pantaleoni to Adolf Berle, 9 May 1933, AAB, box 20; *Securities Act: Hearings Before the Committee on Banking and Currency, United States Senate* (Washington, D.C.: Government Printing Office, 1933), 177; *Address of Hon. Joseph P. Kennedy, Chairman of Securities and Exchange Commission, at National Press Club July 25, 1934* (Washington, D.C.: Government Printing Office, 1934), 4.

32 Alfred I. du Pont to Frederic C. Walcott, 10 June 1932, HHL, box 159A, folder 3; Michael Perino, *The Hellhound of Wall Street: How Ferdinand Pecora's Investigation of the Great Crash Forever Changed American Finance* (New York: Penguin Press, 2010); Ferdinand Pecora, *Wall Street Under Oath: The Story of Our Modern Money Changers* (New York: Simon & Schuster, 1939).

THE BEST OF DISINFECTANTS

"When Wall Street took that tail spin," Will Rogers cracked, "you had to stand in line to get a window to jump out of, and speculators were selling space for bodies in the East River." But his next line was no joke, especially not to the Hoover administration. "You know there is nothing that hollers as quick and as loud as a gambler," Rogers noted. "They even blame it on Hoover's fedora hat." The very next day, one of Hoover's advisors remarked that "when each individual is explaining to his wife how he lost the family funds or to partners the disappearance of the concern's assets, the blame, of course, must be placed on someone and, as Will Rogers said 'It might be on Hoover's fedora hat.' "[33]

The administration was in something of a bind. On one hand, Hoover viewed the boom-and-bust cycle as a natural phenomenon that defied human intervention. "These vast contagions of speculative emotion have hitherto throughout all history proved themselves un-controllable by any device that the economist, the business man, or the Government has been able to suggest," he told the Chamber of Commerce in 1930. Even the government's power to raise interest rates, he recalled, had "offered little real retardation to the speculative mania of the country." And a downturn was a particularly inopportune time to attack the stock market or to propose new restrictions on trading, because such moves might cause prices to fall even more. Even an in-vestigation of traders would be risky, as one member of the administra-tion pointed out. "If the principal bear raiders were put on the stand," he predicted, "they would attempt to show that stocks were much over valued at the present time, . . . which would greatly disturb business." This tendency to avoid major change was reinforced by the fact that the Republicans held majorities in both houses of Congress between 1929 and 1931 and still controlled the Senate between 1931 and 1933. As one of Hoover's supporters observed, "the Stock Exchange is one of the most powerful and far reaching institutions in the country, and twenty out of

33 James M. Smallwood and Steven K. Gragert, eds., *Will Rogers' Daily Telegrams* (1978) (Claremore, Okla.: Will Rogers Memorial Museums, 2008), 2:1929; Anonymous memorandum, 25 Oct. 1929, HHL, box 154, folder 14.

every twenty five of its members are republicans and contribute toward republican campaigns."[34]

On the other hand, *not* proposing new restrictions opened the administration up to considerable criticism. Roosevelt's strategy in the 1932 election "was to allege that I had made the depression and then done nothing about it," Hoover later complained—"that I was personally responsible for the stock market boom and the orgy of speculation." The Hoover administration had pursued none of the regulatory options that were on the table. Roosevelt took the opportunity to campaign on a vague promise to clean up Wall Street. "The money changers have fled from their high seats in the temple of our civilization," he declared in his inaugural address. "We may now restore that temple to the ancient truths. The measure of the restoration lies in the extent to which we apply social values more noble than mere monetary profit." Among the needed "safeguards against a return of the evils of the old order," Roosevelt announced, was "a strict supervision of all banking and credits and investments, so that there will be an end to speculation with other people's money."[35]

Roosevelt became president on March 4, 1933. By March 29, securities bills had been introduced in both houses of Congress, and the Securities Act of 1933 was enacted in late May, as part of the flurry of legislation in the first hundred days of Roosevelt's presidency. The act required a company issuing securities to file with the Federal Trade Commission a registration statement containing a great deal of information about the company's financial condition. (The FTC would be replaced in this role a year later by a new agency, the Securities and Exchange Commission.) Companies also had to disclose much of the same information to prospective purchasers. In broad outline, corporate insiders would be liable to purchasers of the stock for their losses if their disclosures included any material falsehoods or omitted any important facts.[36] The Securities

---

34 *Address of President Hoover at the Annual Dinner of the Chamber of Commerce of the United States* (Washington, D.C.: Government Printing Office, 1930), 3, 6; Anonymous memorandum, 2 Mar. 1932, HHL, box 159A, folder 10; Frank W. Blair to Robert D. Hatch, 23 Apr. 1932, HHL, box 159A, folder 3.

35 Hoover, *Memoirs*, 3:240; Roosevelt's inaugural address at http://www.presidency.ucsb.edu/ws/index.php?pid=14473.

36 48 Stat. 74 (1933).

Act did not impose any substantive limits on trading: it did not regulate short selling or margin trading, it did not prohibit corporate insiders from taking advantage of their positions, and it said nothing about what kinds of transactions would be permitted or forbidden. Nor did the Securities Act empower government officials to protect investors by reviewing the merits of a proposed offering. Instead, the act required only the disclosure of information before selling stock.

Why this reliance solely on disclosure? Disclosure had been a favored regulatory strategy of the progressive reformers earlier in the century. "Sunlight is said to be the best of disinfectants," Louis Brandeis had famously written in 1913. Indeed, Brandeis coined this metaphor while arguing that investment bankers should be forced to reveal to investors the commissions they had received for their services.[37] Progressive reformers, who had long looked across the Atlantic for inspiration, could cite the example of the British Companies Act, which required corporations issuing stock to publish a prospectus containing specified information.[38] The second wave of state blue sky laws, from the mid-1910s forward, had required many new companies to make various disclosures before selling stock. In the intervening years, others had applied this principle to corporate information more generally. The economist William Ripley contended in 1926 that shareholders even in established companies had a "right to adequate information" and that official corporate pamphlets fell woefully short of telling shareholders what they needed to know. During the 1932 presidential campaign, Ripley urged Herbert Hoover to make corporate disclosure part of his platform and warned that if Hoover did not, Roosevelt would.[39]

37 Louis D. Brandeis, "What Publicity Can Do," *Harper's Weekly*, 20 Dec. 1913, 10–12. This essay was later published as a chapter in Louis D. Brandeis, *Other People's Money and How the Bankers Use It* (New York: Frederick A. Stokes Co., 1914), 92–108.

38 On Progressive reformers' use of European models, see Daniel T. Rodgers, *Atlantic Crossings: Social Politics in a Progressive Age* (Cambridge, Mass.: Harvard University Press, 1998).

39 William Z. Ripley, "Stop, Look, Listen! The Shareholder's Right to Adequate Information," *Atlantic Monthly*, Sept. 1926; William Z. Ripley, *Wall Street and Main Street* (Boston: Little, Brown and Co., 1927), 156–207; William Z. Ripley to Herbert Hoover, 11 July 1932, HHL, box 159A, folder 3.

And Roosevelt did. In his acceptance address at the Democratic convention in July, Roosevelt sounded like Brandeis. He called for "the letting in of the light of day on issues of securities, foreign and domestic, which are offered for sale to the investing public." Such a measure, he declared, "would help to protect the savings of the country from the dishonesty of crooks and from the lack of honor of some men in high financial places. Publicity is the enemy of crookedness." The Democratic Party platform advocated "protection of the investing public by requiring to be filed with the government and carried in advertisements of all foreign and domestic stocks and bonds true information as to bonuses, commissions, principal invested, and interests of the sellers." As Joel Seligman has observed, Roosevelt took a Brandeisian approach to the stock market: in his speeches while campaigning and as president, Roosevelt often paraphrased Brandeis in calling for greater disclosure by sellers of securities.[40]

The primary intellectual influence on the 1933 act was the Harvard law professor Felix Frankfurter, a longtime Brandeis disciple and a frequent advisor to Roosevelt dating back to Roosevelt's days as governor of New York. Frankfurter was assisted in the actual drafting by his Harvard colleague James Landis and by two former students, Thomas Corcoran and Benjamin Cohen. At times they even received suggestions from Justice Brandeis himself. This was a group predisposed to favor disclosure as a regulatory tool. As Roosevelt's advisor Raymond Moley recalled, "there was a deep split in the early New Deal between the so-called Brandeis school—consisting of Frankfurter, Samuel Untermyer, James M. Landis, and Benjamin V. Cohen—and believers in national economic planning like Hugh Johnson, [Rexford] Tugwell, and [Henry] Wallace."[41] By putting the former faction in charge of

---

40 http://www.presidency.ucsb.edu/ws/?pid=75174; http://www.presidency.ucsb
    .edu/ws/index.php?pid=29595; Seligman, *Transformation*, 19–20, 41–42.

41 James M. Landis, "The Legislative History of the Securities Act of 1933," *George Washington Law Review* 28 (1959): 29; Donald A. Ritchie, *James M. Landis: Dean of the Regulators* (Cambridge, Mass.: Harvard University Press, 1980), 43–61; William Lasser, *Benjamin V. Cohen: Architect of the New Deal* (New Haven, Conn.: Yale University Press, 2002), 65–85; Bruce Allen Murphy, *The Brandeis/Frankfurter Connection: The Secret Political Activities of Two Supreme Court Justices* (New York: Oxford University Press, 1982), 132–38; Raymond Moley, *The First New Deal* (New York: Harcourt, Brace & World, 1966), 306.

drafting the Securities Act, Roosevelt effectively decided in favor of disclosure and against more substantial government involvement in the securities market.

Frankfurter's group deliberately shut other voices out of the drafting process, especially voices from the New York legal and financial community. As the New Yorker Adolf Berle explained to William Woodin, Roosevelt's first Treasury secretary, "the new draft has been made up by Felix Frankfurter, apparently without consulting any of the banking or accounting people here. Conceding that all of the banking community are villains (they are not), it still would be useful to have their experience." Berle acknowledged that "Felix is a brilliant man with excellent ideas, but some experience sometimes helps in these matters." (Berle was less complimentary when he complained to Roosevelt that Frankfurter "would like to do nothing unless he can have everything he wants.") Arthur Dean, one of the leaders of the New York corporate bar, was apoplectic about Frankfurter's utter lack of interest in the views of securities lawyers. "Last Spring I offered to sever myself for a period of months from the work in the office and place myself entirely at Felix Frankfurter's disposal in working on a draft of the Act," he sputtered to the banker Alexander Sachs. But Frankfurter "declined the offer and I have since learned that he seriously questions whether any one who is actively engaged in passing on security issues can have a sufficiently objective mind in drafting such legislation." ("Unfortunately, Dean seems to be incapable of being satisfied by any reasonable measures," James Landis explained to Sachs, who had left Lehman Brothers to work at the National Recovery Administration. "He represents one point of view; the Securities Act another."[42]) Drafted very quickly and in private by a small group of Harvard law graduates under the leadership of Felix Frankfurter, the Securities Act of 1933 embodied a philosophy of disclosure as a means to cure the stock market.

The purpose of disclosure was to protect the ordinary person, who had no expertise in financial matters and who would otherwise lack

42 Adolf Berle to William H. Woodin, 12 Apr. 1933, AAB, box 20; Adolf Berle to Franklin Roosevelt, 11 Jan. 1933, FDR, PPF 1306; Arthur H. Dean to Alexander Sachs, 16 Sept. 1933, AS, box 150; James Landis to Alexander Sachs, 5 Oct. 1933, JML-HLS, box 9, folder 7.

access to the information he needed to make an intelligent investment. "Today the need to protect the public against itself and against speculation in stocks is far more urgent than ever before, because the entire country has become ticker-minded," the broker Edwin Lefèvre argued. "In the old days the stock market was more like a battlefield where one professional or group of professionals fought against other professionals," but by the late 1920s, "the man or woman who wasn't trading in the stock market was a freak, a coward, a pauper or a great but unrecognized artist." With this greatly expanded participation in the market, argued Joseph Kennedy, "the average American stockholder obviously is a man of such small means that he needs governmental protection." With "every widow or doctor in Podunk or Oshkosh" buying stock, noted Jerome Frank, one of Kennedy's successors, "it is precisely that kind of poor sucker that the statute is designed to protect." But rather than protect investors by guiding their decisions, as the initial blue sky laws had tried to do, the Securities Act would protect investors by supplying them with enough knowledge to make their own decisions. "Government can't provide any substitute for investors' judgment," insisted William Douglas. "We can demand full disclosure of the facts, but we cannot provide sound business judgment, nor can we save a fool from his folly." Ordinary stockholders should "get the same kind of fair treatment they would get if they were big partners instead of little partners in industry."[43]

Mandating disclosure on the part of issuers was hardly an obvious response to the crash. For one thing, the crash could not plausibly be blamed on a lack of disclosure, because corporate insiders lost just as much as anyone. "The great losses suffered through securities purchased in the boom years have been due primarily to the effect of the world-wide depression, which has caused values and prices not alone of securities but of all commodities to fall precipitously," noted the

---

43 Edwin Lefèvre, "Blame the Broker," *Saturday Evening Post*, 9 Apr. 1932, 26; *Address of Hon. Joseph P. Kennedy, Chairman of Securities and Exchange Commission, at Meeting of the Boston Chamber of Commerce* (Washington, D.C.: Government Printing Office, 1934), 2; Jerome Frank to Emanuel Celler, 28 Aug. 1939, JNF, box 23, folder 90; Press conference, 22 Sept. 1937, 2–3, WOD, box 24, folder 3.

New York lawyer Eustace Seligman. "With comparatively few exceptions, the losses suffered by investors in securities have been due to the fact that the investors and the investment bankers, like everyone else in the country, mistakenly believed that the New Era was here to stay." Seligman thought disclosure was a good idea, and indeed, as early as 1925, he had favored requiring corporations to publish regular statements of their financial condition. But he had no illusions that a disclosure requirement would have saved anyone from losing much money.[44]

Moreover, it was not clear that the ordinary investors the Securities Act sought to protect would actually read the financial information that companies had to disclose, or that they would understand it if they did read it. "Investors by and large are woefully ignorant," lamented the investment banker E. G. Parsly. "While there are a few exceptions investors in the main depend on someone for advice and are for the most part incapable of forming any opinion of their own as to the merits of a security on the basis of cold facts submitted to them." What would investors make of the prospectus required by the Securities Act? It "will be beyond the comprehension of the vast majority," Parsly concluded, "and I am satisfied that a very large percent of investors will not even attempt to read such prospectuses. I know from experience that it is hard to get them to read a circular of even the briefest character." The investment banker Alexander Sachs was an early New Dealer—he ran the economic research division at the National Recovery Administration—but he was just as skeptical about the value of disclosure. The prospectus was bound to be "as elaborate as an insurance policy or a real estate lease," Sachs worried, "which have become so complicated that the average man signs them without reading."[45] If investors would not read a prospectus, or if they could not understand what they were reading, what good would disclosure do?

Bankers and corporate insiders had a very different concern—not that the Securities Act would be ineffective but that it would be *too* effective. They "are afraid," Russell Leffingwell of the Morgan bank told his old friend Franklin Roosevelt. "They are really afraid." The act imposed

44 Eustace Seligman, "Amend the Securities Act," *Atlantic Monthly*, March 1934.
45 E. G. Parsly to Baldwin B. Bane, 15 Sept. 1933, JML-LC, box 149; Alexander Sachs to James Landis, 6 Feb. 1934, AS, box 150.

liability for "an untrue statement of a material fact" or the omission "to state a material fact." But how could anyone be 100 percent sure that every single sentence in a long document was exactly correct? "Officers and directors of a company must rely upon engineers, accountants and attorneys for information," D. F. Kelly of Chicago protested. "No man who values his good name would be willing . . . to jeopardize his reputation and accept the responsibility for the errors of his professional advisers." And of the infinite number of facts that were not included in a registration statement or a prospectus, how could anyone predict which ones a court, years later, might deem "material"? The banker W. B. Neergaard worried that "if we sell to an investor, bonds, even of such quality of those of the American Telephone & Telegraph Company or first mortgage bonds of the Union Pacific Railway, and the bond market, as a whole, should decline ten points, that investor could bring an action against us to recover his loss marketwise on the grounds that we did not disclose to him all of the material facts." The law "would effectively cripple the financing of all corporations," complained the Merchants' Association of New York, "because of the excessively drastic responsibilities imposed . . . upon directors and professional advisors." The Boston investment banker Waldo Kendall concluded that "if the intent of the Act had been to put all reputable investment bankers out of business it could not have been better framed."[46]

Not long after the law's enactment, it was already a common view among the New York investment banking and legal community that the liability provisions in the Securities Act were deterring companies from issuing securities. The banker W. C. van Antwerp told Felix Frankfurter in June that the act had already driven one investment bank out of business. "In my own certain knowledge," thundered the lawyer Henry Stimson, "that Act today, by reason of the dangerous liability which it imposes upon those who must sign the registration statements for all

---

46 Russell Leffingwell to Franklin Roosevelt, 4 Jan. 1934, FDR, PPF 866; D. F. Kelly to Franklin Roosevelt, 11 May 1933, FDR, POF 242, box 1; Barrett Wendell Jr. to William Phillips, 3 June 1933, FDR, POF 242, box 1; W. B. Neergaard to Duncan U. Fletcher, 15 Dec. 1933, JML-LC, box 149; S. C. Mead to Franklin Roosevelt, 12 May 1933, FDR, POF 242, box 1; Waldo Kendall to James Landis, 18 Jan. 1934, JML-HLS, box 7, folder 12.

new flotations of capital bonds, is preventing not only the embarkation of new capital but the refunding of short term indebtedness to an extent which is most seriously preventing the revival of business." John W. Prentiss's firm "are both stock brokers and investment bankers, or perhaps I might more correctly say that we *were* investment bankers until the Securities Act," he chided Roosevelt. The problem, as Prentiss saw it, was "the penalty clauses in the Securities Act of 1933 which are preventing us all from attempting to do any business." The banker Otto Kahn likened the act to Prohibition, as an example of legislation with a laudable goal that nevertheless "overshoots the mark and is not guided by practical knowledge and by a sound and informed appraisal of the consequences." In early 1934, the Chamber of Commerce published a pamphlet insisting that the act had caused "a virtual cessation of high-grade and sizable corporate issues," because "the civil liabilities are so extreme." Even Daniel Roper, Roosevelt's own secretary of commerce, concluded that the act had brought financing to a standstill. The Washington businessman E. L. Rice thought the economic slump that would ensue would be enough "to bury the Democratic party at the next and succeeding elections for another twelve years."[47]

Among the Roosevelt administration and its supporters, such concerns were dismissed as nonsense. "A banker or corporation director expects his Rolls-Royce dealer to take back from him a limousine not of the kind or quality it was represented to be," needled the lawyer Bernard Flexner, "but for his own customer to ask him to take back sour securities is sheer cheek!" When Eustace Seligman informed Frankfurter that there was no reason to punish bankers for failing to

---

47 Arthur F. Dean, "Economic and Legal Aspects of the Federal Securities Act of 1933" (19 Sept. 1933), 2–3, AS, box 150; W. W. Dulles to Alexander Sachs, 12 Sept. 1933, JPL, box 68; Henry Bruère to Franklin Roosevelt, 1933, JPL, box 68; W. C. van Antwerp to Felix Frankfurter, 9 June 1933, FF, reel 84; Henry Stimson to Felix Frankfurter, 5 Dec. 1933, FF, reel 84; John W. Prentiss to Franklin Roosevelt, 15 Feb. 1934, FDR, POF 242, box 1 (emphasis added); Otto H. Kahn to Franklin Roosevelt, 12 May 1933, FDR, POF 242, box 1; *The Federal Securities Act of 1933* (Washington, D.C.: Chamber of Commerce, 1934), 5, 9, in JML-HLS, box 9, folder 2; Daniel Roper to Franklin Roosevelt, 2 Feb. 1934, FDR, POF 34, box 1; E. L. Rice to Franklin Roosevelt, 24 May 1933, FDR, POF 242, box 1.

disclose information, because "bankers of standing and of financial responsibility have in every case that I have had any connection with, gone to the extreme caution to insure that the circular was correct and complete," Frankfurter rather snidely retorted: "What a pity that you have not been connected with all security issues, for then there would be no need for any corrective legislation on the subject."[48]

The New Dealers interpreted the slowdown in securities issues as a deliberate effort by the bankers and securities lawyers to blackmail Congress into repealing the Securities Act. Frankfurter told Roosevelt that he had been told that the "leading bankers and the big law firms are trying to create a bankers' strike." As Roosevelt complained, "some of these so-called bankers would be perfectly willing to let ten million people starve if they could continue to sell securities for a nice commission." Frankfurter thought "the real culprit of the drive against the Securities Act are some of the leading law firms who made such a fat killing out of the abuses which brought the Securities Act into existence. They really want to do business at the old stand."[49]

A year later, the Securities Exchange Act of 1934 took more direct aim at the speculation commonly said to have caused the crash, but even the 1934 act imposed limits that were mild relative to the proposals that had circulated in the preceding years. Rather than prohibiting margin trading altogether, or even requiring customers to deposit a certain percentage of the purchase price with the broker, the act delegated to the Federal Reserve the power to prescribe rules to govern margin requirements. Rather than barring or limiting short selling, the act delegated to the new Securities and Exchange Commission the authority to prescribe rules to govern short selling. And rather than banning corporate insiders from trading on their superior information, the

48 Franklin Roosevelt to Felix Frankfurter, 2 Nov. 1934, FDR, PPF 866; Franklin Roosevelt to Otto H. Kahn, 22 May 1933, FDR, POF 242, box 1; Bernard Flexner, "The Fight on the Securities Act," *Atlantic Monthly*, Feb. 1934; Eustace Seligman to Felix Frankfurter, 24 Apr. 1933, and Felix Frankfurter to Eustace Seligman, 25 Apr. 1933, FF, reel 84.

49 Max Freedman, ed., *Roosevelt and Frankfurter: Their Correspondence 1928–1945* (Boston: Little, Brown and Co., 1967), 158; Franklin Roosevelt to Walter Nesbit, 11 Dec. 1933, FDR, PPF 1057; Felix Frankfurter to Louis Howe, 13 Sept. 1933, FF, reel 84.

act merely required insiders to disclose trades in their own companies' stock and prohibited insiders from profiting from purchases and sales (or sales and repurchases) within a six-month period.[50]

The Securities Exchange Act also prohibited various kinds of fraud, but fraud was already illegal and had no defenders, so the act's main target was speculation. The object, as Roosevelt put it, was to make stock prices "represent what is going on in the business and in our economic life rather than mere speculative or 'technical' conditions in the market." All the act would do, Sabath insisted, was "restrict the gambling activities of a small group of men who have no interest in the welfare of the Nation." Representative Carl Mapes of Michigan explained that the act made no "attempt to draw any distinction between speculation and investment, or to tell when speculation ends and investment begins. It aims only to prevent excessive speculation." Had such limits been in effect a decade earlier, declared John Cochran of Missouri, "the crash of 1929 would never have happened."[51]

Critics doubted that such modest measures would have much effect on the quantity of speculation. "It is quite ingenuous to suppose that people can be wholly freed from the speculative urge merely by giving a bureau in Washington regulatory power over stock exchanges," scoffed the *Saturday Evening Post*. Elmer Studley, whose congressional district included Wall Street, cautioned that speculation "is as old as the human race itself. To control it is quite beyond the powers of an act of Congress." Even Samuel Rayburn, the House sponsor of the act, admitted that regulating the stock exchanges was at most a partial solution to the problem of overspeculation. "I also recognize another man who is very largely responsible for the misfortunes of the country and the excessive stock speculation and debacle," Rayburn conceded. "That is Mr. American Citizen who wants to get something for nothing."[52] This kind

50 48 Stat. 881 (1934), sections 7, 10, 16.

51 *Stock Exchange Regulation: Letter from the President of the United States to the Chairman of the Committee on Banking and Currency* (Washington, D.C.: Government Printing Office, 1934), 5; *Congressional Record* 78 (1934): 7689, 7921, 7693.

52 "More Regulation," *Saturday Evening Post*, 17 Mar. 1934, 22; *Congressional Record* 78 (1934): 7942, 7862.

of criticism came from two camps—those who favored no additional regulation of the market (because such regulation would be pointless) and those who favored much stronger regulation (to curtail speculation in a significant way). From either perspective, the 1934 act was weak medicine indeed.

Much of the financial community had the opposite criticism—that the act would be too strong. "Had not conceived that any bill could be drawn so adverse to our business," a New York investment banker cabled Roosevelt. "In eliminating or punishing crookedness it hamstrings every honest banker corporation officer and director." "This is going from no control at all to over control," complained the president of a Virginia bank. "This bill places in the hands of a small commission dictatorial powers similar to those enjoyed by Mr. Hitler and Mr. Mussolini." Another banker predicted that the 1934 act "will bring on a panic, ruin the country, and be the death of the Democratic party."[53]

Brokers worried about the imminent margin requirements, which would make it harder to make loans on securities than on any other kind of asset. "The bill is an attempt to treat what is really a credit matter as a problem of morality," one broker argued. "In attempting to prohibit gambling, Congress is really tinkering with the credit problem of the country." By reducing the quantity of trading, warned the owners of an Ohio company, the margin requirements would widen the spread between prices bid and asked on the stock exchanges, which would only cause stock prices to fluctuate even more.[54]

Corporate officers and directors worried about the ban on profiting from purchases and sales of their own company's stock within a six-month period. "It has always been regarded as important that those running a company have a large financial interest at stake," declared the banker and director Waddill Catchings. "How can a man afford to buy stock in a company if he carries the risk of loss for six months but must

---

53 John M. Hancock to Franklin Roosevelt, 1 Feb. 1934, AS, box 150; L. M. von Schilling to Carter Glass, 26 Feb. 1934, CG, box 316; Henry A. Miller to Carter Glass, 28 Feb. 1934, CG, box 316.

54 Frazier Jelke & Co., "Morning Stock Letter" (22 Mar. 1934), FDR, POF 34, box 1; Robert Patterson Jr. and M. M. Harrod to Carter Glass, 27 Feb. 1934, CG, box 316.

pay any gain to the Corporation?" Catchings predicted that "men of affairs will be reluctant to act as directors." His concern was shared by the vice president of a cement company, who feared that "responsible and able corporate directors and executives throughout the country will feel constrained to tender their resignations."[55]

The New York Stock Exchange complained about the regular reports that listed corporations would have to file, a burden the exchange considered so onerous that the government "might dominate and actually control the management of each listed corporation." And many worried that the 1934 act would discourage so much capital from entering the market that the value of all stocks would plummet. "Is it fair to the people who own securities?" asked one of Carter Glass's correspondents. "It may be popular at the minute to punish Wall Street, but I am wondering how popular this bill will be with investors all over the country, when they see the marketability and prices of their securities perhaps seriously affected."[56]

In practice, the 1934 act's bite would depend on how much of a margin the Federal Reserve required and on the precise nature of the short-selling regulations that would be promulgated by the Securities and Exchange Commission. The Federal Reserve initially required a minimum margin of only 25 percent—that is, brokers could still lend their customers 75 percent of the value of what the customers were buying. The margin requirement fluctuated thereafter, to 55 percent in 1936, then back down to 40 percent in 1937. Since World War II it has been at 50 percent or higher, and it has stayed right at 50 percent since 1974.[57] The purpose of giving the Federal Reserve the authority to set a margin requirement was to reduce the volatility of stock prices, which was widely thought to be a product of speculative trading on credit. In fact, however, the effect of the margin requirement has been

55 Waddill Catchings to Marvin H. McIntyre, 23 Apr. 1934, FDR, POF 34, box 2; Dwight Morgan to Carter Glass, 5 Mar. 1934, CG, box 316.
56 Richard Whitney to the Presidents of All Listed Corporations, 14 Feb. 1934, AAB, box 22; Frank McNulty Ransom to Carter Glass, 29 Mar. 1934, CG, box 316.
57 Susan B. Carter et al., eds., *Historical Statistics of the United States* (Cambridge University Press Online Edition, 2006), table Cj863.

studied extensively over the years by economists, who have been nearly unanimous in concluding that the margin requirement has had little or no effect on the volatility of stock prices.[58] Even without a margin requirement, brokers may well be careful about lending their money to customers engaging in risky purchases. And of course borrowing from a broker is not the only way to speculate. The margin requirements authorized by the 1934 act thus appear not to have done much to curtail speculation.

The same is true of the short-selling regulations authorized by the 1934 act. The Securities and Exchange Commission did not regulate short selling until 1938, and even then, all it did was promulgate the "uptick rule," which prohibited short sales only at prices lower than the last sale price.[59] The consensus among economists is that the uptick rule imposed a cost on traders without producing any corresponding benefit: it made short selling slightly more difficult, but it had no effect whatsoever on the speed with which prices declined in a downturn.[60] For this reason, the SEC repealed the uptick rule in 2007.

58 Thomas Gale Moore, "Stock Market Margin Requirements," *Journal of Political Economy* 74 (1966): 158–67; Michael A. Goldberg, "The Relevance of Margin Regulations," *Journal of Money, Credit and Banking* 17 (1985): 521–27; Michael L. Hartzmark, "The Effects of Changing Margin Levels on Futures Market Activity, the Composition of Traders in the Market, and Price Performance," *Journal of Business* 59 (1986): S147–S180; David A. Hsieh and Merton H. Miller, "Margin Regulation and Stock Market Volatility," *Journal of Finance* 45 (1990): 3–29; Paul J. Seguin and Gregg A. Jarrell, "The Irrelevance of Margin: Evidence from the Crash of '87," *Journal of Finance* 48 (1993): 1457–73; Christian E. Weller, "Policy on the Margin: Evaluating the Impact of Margin Debt Requirements on Stock Valuations," *Journal of Economics and Finance* 26 (2002): 1–15.

59 Jonathan R. Macey et al., "Restrictions on Short Sales: An Analysis of the Uptick Rule and Its Role in View of the October 1987 Stock Market Crash," *Cornell Law Review* 74 (1989): 799–835.

60 Lynn Bai, "The Uptick Rule of Short Sale Regulation: Can It Alleviate Downward Price Pressure From Negative Earnings Shocks?," *Rutgers Business Law Journal* 5 (2008): 1–63; Karl B. Diether et al., "It's SHO Time! Short-Sale Price Tests and Market Quality," *Journal of Finance* 64 (2009): 37–73; Gordon J. Alexander and Mark A. Peterson, "Short Selling on the New York Stock Exchange and the Effects of the Uptick Rule," *Journal of Financial Intermediation* 8 (1999): 90–116.

The New Deal securities acts thus imposed only relatively mild restrictions on speculation, certainly much milder than might have been expected given the severity of the Depression and the extent to which speculation was considered responsible for it.

CAPITALISTIC REFORMERS

Part of the reason for this mildness was of course the countervailing pressure from the New York financial community, a powerful lobby with a strong and focused interest in fending off regulation.[61] But this is hardly a complete explanation. The big New York banks were unable to prevent Congress from erecting a wall between investment banks and commercial banks. The banks and the stock exchange were unable to exert much influence on the disclosure requirements of the Securities Act of 1933, which they opposed just as strongly. And while they succeeded somewhat in weakening the initial draft of the Securities Exchange Act of 1934, they could not stop that legislation either. There was considerable sentiment in Congress to strike hard at Wall Street. If the New Dealers had wanted to impose stricter limits on speculation, they probably could have.

But they did not want to. The primary reason for the moderation of the New Deal securities acts lies in the backgrounds and interests of the New Dealers themselves. They were, by and large, urban intellectuals who accepted the existence of big financial institutions as necessary. They had no desire to change the structure of the nation's financial system in any significant way. They recognized that they differed in this regard from the earlier generation of Progressive reformers, epitomized for the New Dealers by the octogenarian Louis Brandeis, who was still active on the Supreme Court. Brandeis "wants drastic taxation of big business units, accompanied by leaving small business . . . strictly alone," Berle informed Roosevelt. "His view, if ever stated, would command wide popular support." But Berle made clear that he disagreed. "As long as people want Ford

---

61 Ron Chernow, *The House of Morgan: An American Banking Dynasty and the Rise of Modern Finance* (New York: Simon & Schuster, 1990), 379–81.

cars," he told Roosevelt, "they are likely to have Ford factories and finance to match."[62]

From the New Dealers' perspective, the goal of regulating the securities markets was not to transform them but to preserve them, by warding off more serious changes. The New Deal took place while European countries were turning to communism and fascism. Much of the motivation for the securities acts, as with the rest of the New Deal, was to prevent such threats to capitalism from taking root in the United States. The 1934 act "is conceived in a spirit of the truest conservatism," declared the House report that brought it to the floor of Congress. "This bill seeks to save, not destroy, stock markets and business, by making necessary changes in time." As one investment bank approvingly observed, the New Dealers "who drafted the bill in its original form are not Bolsheviks or Communists, but Capitalistic Reformers." Or as Berle explained, the SEC "is in existence primarily to preserve the capitalist form."[63]

This was a major theme in the correspondence of the veteran New Dealer Jerome Frank, who chaired the SEC from 1939 to 1941 after serving in the Agricultural Adjustment Administration and the Reconstruction Finance Corporation. "Unfairness certainly arouses the ire of investors," he declared. "If they are seriously mulcted, they will grow impatient with a government that allows such things to happen. Such an attitude will pave the way for Fascism—and a Fascism which will lead to a deadly attack on the very investment bankers and security traders who are today loudest in their protests against regulation." As he explained on another occasion, "loss of public confidence in the integrity of our securities markets might be fatal to the existence of such markets." For this reason, he proudly informed the *New York Times* reporter Arthur Krock, Frank considered the SEC "a conservative institution,

62 Adolf Berle to Franklin Roosevelt, 23 Apr. 1934, FDR, PPF 1306. See also Jerome Frank to Morris Ernst, 30 Sept. 1939, JNF, box 21, folder 15; Jerome Frank to Randolph Paul, 24 Sept. 1938, JNF, box 36, folder 554.

63 Ira Katznelson, *Fear Itself: The New Deal and the Origins of Our Time* (New York: W. W. Norton, 2013); H.R. Rep. No. 1383, 73rd Cong., 2nd Sess., 3 (1934); Grant & Co., "Weekly Investment Letter," 1934, FDR, POF 34, box 2; Adolf Berle to Jerome Frank, 8 Feb. 1939, JNF, box 22, folder 41.

striving in its own legitimate field, patiently, sensibly, but persistently, to assist in the work of conserving, by improving, our profit system."[64]

Reinforcing this mindset was the fact that many of the New Dealers came from the same social circles as the financiers and lawyers they sought to regulate. At the top, Franklin Roosevelt was born into a wealthy family and attended Groton and Harvard, just like Richard Whitney, the president of the New York Stock Exchange. (Roosevelt was a few years older.) In 1934, in the midst of the controversy over the new SEC, Whitney and Roosevelt attended the same sailing race. When Whitney wanted to speak to Roosevelt, he simply called on the telephone. Roosevelt maintained many other friendships with prominent bankers and stockbrokers. Down in the trenches, many of the lawyers who drafted the legislation and staffed the SEC had gone to the same law schools and worked at the same law firms as the Wall Street lawyers they were regulating. Thomas Corcoran graduated from Harvard Law School, clerked for Oliver Wendell Holmes on the Supreme Court, and spent five years as a securities lawyer in New York before joining the Roosevelt administration. Benjamin Cohen, also a Harvard graduate and a New York lawyer, had been a successful stock speculator before he lost it all in the crash. William Douglas taught corporate law at Yale, while Jerome Frank was a corporate reorganization lawyer in New York. Daniel Ernst has discovered that the first twenty-four lawyers hired at the SEC included twelve with Harvard law degrees and four others from Columbia or Yale, that the agency's first three general counsels were all Harvard graduates, and that several early SEC lawyers had worked at leading securities law firms in New York. As Milton Freeman, one of these early lawyers, recalled, "the general counsel's office soon became the roosting place of the Class of 1925 of Harvard Law School." In 1932, when Hoover was still president, James Landis—then a young Harvard professor—had even been paid by the venerable New York law firm of Carter, Ledyard & Milburn to opine that Congress lacked the constitutional authority to regulate short selling, an opinion the firm happily transmitted to its client, the New York

---

64 Attachment to Jerome Frank to William O. Douglas, 13 Oct. 1938, WOD, box 25, folder 166; Jerome Frank to Cyrus S. Eaton, 29 Apr. 1938, JNF, box 27, folder 247; Jerome Frank to Arthur Krock, 10 June 1939, JNF, box 31, folder 384.

Stock Exchange.[65] These regulators were not anti–Wall Street; they were Wall Streeters themselves, the same sorts of people as the ones they were regulating. Things might have been very different if the new president taking office in 1933 had been from a different part of the country and had staffed the executive branch with people from a different background.

An additional factor tending toward mildness in regulation was that the New Dealers all had strong personal and ideological motives to support Roosevelt's re-election. They knew that a stronger economy would help Roosevelt and that overregulation would weaken the economy. "Since we are all diligently trying to help the President in his program of recovery," SEC Commissioner John W. Hanes remarked, "the machinery must be well oiled in order to bring forward a continuous flow of private capital to the market." William Douglas declared that "it is highly imperative that the jam now obstructing the flow of private savings to industry for capital investments should be broken."[66] Preserving the mechanisms of finance was not just good for the country; it would be good for the New Deal and its administrators too.

Up to a point, regulation might have facilitated the flow of capital, if it made investors more confident about stepping into the market after the disaster of the previous few years. But the New Dealers' private correspondence makes clear that they thought they were past that point. They understood that there was a tradeoff between regulation and market activity—that placing new burdens on sellers of securities meant that fewer securities were likely to be sold. Jerome Frank declared

65 Richard Whitney to Franklin Roosevelt, 10 Oct. 1934, FDR, PPF 1275; Marvin H. McIntyre to Franklin Roosevelt, 7 Feb. 1934, FDR, PPF 1275; Richard Whitney to FDR, 8 Feb. 1934, FDR, PPF 1275; James L. Houghteling to Franklin Roosevelt, 19 Apr. 1934, FDR, POF 242, box 1; Henry McVickar to Franklin Roosevelt, 27 Feb. 1934, FDR, POF 34, box 1; Daniel R. Ernst, "Lawyers, Bureaucratic Autonomy, and Securities Regulation During the New Deal" (unpublished paper, 2009), 7; Katie Louchheim, ed., *The Making of the New Deal: The Insiders Speak* (Cambridge, Mass.: Harvard University Press, 1983), 141; James Landis to William Harding Jackson, 22 Feb. 1932, Jackson to Landis, 25 Feb. 1932, and Jackson to Landis, 14 Apr. 1932, all in JML-LC, box 6.
66 John W. Hanes to Jerome Frank, 15 Apr. 1938, JNF, box 28, folder 290; William O. Douglas to Henry A. Wallace, 11 Apr. 1936, WOD, box 24, folder 1.

that the government's goals should be "(a) to protect investors, and also, (b) always to avoid substantial impediments to expansion of capital," but he acknowledged that "those two objectives frequently cannot be reconciled." The New Dealers were willing to sacrifice a measure of economic activity to protect investors. "Speculative trading must be very greatly curtailed," Franklin Roosevelt remarked to Henry Morgenthau in early 1934. "That means, inevitably, a much smaller volume of trading on the stock exchanges." Not long after, at a question-and-answer session at the Economic Club of Chicago, James Landis likewise conceded that it was "inevitable that in the case of some stocks the spread between bid and asked prices will be somewhat increased due to lessened volume."[67]

Roosevelt and Landis were right: trading volume did decline as a result of the securities acts. As the SEC staffer (and future chairman) Ganson Purcell recognized in 1938, "volume has been considerably reduced in recent years, and other elements of what has traditionally been known as liquidity are presently absent from our market." But Purcell thought this reduction in volume a worthwhile price to pay "for the elimination of undesirable manipulative activity" and "restriction on the irresponsible in and out speculation." Frank conceded that "there can be no doubt that prior to the 1929 crash we had a thicker market," but he too preferred a thinner market if it meant avoiding a return to the practices of the 1920s. "If those practices are sufficiently unfair to investors," Frank warned, "they will revolt not only against investing, but against the economic and political system which permits them to be injured."[68]

Opposition from brokers waned over time. "I think I am in pretty close touch with the brokerage and investment banking community

---

67 Jerome Frank to "the Commission," 11 June 1938, JNF, box 22, folder 62; Henry Morgenthau Jr. to Franklin Roosevelt, 22 Mar. 1934, FDR, POF 34, box 1; James Landis, untitled document with answers to questions from the audience after a speech at the Economic Club of Chicago, 5 June 1934, JML-HLS, box 6, folder 2.

68 James C. Dolley, "The Effect of Government Regulation on the Stock-Trading Volume of the New York Stock Exchange," *American Economic Review* 28 (1938): 8–26; Ganson Purcell to Jerome Frank, 18 Nov. 1938, JNF, box 37, folder 580; Jerome Frank to Elisha M. Friedman, n.d., JNF, box 27, folder 233.

in Boston," the broker Lester Watson recalled as early as 1935, "and I am not stretching it a bit when I say that we were very fearful when the Securities & Exchange Act became a law that its administration would definitely and severely interfere with if not indeed cripple our business. Of course, the actual experience has been all the other way." After a meeting of the board of governors of the Boston Association of Stock Exchange Firms, Watson told SEC chairman Joseph Kennedy that "it was their unanimous opinion that you and your Commission are doing one hell of a good job and they wanted me to pass that word along to you." Opposition from the New York brokers declined sharply after 1938, when Richard Whitney, the former president of the New York Stock Exchange, was convicted of embezzlement. The Whitney scandal prompted something of a generational turnover at the stock exchange. William McChesney Martin, the exchange's new president, was only thirty-one years old, and he was far more cooperative with the government than Whitney and his colleagues had been. "The New York Stock Exchange, under the domination of a backward-looking management, continued to oppose" the New Deal legislation, William Douglas recalled in 1938. "That former management was finally discredited by the Whitney episode. Now there is a new management in the Exchange which accepts the philosophy of the legislation; which understands that it is better business to work with established law than against it." Jerome Frank paid Martin the ultimate compliment; he said that Martin "represents a sort of New Deal in the Exchange."[69]

The leading New York investment bankers, who had vociferously protested against the requirements imposed by the 1933 act, turned out to be unintended beneficiaries of those requirements. By making the sale of stock more complicated, the act gave an advantage to the more prestigious New York banks over their smaller out-of-town competitors. The detailed procedures required by the act suppressed competition

69 Lester Watson to Joseph P. Kennedy, 20 Sept. 1935, JPK, box 83; Lester Watson to Joseph P. Kennedy, 7 Feb. 1935, JPK, box 83; Vincent P. Carosso, *Investment Banking in America: A History* (Cambridge, Mass.: Harvard University Press, 1970), 380–81; William O. Douglas to Stephen A. Early, 31 Oct. 1938, FDR, POF 1060, box 2; Jerome Frank to Frank Murphy, 15 Mar. 1939, JNF, box 34, folder 508.

among investment banks, which likewise benefitted the established banks.[70] In 1933, the leading investment bankers had gone on strike to fight the Securities Act (at least that's how it looked from inside the Roosevelt administration), but within a few years that opposition had evaporated.

The New York securities lawyers, who had led the fight against the 1933 and 1934 acts, also quickly adapted to the new laws. After all, these were rules that issuers and investment banks could scarcely follow without the paid assistance of securities lawyers at each step of the way. Arthur Dean, who in 1933 had fumed about being shut out of the drafting process, concluded by 1937 that he was "in full sympathy with the underlying purposes of both the Securities Act of 1933 and the Securities Exchange Act of 1934 and with the administrative problems facing the Commission." After three years of practicing under the two laws, Dean had come to believe that "the financial community, purely from a selfish standpoint, cannot afford to be without them."[71] The new regulatory requirements had become the bread and butter of the New York corporate bar.[72]

SPECULATING BANKS

For all the discussion in the early 1930s about prohibiting various speculative transactions, the most significant limit on speculation to arise from the crash of 1929–33 concerned not types of *speculation* but types of *speculators*. In four scattered sections of the Banking Act of 1933 that have been known ever since as the Glass-Steagall Act, Congress prohibited deposit-taking banks from selling or underwriting securities.[73] For the rest of the twentieth century, commercial banks (which take deposits and make loans) would be separate enterprises from investment

---

70 Paul G. Mahoney, "The Political Economy of the Securities Act of 1933," *Journal of Legal Studies* 30 (2001): 1–31.

71 Arthur H. Dean, "The Lawyer's Problems in the Registration of Securities," *Law & Contemporary Problems* 4 (1937): 155.

72 Thomas McCraw makes a similar point about accountants in *Prophets of Regulation* (Cambridge, Mass.: Harvard University Press, 1984), 188–92.

73 48 Stat. 162, §§ 16, 20, 21, 32 (1933).

banks (which assist firms in selling securities to investors). This separation was bitterly opposed by many bankers at the time.

The economy has changed so much since 1933 that to understand the rationale behind the Glass-Steagall Act, one has to reconstruct the world of thought in which it was embedded. Why did people in the early 1930s blame the Depression on what seems like a technical issue of banking regulation? And why did they think that separating commercial banks from investment banks was a likely way of preventing such a disaster from happening again?

One of the most visible and troubling features of the Depression was the unprecedentedly large number of bank failures. More than nine thousand banks went under between 1930 and 1933. By the end of 1933, nearly half of the banks that had existed in 1929 were gone.[74] The human cost of a bank failure was far greater than it would be today. The government did not insure bank deposits, so when a bank failed, the depositors lost all they had.

A bank could fail for any number of reasons. Too many borrowers might not be able to repay their loans, especially during a depression. Too many depositors might try to take their money out of the bank at once, again especially during a depression, when rumors that a bank was teetering toward insolvency could be enough to cause a run on the bank. These were the normal hazards of commercial banking. But some of the bank failures of 1929–33 were attributable to a different cause. In some cases, the bank had made speculative investments with the depositors' money, investments that went sour during the stock market crash.

The ability of banks to speculate in this way was a product of a slow evolution in the banking business over the previous thirty years. The major urban banks began establishing or acquiring securities affiliates in the first two decades of the twentieth century. These affiliates grew steadily larger. In 1916, for example, the National City Company—the securities affiliate of the National City Bank of New York—purchased a

74 H. Parker Willis and John M. Chapman, *The Banking Situation: American Post-War Problems and Developments* (New York: Columbia University Press, 1934), 3–20; Elmus Wicker, *The Banking Panics of the Great Depression* (New York: Cambridge University Press, 1996), xv; Ben S. Bernanke, *Essays on the Great Depression* (Princeton, N.J.: Princeton University Press, 2000), 44.

well-established investment bank, N. W. Halsey and Company, which had placed more than $100 million in securities the previous year. All of N. W. Halsey's two hundred employees except the president and vice president became employees of the National City Company, which instantly became one of the largest investment banks in the country. Other banks followed suit. Throughout the 1920s, the securities affiliates of major commercial banks gradually took over much of the underwriting business from private investment banks. Income from securities began to rival interest on loans as a source of profits for commercial banks.[75]

Well before the crash, some expressed concern about these securities affiliates, because they allowed banks to take risks with their depositors' money. The Annual Report of the Comptroller of the Currency was normally a mild document, but in 1920, Comptroller John Skelton Williams took the opportunity to excoriate the affiliates as "instruments of speculation" that were endangering the soundness of the banks under his supervision. "A national bank lends not only its own capital but the money of its depositors, and in doing this is not expected to tie up its funds in long-time and unliquid loans in doubtful ventures," Williams argued. "The operations and practices of these 'securities companies' as now conducted are often directly opposed to the elementary principles of sound banking." Williams urged Congress to bar commercial banks from underwriting new issues of securities and from making speculative investments. But the only relevant legislation in the 1920s, the McFadden Act of 1927, strengthened the ability of commercial banks to enter the securities market.[76] When stock prices were on the way up, there was little sentiment for keeping banks out of a line of business that was growing ever more profitable.

The bank failures that followed the stock market crash brought the issue into the spotlight. "Bankers should be forbidden by statute to speculate, directly or indirectly, with the money of depositors," urged William Deming, who had recently stepped down as president of the

75 W. Nelson Peach, *The Security Affiliates of National Banks* (Baltimore: Johns Hopkins Press, 1941).

76 *Annual Report of the Comptroller of the Currency* (Washington, D.C.: Government Printing Office, 1921), 1:55–57; 44 Stat. 1224 (1927).

Civil Service Commission. The Columbia economist Henry Parker Willis, who had been an advisor to the congressional committee that created the Federal Reserve System and then the first secretary of the Federal Reserve Board, emphasized the same point in the popular press. "The one change which is most to be deplored in our entire banking system of recent years has been the introduction of 'department-store banking,' or multiple-function banking, in lieu of the older plan of sharp division between financial types," Willis argued. Safe commercial banks had "become stock market banks," a fact Willis believed was "primarily responsible for the unliquid conditions which have come to exist in many banks and which today constitute the greatest obstacle perhaps to the restoration of financial soundness."[77]

Of all the people newly interested in keeping banks out of the securities business, the most important was the Virginia senator Carter Glass. Although Glass had never been a banker himself, he probably knew more about banking than anyone else in Congress. Glass had been the chair of the House Banking Committee in 1913, when Congress passed the Federal Reserve Act. He had been secretary of the Treasury under Woodrow Wilson. As a senator from 1920 until his death in 1946, Glass took a special interest in banking issues. In 1931, he chaired a subcommittee charged with surveying the national banking system, and from 1931 to 1933, he sponsored legislation to separate commercial banks from investment banks. Although his name today, if it is remembered at all, is virtually always paired with that of the Alabama representative Henry Bascom Steagall, who was chair of the House Banking Committee all through the 1930s and early 1940s, Steagall was primarily interested in deposit insurance, which would become another important feature of the Banking Act of 1933. The divorce of commercial banking and investment banking was Glass's project, not Steagall's. In the contemporary

---

77 William C. Deming to Herbert Hoover, 19 June 1931, HHL, box 154, folder 15; H. Parker Willis, "Reforms Due in Investment Banking—and in Bank Relations to Affiliates," *The Annalist*, 17 Jan. 1930, 44; H. Parker Willis, "Who Caused the Panic of 1929?," *North American Review* 229 (1930): 179. Willis made the same argument in academic journals, e.g., H. Parker Willis, "The Banking Act of 1933—An Appraisal," *American Economic Review* 24 (1934): 108–9.

press, congressional efforts to accomplish that goal were always referred to as "the Glass bill."

Glass's 1931 subcommittee produced a lengthy report on the banking system. One of its conclusions was that the securities affiliates had made banks riskier enterprises than before. "There can be no objection to the stockholders of a bank engaging in any other business they prefer with their own funds," the report observed. "However, if such activities tend to affect directly the position and soundness of the bank itself, they become of prime importance in the regulation of banking." In early 1932, Glass produced another report recommending that banks be separated from their securities affiliates as much as possible. Glass deplored "the dangerous use of the resources of bank depositors for the purpose of making speculative profits."[78] At Glass's urging, the Democratic Party platform of 1932 included a declaration of support for "the severance of affiliated securities companies from, and the divorce of the investment banking business from, commercial banks."

The hearings conducted by Glass's subcommittee elicited widespread concern about the dangers of speculating banks. William Randolph Hearst published an editorial in his newspapers supporting the separation of commercial banking from investment banking. "You know that the crash and subsequent depression were very largely caused by the overcapitalization and speculation encouraged by many important banks and their affiliates," Hearst told his readers. "Perhaps you do not know that the high financiers do not want their highway robbery interfered with. So they went to Congress to kill the Glass bill." The Democratic lawyer Samuel Untermyer, who had been counsel to the House Banking Committee during the "Money Trust" investigation of 1912, declared that "nothing could more forcibly demonstrate the extent to which the country is being ruled by financial interests than the long years of toleration of this vicious partnership between the banks and these speculative affiliates without a word of warning

---

78 *Operation of the National and Federal Reserve Banking Systems: Hearings Before a Subcommittee of the Committee on Banking and Currency, United States Senate, Seventy-First Congress, Third Session, Pursuant to S. Res. 71* (Washington, D.C.: Government Printing Office, 1931), 1063; S. Rep. No. 584, 72nd Cong., 1st Sess. (1932), 9–10.

or protest from the government authorities." Glass received letters of support from all over the country cheering on his efforts "to protect the savings of millions of people," as one Boston man put it, from the "speculative tendencies" of securities affiliates.[79]

Glass's correspondents, like the witnesses at his hearings, provided numerous stories of banks that had been undone by speculation. Robert Carson, the former president of the Iowa Chamber of Commerce, reported that all four banks in Iowa City had failed, one because it had made heavy investments in South American bonds that were now worthless. Depositors had received only 10 percent of what had once been their money. From Los Angeles, the lawyer Ralph Lindstrom related how one defunct local bank, the United States National Bank, had joined in "the drunken orgy of our recently closed speculative era." Thousands of depositors in New York's National City Bank were ruined, explained a local insurance broker, because of the bank's investments in the new aircraft industry. "If you will look up how many bank failures there have been," suggested a Boston broker, "you will find, I believe, that eight out of ten are the ones that have been putting out Investment Trusts and securities, which have gone about as bad as anything could."[80]

The problem, as these critics saw it, was that bankers had become speculators—with their depositors' money. A Chicago engineer named Edgar Rossiter recalled that "when the stock gambling started late in 1928 it was impossible to obtain a loan in Chicago." Rossiter went from bank to bank offering $125,000 in securities as collateral for a loan of $16,500. At each bank the loan officer refused to make a loan but offered to buy the securities instead. "At last one of the bankers said— why should we loan you $16,500 at six per cent when we are getting

---

79 *Washington Herald*, 18 Jan. 1933, CG, box 305; "Untermyer on the Glass Bill," *Bankers' Magazine* 124 (1932): 510; Richard Feakes to David I. Walsh, 5 Jan. 1932, CG, box 284; see also Raymond E. Herman to Carter Glass, 13 Feb. 1932, CG, box 293; Carter Glass to Garland A. Tunstill, 20 Jan. 1932, CG, box 285.

80 Robert N. Carson to Carter Glass, 10 May 1932, CG, box 296; Ralph G. Lindstrom to Carter Glass, 7 Mar. 1933, CG, box 308; Samuel Berman to Carter Glass, 13 May 1932, CG, box 296; L. R. Packard to Carter Glass, 20 May 1932, CG, box 297.

from 15 to 20 percent on the stock exchange in New York?" Frederick Wells spent thirty years as the director of a Minneapolis bank and had come to realize that "bank officials frequently feel a greater obligation to stockholders than to depositors, and that many of the unfortunate conditions which have developed are the result of attempts to increase earnings at the expense of conservative operation."[81]

On this view, the solution was to force bankers to be conservative with their depositors' funds by restricting deposit-taking banks to the commercial banking business. "It seems to me that the country has a right to expect of its Bankers high devotion to conservative principles of banking," insisted a man in Cleveland. The time had come "to force the banks out of the security business."[82]

This concern about bankers taking risks with their depositors' money was by far the most often cited reason for separating commercial banking from investment banking, but once Glass started holding hearings, proponents of the bill had several other arguments in its favor. How had stock prices become so inflated in the late 1920s? Senator Frederic Walcott of Connecticut, a former banker himself, blamed the entry of commercial banks into the stock market, which he argued had triggered the speculative boom by flooding the market with money. Glass agreed that one benefit of keeping the two kinds of banks separate was to avoid another stock bubble "by forbidding people to use the facilities of Federal reserve banks to inflate prices on the stock exchange to almost an inconceivable degree." Depressions always followed overspeculation, reasoned Robert Hopkins, a furnace maker in Ohio, and it was money from the big banks that had fueled the New York Stock Exchange in the 1920s. The country needed "legislation which will put banks on a business basis instead of the main support of the biggest gambling institution in the country."[83]

81 Edgar A. Rossiter to Carter Glass, 12 May 1932, CG, box 297; Frederick B. Wells to Carter Glass, 21 Mar. 1933, CG, box 310.

82 Julian W. Tyler to Carter Glass, 5 Apr. 1932, CG, box 285.

83 *Congressional Record* 75 (1932): 9904; *Operation of the National and Federal Reserve Banking Systems*, 52; Robert C. Hopkins to Carter Glass, 31 Mar. 1932, CG, box 284. See also F. W. Buell to Carter Glass, 3 Jan. 1933, CG, box 296;

Other critics alleged that a commercial bank faced a conflict of interest when it ventured into the securities business, because while the bank was entrusted with the care of its depositors' money, it was also selling securities to those very same depositors. "The trusting public is being misled," complained L. C. Irvine of Mobile, Alabama. "After the age-old education of the public to TRUST THE BANKER for impartial advice in financial matters it is little less than particeps criminis for the Government to permit this confidence to be betrayed." Critics suspected that the banks were "more interested in the profit in the sale of the securities, than they were in protecting the funds" of their depositors, as one banker from East St. Louis, Illinois, put it. A. H. Eckles, the president of the Planters Bank & Trust Company in Hopkinsville, Kentucky, lamented that his neighbors placed undue trust in the "prestige and influence" of the big banks, which had induced them to buy "securities that have proved in many cases to be practically worthless." Worse, the banks knew exactly how much was in their customers' accounts, which gave the banks an extra edge in pressuring customers into buying whatever they had to sell. "The sales counter across which they are hawking bonds and stocks is the curse of the banking system of this country," declared the Rev. W. A. Matthews, of the First Presbyterian Church of Seattle. "Make it impossible for banks to be anything except pure, simple banks."[84]

Banks that sold securities also faced a conflict of interest with respect to borrowers, many argued, because when a firm was indebted to a bank, it was in the bank's interest for the firm to sell securities to the public (which would raise capital to repay the loan), even if an offering of securities would benefit neither the firm nor the purchasers of the securities. The very first issue of *Fortune* magazine, published in February 1930, worried for this reason that the sale of securities was "getting the

George M. Coffin to Carter Glass, 22 Mar. 1932, CG, box 284; Walter Schaffner to Carter Glass, 10 Oct. 1931, CG, box 302.

84 L. C. Irvine to Henry B. Steagall and Carter Glass, 1932, CG, box 293; J. F. Galvin to Carter Glass, 12 May 1932, CG, box 296; A. H. Eckles, "A Country Banker Looks at the Glass Bill," *Bankers' Magazine* 125 (1932): 136; Winthrop A. Mandell to Carter Glass, 1 Apr. 1932, CG, box 285; W. A. Matthews to Carter Glass, 12 Feb. 1932, CG, box 285.

bank into promotional activities of which it should be judge rather than advocate." William Stark Smith of Milwaukee reported that "these investment departments are frequently used to transfer poor bank loans to the public through the issue of bonds or preferred stock." In 1931, Carter Glass received an anonymous letter from an employee of the securities affiliate of a national bank, who revealed that the bank was doing just that. "The sales talk was just DOPE to lull the unwary into buying," he disclosed. "One issue was put out to liquidate a bad loan of the bank." Until investment banks were kept separate from commercial banks, warned the journalist John Flynn, "the function of the guardian is submerged in that of adventurer and speculator."[85]

These critiques of banks had a particularly sharp edge in the early 1930s. As banks failed left and right, it was a common concern that the public was losing confidence in the banks that were still standing, which would cause people to pull their money out of banks and keep it at home, which would cause even more banks to fail. If shady practices on the part of securities affiliates were making the public suspicious of banks, some argued, that was reason enough to get banks out of the securities business. "Confidence is the very life blood of a bank," declared a banker in Fort Worth, Texas. "Unless the security sales of our banks are curbed, and that at once, it will break down the confidence that the people have in our banking institutions, and will be the cause of untold mischief." With all the reports of banks selling bad investments, wondered a Shriner from Memphis, "can one be blamed for putting his funds in a lock box and hoarding?"[86]

The idea of banning commercial banks from selling securities thus seems to have enjoyed widespread support for a few different reasons, all of which had to do with the fear that the ability to sell securities was encouraging banks to look after their own profits at the expense of their customers. Of course, there was one interest group with the most to

85 "Banking, Group and Branch," *Fortune*, Feb. 1930, 140; William Stark Smith to Carter Glass, 27 Apr. 1932, CG, box 291; Anonymous to Carter Glass, 3 Dec. 1931, CG, box 301; John T. Flynn, "The Dangers of Branch Banking," *Forum and Century* 89 (1933), 261.
86 Garland A. Tunstill to Carter Glass, 26 Jan. 1932, CG, box 285; Leon Franks to Carter Glass, 6 Feb. 1932, CG, box 284.

gain from the measure—the investment banks that were not affiliated with a commercial bank. These banks, which were often called "private" banks to distinguish them from the "national" commercial banks that were under the jurisdiction of the Federal Reserve, had lost a big part of their market share when the commercial banks entered the securities business, and the separation of commercial banking from investment banking promised to bring that market share back. Carter Glass could hardly have been surprised to discover that among the heartiest supporters of his banking bill were the investment bankers. "For years it has been a great source of worry to the private banking houses that the banks had, through their affiliates, gobbled up so large a part of the issues of new securities to such a degree that the small houses were being practically starved out of such business," explained Waldo Kendall, an investment banker in Boston. But Kendall could see better days around the corner. "The fact is that all of this work has been done throughout history up to within a few years ago by the private investment houses, who stand ready and willing to do the necessary work," he promised.[87]

The only significant opponents of the bill were, again not surprisingly, the commercial banks. Their primary argument was that they were needed, because the investment banks could not provide enough capital to finance American business. "The long term capital market in the United States has been developed in large part by member banks and their securities affiliates," insisted Charles McCain, the chairman of the Chase National Bank, and William Potter, the president of the Guaranty Trust Company of New York. They warned that forcing commercial banks out of the securities business "will seriously impair the ability of business in the future to get long term capital." At its 1932 annual meeting, the American Bankers Association adopted a resolution emphasizing that "for many years national banks and state member banks through their powers of underwriting and investing in securities have supplied long-term capital to many important industries," and

---

87 Jonathan R. Macey, "Special Interest Groups Legislation and the Judicial Function: The Dilemma of Glass-Steagall," *Emory Law Journal* 33 (1984): 20; E. B. Parsly to Carter Glass, 10 Feb. 1932, CG, box 285; J. F. B. Mitchell to Carter Glass, 22 Nov. 1933, CG, box 311; Waldo S. Kendall to Carter Glass, 4 May 1932, CG, box 291.

that "it has been the history of past depressions that recovery has largely come about through the refinancing of industry and commerce in which the member banks have played a material and important part." Fred Kent, a director of the Bankers Trust Company, testified that the stock market would collapse even more than it already had if banks like his were no longer allowed to sell securities. "It is not conceivable that such a market could exist," Kent reasoned, "if every natural channel through which funds are applied to maintain it was stopped up or curtailed through legislation."[88]

The weakness of this argument, as the investment bankers pointed out, was that the commercial banks had been selling securities in large quantities only for the previous few years. Before that, the business had been in the hands of the investment banks, and no one had thought the investment banks lacked access to sufficient capital. The commercial banks had not added new capital to the system so much as they substituted themselves for the investment banks.

The commercial banks had a second argument against the Glass bill. Commercial banks were regulated by the federal government, but the private investment banks were not. "By divorcing the security business from commercial banking," the commercial banks contended, "the former is turned over either to unregulated dealers, or to those regulated only by such varying laws as the forty-eight states may provide." They suggested that a better plan would be to keep the securities business with the federally regulated commercial banks, perhaps with a new layer of regulation to prevent a recurrence of the abuses of the past few years. "I think you will agree with me," the Detroit banker E. F. Connely wrote to Glass, "that it would be far better to have this business conducted in connection with the banking business where it might be rigidly administered than to have it revert to the hands of private bankers answerable only to state governments subject to no examination and free to do about as they please." But Glass did not agree, no

88 H. H. Preston and Allan R. Finlay, "Era Favors Investment Affiliates," *American Bankers Association Journal* 22 (1930): 1153; Charles S. McCain and William C. Potter to Carter Glass, 29 Apr. 1932, CG, box 291; "Resolution of American Bankers Association Upon Glass Banking Bill, S. 4412," CG, box 296; *Operation of the National and Federal Reserve Banking Systems*, 512.

doubt because the self-interest of the commercial banks was so transparent. "What has the American Bankers' Association ever done in the public interest?" scoffed another of Glass's correspondents. "I have followed the proceedings of their annual conventions for many years. The trend of thought and action is in the interest of those managing the banks, not the depositors or the public."[89]

After the election of 1932, there was no longer any serious political opposition to the separation of commercial from investment banking. Carter Glass's banking bill was incorporated into the Banking Act of 1933. "New Epoch in Banking Opens Under Glass-Steagall Act" ran the headline in the *New York Times*. Some of the biggest banks, seeing the writing on the wall, had already divested themselves of their securities affiliates, which after all had not been particularly profitable during the Depression. Bankers Trust and the Manhattan Company had dropped their affiliates in 1931. But most of the banks waited until near the June 1934 deadline. The First National Bank of Boston let go its affiliate, the First Boston Corporation, which acquired Chase Manhattan's old affiliate. The Guaranty Trust Company, the National City Bank, and the First National Bank all dissolved their affiliates. Most of the private banks that had begun taking deposits stopped doing so and confined themselves to investment banking. These included some of the firms that would be among the most prominent investment banks for most of the remainder of the century, including Kuhn, Loeb and Company; Kidder, Peabody and Company; Lehman Brothers; and Goldman, Sachs and Company. A few of the private banks made the opposite decision to become pure commercial banks, most notably J. P. Morgan and Company, which spun off its securities business into a separate firm that would be called Morgan Stanley.[90] Investment banks and commercial banks would remain separate for decades.

89 "Glass Banking Bill Passes the Senate," *Bankers' Magazine* 126 (1933): 210; E. F. Connely to Carter Glass, 29 Mar. 1932, CG, box 293; T. J. Morrison to Carter Glass, 24 Dec. 1932, CG, box 297.
90 *New York Times*, 25 June 1933, 3; "Wall Street Accepts New Deal in Finance," *Literary Digest*, 23 June 1934, 36; Chernow, *House of Morgan*, 384–88; Carosso, *Investment Banking in America*, 372–75.

The Glass-Steagall Act was a major change in the structure of the financial system, but it was small indeed compared with some of the proposals that were seriously considered after the crash. The biggest catastrophe in American economic history had largely been blamed on speculation, but when the dust had settled, the law governing speculation had scarcely changed.

6

Land and Onions

ONE OF THE BROADWAY hits of 1925 was the Marx Brothers' musical *The Cocoanuts*. It opened during the Florida land boom, which served as the show's setting. Real estate prices in Florida were rising quickly. Speculators were flocking south to buy and sell parcels of land. Irving Berlin wrote the songs for *The Cocoanuts*, one of which, "Florida by the Sea," gently parodied the promotional literature for Florida that was blanketing the rest of the country:

> Down in the land where the trees are tall,
> we're asking you to pay a call
> and live where it is summer all the year round.
> Buy a lot,
> any piece that we've got
> will increase every season;
> ask us why
> everybody wants to lie
> in the sun, there's a reason.

By the time the film version of *The Cocoanuts* appeared four years later, the bubble had burst. Florida land was selling for a small fraction of 1925 prices. "Florida by the Sea" was moved from the middle of the Broadway show to the opening credits of the movie, where it took on a sharper satirical edge, as a reminder of the madness of a few years before. Also acquiring a sharper edge were the words of Groucho Marx, who plays a huckster trying to sell off land he knows is worthless.

"All ye suckers who are gonna get trimmed, step this way for the big swindle!" Groucho announces. "Friends, you are now in Cocoanut Manor, one of the finest cities in Florida. Of course, we still need a few finishing touches, but who doesn't? This is the heart of the residential district. Every lot is a stone's throw from the station. As soon as they throw enough stones, we're going to build a station. Eight hundred wonderful residences will be built right here. Why, they're as good as up. Better. You can have any kind of home you want to. You can even get stucco—Oh, how you can get stuck-o!"

Everyone remembers the stock market boom and bust of the 1920s, but only historians and film buffs remember that there was a nearly simultaneous boom and bust in the real estate market, most vividly in Florida, but not only there. The rise and fall of the stock market gave rise to a national debate about limiting speculation in financial assets, a debate that produced the New Deal financial regulation that continues to structure the market today. But the rise and fall of the real estate market did not give rise to an analogous debate or any analogous regulation. And of course the real estate bubble of the 1920s was not the first in American history, and it would not be the last. A similar episode took place in the first decade of the twenty-first century, as real estate prices soared upward, amidst considerable speculation, only to plummet back down to earth. Once again, there would be considerable discussion about speculation in financial assets, especially securities backed by loans on real estate, but scarcely any debate about speculation in real estate itself. Why the difference? Why have Americans been so much more concerned about financial speculation than about real estate speculation?

FLORIDA FRENZY

Land speculation has been a constant feature of American life since the seventeenth century.[1] So have periodic booms and busts, in both urban

---

1 John Frederick Martin, *Profits in the Wilderness: Entrepreneurship and the Founding of New England Towns in the Seventeenth Century* (Chapel Hill: University of North Carolina Press, 1991); Alan Taylor, *William Cooper's Town: Power and Persuasion on the Frontier of the Early American Republic* (New York: Vintage Books, 1995); A. M. Sakolski, *The Great American Land Bubble: The Amazing*

and rural areas. Recent studies suggest a common dynamic: as the population of an area grows, it takes some time to develop a corresponding quantity of land. Land grows scarcer in the short run. Investors bid up its price, but they underestimate the elasticity of the supply of land in the long run. Eventually more land is developed and its price tumbles back down.[2]

In the 1920s, older investors could still remember the real estate bubbles of the previous generation. Retail space in central Chicago that sold for $1,500 per front foot in 1883 was worth $4,000 in 1889 and reached $7,000 to $10,000 in 1891, only to drop back down in the 1890s. In towns all over Nebraska, speculators poured millions into undeveloped lots in 1886 and 1887, lured by easy credit and the hope that new railroads would turn remote agricultural areas into bustling cities. A 640-acre farm near Omaha that had been bought several years earlier for $2.50 an acre sold in 1887 for $1,000 an acre, and then a 120-acre portion of the farm sold a few months later for $2,500 an acre. Soon after, prices were back where they had started. Similar bubbles blew up and popped up all over the Midwest at around the same time, in Minnesota and the Dakotas, in Kansas, in Texas, and in parts of Iowa, Wisconsin, and Missouri. "The East invested vast sums in Western property," one observer recalled. "The rapid development of the resources of the West lent plausibility to every reckless prophecy of higher prices; the continued inundation of Eastern money seeking chances of speculation falsified the predictions of the foreboding."[3]

Story of Land-Grabbing, Speculations, and Booms From Colonial Days to the Present Time (New York: Harper & Brothers, 1932).

2 Edward L. Glaeser, "A Nation of Gamblers: Real Estate Speculation and American History," *American Economic Review: Papers & Proceedings* 103, no. 3 (2013): 1–42; Robert J. Shiller, "Historic Turning Points in Real Estate," *Eastern Economic Journal* 34 (2008): 1–13.

3 Homer Hoyt, *One Hundred Years of Land Values in Chicago: The Relationship of the Growth of Chicago to the Rise of Its Land Values, 1830–1933* (1933) (Washington, D.C.: Beard Books, 2000), 175–81; Herbert L. Glynn, "The Urban Real Estate Boom in Nebraska During the Eighties," *Nebraska Law Bulletin* 6 (1928): 473–76; Henry J. Fletcher, "Western Real Estate Booms, and After," *Atlantic Monthly* 81 (1898): 689.

Perhaps the sharpest rise and fall in real estate prices during the late nineteenth century took place in Los Angeles during the boom of 1887. When artesian well water began to be used for irrigation, and the coming of the Southern Pacific Railroad introduced competition between railroad lines and thus lower fares, emigrants and speculators swarmed into southern California. Sixty new townsites were put on the market in 1887 alone, most of which consisted of undeveloped land in the middle of nowhere, bordered only by other equally imaginary townsites. Some, including Claremont, actually got built, but most would never exist except on paper. Land was typically purchased with small down payments. Speculators bought and sold options to buy land, and an option on a particular parcel often changed hands several times before it expired. Prices skyrocketed. A thirty-two-acre parcel just south of what is now downtown Los Angeles that sold in 1885 for $8,500 was resold in 1887 for $40,000, to be subdivided. In Hollywood, land worth $100 per acre in 1886 was worth $600 per acre a year later. In Boyle Heights, parcels that had been worth $150 only a few years earlier sold in 1887 for $10,000. By the end of the year, the bubble had burst. Many of the lots purchased at fabulous prices were abandoned by the buyers as worthless.[4]

It happened again in the 1920s. As the stock market rose to new heights in the middle of the decade, so did the real estate market in much of the country. National real estate prices peaked in 1926 and dropped sharply thereafter. In New York, real estate prices closely tracked stock prices, peaking in 1929 and then declining rapidly between 1929 and 1932. The boom of the 1920s gave rise to considerable speculation in real estate and also in a new kind of financial asset, bonds backed by real estate, the forerunners of the mortgage-backed securities that would play a big part in the boom of the early 2000s. By the mid-twenties, issuances of real estate bonds constituted nearly a quarter of all corporate debt issues, an even larger share than bonds issued by railroads. Just as contemporaries worried that there was too much stock speculation in the mid-1920s, they worried that there was too much real

4 Joseph Netz, "The Great Los Angeles Real Estate Boom of 1887," *Annual Publication of the Historical Society of Southern California* 10 (1915–16): 54–68.

estate speculation. In 1925, for example, the economist A. C. Miller, a member of the Federal Reserve Board, urged the bankers of Boston to be more conservative in making loans for the speculative purchase of land. "There is evidence," Miller argued, "that a section of the public is losing its bearings and being drawn into the arena of thoughtless speculation."[5]

Nowhere was real estate speculation more spectacular than in Florida. In Miami, subdivisions that existed only on paper sold out the first day they were offered, most to investors who resold within days, before they had to put any money down. It was hard to walk in downtown Miami because the sidewalks were clogged with realtors. In Palm Beach, reported *Harper's* magazine, "conversation was full of stories of houses built for $5,000 and sold for $18,000; of sea-front lots bought at $20 a foot, and now worth $700." As one correspondent put it in late 1925, "the smell of money in Florida, which attracts men as the smell of blood attracts a wild animal, became ripe and strong last spring. The whole United States began to catch whiffs of it." The result was a "Florida frenzy."[6]

5 Eugene N. White, "Lessons From the Great American Real Estate Boom and Bust of the 1920s," NBER Working Paper 15573 (2009); Alexander James Field, "Uncontrolled Land Development and the Duration of the Depression in the United States," *Journal of Economic History* 52 (1992): 785–805; Tom Nicholas and Anna Scherbina, "Real Estate Prices During the Roaring Twenties and the Great Depression," *Real Estate Economics* 41 (2013): 278–309; William N. Goetzmann and Frank Newman, "Securitization in the 1920s," NBER Working Paper 15650 (2010); *New York Times*, 18 Nov. 1925, 36.

6 William Frazer and John J. Guthrie Jr., *The Florida Land Boom: Speculation, Money and the Banks* (Westport, Conn.: Quorum Books, 1995); Mark S. Foster, *Castles in the Sand: The Life and Times of Carl Graham Fisher* (Gainesville: University Press of Florida, 2000); Raymond B. Vickers, *Panic in Paradise: Florida's Banking Crash of 1926* (Tuscaloosa: University of Alabama Press, 1994); Homer B. Vanderblue, "The Florida Land Boom," *Journal of Land & Public Utility Economics* 3 (1927): 118–19; Paul S. George, "Brokers, Binders, and Builders: Greater Miami's Boom of the Mid-1920s," *Florida Historical Quarterly* 65 (1986): 34; W. L. George, "Humanity at Palm Beach," *Harper's Monthly Magazine* 150 (1924): 221; Gertrude Mathews Shelby, "Florida Frenzy," *Harper's Monthly Magazine* 152 (1925): 177.

While Florida land prices were on the rise, there was no shortage of sober justifications for them. "The bubble will not burst for the very good and sufficient reason that there is no bubble," insisted Elmer Youngman in early 1926, just before the bubble burst. Youngman, the editor of the *Bankers' Magazine*, declared that "some of the ablest men in America are pouring millions into Florida." He attributed the new values being placed on Florida real estate to the increased prosperity of the country, which gave the masses the means to enjoy leisure and travel, and to the invention of the automobile, which gave them an easy way to reach a warm climate. The journalist Frank Stockbridge emphasized the recent drainage of Florida's swamps, which eliminated the mosquito and the attendant threats of malaria and yellow fever. Others simply liked the weather. "One may swim in the surf, pick strawberries and wear roses in December," marveled one correspondent. "You can go fishing, boating and surf bathing when the waters of the north are covered with ice."[7]

Florida's real estate prices came crashing down in 1926. The *New York Times* summed up the situation at the year's end: there was "a large class of investors who, having made payments ranging from a few hundred to several thousand dollars, now have nothing to show for their money except parcels of waste land." Banks all over the state failed within a few months, after making real estate loans that now had no hope of being repaid.[8] The banks and the speculators alike were, as Groucho Marx put it, stuck-o.

By the early 1930s, after similar if less colorful episodes in many cities, there was a general recognition that real estate speculation had gotten out of hand in the previous decade. "Real estate values, we were told, could never go down—only up. You simply *could* not lose out on any real estate investment," the *North American Review* recalled. "Therefore money poured into the real estate field." Chicago was awash in foreclosures because of overspeculation, lamented the vice president

7 Elmer H. Youngman, "Florida: The Last Pioneer State of the Union," *Bankers' Magazine* 112 (1926): 14, 7–8; Frank Parker Stockbridge, "The Florida Rush of 1925," *Current History* 23 (1925): 181–82; J. D. Burke, "Florida–The Material Progress From 1912 to 1926," *Lawyer & Banker and Southern Bench and Bar Review* 19 (1926): 129–30.
8 *New York Times*, 3 Jan. 1927, 3; 16 Mar. 1927, 24.

of the Chicago Title and Trust Company. Land speculation had left "wreckage" all over the New York area, a regional board concluded, in the form of hundreds of thousands of undeveloped lots whose purchasers had defaulted on their loans. The economist Herbert Simpson observed that local governments were victims as well. Most of their revenue came from property taxes, and many had embarked on ambitious public works based on the assumption that property values would continue to rise. As the *Atlantic* magazine despaired in 1931, the nation was now reaping the "whirlwinds of speculation."[9]

Analogous events in the securities markets gave rise to an extensive debate in the late 1920s and early 1930s about how to regulate the markets to prevent another crash. There was no parallel debate concerning real estate. Occasionally, to be sure, someone would call for greater regulation. During the midst of the Florida land boom, for example, at the annual meeting of the Investment Bankers Association, the Chicago banker Walter Greenbaum proposed a national blue sky law for real estate. Greenbaum had become exasperated with the glowing public relations material touting land in Florida. He wanted a federal agency to screen out the bad investments before real estate could be offered to the public, just like the first wave of state blue sky commissions screened out unsound stock offerings.[10] This idea went nowhere. And such calls for regulation of the real estate market seem to have been exceedingly rare. Certainly they were much rarer than calls to regulate the stock market.

THE ONLY HOPE HERE IS INCREASED CAUTION

One obvious form of regulation that would have deterred real estate speculation, if such deterrence had been desired, was a tax on real estate

---

9 Gerhard Hirschfeld, "A Morgue of Mortgages," *North American Review* 232 (1931): 255; Kenneth E. Rice, "A Study of Real Estate Cycles," *Lawyer & Banker and Central Law Journal* 24 (1931): 254; *New York Times*, 11 Feb. 1929, 14; Herbert D. Simpson, "Speculation and the Depression," *American Economic Review: Papers and Proceedings* 23 (1933): 165–66; Samuel Spring, "Whirlwinds of Speculation," *Atlantic*, 1 Apr. 1931.

10 *New York Times*, 23 Oct. 1925, 31.

transfers. In the early 1930s, there were many calls to tax stock transfers for the same purpose, to deter speculation in stock. In more recent times, a few jurisdictions imposed taxes on real estate transfers in an effort to dampen real estate speculation. Vermont established such a tax in 1973, for example, and Ontario did the same in 1974. In earlier eras, frontier residents had clamored for special property taxes on absentee land speculators, and the available evidence suggests that at least some jurisdictions satisfied that demand indirectly, by assessing absentee-owned property at higher values than comparable property owned by residents. Taxing land speculation to reduce its quantity was thus well within the realm of possibility in the late 1920s and early 1930s. D. E. French, a West Virginia lawyer, suggested in 1931 that the federal government could curtail real estate speculation by imposing a special income tax on the profits of sales of real estate held for less than twelve months. Booms were always followed by depressions, French pointed out, so "if we can find a way to eliminate booms we will thereby eliminate the depression."[11] But no such tax was seriously considered by Congress or any state legislature.

There *was* a debate about real estate taxation during the period, one that bore tangentially upon speculation, but it had little to do with the boom and bust of the 1920s. In the late nineteenth century the political economist Henry George had proposed his famous "single tax," a tax on increases in the value of land. The primary reason George favored this tax was to reduce inequality, but, he contended, the single tax had the additional advantage of deterring real estate speculation. "That land speculation is the true cause of industrial depression is, in the United States, clearly evident," George argued. He thought his tax would "tend to increase production, by destroying speculative rent," because "if land were taxed to anything near its rental value, no one could afford to hold land that he was not using, and, consequently, land not in use

---

11   R. Lisle Baker and Stephen O. Andersen, "Taxing Speculative Land Gains: The Vermont Experience," *Urban Law Annual* 22 (1981): 3–69; Lawrence B. Smith, "The Ontario Land Speculation Tax: An Analysis of an Unearned Increment Land Tax," *Land Economics* 52 (1976): 1–12; Robert P. Swierenga, "Land Speculation and Frontier Tax Assessments," *Agricultural History* 44 (1970): 253–66; D. E. French to Carter Glass, 28 Apr. 1931, CG, box 278.

would be thrown open to those who would use it." By the 1920s, this claim does not appear to have been widely believed, at least among economists and those with experience collecting taxes. But there was always a small cohort of ardent Georgists who kept the faith, like the economist Harry Gunnison Brown, who still argued that the single tax really would discourage speculation.[12] The debate over the single tax had mostly petered out by the 1920s, however, and the effect of the single tax on speculation was, in any event, a minor issue within that debate.

Why were contemporaries so much more interested in limiting speculation in securities than in real estate? Any answer to this question requires some guessing, because there does not appear to have been much discussion of the question at the time, but it is not hard to identify five related reasons for the disparity. None provides a full explanation, but together they can explain why there was no new regulation for land comparable to the New Deal limits on speculation in securities.

First, while securities were intangible, man-made, and a bit mysterious to the average person, land was a physical, natural thing with qualities that were easily understood. Many more people owned land than securities, and while most people had never seen securities and may have had only a vague sense of what they were, everyone had seen land and knew exactly what it was. The buying and selling of land was a well-known part of everyday life, from the biggest cities to the smallest towns. The same was not true of securities.

Second, speculators in securities engaged in all sorts of arcane and unnatural-seeming transactions. They made short sales, of items they did not even own, to profit from price declines, which gave some speculators the unneighborly incentive to make their fellows poorer.

12 Henry George, *Progress and Poverty: An Inquiry Into the Cause of Industrial Depressions and of Increase of Want with Increase of Wealth* (1879) (San Francisco: National Single Tax League, 1905), 266, 411; Adam Shortt, "Municipal Taxation in Relation to Speculative Land Values," *Annals of the American Academy of Political and Social Science* 58 (1915): 214–21; J. Hamilton Ferns, "Single Tax in Theory and Practice," *Bulletin of the National Tax Association* 5 (1919): 75–80; Harry Gunnison Brown, "Land Speculation and Land-Value Taxation," *Journal of Political Economy* 35 (1927): 390–402.

They entered into futures contracts, for things they might never even see. They hedged against price movements by buying and selling at the same time. The repertoire of transactions in real estate was much smaller. There were no short sales, so there was no way to profit from a decline in real estate prices, and there were no real estate speculators hoping for a crash. There were no futures and there was no hedging. Real estate speculators could buy options, and in the bubblier locations, like Florida, options were bought and sold in their own right, but this was small stuff compared with the transactions on the stock and commodity exchanges. The main way to speculate in real estate was straightforward: buy land and hope it rose in price so it could be sold to someone else. The transactions in securities that seemed artificial and even pernicious had no parallels in real estate.

Third, real estate seemed like a more level playing field than securities for the average investor. An ordinary person venturing into the stock market was competing with corporate insiders, who knew much more about their own firms than anyone on the outside possibly could. And he was competing with professionals who were widely suspected to have tricks up their sleeves that allowed them to manipulate prices, at least in the short run, to fleece the amateurs. Not so with land. "Generally speaking, the prudent purchase of land is a better investment for the ordinary man than stocks and bonds, because in the former case he does not pit his judgment against the machinations of a board," advised the economist Richard Ely. "For example, you buy some stock. You know some of the facts with regard to the stock, but you cannot know all the facts which are known to the president and the board of directors, even supposing they are honest and do not want to swindle anyone. But, if they do not want to be honest, the buyer is playing with dice loaded against him."[13] Real estate was more transparent. Its value might fluctuate, but the average investor could see why.

Fourth, crashes in securities markets affected the country as a whole, all at once, while crashes in real estate markets, although often correlated, were local events. When the Florida land bubble burst in 1926, it harmed only people who had bought land in Florida. When the

13   Richard T. Ely, "Land Speculation," *Journal of Farm Economics* 2 (1920): 123.

stock market crashed three years later, it harmed everyone. Real estate downturns were less likely than stock market downturns to mobilize political support for regulation.

Finally, with real estate, there was no interest group that was always on one side of a transaction. Anyone who was a buyer of land one day could be a seller of land another day; there was no group of people who were always one or the other. That made land very different from commodities, where farmers were always sellers and their customers were always buyers. Arguments that speculation pushed prices up or down had a sharp impact for commodities, because if those arguments were true, there would be clear winners and losers. Not so with real estate, where if speculation pushed prices up, any given participant would gain as a seller whatever he lost as a buyer, and vice versa if speculation pushed prices down. Corporate stock was somewhere in the middle. Anyone who bought stock one day might sell it another day, so in that sense stock was like land. But when new stock was issued, corporate insiders were always sellers, and members of the general public were always buyers. In that sense, stock was like commodities. All else equal, one would expect interest groups to form most readily to regulate speculation in commodities, least readily to regulate speculation in real estate, and somewhere in the middle to regulate speculation in stock.

Real estate speculation thus seemed more natural and less dangerous than speculation in securities. "Real-estate booms probably will constantly recur," the *Atlantic* observed in 1931, "because the real-estate men involved—drifters from other industries—naturally will cooperate with local interests to sell through high-pressure sales methods as many lots as the public can possibly be induced to buy." But the magazine did not think any regulation was needed to prevent the next bubble from inflating and bursting. "The only hope here is increased caution, born of experience, on the part of the public," the *Atlantic* concluded, "and the influence of the established and more experienced local real-estate firms in checking boom tendencies."[14] With land, unlike with the stock market, contemporaries perceived nothing for regulators to do.

14 Spring, "Whirlwinds."

AN ONION RING

To gain some perspective on the lack of interest in limiting speculation in real estate, it is useful to look at a very different market, one in which Congress, in relatively short order, completely banned speculation. In the Onion Futures Act of 1958, Congress made it a crime to enter into a contract for the sale of onions for future delivery.[15] To this day, onions are the one agricultural commodity in which futures trading is illegal.

Onion futures were relatively new in 1958. The Chicago Mercantile Exchange began trading onion futures in 1942, and the New York Mercantile Exchange followed suit in 1946. By the mid-1950s, the Chicago exchange hosted nearly all of the transactions, in what was still a tiny market compared with more established commodity futures like wheat or corn.[16]

Then disaster struck—disaster from the perspective of an onion farmer. In August 1955, a fifty-pound bag of onions was worth $2.75. By March 1956, the same onions were worth 10 cents, less than the cost of the bag. It turned out that two onion dealers, Sam Siegel of Chicago and Vincent Kosuga of New York, had outmaneuvered the onion market. In the fall of 1955, Siegel and Kosuga bought virtually the entire onion crop available on the Chicago market. Once they had the onions, they threatened the leading onion growers that they would flood the market, and depress the price, unless the growers bought about a third of the onions back from them at high prices. The growers agreed to buy a third of the onions back. Siegel and Kosuga then double-crossed the growers. They sold onions short on the Chicago Mercantile Exchange, to the point where they acquired short positions that exceeded the amount of onions they had originally purchased. They then flooded the market with the remaining two-thirds of the onions. They even shipped some of their onions out of town, repackaged them, and shipped them back to Chicago to make it appear as if still more new onions were coming on the market. Onion prices fell through the floor. The growers

15 72 Stat. 1013 (1958).

16 Emily Lambert, *The Futures: The Rise of the Speculator and the Origins of the World's Biggest Markets* (New York: Basic Books, 2011), 33–44; *Prohibiting Futures Trading in Onions*, H.R. Rep. No. 1036, 85th Cong., 1st Sess. (1957).

were left holding very expensive onions, while Siegel and Kosuga made millions on their short positions.[17]

Onion farmers were devastated by the fall in prices. Within a few months, the Commodity Exchange Authority (the agency within the Department of Agriculture that administered the Commodity Exchange Act of 1936) set sharp limits on trading in onion futures. Under the new rules, no trader could hold net long or short positions of more than two hundred car lots of onions, about a sixth of the short position accumulated by Siegel and Kosuga.[18] But this was not enough for the onion farmers, who urged Congress to ban the futures trade completely. Their testimony before Congress demonstrated that the market in onions was very different from the market in real estate in each of the respects that made limiting speculation in real estate so unlikely.

Onion farmers, unlike real estate investors, were a tightly focused interest group who were always on the same side of the transaction. They sold onions and never bought them. Their livelihood thus depended on keeping onion prices up. Anything that was perceived to depress onion prices was a menace. Farmers had long believed that commodity speculation depressed prices, and the events of 1955–56 had confirmed for the onion farmers that this was indeed the case. There was no comparable interest group on the other side of the transaction. Lower onion prices were good for consumers, who were always onion buyers and never onion sellers, but of course onions made up a negligible portion of their food budget, so they had little reason to lobby for lower prices.

Onions, unlike real estate, traded in a national market. A fall in prices affected onion farmers everywhere. And onions were grown all over the country. Letters poured into the Senate from onion growers in Oregon and Wisconsin, Texas and Michigan, Idaho and New York. The growers were represented by the National Onion Association, which gained the support of larger agricultural organizations like the Vegetable Growers of America and the National Farm Bureau, who had members in all

---

17 "Odorous Onions," *Time*, 2 July 1956, 70; *Chicago Daily Tribune*, 22 June 1956, B7.
18 *Wall Street Journal*, 23 July 1956, 15.

but the most urban congressional districts.[19] The Florida real estate bust was well known throughout the country, but it personally affected only those who had bought land in Florida. The great onion bust was probably less famous, outside the onion trade. It did not serve as the setting for any Marx Brothers movies or Irving Berlin songs. But it affected onion growers nationwide.

Onions, like land, were an easily understood physical commodity, but onion futures were not. Most onion farmers did not hedge, testified Veril Baldwin of Stockbridge, Michigan, the president of the National Onion Association. "Onions are not processed or used in manufacturing to any extent," he explained, "so buying to hedge for future use is almost nonexistent," and "the average grower cannot successfully use the market to hedge his sales." The onion farmers had little or no experience with onion futures, which were primarily the province of speculators. Onion futures, sneered the Texas grower Austin Anson, were traded by "smart boys who had never owned an onion in their lives."[20]

And those smart boys were engaging in unnatural-seeming transactions that seemed to flout the laws of supply and demand, by causing the price of onions to fluctuate wildly when neither the supply of onions nor the demand for them was changing. "It is only in a futures market," Baldwin complained, that a person "can make money by depressing the market, and that is what is the matter with it." John Hardwicke, another Texas grower, emphasized how little the onion farmers were asking for. They were "not asking for a handout or subsidy, not asking for price supports," he noted. The industry was "simply asking for its God-given right to conduct its own free business according to the laws of supply and demand without some speculators being in a position to often make a lot of money by scheming up to demoralize and ruin the onion growers' market."[21]

19 *Onion Futures Trading: Hearing Before a Subcommittee of the Committee on Agriculture and Forestry, United States Senate* (Washington, D.C.: Government Printing Office, 1957) ("1957 Hearings"), 2–6, 23–24.

20 *Onion Futures Trading: Hearings Before the Committee on Agriculture and Forestry, United States Senate* (Washington, D.C.: Government Printing Office, 1958) ("1958 Hearings"), 141–43; 1957 Hearings, 61.

21 1958 Hearings, 143, 168.

Onion futures were thus a much more likely target of antispeculative regulation than real estate. The farmers' case was not very strong from an economic perspective. Onion prices were actually *more* stable during the period in which onion futures were traded on the Chicago Mercantile Exchange than they had been before or would be after. As the economist Roger Gray pointed out, wide swings in prices were indicative of too *little* speculation in onions rather than too much, because a thicker market in onion futures would have dampened price movements in both directions. A thicker market would also have been harder for Siegel and Kosuga to manipulate. But this kind of argument had little effect on Congress, where the prevailing view was that trading in onion futures was an injustice to the farmers. The farmer did all the work, reasoned the Michigan congressman Clare Hoffman, but "it's those Chicago birds, those city slickers, who get the money."[22] The point of banning onion futures was to give the money back to the farmers.

THE SUBPRIME CRISIS

Real estate speculation returned to the headlines in the first decade of the twenty-first century, which saw the biggest rise and fall in real estate since the 1920s. Nationally, home prices more than doubled between 1995 and 2007. As in the 1920s, rising prices attracted purchasers who hoped to own real estate only briefly before selling it on to someone else. By 2005, according to the National Association of Realtors, 28 percent of the people buying homes were seeking investments rather than places to live. Perhaps the best barometer of the public interest in real estate speculation was the proliferation between 2005 and 2007 of reality television programs devoted to "flipping" houses, in which purchasers with no real estate experience were depicted as making quick profits by speculating in single-family homes.

22 Roger W. Gray, "Onions Revisited," *Journal of Farm Economics* 45 (1963): 273–76; Roger W. Gray, "Some Current Developments in Futures Trading," *Journal of Farm Economics* 40 (1958): 344–51; *Washington Post and Times Herald*, 14 Mar. 1958, A19.

Lenders extended credit to homebuyers who had no prospect of ever repaying their loans unless the value of their homes rose enough so they could borrow even more a few years later. But the bubble burst in 2007. Within three years, national housing prices fell by a third. And these were national averages; in some cities, prices rose and fell much more sharply. By 2010, four million homes were in foreclosure, and several million more foreclosures seemed to be on the way. Nearly a quarter of the surviving borrowers owed more on their mortgages than their homes were worth.[23]

Unlike previous real estate bubbles, this one nearly brought down the entire financial system, because of innovations in the ways that money flowed from lenders to borrowers. Mortgages existed at least as early as the nineteenth century, and in the later part of the century eastern financial institutions began investing in western farm mortgages. But the mortgage market remained very small by modern standards until the middle of the twentieth century. During the real estate boom of the 1920s, the main mortgage lenders were banks, insurance companies, and building and loan associations, cooperative organizations in which members would pool their funds to lend to members buying homes. Mortgages were not the norm; only around 40 percent of owner-occupied housing units had a mortgage. And these mortgages were stingy by modern standards. They typically covered no more than half of a home's value, lasted only three to five years, and left the homeowner owing a large lump sum at the loan's expiration. In the 1920s, many of these loans were securitized—broken into small pieces and sold to investors—but these were relatively simple transactions, in which investors essentially bought shares of the mortgage for a single

---

23 National Association of Realtors survey quoted in Todd J. Zywicki and Joseph D. Adamson, "The Law & Economics of Subprime Lending," *University of Colorado Law Review* 80 (2009): 33; *New York Times*, 18 Mar. 2007, F90; *S&P/Case-Shiller U.S. National Home Price Index*, http://us.spindices.com/index-family/real-estate/sp-case-shiller; *The Financial Crisis Inquiry Report: Final Report of the National Commission on the Causes of the Financial and Economic Crisis in the United States* (Washington, D.C.: Government Printing Office, 2011), 402, 23.

building (usually a large apartment building or commercial building) rather than for an assortment of properties.[24]

The collapse of the real estate market and the failure of many lenders in the late 1920s and early 1930s gave rise to new government institutions intended to encourage mortgage lending. The Federal Home Loan Bank Act of 1932 established regional home loan banks, which could borrow from the government and issue tax-free bonds to raise money that could be lent to homeowners. The Home Owners' Loan Act of 1933, part of the flurry of New Deal legislation in the first hundred days of the Roosevelt administration, created the Home Owners' Loan Corporation, which used government funds to refinance existing mortgages that were near foreclosure. A year later, the National Housing Act of 1934 established the Federal Housing Administration as an insurer of mortgages. In 1938, the Housing Act was amended to establish another federal agency, the Federal National Mortgage Association ("Fannie Mae"), for the purpose of buying mortgages from private lenders. Federal government support transformed housing finance. By the middle of the century, the standard mortgage lasted up to thirty years, covered up to 80 percent of the home's value, and left the homeowner owing nothing when it came to an end. With the availability of these mortgages, homeownership rates rose from 44 percent in 1940 to 64 percent by 1980.[25]

The pervasive securitization of mortgages has its roots in the 1968 reorganization of government support of the mortgage market, when Fannie Mae was converted into a formally private firm, and the Government National Mortgage Association ("Ginnie Mae") was created as a federal agency to securitize the mortgages insured by the Federal Housing Administration. The Emergency Home Finance Act

24 Jonathan Levy, *Freaks of Fortune: The Emerging World of Capitalism and Risk in America* (Cambridge, Mass.: Harvard University Press, 2012), 150–90; Kenneth A. Snowden, "The Anatomy of a Residential Mortgage Crisis: A Look Back to the 1930s," NBER Working Paper 16244 (2010).

25 Richard K. Green and Susan M. Wachter, "The American Mortgage in Historical and International Context," *Journal of Economic Perspectives* 19 (2005): 93–114; Kent W. Colton, "Housing Finance in the United States: The Transformation of the U.S. Housing Finance System," Harvard University Joint Center for Housing Studies, W02-5 (2002).

of 1970 established another nominally private firm, the Federal Home Loan Mortgage Corporation ("Freddie Mac"), to purchase mortgages. Before long, Freddie Mac and Fannie Mae began securitizing mortgages just like Ginnie Mae did. By the 1990s, both organizations were securitizing most of the mortgages they purchased—that is, they were selling to investors bonds that were backed by the flow of payments from homeowners. Private companies (typically investment banks) unaffiliated with the government soon began securitizing mortgages that were not guaranteed by Fannie Mae, Freddie Mac, or Ginnie Mae, a development encouraged by the Secondary Mortgage Market Enhancement Act of 1984, which removed regulatory obstacles to such "private label" securitization. All this securitization allowed homebuyers to tap into vast sums of money that had previously been unavailable for mortgage lending, which almost certainly caused more money to be borrowed, at lower interest rates, than would otherwise have been possible.[26]

Securitization also increased the number and size of the participants in the financial system who depended on homeowners paying their mortgages. Previous downturns in the housing market had bankrupted mortgage lenders, but now there were, in effect, many more mortgage lenders than ever before. The number of actors potentially exposed to mortgage defaults multiplied in the first decade of the twenty-first century, when banks began assembling collateralized debt obligations (CDOs)—slices of pools of mortgage-backed securities—which were then sold to other investors. That exposure multiplied again with the development of credit default swaps (essentially insurance against defaults on CDOs), and then synthetic CDOs, which were slices of pools of the credit default swaps. By the time the housing bubble burst, an enormous financial superstructure had been built on a rickety base of borrowers' ability to make their mortgage payments.

This was why the downturn in real estate prices that began in 2007 had such a dramatic effect on the financial system. Major financial institutions were more tightly connected to the housing market,

---

26 Congressional Budget Office, *Fannie Mae, Freddie Mac, and the Federal Role in the Secondary Mortgage Market* (2010), S1–S4, 4–7.

through the securitization of mortgages and the reassembly of the resulting bonds into various flavors of derivatives, than they had been in earlier episodes of real estate speculation. The Florida land bust of 1926 wiped out some Florida banks, but the nationwide land bust of 2007 nearly wiped out the largest financial institutions in the country.

Before one could think intelligently about how to prevent such a catastrophe from occurring again, one had to understand why real estate prices had risen and fallen so sharply. On this question there was, unsurprisingly, a wide range of opinion. Some blamed land use regulation that limited the supply of buildable land, thus forcing up its price. If such regulation was indeed the disease, the cure would be to have less of it. Then again, while land use regulation was a plausible explanation for why land was more expensive in some places than in others, it was far less plausible as an explanation for the sharp rise in real estate prices (because regulation had not become any more intense while prices were on the way up), and it could scarcely explain why real estate prices had plummeted (because regulation had not become any less intense during the fall). Others, especially in the immediate aftermath of the financial crisis, blamed government policies that encouraged homeownership in less affluent communities, which they contended led to the deterioration of lending standards. But more careful study afterward revealed that the homeowners in the communities in which these policies were implemented were actually *less* likely to default on their loans.[27]

A more persuasive set of explanations focused on the rapid expansion of the practice of securitizing mortgages. The housing bubble coincided with the influx of capital from the "private label" securitization

---

27 Edward L. Glaeser et al., "Housing Supply and Housing Bubbles," *Journal of Urban Economics* 64 (2008): 198–217; Randal O'Toole, "How Urban Planners Caused the Housing Bubble," *Policy Analysis*, no. 646 (2009); Thomas Sowell, *The Housing Boom and Bust* (New York: Basic Books, 2009); R. Christopher Whalen, "The Subprime Crisis—Cause, Effect and Consequences," Indiana State University Networks Financial Institute Policy Brief 2008-PB-04 (2008); Peter J. Wallison and Arthur F. Burns, "Dissenting Statement," *Financial Crisis Inquiry Report*, 443–533; Robert B. Avery and Kenneth P. Brevoort, "The Subprime Crisis: Is Government Housing Policy to Blame?" (2011), http://ssrn.com/abstract=1726192.

of mortgages that were too risky to be insured or securitized by the government or by the nominally private government-sponsored entities. Securitization reduced lending standards, as a greater supply of money became available for lending. Borrowers took on more debt than they had a rational hope of repaying, in part because many of them did not fully understand the terms of their loans, and in part because unscrupulous lenders took advantage of their ignorance by steering them into loans at higher interest rates than they could otherwise have obtained. Many of the originators of these loans had little incentive to inquire into the creditworthiness of the borrowers, either because they were mortgage brokers who were compensated per loan regardless of repayment or because the securitization process allowed them to pass the risk of default on to investors.[28]

These institutional changes had been facilitated by legal changes. It was lawful to make such subprime loans because of the liberalization of federal banking laws in the early 1980s. The Depository Institutions Deregulation and Monetary Control Act of 1980, the statute that removed interest rate caps on bank accounts, also deprived the states of their traditional power to limit the interest rates that mortgage lenders could charge. The availability of higher rates made lenders more willing to extend credit to riskier borrowers. The Garn–St. Germain Depository Institutions Act of 1982 permitted "alternative mortgage transactions," including loans with adjustable rates and balloon payments.[29] These became common features of subprime loans.

---

28 Atif Mian and Amir Sufi, "The Consequences of Mortgage Credit Expansion: Evidence From the U.S. Mortgage Default Crisis," *Quarterly Journal of Economics* 124 (2009): 1449–96; Benjamin J. Keys et al., "Did Securitization Lead to Lax Screening? Evidence From Subprime Loans," *Quarterly Journal of Economics* 125 (2010): 307–62; Oren Bar-Gill, "The Law, Economics and Psychology of Subprime Mortgage Contracts," *Cornell Law Review* 94 (2009): 1073–151; Sumit Agarwal et al., "Predatory Lending and the Subprime Crisis," NBER Working Paper 19550 (2013); Alan M. White, "The Case for Banning Subprime Mortgages," *University of Cincinnati Law Review* 77 (2008): 617–44; Antje Berndt et al., "The Role of Mortgage Brokers in the Subprime Crisis," NBER Working Paper 16175 (2010).

29 Cathy Lesser Mansfield, "The Road to Subprime 'HEL' Was Paved With Good Congressional Intentions: Usury Deregulation and the Subprime Home Equity Market," *South Carolina Law Review* 51 (2000): 473–587; Patricia

Of course, none of these factors could have brought about the financial crisis without the investors who were willing to buy the mortgage-backed securities and CDOs that were made up of sub-prime mortgages. These were sophisticated investors, including some of the large banks that would be bailed out by the government when these investments went sour. Why were they so eager to buy securities that rested on such a flimsy base of mortgages? There are two likely answers to this question.

First, while it might not have been difficult to estimate the value of any single loan, the outputs of securitization were pools consisting of thousands of heterogeneous loans. It was not a simple matter to figure out what they were worth. Assessing their value required constructing models of the probability that given numbers of individual borrowers would default, but these securities were so new that there was not much historical data against which to test the models, and the existing data were mostly from the recent past, when real estate prices were consistently rising. Mortgage-backed securities were rated by the credit-rating agencies, but in retrospect it is clear that these agencies did a very poor job, perhaps in part because they were compensated by the issuers and so had an incentive to downplay the risk. As a result, even sophisticated investors seem to have underestimated the risk of these securities and thus paid too much for them.[30]

Second, the human psychology of this bubble was no different from that of previous bubbles. Just as in Florida in 1925 or Los Angeles in 1887, participants genuinely believed that prices would continue to rise. This belief seems to have been just as prevalent among the sophisticated suppliers of finance as among the unsophisticated borrowers. While inexperienced "flippers" were increasing their exposure to a real estate market that was nearing unsustainable heights, so were many of the managers of the Wall Street banks that were securitizing the flippers'

A. McCoy, Andrey D. Pavlov, and Susan M. Wachter, "Systemic Risk Through Securitization: The Result of Deregulation and Regulatory Failure," *Connecticut Law Review* 41 (2009): 1327–75; 94 Stat. 161 (1980); 96 Stat. 1545–46 (1982).

30 Adam J. Levitin and Susan M. Wachter, "Explaining the Housing Bubble," *Georgetown Law Journal* 100 (2012): 1177–258.

mortgages.[31] As in the 1920s, the insiders were just as optimistic as the outsiders.

Previous bursts of real estate speculation had not given rise to any substantial proposals for regulating the market, but this episode was simultaneously a real estate bubble and a much more dangerous financial bubble in securities backed by real estate. Congress was busy in the aftermath, and its response to the twin bubbles followed the pattern of previous crises. The flurry of ensuing legislation did little or nothing to limit speculation in land, but it placed new limits on speculation in the securities whose value derived from land.

The Housing and Economic Recovery Act of 2008 was the primary legislation for the housing market. It was intended to ease the foreclosure crisis rather than to restrain speculation in real estate, and to that end it provided government insurance for new mortgages to replace loans to homeowners at risk of foreclosure. Indeed, to the extent the new law had any effect on speculation, it was to make purchasing real estate even *easier* than it had been before, by raising the limits on the size of loans that could be insured by the Federal Housing Administration, and by providing a tax credit for first-time homebuyers.[32]

By contrast, the Dodd-Frank Act of 2010, the primary legislation addressing securitization, was more restrictive. The act required securitizers to retain at least 5 percent of the risk of the mortgages being securitized, in the hope that being forced to hold this risk would make securitizers more careful about the soundness of the mortgages. The act also required issuers of mortgage-backed securities to disclose information about the securities. The precise nature of that information was left to the Securities and Exchange Commission, but the point was to help investors assess the risk that the underlying mortgages would go

31 Robert J. Shiller, *The Subprime Solution: How Today's Global Financial Crisis Happened, and What to Do about It* (Princeton, N.J.: Princeton University Press, 2008), 39–68; Yuliya Demyanyk and Otto Van Hemert, "Understanding the Subprime Mortgage Crisis," *Review of Financial Studies* 24 (2011): 1848–80; William M. Goetzmann et al., "The Subprime Crisis and House Price Appreciation," *Journal of Real Estate Finance and Economics* 44 (2012): 36–66; Ing-Haw Cheng et al., "Wall Street and the Housing Bubble," NBER Working Paper 18904 (2013).

32 122 Stat. 2264 (2008).

into default. The Dodd-Frank Act also included provisions intended to abolish some of the darker arts of lending that took place during the bubble. Mortgage originators were barred from receiving compensation that varied based on the terms of the loan other than the amount, to remove the incentive to steer borrowers into loans with higher interest rates. Lenders were required to make a good-faith effort to verify the borrower's ability to pay. Exceptionally large balloon payments and fees were banned. These measures were intended in part to protect less sophisticated borrowers against what had come to be called "predatory" lending, but also in part to protect investors in mortgage-backed securities, by weeding out the lowest-quality loans.[33]

Had there been more interest in limiting speculation in real estate itself, in addition to limiting speculation in securities backed by real estate, a few measures would have been available for consideration. The phenomenon of "flipping" might have been deterred by imposing a special tax on gains from short-term holdings of real estate. Congress might have reduced the availability of subprime mortgages by reallowing states to set maximum interest rates for home loans, a power Congress had taken away in 1980. The terms of mortgage loans that seemed to cause the most trouble, like adjustable rates and balloon payments, might have been further regulated by revisiting the 1982 statute that authorized such terms. None of this was done, because there was no public outcry for restricting land speculation.

The experience of 2007–10 thus replicated the experience of 1926–33. The real estate market and the securities market rose together and then fell together. It was widely believed in retrospect that there had been too much speculation in both. The law quickly responded with new rules governing speculation in securities. But there were no new rules governing speculation in land, which has always seemed more natural and less dangerous than speculation in intangible assets.

33 124 Stat. 1376 (2010).

7

Inside Information

RODOLPHE AGASSIZ WAS THE consummate insider. He was an elite
Bostonian, grandson of the distinguished Harvard naturalist Louis
Agassiz and son of Alexander Agassiz, the founder of the Calumet and
Hecla Mining Company, one of the leading mining firms of the early
twentieth century. As a young man, Rodolphe Agassiz was one of the
best polo players in the world. He became chairman of the board of the
family mining company after his father's death. Meanwhile, he held
prominent positions in several Boston institutions: he was a director of
the State Street Trust Company, the Old Colony Trust Company, the
First National Bank, and the Edison Electric Illuminating Company.
Agassiz was also an active member of the Republican Party until the
mid-1920s, when he broke with the Republicans because of their support for Prohibition. Few Americans were better placed to profit from
inside information than Rodolphe Agassiz.[1]

The Calumet and Hecla Mining Company owned a bit less than half
of the shares of the Cliff Mining Company, a firm with copper mines
in northern Michigan. The rest of the shares were dispersed among a
large number of stockholders, so Cliff Mining was in effect a subsidiary
of Calumet and Hecla. Agassiz was the president of Cliff Mining. In
1924, he hired the Harvard geologist Louis Graton to study the property in Michigan and to report on the likelihood of finding copper ore.[2]

1 *New York Times*, 1 Aug. 1933, 17.
2 *Wall St. Journal*, 22 Sept. 1928, 7; 18 Oct. 1929, 13; C. S. Hurlbut Jr., "Memorial
of Louis Caryl Graton," *American Mineralogist* 57 (1972): 638–43.

Graton came back with a highly positive confidential report in March 1926. The Michigan mines were far more valuable than anyone had realized.

Agassiz put this information to immediate use. He and James MacNaughton, the local manager of Cliff Mining, promptly purchased on their own behalf nine thousand shares of the company, which was more than a quarter of the outstanding shares that were not owned by Calumet and Hecla. They were able to make these purchases at approximately $2.50 per share. While Agassiz and MacNaughton were buying up the stock of Cliff Mining, they shut down Cliff Mining's exploratory operations in Michigan and announced that the mine was being abandoned as unprofitable, an announcement that prevented Cliff Mining's stock price from rising. All the while, Calumet and Hecla was quietly obtaining options to buy the land adjacent to the Cliff Mining properties. In October 1926, once they had finished their stock purchases, Agassiz and MacNaughton reopened the mine and made the geologist's report public. Shares in Cliff Mining rose to $12.50. Agassiz and MacNaughton sold their shares and made roughly $90,000, or well over $1 million in today's money. Agassiz most likely did not think he had done anything wrong. He had not tried to conceal his identity as the purchaser or seller of the stock in his company. It was simply a matter of common sense to speculate where one had the best information.

Homer Goodwin was furious. Goodwin was a local stockbroker, a member of the Boston Stock Exchange. He had owned seven hundred shares of the Cliff Mining Company, but he sold them in May, while Agassiz and MacNaughton were snapping up the firm's shares, and while the share price was still $2.50. He sued Agassiz to get the shares back. (Goodwin initially sued MacNaughton too, but he never followed through, most likely because MacNaughton lived in Michigan while Agassiz was close at hand in Boston.) Had he known what Agassiz had known, Goodwin argued, he never would have sold his stock at $2.50 per share. He would have waited for the inevitable rise in price once the mine was reopened and the geologist's report was disclosed. Goodwin contended that Agassiz had an obligation to the shareholders of the Cliff Mining Company to refrain from using his superior information to take advantage of them by purchasing their stock for less than its true value.

The Massachusetts Supreme Court held that Agassiz had not broken the law. Corporate directors and officers owed a duty *to the corporation*, explained Chief Justice Arthur Prentice Rugg in his opinion for the court, but not to each of the corporation's shareholders as individuals. Besides, directors bought and sold their own company's stock all the time. "An honest director would be in a difficult situation," Rugg worried, "if he could neither buy nor sell on the stock exchange shares of stock in his own corporation without first seeking out the other actual ultimate party to the transaction and disclosing to him everything which a court or jury might later find that he then knew." Disclosure might be morally right, but it was not a legal requirement. "Business of that nature is a matter to be governed by practical rules," Rugg observed. "Law in its sanctions is not coextensive with morality." And who would serve as the director of a corporation if he had to pay the heavy price of not dealing in the corporation's stock? The court concluded: "Fiduciary obligations of directors ought not to be made so onerous that men of experience and ability will be deterred from accepting such office."[3]

Rugg pointed out that most transactions in the economy were just like the one between Goodwin and Agassiz, in that they involved one party who possessed more information than the other. Inequality was inherent in contracting. The law "cannot undertake to put all parties to every contract on an equality as to knowledge, experience, skill and shrewdness," Rugg insisted. Sometimes the party with superior information got the better of the deal, but that was life. A court "cannot undertake to relieve against hard bargains made between competent parties without fraud." Agassiz knew more about the financial condition of the Cliff Mining Company than Goodwin did, but Goodwin's remedy was not to force Agassiz to share what he knew. Rather, it was to find out the information for himself. Goodwin "was no novice," Rugg lectured. "He was a member of the Boston stock exchange." Before selling his stock, "he made no inquiries of" Agassiz "or of other officers of the company." If he had asked about the

3 *Goodwin v. Agassiz*, 186 N.E. 659, 661 (Mass. 1933).

mines in Michigan, and if Agassiz had lied to him, that would have been fraud, and Goodwin would have been entitled to rescind the transaction. As Rugg put it, "directors cannot rightly be allowed to indulge with impunity in practices which do violence to prevailing standards of upright business men." But Agassiz had not lied to anyone, much less to Goodwin. He had merely stayed quiet about what he knew, and that did not disable him from dealing in the stock of his own company.[4]

Seventy years later, Samuel Waksal found himself in the same position as Rodolphe Agassiz. Waksal, a former immunologist, had started a company called ImClone, whose primary product was a promising cancer treatment called Erbitux. But Waksal learned, to his disappointment, that the Food and Drug Administration would not permit Erbitux to be sold. When the rest of the world found out, ImClone's share price would plummet. Just as Rodolphe Agassiz had taken advantage of his access to good news, Waksal sought to take advantage of his own access to bad news. He immediately tried to sell $5 million of ImClone stock before the FDA announced its decision. But times had changed. Waksal's brokers refused to execute his sell order, because they knew he was not allowed to sell his ImClone stock until the news reached the public. Waksal was arrested a few months later. He pled guilty to securities fraud and several other crimes, and he was sentenced to seven years in prison. While he was trying to sell his own shares, Waksal had urged friends and family members to sell their shares too. One of those friends was the celebrity homemaker Martha Stewart, who ended up serving a five-month prison sentence for making false statements during the investigation of the incident.[5]

Over the course of the twentieth century, the law's treatment of inside information had changed dramatically. At the beginning of the century, speculators' ability to exploit their superior access to knowledge was considered at worst inevitable, and at best a positive good. By the end of the century, at least in certain circumstances, exploiting one's knowledge in this way was a serious crime. Rodolphe Agassiz had been esteemed a shrewd businessman. Although he died a mere two months after the Massachusetts Supreme Court decided his case, his lengthy obituary in

---

4 *Id.* at 661–62.
5 Daniel Kadlec, "Sam's Club," *Time*, 17 June 2002.

the *New York Times* discussed his polo playing and his service on corporate boards but did not even mention Homer Goodwin's lawsuit against him. Samuel Waksal did the same thing Agassiz had done, but when his obituary is written he will likely be remembered as a criminal. Between Agassiz's era and Waksal's, speculating on inside information had been transformed from a normal, sound business practice into a vice.

ONE-SIDED KNOWLEDGE

Insider trading in the shares of a corporation is just one instance of a much broader and much older question of commercial morality. Where a buyer or a seller knows more than his counterpart, when should he be able to use that knowledge to his advantage, and when should he be required to disclose the information before entering into a transaction? This was an important and unsettled question in the early United States.

The issue was sharply presented to the US Supreme Court in 1817 in *Laidlaw v. Organ*, which became one of the court's most well-known commercial cases in its early years. During the War of 1812, tobacco prices were much lower than normal due to the British blockade of southern ports, which deprived tobacco growers of foreign markets. The war formally ended in December 1814 with the signing of the Treaty of Ghent, but it took some time for news of the treaty to reach the United States. In the evening of February 18, 1815, Hector Organ, a New Orleans tobacco merchant, learned about the treaty. He realized that the news would spread quickly, and that tobacco prices would rise with the lifting of the blockade. Early the next morning, just after sunrise, he called on another tobacco merchant in the city, Peter Laidlaw & Company, and offered to buy approximately 120,000 pounds of tobacco. Francis Girault, a member of Laidlaw & Company, asked Organ if there was any news that might influence the price of tobacco. Organ did not respond. Girault nevertheless sold Organ the tobacco. Within a day, as news of the treaty filtered through New Orleans, the price of tobacco rose 30 to 50 percent. Laidlaw & Company seized the tobacco it had just delivered to Organ. Organ sued.[6]

---

6 *Laidlaw v. Organ*, 15 U.S. 178 (1817); M. H. Hoeflich, "*Laidlaw v. Organ*, Gulian C. Verplanck, and the Shaping of Early Nineteenth Century Contract

Was Laidlaw & Company bound by the contract? The company's lawyer insisted it was not. "The parties [were] treated on an unequal footing," he argued, "as the one party had received intelligence of the peace of Ghent, at the time of the contract, and the other had not." Organ's lawyer was Francis Scott Key, who had written the lyrics to *The Star-Spangled Banner* while watching the British bomb Baltimore only a few months before his client had bought the tobacco. Organ's failure to disclose that the war was over might have been immoral, Key acknowledged, but "human laws are imperfect in this respect, and the sphere of morality is more extensive than the limits of civil jurisdiction." Indeed, he continued, Organ deserved praise rather than censure. He had done nothing wrong, "unless rising earlier in the morning, and obtaining by superior diligence and alertness that intelligence by which the price of commodities was regulated, be such." In any event, Key contended, it would be futile to require disclosure, because virtually every contract involved one party who knew things the other did not. "It is a romantic equality that is contended for on the other side," Key declared. "Parties never can be precisely equal in their knowledge."[7]

The court agreed with Key. Chief Justice John Marshall wrote a very short opinion, only a few sentences long. Organ "was not bound to communicate" his knowledge of the treaty, the court concluded. "It would be difficult to circumscribe the contrary doctrine within proper limits, where the means of intelligence are equally accessible to both parties. But at the same time, each party must take care not to say or do any thing tending to impose upon the other."[8] That is, a rule requiring disclosure in this particular case would lead to chaos. It would open up all contracts to challenge, because there would be no way to draw a principled line distinguishing the situations in which information had to be disclosed from those in which information could be kept secret. Contracting parties could not lie to each other, but they were under no

Law: A Tale of a Case and a Commentary," *University of Illinois Law Review* 1991 (1991): 55–66.

7 *Laidlaw*, 15 U.S. at 185–86, 193.

8 *Id.* at 194.

obligation to reveal what they knew. As the old Latin expression put it, *caveat emptor*—let the buyer beware.

But this view was controversial. In a similar case a few years earlier, for example, a Kentucky court had reached the opposite result. A Virginian named Bowman owned a tract of land in Illinois that he had never seen. (This was not unusual at the time. Bowman was apparently a war veteran who had received the land as part of the compensation for his military service.) John Bates lived near the tract. He knew that it included salt water, which made it more valuable, and he knew that Bowman was unaware of the salt water. Bates communicated this information to his brother James, who lived near Bowman. James Bates purchased the land from Bowman without telling him about the salt water. Bowman sued, and the court set aside the sale. To allow one person to take advantage of another's ignorance "might become pernicious in practice," the court worried. It would allow "the dishonesty and cunning of some to operate upon the honest credulity of others."[9]

Indeed, a year after *Laidlaw v. Organ*, the Mississippi Supreme Court disagreed with the US Supreme Court even more directly. *Frazer v. Gervais* was nearly a carbon copy of *Laidlaw*: a merchant who knew of the Treaty of Ghent bought cotton from a merchant who did not, at a price that seemed far too low once the news of the treaty had spread. The Mississippi court refused to enforce the transaction. Once the purchaser heard information that would affect the price of cotton, the court concluded, he could not buy cotton without first divulging the information to the seller.[10]

The lawyer and future congressman Gulian Verplanck was so outraged by *Laidlaw v. Organ* that he wrote an entire book criticizing it. Verplanck's *Essay on the Doctrine of Contracts* was devoted to answering the question posed by *Laidlaw* and similar cases. "We shall find numberless cases of the most opposite moral character, from the arts of deliberate knavery to the fairest gains of industry and enterprise, all agreeing in this one prominent feature: that the profits of the transaction arose from the superiority of one party to the other in some material

9 *Bowman v. Bates*, 5 Ky. 47, 53 (1810).
10 *Frazer v. Gervais*, 1 Miss. 72, 73 (1818).

knowledge respecting the subject of the contract," Verplanck noted. "Where then shall we draw the line of fair and unfair, of equal and unequal contracts?" Verplanck thought the line should be drawn between information about a person's own desires and capacities, which would not have to be disclosed, and information about the external world, which would. "My knowledge of my own interests, and my personal necessities, my sagacity, natural or acquired, in forming judgments of the state of the market," he reasoned, "can never be expected by the other party to be communicated; and in most instances it would be impracticable or silly to do so." People differed widely in their motivations and their skills, but it could not be unlawful to exploit such advantages, or else commerce would cease entirely. "Not so with regard to the *common* facts, which immediately and materially affect price," Verplanck continued. "It is true, that strict equality of knowledge, as to these points, is just as difficult as with regard to other matters. But the contract is entered into on the supposition, that whatever superiority of knowledge one may have over the other, *no advantage will be taken of it.*" Verplanck provided some examples. When he purchased a hat from his hatter, the hatter knew much more about the value of hats than he did. But if the hatter tried to exploit this informational advantage by charging him $10, when better-informed customers paid only $5, the hat-buying contract would be unenforceable, because hat purchasers were entitled to presume that the hatter would treat them equally. And of course, if a purchaser of tobacco or cotton knew that the War of 1812 had ended, he could not gain an edge on a seller who had not yet heard the news. On the other hand, if a merchant discovered a new use for a product, or if a scientist developed a new invention, there was nothing wrong with exploiting these informational advantages, because customers would "take it for granted, that such advantage, if possessed, would be used."[11]

Verplanck was hardly alone in believing that knowledge should not be kept secret to the commercial detriment of others. Caveat emptor was "a most demoralizing principle," complained the lawyer-scientist

---

11   Gulian C. Verplanck, *An Essay on the Doctrine of Contracts* (New York: G. & C. Carvill, 1825), 10, 119–21.

Thomas Cooper. "It is a disgrace to the law that such a maxim should be adopted." Cooper thought the court opinions applying the doctrine "ought to be classed as cases in support of falsehood and fraud." An admiring reviewer of Verplanck's book blamed the doctrine on the American inheritance of English common law, which had been formed long before under primitive circumstances. "A savage race, like the Saxons, and a nation of military barbarians, like the Normans," he scoffed, "could hardly be expected to derive their law of contracts from a very pure and enlightened source, or to found it upon the enlarged principles of civilized morality." A Kentucky court refused to enforce a contract for the sale of a horse when the seller failed to tell the buyer that the horse was blind. "It will better comport with morality and sound policy," the court insisted, "to subject the seller to an action at law, and thereby impose upon him the legal, as well as moral duty of telling the whole truth." James Kent, whose four-volume treatise on American law was a standard reference work for decades after its publication in the 1820s, declared that "as a general rule, each party is bound in every case to communicate to the other his knowledge of material facts, provided he knows the other to be ignorant of them, and they be not open and naked, or equally within the reach of his observation."[12] On this view, information was not a weapon to be wielded in the marketplace. The law, like common morality, should forbid the informed from taking advantage of the ignorant.

But if there were many voices speaking against the caveat emptor doctrine in the early nineteenth century, there were also many, probably more, speaking in its favor. "It would certainly be well, for the best interests of society, if the pure principles of morality ... could be established as the law of the land, and practically enforced in the ordinary transactions of life," one Mississippi lawyer acknowledged. But requiring that contracting parties tell each other all they knew would be "replete with difficulties." Was a buyer bound to tell a seller "*every* fact or rumor calculated to enhance the price of the article—or if not every

---

12 Thomas Cooper, *The Institutes of Justinian* (Philadelphia: P. Byrne, 1812), 610–11; Book Review, *North American Review* 22 (1826): 262; *Hughes v. Robertson*, 17 Ky. 215, 217 (1824); James Kent, *Commentaries on American Law* (New York: O. Halsted, 1826–30), 2:377.

fact, what facts, and who is to be the judge?" The law had to facilitate commerce, not just promote morality, and the most moral rule was not always the most practical. "In some special cases the *law of the land* and *morality* are the same," reasoned the Boston lawyer Nathan Dane, but the two differed when "policy" was taken into account. Thus, every "undue advantage in a bargain, to the hurt of another party, practised by one, is an act of injustice in the eyes of *morality*; yet it is not the means of restitution in the eyes of the *law*." As another commentator put it, caveat emptor "furnishes a plain, simple and practical rule for the decision of all controversies of this nature," even if "it is said by some to be a hard, inequitable doctrine, repugnant to sound morality, and productive of fraud, injustice and oppression."[13] Buyers or sellers could not lie, but they had no duty to volunteer the truth.

Between the 1830s and 1850s, several courts accordingly declared that American law embodied the principle of caveat emptor. A contract for the sale of coffee beans was enforceable, held the US Supreme Court Justice Henry Baldwin, even if one party failed to disclose his superior knowledge of the state of the coffee market. "A purchaser may avail himself of information which affects the price of the article, though it is not known to the seller," Baldwin explained. "Though the latter inquires if there is any news which affects the price, the purchaser is not bound to answer, and the contract is binding, though there was news then in the place which raised the price." As Baldwin saw it, acquiring and exploiting information was a normal part of conducting business. "The buying and selling [of] merchandize being for mutual profit," he reasoned, "one is not bound to impart to another his views of speculation, his opinion of the effect of news or events, the bearing of the rise of one article on another, or the results of his mercantile skill and knowledge of the markets." A few years later, the Indiana Supreme Court agreed, in enforcing a contract in which a professional pork dealer bought approximately a thousand hogs, at a price well below market value, from an elderly man unfamiliar with the value of pork. "However justly the

---

13 Note appended to *Frazer v. Gervais*, 1 Miss. 72, 73 (1818); Nathan Dane, *A General Abridgment and Digest of American Law* (Boston: Cummings, Hilliard & Co., 1823–29), 1:100; "Caveat Emptor—The Rule of the Common Law—Not of the Civil Law," *American Jurist* 12 (1834): 95.

moralist may censure the address sometimes resorted to by men of keen business habits to effect advantageous contracts," the court observed, "misrepresentations as to the value or quantity of a commodity in market, when correct information on those subjects is equally within the power of both contracting parties with equal diligence, do not in contemplation of law constitute fraud." A contrary rule, the court worried, would lead to results much worse than the hard bargain it was enforcing. "To deprive the better informed, more enterprising, and more cautious party of the benefit of his contract, on account of representations, of the correctness of which the other party ought to judge for himself, would tend more to encourage ignorance, sloth, and recklessness, than to repress dishonesty." The Pennsylvania Supreme Court took the same view while enforcing a land sale in which an experienced miner, who knew that the land contained valuable chrome deposits, purchased it from a family of poor and sickly farmers who were unaware of the chrome, at a price suitable for barren farmland rather than for a valuable mining property. "A person who knows that there is a mine on the land of another may nevertheless buy it," the court held. "The ignorance of the vendor is not of itself fraud on the part of the purchaser. A purchaser is not bound by our laws to make the man he buys from as wise as himself."[14]

As caveat emptor became the general rule, however, many of the judges and commentators who espoused it remained uncomfortable with some of the more unsavory transactions it seemed to permit. They increasingly began to suggest that the doctrine should not apply in circumstances where the less knowledgeable person had a particular reason to place trust in the more knowledgeable. The US Supreme Court Justice Joseph Story was one of the first to spell out these circumstances at length, in his widely read 1836 treatise on equity jurisprudence. "If a vendor should sell an estate, knowing that he had no title to it," Story argued, the purchaser should be able to void the transaction, because "the very purchase implies a trust and confidence" on the part of the purchaser that the seller actually owns what he purports to sell.

14 *Blydenburg v. Welsh*, 3 F. Cas. 771, 773 (C.C.D. Pa. 1831); *Foley v. Cowgill*, 5 Blackf. 18, 20 (Ind. 1838); *Harris v. Tyson*, 24 Pa. 347, 359–60 (1855).

"The like reason would apply," Story added, "where the vendor should sell a house, situate[d] in a distant town, which he knew at the time to be burnt down." Story maintained that cases like these were exceptions to the general rule of caveat emptor, because "there are circumstances of peculiar trust and confidence, or relation between the parties."[15]

Story's view soon became orthodoxy. It was a middle ground between a strict rule of caveat emptor and a rule requiring disclosure. In the 1820s, James Kent had argued that disclosure should always be required, but in later editions of his treatise, beginning in the 1840s, he conceded that such a requirement, "though one undoubtedly of moral obligation, is perhaps too broadly stated, to be sustained by the practical doctrine of the courts." He agreed with Story that disclosure was required only where the person knowing the facts was "under some special obligation, by confidence reposed, or otherwise, to communicate them truly and fairly." The courts agreed as well. In Maine, for example, the state supreme court considered the case of a man who had paid for a carriage with a note (that is, a promise to pay) from a third party. He failed to tell the carriage seller that it would be impossible to collect on the note. The court required him to give the carriage back to the seller. A person had to disclose such information "if the means of information are not equally accessible to both" the buyer and the seller, the court held, "and especially when one of the parties relies upon the other to communicate to him the true state of facts to enable him to judge of the expediency of the bargain."[16] By the middle of the nineteenth century, it was fairly well settled that one party to a contract had no obligation to disclose information to the other, even information that might have a big effect on the price of whatever was being sold, unless there was some special relationship between the parties that imposed such a duty.

15 Kim Lane Scheppele, *Legal Secrets: Equality and Efficiency in the Common Law* (Chicago: University of Chicago Press, 1988), 269–98; Paula J. Dalley, "The Law of Deceit, 1790–1860: Continuity Amidst Change," *American Journal of Legal History* 39 (1995): 405–42; Joseph Story, *Commentaries on Equity Jurisprudence* (Boston: Hilliard, Gray & Co., 1836), 1:218–19, 221.

16 James Kent, *Commentaries on American Law*, 5th ed. (New York: Printed for the author, 1844), 2:482 note a; *Prentiss v. Russ*, 16 Me. 30, 32–33 (1839); William W. Story, *A Treatise on the Law of Contracts Not Under Seal* (Boston: Charles C. Little and James Brown, 1844), 109.

As shares in business corporations became more frequently bought and sold, they were just one more asset to which general commercial principles would apply. The question of how to deal with unequal information often arose in stock transactions. Everyone recognized the importance of timely information to stock prices. A successful investor "must watch the telegraph instruments which bring news from various parts of the world, and be prepared to act promptly," advised the president of the New York Stock Exchange. "Opinions formed in the morning must be changed at noon, and the evening's news furnishes no safe basis for the next day's operations."[17] But some shareholders could acquire information before others, because some were actively involved in directing the corporation's activities, while others were mere investors who knew scarcely anything about the day-to-day operations of the company. When insiders bought stock from or sold stock to outsiders, did they have an obligation to reveal their superior knowledge of the company? If the general rule of caveat emptor applied to these transactions, corporate directors could buy and sell without disclosing what they knew. But if the directors of a corporation owed a duty to the corporation's shareholders not to take actions that would harm them, the general rule of caveat emptor would not apply, and the directors would have to disclose before transacting. The disclosure question thus hinged on a question of corporate law. Did directors owe any duties to shareholders?

Corporate law was itself in the process of forming, so this too was an unsettled question. In 1836, for example, the Alabama Supreme Court considered a lawsuit filed by the estate of Joseph Spence, who had owned six shares of the Courtland Land Company, a corporation that owned land it planned to subdivide into lots and sell. The company was managed by William Whitaker, who although nominally the treasurer, failed to keep any accounts. Shortly before Spence's death, Whitaker purchased Spence's shares for $93.50 each, an amount far lower than their actual value. The Alabama Supreme Court held that the transaction was void because of Whitaker's failure to disclose the true financial

---

17 Edwin T. Freedley, *A Practical Treatise on Business* (Philadelphia: Lippincott, Grambo & Co., 1853), 168–69; Brayton Ives, "Wall Street as an Economic Factor," *North American* Review 147 (1888): 569.

condition of the company. The court determined that Whitaker was "a trustee, in whom faith and confidence have been reposed, and whose agency imparted to him a more intimate knowledge of the condition and value" of the shares than Spence, an ordinary shareholder, could possess. Whitaker had "taken advantage of his superior knowledge, to force an unequal bargain." The court accordingly rescinded the sale of Spence's shares.[18]

But the large majority of cases in the second half of the century held precisely the opposite—that a corporate director had no obligation to disclose anything when transacting with shareholders, because directors owed a duty to shareholders with respect only to the management of the corporation, not with respect to property (including shares in the corporation) owned by the shareholder or the director as individuals. In 1862, for instance, the administrator of Lloyd Glover's estate was selling off Glover's assets, after Glover accidentally killed himself while hunting when he tried to board a boat with a loaded gun. Glover had been an employee of the National Bank Note Company, and among his assets were 136 shares of the company's stock. Glover's administrator sold the shares to George Danforth, one of the company's directors. Not long after, the company declared an extraordinary dividend, most likely because it had the lucrative contract to print the federal government's new paper currency, and the administrator realized he had sold the stock for far less than its actual value. His suit against Danforth raised the same question the Alabama Supreme Court had considered: was caveat emptor the governing rule, or did Danforth, as a director, owe a duty to shareholders not to exploit his superior information?[19]

A New York court decided that there was nothing unlawful about the transaction. There is "a certain trust relation between the shareholders and the directors of a corporation," the court reasoned, "but the trust put in the directors usually extends . . . only to the management of the general affairs of the corporation." Danforth owed shareholders a duty to manage the corporation properly, but not a duty to help the

---

18 *Spence v. Whitaker*, 3 Port. 297, 325 (Ala. 1836).
19 *New York Times*, 7 Aug. 1862, 3; *Carpenter v. Danforth*, 52 Barb. 581 (N.Y. Sup. 1868).

shareholders sell their shares at an appropriate price. That was their business. Danforth knew much more about the company's financial condition than Glover's administrator, but it was the administrator's "right to judge for himself as to the value of the stock, and to enable him to do so, it was his right, and perhaps his duty, to inform himself as to facts material on the question of value." If a shareholder desired information about the state of a corporation, he had to find it out for himself before buying or selling. Transactions with directors were no different from transactions with anyone else.[20]

This view soon became standard. Directors were trustees for shareholders "in respect to the property of the corporation," not the property of the shareholders, declared the Indiana Supreme Court, in the course of upholding a transaction in which the president of a railroad company bought up company stock while, unbeknownst to the shareholders, he was negotiating a sale of the corporation to another railroad at a much higher price per share. The Tennessee Supreme Court agreed in another case in which several directors of a railroad purchased stock from shareholders because, due to their positions, they knew the stock was worth more than the sale price. "A director or the treasurer of a corporation is not, because of his office, in duty bound to disclose to an individual stockholder, before purchasing his stock, that which he may know as to the real condition of the value of that stock," New Jersey's highest court concluded. It was thus not unlawful for a director of a printing company to buy shares when he knew, but the shareholders did not, that the company had just "made a favorable sale of property, which enhanced the value of its stock."[21] When the New York lawyer William Cook summed up the cases in 1887, in his *Treatise on the Law of Stock and Stockholders*, it took him only a few sentences. "A director of the corporation itself may buy and sell its stock like any other individual," Cook explained. "The information which he has of the affairs of the corporation, whereby he is enabled to buy or sell at an advantage

---

20 *Id.* at 584, 589.
21 *Board of Commissioners of Tippecanoe County v. Reynolds*, 44 Ind. 509, 513 (1873); *Deaderick v. Wilson*, 67 Tenn. 108 (1874); *Crowell v. Jackson*, 23 A. 426, 427 (N.J. 1891). See also *Grant v. Attrill*, 11 F. 469, 470 (C.C.S.D.N.Y. 1882); *Gillett v. Bowen*, 23 F. 625, 626 (C.C.D. Colo. 1885).

over the person with whom he deals, does not affect the validity of the transaction."[22]

While the judges tended to emphasize the doctrinal justification for allowing corporate directors to trade on inside information—the lack of any duty they owed to shareholders with respect to their ownership of shares—the judges also sometimes provided practical reasons for permitting insider trading. Stocks were constantly fluctuating in value, the Utah Supreme Court reasoned, and one "who assumes to know the most about them is frequently the first one to be deceived." Information was money in this uncertain world, so a director, like anyone, "is entitled to the benefit of his facilities for information." The solution to the problem of unequal information was not compelled disclosure, argued the Michigan Supreme Court. It was for the less-informed party to find out what the insiders already knew. "The books of the corporation are open to all stockholders alike," the court noted, "and each may inform himself of the condition of the company." If a shareholder did not avail himself of this opportunity, lectured Maryland's highest court, he had only "his own lack of business prudence" to blame.[23]

In reaching this conclusion, American courts were both ratifying a pervasive practice and ensuring that it would continue. By all accounts, insider trading was very common. Guides for investors routinely warned that the market was an uneven playing field, where newcomers would be up against better-informed insiders. In eighteenth-century England, when government debt securities (then also called "stocks") were traded more widely than shares of businesses, Thomas Mortimer's oft-reprinted *Every Man His Own Broker* cautioned that government officials "have the earliest intelligence of all events that can tend either to raise or fall the STOCKS," and that an official, "if he should be a JOBBER," might "settle a great account . . . to his advantage." In the nineteenth century, as corporate shares became an ever-larger part of the market, American authors repeated the same warning. "Sometimes the funds of a Bank are employed in purchasing its own stock," lamented the

---

22 William W. Cook, *A Treatise on the Law of Stock and Stockholders* (New York: Baker, Voorhis & Co., 1887), 330.

23 *Haarstick v. Fox*, 33 P. 251, 153 (Utah 1893); *Walsh v. Goulden*, 90 N.W. 406, 410 (Mich. 1902); *Boulden v. Stilwell*, 60 A. 609, 612 (Md. 1905).

economist and journalist William Gouge, "and then, if the price offered be sufficiently high, those who have the management contrive
to sell their own shares." The same was true of all corporations, which
were "liable to be abused," cautioned the economist Daniel Raymond.
"This is mostly done by speculators and stock-jobbers, getting control
and management of them, and then managing them with a view to
their own speculations," a feat they could accomplish by keeping "the
stockholders and the public in the dark respecting the conditions of the
corporation, while they are themselves in the light."[24]

The difficulty of matching wits with wily insiders was a staple of
the breathless exposés of Wall Street published at midcentury. "Certain
Stockholders are the losers," one such publication reported, while "those
most active in getting up the concern are greatly improved in circumstances." For this reason, "we advise those not acquainted with active
business, widows, orphans, &c. to leave *all* new undertakings to business men." Another cautioned that Wall Street was no place for "small
victims and outsiders." "Don't let speculators have anything to do with
the management," insisted another. "Ask for the accounts; examine well
the details. . . . You have certainly a right to inquire about investing
your own money."[25] It was well understood, although often deplored,
that one of the customary perks of being the director of a corporation
was the opportunity to profit from trading in the corporation's stock.

Two New York stockbrokers published books in 1888 that were
part memoir and part investment guide, and both brokers discussed
the prevalence of insider trading. "Incomplete or insufficient information is especially dangerous," Henry Clews explained in an account of
his twenty-eight years on the New York Stock Exchange. "One-sided
knowledge is nowhere as deceiving as here." Clews recalled examples

24 Thomas Mortimer, *Every Man His Own Broker* (London: S. Hooper, 1761), 44;
William M. Gouge, *A Short History of Paper Money and Banking in the United
States* (Philadelphia: T. W. Ustick, 1833), 76; Daniel Raymond, *The Elements
of Constitutional Law and of Political Economy*, 4th ed. (Baltimore: Cushing &
Brother, 1840), 276.

25 William   Armstrong,   *Stocks   and   Stock-Jobbing   in   Wall-Street*
(New York: New York Publishing Co., 1848), 28; George G. Foster, *New York
in Slices* (New York: W. F. Burgess, 1849), 16; George Francis Train, *Young
America in Wall-Street* (New York: Derby & Jackson, 1857), 212–13.

in which "a stock is bought up freely at New York because London is taking large amounts of it; a day or two later, the deliveries show that large holders connected with the management are unloading on the foreign market upon knowledge of facts damaging to the prospects of the property." J. F. Hume likewise revealed "how certain great railroad magnates, who are leading operators in Wall street, have amassed such colossal fortunes." It was by speculating in the stock of their own companies. "Had they, like ordinary speculators, confined themselves to other people's goods," Hume remarked, "it is questionable whether they would have grown exceptionally rich."[26]

In 1915, a magazine called *The Annalist* interviewed several directors of large corporations to learn their opinions of insider trading. Nearly all of them believed that there was nothing wrong with the practice. They offered a variety of defenses. One bank director reasoned that it was only fair. If a director "knows of a profitable contract about to be closed," he argued, "he has more right than any one else to benefit by a rise in the stock on the announcement, because he has helped to get the contract." Another who was a director of many large corporations characterized the profit from trading as a form of compensation to which directors were due. "A Director gives his time and ability to the management of a corporation and gets $20 a week if weekly meetings are held," he explained. "That is surely not compensation enough. What the Director can make in the market on the basis of what he learns as a Director is part of the pay which he gets for his work." Another director argued that shareholders were not harmed when directors speculated in their companies' stock. A director *should* "buy stocks on the knowledge which he has of good things to come," he suggested. "The more stock he holds the better qualified he is to serve on the board." Finally, the directors feared that a ban on buying and selling shares would make it difficult for firms to find directors. "If it were held that a man's holdings of a stock should be frozen up the moment he becomes a Director," one worried, "I fancy very few could be induced to become Directors." But

---

26 Henry Clews, *Twenty-Eight Years in Wall Street* (New York: Irving Publishing Co., 1888), 202–3; J. F. Hume, *The Art of Investing* (New York: D. Appleton & Co., 1888), 128–29.

whether one welcomed or deplored insider trading, everyone recognized it as, in the words of one director, something that "as a practical matter nearly all Directors do."[27]

A CONTRARIETY OF JUDICIAL OPINION

Insider trading was legal and commonplace, but it had its critics, who thought it gave an unfair advantage to a privileged few. "Directors and officers of our large corporations have peculiar means for obtaining information with regard to the company with which they are connected," the *Commercial & Financial Chronicle* editorialized in 1872. "This speculating upon information which all the stockholders are equally entitled to is a very great evil."[28] On this view, insider trading was common in the same way that rudeness or lying was common: it was an ethically dubious but seemingly inescapable part of life. In a legal environment in which caveat emptor was the governing rule for most commercial transactions, and in which corporate directors owed no duties to shareholders that might render caveat emptor inapplicable, there was no ground for requiring directors to disclose information to shareholders before they bought and sold the stock of their own companies. A prudent shareholder had to assume the worst when dealing with an insider. Yet this conclusion was intuitively unappealing to many, including many judges.

The judges accordingly pressed back against the rule. In case after case in the late nineteenth and early twentieth centuries, judges identified special circumstances that took the case outside the doctrine of caveat emptor and imposed on insiders a duty of disclosure. For example, when the president of the Commercial Insurance Company told shareholders that he had found a purchaser for their stock, but the ostensible purchaser turned out to be an agent for the president, who was really trying to buy up the shares for less than their true worth, the Rhode Island Supreme Court refused to allow the transactions to stand. If the president had merely offered to buy the stock himself, the court

27 "Should Directors Speculate?," *The Annalist*, 19 July 1915, 65.
28 "Railroad Officers as Stockholders and Speculators," *Commercial & Financial Chronicle*, 8 Feb. 1872, 145.

reasoned, a shareholder "could have no right to complain. As a matter of common sense, the fact that the president of the company, presumed to be fully acquainted with its condition, offered a certain sum, would put the seller on his guard, and he might in most cases reasonably consider that he might get more." But this case was different, in the court's view, because the president had concealed his identity as the purchaser. He had claimed to be helping the shareholders, and by doing so he had caused each shareholder "to repose a trust and confidence" in him. That was enough, the court held, to impose on the president a duty to act on the shareholders' behalf. Caveat emptor was the ordinary rule, "yet if there be any peculiar relation implying confidence or leading to confidence, it would take the case out of the ordinary rule," the court concluded. "In the present case there are peculiar circumstances."[29]

In another case, the directors of a mining company had intentionally driven down the value of the stock by refusing to develop the mines, so that they could buy up stock from shareholders at an artificially depressed price. This would not have been illegal, explained the judge, a young William Howard Taft, if there had been no relationship between the buyers and sellers other than director and shareholder. A director owed a duty to the corporation, not to the corporation's shareholders. But in this case the shareholders had pledged the stock to the directors as collateral for a loan, so there *was* another relationship. The directors owed a duty to the shareholders—not as directors but as custodians of the shares—to refrain from taking actions that would reduce the value of the stock.[30]

Judges were quick to find special circumstances that would prohibit insider trading in a given case, without casting doubt on the general principle permitting insiders to buy and sell without disclosing information. In Kansas, the president of the Topeka Water Supply Company bought stock from shareholders without telling them that he had received an offer to buy the entire company at a much higher price per share. But the president was not just a corporate officer, the state

29 Paula J. Dalley, "From Horse Trading to Insider Trading: The Historical Antecedents of the Insider Trading Debate," *William & Mary Law Review* 39 (1998): 1289–1353; *Fisher v. Budlong*, 10 R.I. 525, 527–29 (1873).
30 *Ritchie v. McMullen*, 79 F. 522, 532–34 (6th Cir. 1897).

supreme court determined. Once he had received the offer to buy the company, he also had "a special agency for the sale," under which "he was specially authorized to find a purchaser," and that special agency imposed an obligation of candor toward the shareholders greater than that of an ordinary insider. In Utah, when Alviras Snow, the treasurer of a mining company, bought shares from C. D. Morrison for much less than their true value, the state supreme court rescinded the transaction. Snow was "a dealer in mines and mining stock" who had "almost absolute control of the business affairs." Morrison, by contrast, "was a poor man, with a family, and had to keep constantly at work. He resided at a wayside station on the railroad 500 miles from Salt Lake City, where the books of the company were kept." Morrison had never even been to Salt Lake City. He knew little or nothing about the business. He was entirely dependent on Snow for information. The stock sale was "the culmination or final act of a scheme conceived by Snow, weeks before, to defraud Morrison out of his stock." These special facts sufficed to render the normal caveat emptor rule inapplicable. "Under these circumstances," the court held, "Snow was both morally and legally bound to refrain from doing anything . . . to mislead or deceive Morrison."[31] Where an insider's conduct seemed especially reprehensible, or where a shareholder was particularly sympathetic, it did not take much for courts to find special circumstances that allowed them to disregard the usual rule.

The most famous of these "special facts" cases, *Strong v. Repide*, was decided by the US Supreme Court in 1909. It came from the Philippines, which had become an American colony shortly before. When the United States assumed control of the Philippines, one of its first acts was to purchase much of the colony's land. One of the big landowners was the Philippine Sugar Estates Development Company, which, after protracted negotiations, reached an agreement in 1903 to sell a large parcel to the government at a price favorable to the company, a deal that would cause the company's stock price to rise. Francisco Repide, a director of the company and the owner of nearly three-quarters of

31 *Mulvane v. O'Brien*, 49 P. 607, 613 (Kan. 1897); *Morrison v. Snow*, 72 P. 924, 927–28 (Utah 1903).

the company's stock, conducted the negotiations. While doing so, he purchased shares in the company from Eleanor and Richard Strong. Repide bought the stock in a sneaky way, so that the Strongs would not realize he was the purchaser and raise their asking price. He hired a relative by marriage named Kauffman, who hired a broker, who told the Strongs that the stock was for a member of Kauffman's wife's family. The Supreme Court concluded that while, in the ordinary case, a director need not disclose inside information when buying shares, this was not an ordinary case. "Concealing his identity when procuring the purchase of the stock," the court held, "was strong evidence of fraud." Repide may not have committed fraud in the strict sense—he really *was* a member of Kauffman's wife's family, so the broker's statement was technically true—but his actions were devious, and that was enough. A director normally owed no duty of disclosure to shareholders, "yet there are cases where, by reason of special facts, such duty exists." This was one of them.[32]

At the turn of the century, the general rule was that insiders need not disclose information when buying and selling stock, but that rule was heavily qualified by judges' willingness to find special circumstances that required disclosure. Beginning in the first decade of the century, courts in several states went one step further. They began to say that corporate insiders *did* have a duty of disclosure, in *all* circumstances. In the view of these courts, the directors of corporations were trustees not just for the corporation, but for the shareholders as well. The courts that took this step were in the South and the rural Midwest, far from the nation's financial centers.

The first court to prohibit insider trading was the Georgia Supreme Court, which in 1903 considered a case involving the Gate City Oil Company. The company's president, William Oliver, had acquired options to purchase stock in the company from several shareholders for $110 per share, while he was negotiating the sale of the company's plant for a sum that made the stock worth $185 per share. Oliver had not disclosed the impending transaction to the shareholders. Once he signed

---

32 *Strong v. Repide*, 213 U.S. 419, 431–33 (1909).

the contract to sell the plant, he exercised the options and immediately resold the shares, yielding him an instant profit of nearly $50,000.

This scheme did not sit right with Joseph Lamar of the Georgia Supreme Court. Lamar had just been appointed to the court. He was a corporate lawyer from Augusta, who would stay on the court for only two years before returning to his law practice. (In 1911, President Taft would appoint him to the US Supreme Court, where he would serve until his death five years later.) Lamar knew full well that under existing law there was nothing illegal about Oliver's transactions. But he did not like it. "It is a matter of common knowledge," Lamar noted, "that the market value of shares rises and falls, not only because of an increase or decrease in tangible property, but by reason of real or contemplated action on the part of managing officers." To allow an insider to trade on his superior knowledge, "without making a full disclosure, and putting the stockholder on an equality of knowledge as to those facts, would offer a premium for faithless silence, and give a reward for the suppression of truth." Lamar was dismayed that the law would allow a director "to take advantage of his own wrong—a thing abhorrent to a court." So he and his colleagues established a new rule. In Georgia, Lamar explained, the inside information obtained by a corporate director "is a quasi asset of the company, and the shareholder is as much entitled to the advantage of that sort of asset as to any other regularly entered on the list of the company's holdings." Information about corporate dealings belonged to the corporation, not to the director. "Where the director obtains the information giving added value to the stock by virtue of his official position," Lamar declared, "he holds this information in trust for the benefit of those who placed him where this knowledge was obtained." The director was thus "a quasi trustee as to the shareholder's interest in the shares." He could not use inside information to take advantage of the shareholders.[33]

Kansas followed suit the next year. "The managing officers of a corporation are not only trustees in relation to the corporate entity," the state's supreme court held, "but they are also to some extent and in many respects trustees of the corporate shareholders." John Stewart,

33 *Oliver v. Oliver*, 45 S.E. 232, 233–35 (Ga. 1903).

the president of the Wellington National Bank, had purchased shares in the bank for much less than their actual value from an eighty-year-old stockholder who knew nothing about banking. The Kansas Supreme Court rejected existing law, which, in the court's view, left stockholders "the legitimate prey" of insiders. In a later case, the court required insiders not merely to disclose information before they traded, but also to explain it for the benefit of shareholders who would not otherwise understand it.[34]

By the 1910s, insider trading was illegal in Nebraska and Iowa as well. The law had once been clear, but now lawyers faced "a contrariety of judicial opinion," one law professor lamented. Some thought the trend a bad one. "If a seller understands that the buyer is in a position to know more about the subject of sale than he does," insisted Clarence Laylin of Ohio State University, "there is nothing morally or legally wrong, according to present-day standards, in laying upon him the burden of making inquiry of the buyer." Roberts Walker, a New York corporate lawyer and a director in several large corporations, sniffed that the newer view, "particularly at a distance from salt water, seems to have beclouded rather than clarified the state of the law." Walker complained that "courts, in the Mississippi basin especially, seem to cherish a mental picture of shrewd, sharp, scheming directors craftily trading with inexperienced, female, infant, defective stockholders." Walker worried that a ban on insider trading "would be most unsettling if enforced in financial centers, or respecting great corporations with hosts of stockholders."[35]

Others thought the trend was a positive development. Insider trading "offends the moral sense," declared H. L. Wilgus of the University of Michigan. "No shareholder expects to be so treated by the director he selects; no director would urge his friends to select him for that reason;

34 *Stewart v. Harris*, 77 P. 277, 279–81 (Kan. 1904); *Hotchkiss v. Fischer*, 16 P.2d 531, 534 (Kan. 1932).

35 *Jacquith v. Mason*, 156 N.W. 1041 (Neb. 1916); *Dawson v. National Life Ins. Co.*, 157 N.W. 929 (Iowa 1916); Clarence D. Laylin, "The Duty of a Director Purchasing Stock," *Yale Law Journal* 27 (1918): 732, 739–40; Roberts Walker, "The Duty of Disclosure by a Director Purchasing Stock from His Stockholders," *Yale Law Journal* 32 (1923): 639–40.

that the law yet allows him to do this, does more to discourage legitimate investment in corporate shares than almost anything else." Adolf Berle approvingly predicted that the recent cases classifying directors as trustees for the shareholders "are merely specific applications of a much wider fiduciary relationship which will ultimately transform the publicly financed corporations of today into organisms having many of the characteristics of investment trusts."[36]

The Securities Exchange Act of 1934 addressed the propriety of insider trading only indirectly. The act did not prohibit insiders from buying or selling stock or require them to disclose their inside information before trading. Instead, section 16(a) of the act required directors, officers, and large shareholders (those who own more than 10 percent of the stock) to file monthly statements revealing any purchases or sales. This requirement was "based upon the theory that if such transactions were publicized they would be discontinued," explained Securities and Exchange Commission Chairman Donald Cook. In addition, "for the purpose of preventing the unfair use of information," section 16(b) of the act barred directors, officers, and large shareholders from profiting from purchases and sales (or sales and purchases) within a six-month span. The corporation itself could sue to recover any such short-swing profits. Finally, section 16(c) of the act prohibited directors, officers, and large shareholders from making short sales of shares they did not yet own.[37]

This was an extremely oblique way of preventing insider trading. The Securities Exchange Act applied only to the largest corporations, those traded on a stock exchange, so it did not limit insider trading in the shares of smaller companies. As for the largest corporations, the act made insider trading more difficult. Insiders could not profit secretly or

36 H. L. Wilgus, "Purchase of Shares of a Corporation by a Director from a Shareholder," *Michigan Law Review* 8 (1910): 297; A. A. Berle Jr., "Publicity of Accounts and Directors' Purchases of Stock," *Michigan Law Review* 25 (1927): 831. Berle would later make a similar argument in Adolf A. Berle Jr. and Gardiner C. Means, *The Modern Corporation and Private Property* (New York: Macmillan, 1932), 327–30.

37 Donald C. Cook and Myer Feldman, "Insider Trading Under the Securities Exchange Act," *Harvard Law Review* 66 (1953): 386; 48 Stat. 881, 896–97 (1934).

quickly. But they could still profit, by buying shares before publicizing good news or selling before publicizing bad, so long as they were willing to hold the shares (or refrain from repurchasing them) for more than six months. And as a committee of the American Bar Association pointed out a few years after the law's enactment, the act "does not meet the problem squarely, for it neither compensates the losing party to a trade nor confines its punitive effect to actual instances where information confidentially obtained is used for private profit."[38] Section 16 failed to reach many instances of insider trading, while it forced insiders to disgorge profits even if they were not acquired by virtue of inside information. In retrospect, the strategy pursued in the Securities Exchange Act can be understood as a snapshot of informed opinion during an era of transition. Just as the states were dividing over the propriety of insider trading, the federal government occupied an intermediate position as well, neither fully approving nor fully forbidding it.

WE ARE AGAINST FRAUD, AREN'T WE?

The legality of insider trading before the mid-twentieth century was a special case of a more general rule of caveat emptor governing commercial transactions. The general rule would change over the course of the century, however, and as it did, so did the rules governing insider trading.

One of the overarching legal developments of the twentieth century was the gradual loss, in a wide variety of contexts, of the ability to exploit an informational advantage to the detriment of one's contractual counterparts. Merchants were no longer allowed to sell defective products: they were held to an implied warranty of the quality of their wares, and they were made strictly liable for the harms their products caused to consumers. House builders and house sellers were required to reveal unfavorable information to prospective purchasers. Mandatory disclosures became familiar parts of commercial life—disclosures of the ingredients in food, the attributes of automobiles, the terms of credit

---

38 "Report of the Special Committee on Securities Laws and Regulations," *Annual Report of the American Bar Association* 66 (1941): 356.

cards, and much more. If caveat emptor was the background rule of commercial law in the late nineteenth century, disclosure—the opposite of caveat emptor—had become the background rule by the late twentieth.[39]

These legal changes reflected a growing ethical interest in protecting consumers against sharp practices by knowledgeable insiders in the marketplace. In the stock market, ordinary shareholders were consumers of a sort; they were buying (and selling) a product they often knew much less about than the person on the other side of the trade. The law's treatment of insider trading began to change accordingly.

Courts in rural states had already condemned insider trading, but in the late 1940s, the practice came in for condemnation by judges in urban states and eastern financial centers as well. The California Supreme Court held that "an officer, in buying or selling to a shareholder, must inform him of those matters relating to the corporate business of which the officer has knowledge." A court in Chicago required a director to reveal his advance knowledge of the sale of the corporation's assets before buying stock. The Delaware Court of Chancery, an important decision maker because of the many corporations chartered in Delaware, held that a corporate employee could not purchase the corporation's stock when he knew that the price would soon rise because the corporation itself planned to purchase its own stock. Louis Loss, the associate general counsel for the Securities and Exchange Commission, concluded in 1951 that "the so-called 'majority' view," which permitted insiders to buy and sell freely without disclosure, "is gradually giving way to the generally growing feeling of responsibility of corporate insiders—the development of a status of 'trusteeship' in a non-technical sense."[40]

The SEC helped this development along. In 1942, the SEC promulgated Rule 10b-5, a catch-all provision that prohibited "any act,

---

39 William L. Prosser, "The Implied Warranty of Merchantable Quality," *Minnesota Law Review* 27 (1943): 117–68; Alan M. Weinberger, "Let the Buyer Be Well Informed? Doubting the Demise of Caveat Emptor," *Maryland Law Review* 55 (1996): 387–424.

40 *Hobart v. Hobart Estate Co.*, 159 P.2d 958, 970 (Cal. 1945); *Agatucci v. Corradi*, 63 N.E.2d 630, 632 (Ill. App. 1945); *Brophy v. Cities Service Co.*, 70 A.2d 5, 8 (Del. Ch. 1949); Louis Loss, *Securities Regulation* (Boston: Little, Brown and Co., 1951), 826.

practice, or course of business which operates or would operate as a fraud or deceit upon any person." The rule was not written with insider trading in mind. "I was sitting in my office," recalled the SEC lawyer Milton Freeman,

> and I received a call from Jim Treanor who was then the Director of the Trading and Exchange Division. He said, "I have just been on the telephone with Paul Rowen," who was then the S.E.C. Regional Administrator in Boston, "and he has told me about the president of some company in Boston who is going around buying up the stock of his company from his own shareholders at $4.00 a share, and he has been telling them that the company is doing very badly, whereas, in fact, the earnings are going to be quadrupled and will be $2.00 a share for the coming year. Is there anything we can do about it?"

The Boston company president was committing a garden-variety fraud by lying to the shareholders about the company's prospects, but nothing in the SEC's rules covered the situation. The SEC lawyers hastily put together a new rule prohibiting all frauds and presented it to the agency's five commissioners. "All the commissioners read the rule," Freeman remembered. "Nobody said anything except Sumner Pike who said, 'Well,' he said, 'we are against fraud aren't we?' That is how it happened."[41]

Although the new rule did not mention insider trading, within a year the SEC had already concluded that insider trading violated the rule. In 1943, the SEC investigated the Ward La France Truck Corporation, which was making unprecedented profits from truck sales to the military during the war. The company planned to sell its entire business to the Salta Corporation, a transaction that would greatly increase the value of the shares in the Ward La France Corporation. Without disclosing this plan to shareholders, both companies were busy buying up Ward La France shares at prices much lower than the shareholders would have received if they had known to wait for the merger. The SEC determined that these share purchases "unaccompanied by appropriate disclosure of

---

41 Milton Freeman, "Administrative Procedures," *Business Lawyer* 22 (1967): 922.

material facts" constituted a violation of the new Rule 10b-5.[42] This was just an administrative decision, not the judgment of a court, but it was important nonetheless, because as a practical matter many of the cases before the SEC never reached a court. In the view of the SEC, at least, insider trading was now illegal.

Investors soon began using the rule to sue insiders to recover the insiders' profits from such trades. In 1946, the managers of the Western Board and Paper Company bought company stock from fellow shareholders without telling the shareholders that they had reached an agreement to sell the company's plant and equipment to another firm. The shareholders sued the managers under Rule 10b-5 and won. "Under any reasonably liberal construction" of the rule, the judge explained, "these provisions apply to directors and officers who, in purchasing the stock of the corporation from others, fail to disclose a fact coming to their knowledge by reason of their position, which would materially affect the judgment of the other party to the transaction." In a similar case a few years later, another judge declared that "the rule is clear. It is unlawful for an insider, such as a majority stockholder, to purchase the stock of minority stockholders without disclosing material facts affecting the value of the stock, known to the majority stockholder by virtue of his inside position." The judge reasoned that "the duty of disclosure stems from the necessity of preventing a corporate insider from utilizing his position to take unfair advantage of the uninformed minority stockholders. It is an attempt to provide some degree of equalization of bargaining position." By the late 1950s, the leading treatise on closely held corporations advised the victims of insider trading to sue under Rule 10b-5 rather than state common law, because the rule imposed stricter duties of disclosure on insiders.[43]

The norms of corporate insiders changed accordingly. In the early twentieth century, Donald Cook recalled, profits from insider trading

---

42 *In the Matter of Ward La France Truck Corp.*, 13 S.E.C. 373 (1943).
43 "The Prospects for Rule X-10B-5: An Emerging Remedy for Defrauded Investors," *Yale Law Journal* 59 (1950): 1140–49; *Kardon v. National Gypsum Co.*, 73 F. Supp. 798, 800 (E.D. Pa. 1947); *Speed v. Transamerica Corp.*, 99 F. Supp. 808, 828–29 (D. Del. 1951); F. Hodge O'Neal, *Close Corporations: Law and Practice* (Chicago: Callaghan & Co., 1958), 2:156; see also Elvin R. Latty, "The Aggrieved Buyer or Seller or Holder of Shares in a Close Corporation

had been "regarded by members of the financial community as one of the usual emoluments of office." But a 1961 survey conducted by the *Harvard Business Review* revealed a very different picture. The *Review* posed this scenario to seventeen hundred executives: "Imagine that you are a member of the board of directors of a large corporation. At a board meeting you learn of an impending merger with a smaller company which has had an unprofitable year, and whose stock is presently selling at a price so low that you are certain it will rise when news of the merger becomes public knowledge." A few decades earlier, this question would probably not even have been asked in a survey of ethics, because it would hardly have been thought to raise an ethical issue. But in 1961, 56 percent of respondents declared that they would "do nothing" in this situation. Only 42 percent said they would buy shares in the smaller company for themselves. Only 61 percent thought that the "average executive" would buy shares for himself. A few decades earlier, both figures would have been close to 100 percent.[44]

While the *Harvard Business Review* was conducting its survey, the SEC was extending the reach of its prohibition on insider trading. At a 1959 board meeting of the Curtiss-Wright Corporation, a manufacturer of airplane parts, the directors voted to cut the company's quarterly dividend by nearly half. Curtiss-Wright's normal policy, in keeping with the rules of the New York Stock Exchange, was to send telegrams immediately to the stock exchange and to the Dow Jones News Ticker Service, so that everyone would know about the dividend. (The stock exchange was marketing itself to small investors as a safe place for their money.[45] The notification rule was part of that effort.) In this instance, however, there was an inadvertent delay in sending the telegrams. The board vote took place at 11:00 a.m., but the telegram did not reach Dow

Under the S.E.C. Statutes," *Law & Contemporary Problems* 18 (1953): 527–32; Robert M. Desky, "Corporations: Fiduciary Duties: Application of SEC Rule X-10B-5 to Prevent Nondisclosure in the Sale of Corporate Securities," *California Law Review* 39 (1951): 429–39.

44 Cook and Feldman, "Insider Trading," 386; "How Ethical Are Businessmen?," *Harvard Business Review*, July–August 1961, 16.

45 Janice M. Traflet, *A Nation of Small Shareholders: Marketing Wall Street after World War II* (Baltimore: Johns Hopkins University Press, 2013).

Jones until 11:45, and it did not reach the stock exchange until 12:29. In the interim, a Curtiss-Wright director named J. Cheever Cowdin left the meeting. Cowdin was also a representative of a brokerage firm called Cady, Roberts and Company. He phoned Robert Gintel, a colleague at Cady Roberts, and told Gintel about the reduction of the dividend. Gintel promptly sold Curtiss-Wright stock on behalf of several of the brokerage firm's customers, and sold the stock short on behalf of several others. One of the customers was Gintel's wife. When the news of the dividend was finally made public, Curtiss-Wright's stock price plummeted. By selling as soon as Cowdin told him about the dividend, Gintel had saved his clients a bundle.

William Cary had just been appointed by President Kennedy as chairman of the SEC. Cary had spent most of his career as a law professor at Columbia. He had a particular interest in stamping out insider trading. The SEC's earlier cases had involved insiders who traded with shareholders in face-to-face transactions, and Cary recognized that the Cady Roberts case presented a chance to extend the ban on insider trading to trades on a stock exchange, where the person on the other side of the trade was unknown. He took the opportunity to write a lengthy opinion spelling out the SEC's view of the law. "The securities acts may be said to have generated a wholly new and far-reaching body of Federal corporation law," Cary declared. Part of that law, he explained, was a ban on insider trading. "We and the courts have consistently held that insiders must disclose material facts which are known to them by virtue of their position but which are not known to persons with whom they deal," he explained. This was just as true for transactions on a stock exchange as for face-to-face transactions. "It would be anomalous indeed," Cary insisted, "if the protection afforded by the antifraud provisions were withdrawn from transactions effected on exchanges," which were the "primary markets for securities transactions." Because neither Cowdin nor Gintel had disclosed the dividend reduction before Gintel sold Curtiss-Wright stock, they had broken the law. Cowdin had died shortly after the incident, so the SEC could not punish him, but the SEC suspended Gintel from the stock exchange for twenty days.[46]

46 Joel Seligman, *The Transformation of Wall Street* (Boston: Houghton Mifflin, 1982), 344–45; *In the Matter of Cady, Roberts & Co.*, 40 S.E.C. 907 (1961).

The case caused considerable alarm in the New York financial community. It was the first in which an upstanding member of that community was punished for insider trading. Robert Gintel was a recent graduate of Harvard Business School who had served in the air force. He would go on to run a small mutual fund named after himself, a fund small enough that he could invite all the shareholders to an annual barbecue at his estate in Greenwich, Connecticut.[47] J. Cheever Cowdin had been the president of Universal Pictures and the Aqueduct Racetrack, and he had been a Curtiss-Wright director for more than thirty years. Unlike some of the insiders in the earlier cases, these were prominent people.

The case was also the first in which the person punished was not himself a director or officer of the corporation, but rather someone who had received a tip from a director. Robert Gintel was a stockbroker who happened to have a partner who sat on the board of a major corporation. Wall Street was full of brokers and bankers and lawyers in the same position, people who knew directors but were not directors themselves. They talked to each other all the time, at work and at play, and some of their conversation involved information that could affect stock prices. Indeed, in an era when the commissions stockbrokers charged their customers were fixed by the exchange, the brokers could not compete on price, so one common way of competing was by offering tips to their customers.[48] If Gintel had broken the law, who else might have done the same?

"The decision raises many troublesome questions and encompasses various shadowy areas," two New York lawyers worried. Investment advisors were *supposed* to gather information about companies, so they could recommend which stocks to buy. But now the SEC was punishing a broker for doing just that. If giving good advice would only "expose the well advised to potential penalties," they feared, "the precept of 'investigate and invest' may be thwarted." The lawyer Carlos Israels wondered whether ordinary small talk had become

47 *New York Times*, 19 Mar. 1990, D6; *New York Times*, 13 Aug. 1982, A14.
48 Stanislav Dolgopolov, "Insider Trading, Chinese Walls, and Brokerage Commissions: The Origins of Modern Regulation of Information Flows in Securities Markets," *Journal of Law, Economics & Policy* 4 (2008): 311–67.

illegal. "How about the case in which the partner of this brokerage house has lunch with his friend, the vice-president, and is told, 'You know, Bill, that new combustion engine that we wrote about in our last report to stockholders, we spent fifteen million dollars on it, but it turned out to be a complete dud.'" Had the broker become an "insider" who owed a duty to the corporation not to trade in its stock? And what about his duty to the clients whose money he was investing—which took priority? The Chicago lawyer W. McNeil Kennedy was a former regional administrator of the SEC, but even he was positive that the decision "foreshadows grave problems for the securities industry."[49]

The view was quite different outside Wall Street. Louis Loss had left the SEC for Harvard Law School, where he would teach for decades. "I think if Professor Cary does nothing else at the SEC he has earned his pay in *Cady*," Loss exclaimed. "I view that as a landmark in the law." As Loss saw it, Cary had said "officially what needed to be said a long time ago. Of course it opens problems—what does not?"[50]

Another set of problems was opened a few years later, when the US Court of Appeals for the Second Circuit, the federal appellate court with jurisdiction over New York and thus the most important to securities law, decided the *Texas Gulf Sulphur* case. Directors and officers of a mining company bought company stock when they, but not the public, knew that the company had found unusually rich ores and thus that the stock price was certain to rise. These directors and officers were paradigmatic insiders, and their knowledge of the ores was information as important to the stock price as any information could be. The difficult thing about the case was not the result, although the case did mark the first occasion in which a court of appeals blessed the SEC's now two-decades-old view that Rule 10b-5 barred insider trading. The problems were caused instead by the court's broad language, which suggested a prohibition on insider trading even wider than the SEC

49 F. Arnold Daum and Howard W. Phillips, "The Implications of Cady, Roberts," *Business Lawyer* 17 (1962): 940, 959; William L. Cary, "Recent Developments in Securities Regulation," *Columbia Law Review* 63 (1963): 866; William L. Cary, "The Direction of Management Responsibility," *Business Lawyer* 18 (1962): 79.
50 Cary, "Recent Developments," 861.

had urged. "The Rule is based in policy on the justifiable expectation of the securities marketplace that all investors trading on impersonal exchanges have relatively equal access to material information," the court declared. "Insiders, as directors or management officers are, of course, by this Rule, precluded from so unfairly dealing, but the Rule is also applicable to one possessing the information who may not be strictly termed an 'insider.'" It was not one's status as an insider that triggered a ban on trading; it was rather the possession of information that the public did not yet have. "Thus, anyone in possession of material inside information must either disclose it to the investing public, or, if he is disabled from disclosing it in order to protect a corporate confidence, or he chooses not to do so, must abstain from trading." The purpose of the rule was that "all investors should have equal access to the rewards of the participation in securities transactions," the court concluded. "It was the intent of Congress that all members of the investing public should be subject to identical market risks."[51]

This was as strong an assertion of commercial morality as the American legal system had seen since the cases rejecting the caveat emptor doctrine in the early nineteenth century. Read literally, it would mean that no securities could be bought or sold unless both parties had equal knowledge of all information affecting the price. The *Texas Gulf Sulphur* rule extended far beyond the devious director who conned his shareholders by buying up their stock on the cheap. It covered *everyone* who knew more than the person on the other side of the transaction. Once the law had allowed anyone to speculate with superior information, but now the pendulum had swung completely in the opposite direction.

"It's going to have a hell of an impact on the financial world," predicted Sterry Waterman, the judge who wrote the opinion. He was right. The printed text of the opinion broke all the sales records for the company with the Second Circuit printing contract. "This thing is hot as hell," exclaimed the printing company's manager. "Almost everybody and his uncle who knows anything about law or the stock

---

51 *Securities and Exchange Commission v. Texas Gulf Sulphur Co.*, 401 F.2d 833, 848, 851–52 (2d Cir. 1968) (en banc).

market wants it." Lawyers, brokers, investors—everyone had to read *Texas Gulf Sulphur*. The brokers did not like it one bit. "This makes for utter confusion," one complained. Another reported that "it's got the whole street disturbed." Brokers had long been accustomed to ferreting out news and passing tips along to their clients, because the brokers had not considered themselves insiders with respect to the corporations whose stock they bought and sold. But if the brokers could not use the information they discovered, how would they make a living? One broker lamented that he and his colleagues would be nothing but "ticket sellers," simply buying whatever stocks their clients requested. Their alarm grew two weeks later, when the SEC commenced administrative proceedings against fourteen employees of the Merrill Lynch broker- age firm for telling clients about an earnings decline at the Douglas Aircraft Company before the decline was reported to the public. The SEC had "put Wall Street on notice," reported the *New York Times*, "that a relatively widespread practice no longer will be tolerated." But a famine for brokers could be a feast for members of other professions. Public relations firms foresaw an increased need for their services, be- cause of the specter of liability from the mistimed release of corporate information. "Every sensible company will have to consider its finan- cial public relations in a new light," chortled the chairman of Hill & Knowlton. Lawyers flocked to conventions to discuss how to advise their clients. The Practising Law Institute held a special session on *Texas Gulf Sulphur* and got the biggest turnout the organization had ever seen. "Nearly every company is re-examining its policy in this area," one satisfied lawyer explained.[52]

Eventually, however, the Supreme Court narrowed the class of people barred from insider trading. In two opinions in the early 1980s, the court rejected the view that the law required both parties to a transaction to have equal information. Both opinions were written by Justice Lewis Powell, who had been a corporate lawyer before joining the court and who had formed a strong belief that the law imposed too many restrictions on businesses. In *Chiarella v. United States*,

52 *Wall Street Journal*, 14 Aug. 1968, 3; 19 Aug. 1968, 5; *New York Times*, 15 Aug. 1968, 54; 18 Aug. 1968, F1; *Wall Street Journal*, 3 Sept. 1968, 30; *New York Times*, 1 Sept. 1968, E5; 25 Aug. 1968, F14; 13 Oct. 1968, F1; 11 Oct. 1968, 67.

the court reversed the conviction of a printer who had learned of an impending takeover while printing the necessary documents. There was no "general duty between all participants in market transactions to forgo actions based on material, nonpublic information," Powell declared. Rather, insider trading was unlawful only where the trader owed a duty to disclose the information to another. Three years later, in *Dirks v. S.E.C.*, the court ruled in favor of a broker who had received tips about a corporate fraud from corporate employees, and who then spread news about the fraud to others, who sold the company's stock before the news became public. Such "tippees" broke the law, the court explained, only where the insider provided the tip to profit from it. Powell again took the opportunity to reject the contention that the law requires equal information among all traders.[53]

Many more difficult questions remained.[54] Who owed duties to whom not to exploit inside information? What was the source of these duties, and what was their content? Were there also non-duty-based grounds for imposing liability for insider trading? These questions were rendered even more difficult by Congress's failure to answer them in legislation. By the early twenty-first century there was a large and complex body of insider trading law, all of which had been created by judges who had little to guide them apart from the 1942 SEC rule banning "fraud or deceit." The judges had rejected both extremes. The law did not permit insider trading across the board, as it had for much of the nineteenth century, nor did it completely forbid traders from exploiting their superior knowledge, as it briefly had in the mid-twentieth. The law of insider trading was somewhere in the middle, but it was no easy matter to say exactly where. "The closer one looks at insider trading law," one expert despaired, "the messier it appears."[55]

53 Adam C. Pritchard, "Justice Lewis F. Powell, Jr., and the Counterrevolution in the Federal Securities Laws," *Duke Law Journal* 52 (2003): 841–949; *Chiarella v. United States*, 445 U.S. 222, 233, 230 (1980); *Dirks v. S.E.C.*, 463 U.S. 646, 655–62 (1983).

54 For an engaging discussion of these questions, see Stephen M. Bainbridge, *Securities Law: Insider Trading* (New York: Foundation Press, 1999).

55 Sung Hui Kim, "Insider Trading as Private Corruption," *UCLA Law Review* 61 (2014): 945.

A handful of high-profile prosecutions in the 1980s made insider trading the white-collar crime perhaps most familiar to the general public. Prominent people charged with insider trading during the era included the entrepreneur Ivan Boesky and the investment bankers Michael Milken and Dennis Levine. Insider trading was a major theme of the popular 1987 film *Wall Street*, which earned Michael Douglas an Academy Award for best actor. The public seemed to take a greater interest in insider trading than in more humdrum offenses like embezzlement or tax fraud, most likely because the existence of insider trading confirmed the widespread sense—one that has always been deeply ingrained in American culture—that the financial markets are rigged in favor of crafty insiders. Despite the attention these cases received, the empirical evidence suggests that they did little to reduce the frequency or the profitability of insider trading.[56]

Meanwhile, there was a raging debate among economists and law professors over whether insider trading should be illegal at all. The debate was sparked in 1966 by the law professor Henry Manne, who argued that insider trading made the stock market more efficient by aligning the price of stocks with their true value, and that allowing entrepreneurs to profit from trading was the most effective way of compensating them for their contributions. Other market participants were not harmed by insider trading, Manne contended. Long-term investors would not care whether stock prices moved before or after the announcement of news, because they were unlikely to buy or sell in the interim. And short-term investors who transacted with an insider were not hurt, because they would have bought or sold anyway.[57] In the old days, when an insider dealt directly with a handful of shareholders, any gain to the insider was a loss to the shareholder, who would have held on to his shares had he not sold them to the insider. But in the modern impersonal market, an insider could buy shares only from a shareholder who had already decided to put them up for sale.

56 H. Nejat Seyhun, "The Effectiveness of the Insider-Trading Sanctions," *Journal of Law and Economics* 35 (1992): 149–82.
57 Henry G. Manne, *Insider Trading and the Stock Market* (New York: Free Press, 1966).

Manne's argument was attacked immediately, by critics who charged that investors *were* harmed by insider trading when they sold at prices less advantageous than they would have otherwise received. The critics worried about the loss of public confidence and participation in the market that might result from a perception that insiders had an advantage.[58] The debate has continued in the pages of economics journals and law reviews for half a century.

But this academic debate about the economic effects of insider trading has made scarcely any dent in the law. Insider trading became illegal because it was widely perceived as unfair, not because of its effects on the efficiency of markets. Whether it is right to use one's superior knowledge to gain an edge in the marketplace is one of our oldest questions of commercial morality. As the law of insider trading has developed over the past century, speculators have been held to the same standards as other merchants. They have gradually lost much, but not all, of their former ability to exploit inside information.

58 A good example of the early criticism of Manne's thesis is Roy A. Schotland, "Unsafe at Any Price: A Reply to Manne, *Insider Trading and the Stock Market,*" *Virginia Law Review* 53 (1967): 1425–78.

8

Speculation or Investment?

WHAT IS THE DIFFERENCE between *speculation* and *investment?* As we have seen, this question lurked behind the commercial regulation of the nineteenth and twentieth centuries, much of which was intended to restrain the former but encourage the latter. But there were also some contexts in which the question was in the foreground. In these situations, lawyers, judges, and legislators routinely had to classify particular transactions as instances of speculation or investment, because important legal consequences flowed from the decision. Over the nineteenth and twentieth centuries, a great deal of thought was devoted to an immediately practical question: where does investment stop and speculation begin?

One of these contexts was the "prudent man" rule that governed the conduct of trustees. A trustee is a person who manages assets for the benefit of someone else. Courts declared over and over again that a trustee was required to act as a prudent man would. In particular, a trustee had to *invest* the trust's assets, but under no circumstances could he *speculate* with them. When a trustee used the trust's funds to buy an asset, like stock in a corporation, and the value of that asset declined, the trustee was not personally responsible for the loss if his purchase of the asset was an investment, but if it was a speculation, the trustee had to make up the loss out of his own pocket. A lot turned on precisely how to draw the line between speculating and investing. But the prudent man rule was much easier to state in the abstract than to apply in concrete cases. How was a judge supposed to tell whether this or that transaction was speculation or investment?

A second context was the capital gains tax. A capital gain is income from the sale of an asset at a price higher than was paid for it. Capital gains have been taxed as income since the birth of the modern federal income tax in the early twentieth century. For nearly as long, Congress has sought to impose higher tax rates on speculators than on investors, so as not to deter investment. Of course, to do so requires some method of telling the two groups apart. The drafters of the tax code have thus faced the same question as judges evaluating the transactions of trustees. How could they distinguish speculation from investment?

A third context in which the question arose was in the design of a securities transaction tax. Since the late nineteenth century, the federal government and the state of New York have, off and on, imposed small taxes on the sale of stock. The primary goal of these taxes has been to raise revenue, not to deter speculation. There have been recurring suggestions, however, that the tax should be increased to the point where it would make speculation uncomfortably expensive, as a way of reducing the amount of it. And these suggestions have inevitably raised the same old nagging questions: Is it possible to deter speculation without also deterring investment? Can one be distinguished from the other?

THE PRUDENT MAN

When the wealthy Boston merchant John McLean died in 1823, he left the then-enormous sum of $50,000 to a trust, the income from which was to support his widow, Ann, for the rest of her life. Upon Ann's death, the fund would be divided evenly between Harvard College and the Massachusetts General Hospital. McLean placed the money in the care of two other Boston merchants, Jonathan and Francis Amory, who used it to purchase the stock of a bank, an insurance company, and two textile firms. A few years later, the value of the insurance stock had fallen from $16,000 to $12,000, and the shares in the two textile companies, which the Amorys had bought for $25,000, were worth only $17,000. Harvard and the Massachusetts General Hospital were not pleased. They sued Francis Amory (Jonathan had died), and they argued that he was responsible for making up the difference. Rather than making "safe and productive" investments in government bonds or bank shares, they contended, Amory had speculated "in trading companies, whereby the principal sum was exposed and still continues to be exposed to great loss."

But the Massachusetts Supreme Court drew a different line between investing and speculating. Government bonds could be risky too, Justice Samuel Putnam pointed out. In times of war, for example, when the government borrowed so much that bondholders feared a default, the value of outstanding bonds could plummet. And "bank shares may be subject to losses which sweep away their whole value." There was simply no place to put money with absolute safety. "It will not do to reject those stocks as unsafe, which are in the management of directors whose well or ill directed measures may involve a total loss," Putnam reasoned. "Do what you will, the capital is at hazard." John McLean himself had owned manufacturing stock—so much that it amounted to nearly half his fortune—and McLean was well known as "a man of extraordinary forecast and discretion." The court concluded that Amory had done nothing wrong. He had been investing, not speculating.[1]

By the time Ann McLean died in 1834, the trust had not recovered. Harvard and the Massachusetts General Hospital ended up with less than $20,000 each. For many years after, they would resent what Amory had done with their money. The real estate lawyer and Harvard graduate Nathaniel Ingersoll Bowditch reported decades later: "It is believed that every Trustee of the Hospital and every Corporator of the College coincided in opinion, that this investment of the trust-funds, though adjudged to be legal, was not made in the exercise of a sound discretion, and with a due regard to the rights of all parties."[2]

But if Harvard and the hospital lost their case, their argument would eventually win general acceptance. Only a handful of American courts in the nineteenth century would agree with Judge Putnam that shares of corporations were investments suitable for trustees. One was the highest court in Mississippi, which recalled that stock in the

1 *Harvard College v. Amory*, 26 Mass. 446, 460–63 (1830).
2 Nathaniel I. Bowditch, *Extracts from a History of the Massachusetts General Hospital 1810–1851* (s.l.: privately printed, 1899), 18.

Commercial Bank of Natchez "was considered safe and profitable . . . by the most prudent men in the country" when a trustee bought $5,000 of it, even after the stock became worthless a few years later. Most American judges, however, would agree with Harvard and the Massachusetts General Hospital that corporate stock was too speculative for trustees to touch. "Stocks are liable to great depression," cautioned New Jersey chancellor Peter Vroom. "The prospects of peace or war, to say nothing of the agitations caused by the spirit of restless and unprincipled speculation, are constantly causing a fluctuation in the stocks." Vroom warned the state's trustees that "the stock of private companies is not considered safe." A New York court ordered a trustee for four children to compensate the children for the trust's losses on shares in the Dutchess County Bank. The property of a trust "cannot be jeopardized and wasted by hazardous speculations," the court lectured. "In a great majority of cases speculations in this country have been productive of disastrous consequences." Such transactions might sometimes yield high incomes for the trust's beneficiaries, but "the law regards the certainty of an income for persons thus situated, more than its magnitude."[3] Real estate and government bonds were investments, but corporate stock was a speculation.

This view was orthodoxy by the middle of the nineteenth century, as was made evident during the protracted litigation over the will of the Philadelphia banker Stephen Girard, who was probably the wealthiest person in the United States when he died childless in 1831. Girard's will is most famous for its bequest of $2 million to the city of Philadelphia for the establishment of a school for orphans, at which Girard specified that no minister of any sect would be allowed to teach. This aspect of the will was challenged by some of Girard's relatives, who hoped to get the $2 million for themselves, but it was upheld by the US Supreme Court in 1844.[4] Litigation over the will did not end there, however. Another clause of the will left $50,000 to a trust for the benefit of Girard's niece, Marie Antoinette Hemphill. Hemphill would receive

3 *Smyth v. Burns,* 25 Miss. 422, 427 (1853); *Gray v. Fox,* 1 N.J. Eq. 259, 266–67 (N.J. Ct. Ch. 1831); *Ackerman v. Emott,* 4 Barb. 626, 646–47 (N.Y. Super. 1848).
4 *Vidal v. Philadelphia,* 43 U.S. 127 (1844).

the interest on this sum for her life, and then on her death the money would be divided among her children. The trustees used part of the money to buy shares of the Bank of the United States. Girard himself had been intimately involved in creating the bank, had been one of the bank's directors, and had owned a significant fraction of the bank's stock. No financial institution, with the exception of Girard's own private bank, was as closely associated with Stephen Girard as the Bank of the United States. But the trustees had the misfortune to buy the shares just before the panic of 1837 shut the bank's doors for good.

"We have not a doubt, that the investment was made in perfect good faith," explained the Pennsylvania Supreme Court. But the court required the trustees to compensate the Hemphills for the loss, because they had speculated with the Hemphills' money. "If a trustee may throw off his responsibility by investing the trust fund in the stock of a corporation, what security is left?" the court asked. "There is no reason why the trustee should not make the investment in some security which cannot fail. It is just as convenient." The court held that the trustees should have invested in land or in government bonds, which were less likely to lose their value. "It is better for trustees that the rule of their conduct should be clearly defined and well understood," the court concluded. "A plain path, though it may be a narrow one, is safer to walk in than a trackless waste, where no man can be sure that he is on the right course."[5]

A few years later the New Hampshire Supreme Court was just as dubious about a trustee's purchase of stock in the Boston, Concord, and Montreal Railroad, stock that soon became worthless. "Safety is the primary object to be secured in an investment of this kind," the court noted, "and the trustee is not chargeable with an income that cannot be realized without hazard to the fund." The construction of a new railway line was the very opposite of safe. "Now it seems to us that the building of a railroad must, from the very inherent nature of the enterprise, have at all times been regarded by prudent men as a doubtful adventure," clucked the court. Even if the purchase of the stock "was advised and approved by . . . judicious and prudent men

5 *Hemphill's Appeal*, 18 Pa. 303, 306 (1852).

whom the trustee consulted," it was simply not the role of a trustee to put funds into any business corporation.[6]

By 1872, when the Salem, Massachusetts, lawyer Jairus Perry published his *Treatise on the Law of Trusts and Trustees*, he could report that nearly all courts drew a sharp line between business corporations, which were too speculative for trustees, and safe investments like land and government bonds. Money put into business corporations "runs the risks and chances of trade, business, and speculation," Perry explained. "Calamities that depress public credit seldom occur, while the risks of trade are constant. It would seem to be the wiser course to withdraw the funds, settled for the support of women, children, and other parties who cannot exercise an active discretion in the protection of their interests, as much as possible from the chances of business."[7] The prudent man would stay away from such risks.

What made corporate stock too speculative? The problem with corporations, a New York court explained, was that a stockholder had to put his faith in the wisdom of other people, the directors and officers of the firm, who were beyond the effective supervision of the trustee. "The moment the fund is invested in bank, or insurance, or railroad stock, it has left the control of the trustees," the court reasoned. "Its safety and the hazard, or risk of loss, is no longer dependent upon their skill, care, or discretion, in its custody or management." A trustee would be abdicating his solemn responsibility if he delegated his duty of care to the managers of such an enterprise. Of course, prudent men bought shares of corporations all the time, with their own money, but in the court's view that was no reason for trustees to speculate with other people's money. "If it be said, that men of the highest prudence do, in fact, invest their funds in such stocks," the court concluded, "the answer is" that "in their private affairs, they do, and they lawfully may, put their principal funds at hazard; in the affairs of a trust they may not."[8]

In many cases, the problem courts perceived was that the particular corporation involved was so new that there was not yet any way to

---

6 *Kimball v. Redding*, 31 N.H. 352, 374–76 (1855).

7 Jairus Ware Perry, *A Treatise on the Law of Trusts and Trustees* (Boston: Little, Brown and Co., 1872), 412.

8 *King v. Talbot*, 40 N.Y. 76, 88–89 (1869).

ascertain whether it would be successful. In Maine, the trustee for a child bought shares of the Union Packing Company, a Portland firm that was only a few years old. The company had scarcely any capital on hand because it had spent nearly all of its money to lease factories. Its business "was sensitive to changes in the markets, the crops, the migrations of fish, the weather, etc., which are always variable and uncertain," lectured the Maine Supreme Court. The Union Packing Company "was liable to be overwhelmed at the first unfavorable turn in affairs," which indeed happened, leaving its stock worthless. The court required the trustee to cover the loss himself, because "a mere business chance or prospect, however promising, is not a proper place for trust funds." The Alabama Supreme Court reached the same conclusion about a trustee's purchase of "stock of a recently-formed land company, organized, as is alleged, as a purely speculative venture." When a gullible dentist in Rochester, New York, acting as a trustee for his own son, bought stock in the Tex-Lahoma Oil Company and in Herschell-Spillman Motors, a judge mocked the dentist as a man "who believes that an investment is something that pays abnormally high rates of interest and promises excessive profits." By the time of litigation, the two companies' short lives had long since ended. "Under no pretext whatever may trust funds be used for engaging in wild speculation," the judge intoned. "To so use them is illegal." Even the Union Pacific Railroad was too unproven an enterprise for the Massachusetts Supreme Court to allow a trustee to buy its shares in the late nineteenth century. "It must have been manifest to any well-informed person," the court declared, "that the Union Pacific Railroad ran through a new and comparatively unsettled country; that it had been constructed at great expense, as represented by its stock and bonds, and was heavily indebted; that its continued prosperity depended upon many circumstances, which could not be predicted, and that it would be taking a considerable risk to invest any part of a trust-fund in the stock of such a road."[9] Novelty meant risk, and risk meant speculation rather than investment.

9 *Mattocks v. Moulton*, 24 A. 1004, 1006–7 (Me. 1892); *Randolph v. East Birmingham Land Co.*, 16 So. 126, 129 (Ala. 1894); *In re Cady's Estate*, 207 N.Y.S. 385, 390 (N.Y. App. Div. 1925); *Appeal of Dickinson*, 25 N.E. 99, 100 (Mass. 1890).

But there were other sources of risk besides novelty. One was distance. When a trustee in New York purchased a mortgage on land in Toledo, Ohio, New York's highest court took the opportunity to establish a general rule forbidding trustees from making investments in other states. When money was sent so far away, the court fretted, "the proper and prudent knowledge of values would become more difficult and uncertain; watchfulness and personal care would in the main be replaced by confidence in distant agents, and legal remedies would have to be sought under the disadvantages of distance, and before different and unfamiliar tribunals." The Missouri Supreme Court was positively scornful, for the same reason, about a trustee who purchased bonds issued by the Mexican state of Jalisco. The court was shocked that a trustee in St. Louis would go "thousands of miles into a foreign country and among a strange people to obtain for his brother an investment in 6 per cent bonds."[10] A prudent man would keep his money closer to home, where he could keep an eye on it himself, and where the rules of the game were familiar and enforced by his own neighbors.

Any number of circumstances could push an investment into the forbidden territory of speculation. Making an investment with borrowed money, for example, was "purely a speculation," one New York judge declared, even where the investment would have been permissible without the borrowing. The judge explained that an investment is "for the purpose of securing an income for the beneficiaries, while a speculation is for the purpose of realizing a profit from the transaction." Making an investment in a business the trustee knew little or nothing about was another circumstance that suggested speculation. When Ezra Curtis died in 1882, he left a friend named Potter in charge of managing the funds of his widow, Mary, who "had no business experience whatever" and thus left all the decisions to Potter. Potter put most of the money into shares of the Housatonic Rolling-Stock Company, a manufacturer of railroad cars. "The stock of the Housatonic Rolling-Stock Company was a speculative stock, of the character or value of which it is found that Mr. Potter knew nothing,"

10 *Ormiston v. Olcott*, 84 N.Y. 339, 344 (1881); *Cornet v. Cornet*, 190 S.W. 333, 340 (Mo. 1916).

a Connecticut judge sneered, after the share price had plummeted from $50 to $5. The firm had never even been properly incorporated, "a fact that Mr. Potter . . . could easily have ascertained, and was bound to have ascertained before assuming to advise an investment in it by Mrs. Curtis." The court concluded that this was "conduct on the part of Mr. Potter that is really inexcusable."[11]

But if the general rule was that the purchase of corporate stock was speculation rather than investment, there were always cases in which courts held the opposite. When Joseph Glover died in Knoxville, he left a trust for his three little children, in the charge of the Fidelity Trust & Safety Vault Company. At his death Glover had owned shares of the East Tennessee National Bank that paid annual dividends of 14 percent, shares that would become part of the trust unless the trust company had to sell them. The trust company accordingly went to court to request permission to keep the stock. The court recognized that the bank "is in a prosperous condition, and as the proof shows is well managed." The stock was "producing a considerable income for the children." The court gave its blessing. "An investment for purposes of speculation, or in such stocks as pay a dividend one month and none the next, and that are thrown day by day on the market for purposes of speculation," would be forbidden to trustees, the court reasoned. But when a trustee invests in "a safe banking institution," where the trust funds are "secure and the dividends regularly paid," it made no sense to require the trustee to sell the stock and reinvest the proceeds, which "might result in an investment not nearly as profitable or secure." The purchase of stock, at least in this case, was an investment suitable for trustees, not a speculation, because the trustee was expecting a steady stream of dividends rather than a rise in the share price.[12]

In other cases, courts likewise distinguished investment from speculation, not by condemning all business corporations as speculative, but by discerning the intentions of the trustee. Where a trustee bought shares for their dividend income, that was investment, but where he

---

11 *In re Hirsch's Estate*, 101 N.Y.S. 893, 899 (N.Y. App. Div. 1906); *Appeal of Potter*, 12 A. 513, 514 (Conn. 1888).

12 *Fidelity T. & S.V. Co. v. Glover*, 14 S.W. 343, 344 (Ky. Ct. App. 1890).

bought shares in the hope that they would appreciate, that was speculation. "The word 'speculate' means to purchase with the expectation of
an advance in price," declared one Ohio judge. "An investment is the
laying out of money with the view of obtaining an income or profit
from the thing bought whether it be an interest in a business, a farm,
stocks or bonds; to place money so that it will be safe and yield a profit."
On this definition, "investments can be made in stocks and stocks can
be taken as security for loans without the transactions becoming speculations." A judge in New Jersey similarly reasoned that "a speculative
investment is one in which there is a substantial danger of loss of principal balanced by a prospect of appreciation of principal." Many stock
purchases were speculative, but not all. "Some few common stocks,
because of the ample assets which they represent, the steady earnings
of the company, and the conservatism of its management, fall into the
class of safe investments, and such the trustee may properly retain."[13]
There was more than one line that could be drawn between investment
and speculation.

Case by case, trustee by trustee, transaction by transaction, courts
were policing the boundary between investment and speculation, by
applying the vague standard of the prudent man to countless unique
factual situations. By the late nineteenth and early twentieth centuries
it was commonplace to observe that the lines the courts drew were not
all consistent. The prudent man standard "is wholly valueless, except as
an indication of the *animus* of the court," complained the Philadelphia
lawyer Jonathan Merrill. "What court could or would name the securities in which, and in which alone, diligent, careful and prudent men of
discretion and intelligence might place their funds?" "The word 'speculation' is not capable of exact legal definition," admitted Mayo Adams
Shattuck, a Boston trust lawyer. "It is a very difficult task to state what
it is that provides the distinction between the fiduciary attitude and
that of the business man or speculator." When the Harvard law professor Austin Wakeman Scott surveyed the field in his magisterial treatise
on the law of trusts, he had to concede that "the line between what

13 *State v. Gibbs*, 18 Ohio Dec. 694, 695–96 (Ohio. Ct. Comm. Pleas 1908); *Wild
v. Brown*, 183 A. 899, 900 (N.J. Ct. Ch. 1936).

constitutes speculation and what constitutes a business man's risk and what constitutes a prudent investment is drawn in different places by different courts."[14] The judges who evaluated the decisions of trustees were no more able to draw a definitive line between investment and speculation than anyone else had been.

The line-drawing problem was complicated by two circumstances that were present in virtually all of these cases. On one hand, it was widely recognized that trustees, unless closely watched, often had a greater incentive to take risks than did the beneficiaries whose money they were managing. This was in part a matter of age, gender, and disposition. Trustees were often men of working age accustomed to taking business risks, while beneficiaries were often elderly widows or children with no experience in the business world. One newspaper complained of "these smart young men, who become the life of trade and speculation—into whose hands come the . . . sacred trusts of widows and orphans." But it was also a matter of how trustees were compensated. Many, particularly the banks that took over much of the trust business, were paid according to how much income the trusts in their care earned each year. "A banker is constantly beset by temptation to yield a little of a customer's safety in favor of more profits for the bank," contended the journalist Fred C. Kelly. "In the trust department, a bank's charges are based on income. If an individual investor has only $50,000, his mode of life will be much the same whether his income is 5 per cent or only 4 per cent. But to a banker, handling many millions, his share of that extra one per cent of other people's incomes is worth thinking about." As a result, Kelly alleged, "bankers became inclined more than ever to take chances" with trust funds.[15] These considerations counseled in favor of strict supervision of trustees by the courts, to rein them in when they tried to cross the line from investment into speculation.

14 Jonathan Houston Merrill, "Investment of Trust Funds," *American Law Register* 34 (1886): 232–33; Mayo Adams Shattuck, "The Massachusetts Prudent Man in Trust Investments," *Boston University Law Review* 25 (1945): 334, 337; Austin Wakeman Scott, *The Law of Trusts* (Boston: Little, Brown and Co., 1939), 2:1206.

15 *Zion's Herald*, 21 May 1884, 164; Fred C. Kelly, "Can Trust Companies Be Trusted?," *Forum and Century* 88 (1932): 241–42.

On the other hand, cases only reached the courts when investments went sour. Beneficiaries never complained when trustees took risks and made money. With hindsight it was easy to condemn a transaction as unduly speculative, after it had already proven disastrous. Judges' awareness that they encountered a biased sample of investments should have counseled in favor of deference to the decisions of trustees, for fear of classifying as speculation a transaction that would have seemed a prudent investment if it had been taken to court when it was made. If many judges were aware of this problem, however, it is not evident in their opinions, which contain few traces of humility. As one judge wrote in 1931, speaking of the state of the stock market two years earlier, just before the crash, "it was common knowledge, not only amongst bankers and trust companies, but the general public as well, that the stock market condition at the time of the testator's death was an unhealthy one, that values were very much inflated, and that a crash was almost sure to occur." The judge accordingly blamed the trustees for lacking the foresight to anticipate the crash, a prescience that had been possessed by very few in 1929.[16]

The line between speculation and investment, always unstable, moved conspicuously in the twentieth century. Virtually all courts began to permit trustees to buy shares of business corporations, so long as the trustees intended to own the shares for a long time. "The difference between speculation and investment," declared an Alabama court, was that "one who buys common stocks with the idea of selling them on the market for higher prices is speculating. One who is making a prudent investment examines the stocks' intrinsic values and purchases them for a long-term investment." As Mayo Shattuck summarized the cases at midcentury, "definitions of 'speculative' participations must vary with time and place and circumstances. The concept of *permanence* of investment, as contrasted with transactions entered into for a quick turnover or profit, is, however, basic."[17] In the nineteenth

---

16 Jeffrey J. Rachlinski, "Heuristics and Biases in the Courts: Ignorance or Adaptation?," *Oregon Law Review* 61 (2000): 79–81; *In re Chamberlain's Estate*, 156 A. 42, 43 (N.J. Prerogative Ct. 1931).

17 Harold B. Elsom, "The Law of Trust Investment," *Financial Analysts Journal* 16, no. 4 (1960): 32; *First Alabama Bank of Montgomery, N.A. v. Martin*, 425 So. 2d 415, 427 (Ala. 1983); Mayo Adams Shattuck, "The Development of the Prudent

century, judges had tended to draw the line between corporate stock and government bonds, but in the twentieth they tended to draw it between short-term and long-term purchases of corporate stock.

One reason for the line's migration was simply that by the middle of the twentieth century there were some corporations that had proven stable and profitable for a long period of time. The St. Louis–based International Shoe Company, for example, had been formed in 1911 by the merger of firms dating back to the 1890s. By the mid-twentieth century it was the largest shoe manufacturer in the nation. Its sales and its revenue had grown continuously for decades, except for a brief downturn at the beginning of the Depression. It had operated at a profit every year since its inception, and its stock had paid dividends every year. It had no debt. In 1946, when a St. Louis court had to decide whether stock in the International Shoe Company was an appropriate investment for a trustee, the court had no doubt that it was. "Generally speaking," explained the Philadelphia lawyer James Moore, shares "in a 'well-seasoned' corporation are acceptable for investment and retention. By 'well-seasoned' (or similar phrases) the courts seem to mean corporations which have been in existence for a substantial period of time, which are leaders in their field, which have a background of steady earnings and growth, and whose securities, listed on a recognized exchange, are not particularly subject to rapid fluctuations in market price." In short, "the background of the corporation will go far toward determining whether the investment is speculative."[18]

Another reason for the courts' growing acceptance of stock purchases as investments rather than speculations was the pervasive inflation of the twentieth century. There had been inflationary periods in the nineteenth century, especially during the Civil War, but these had been more than balanced out by long periods of deflation. Price levels in 1900 were only around two-thirds of what they had been in 1800. The

Man Rule for Fiduciary Investment in the United States in the Twentieth Century," *Ohio State Law Journal* 12 (1951): 517.

18 Louis S. Headley, "Trust Investments: Fundamental Principles Lawyers Should Know," *Trusts and Estates* 71 (1952): 740–41; *Warmack v. Crawford*, 195 S.W.2d 919, 920–21 (Mo. Ct. App. 1946); James A. Moore, "A Rationalization of the Trust Surcharge Cases," *University of Pennsylvania Law Review* 96 (1948): 668.

twentieth century was very different. Prices nearly tripled between 1900 and 1950, even with the sharp deflation of the early 1930s, and in the second half of the twentieth century they would rise even faster. This new economic climate required a rethinking of trustees' investment strategies. In the nineteenth century, when even an investment that paid no interest at all would leave the investor ahead after accounting for deflation, the prudent man had no reason to take risks to seek a higher return. But in the twentieth century, when a long-term investment at low interest rates would lose money in light of inflation, the avoidance of all risk was no longer prudent. "Hardship has overtaken the income beneficiaries of many trusts which, when created, were thought to provide adequate support," one commentator observed after the inflation of the late 1940s. "The trouble with trust funds," agreed the financial journalist H. J. Maidenberg, was that the old standards of prudence had become obsolete. Because of inflation, "in recent years, trust funds have generally performed far worse than the portfolios of most investors who have handled their own trading and investments."[19] The prudent man had to invest in stocks to keep up with inflation.

Finally, in the second half of the twentieth century, advances in economics made the old prudent man rule seem even more outdated. Judges had been in the habit of evaluating investments one by one, when by modern lights the relevant question was not the wisdom of any single investment but rather the wisdom of the entire portfolio of investments chosen by the trustee. A purchase of stock that might have been too risky on its own could be deemed prudent as part of a larger diversified package. Along with the new economic theory came new investment vehicles like index funds, which made it much easier for trustees to diversify their investments. These developments put additional pressure on the always-fragile line between speculation and investment.[20]

19 Susan B. Carter et al., eds., *Historical Statistics of the United States: Millennial Edition On Line* (Cambridge University Press, 2006), table Cc1–2; Harry L. Fledderman, "Prudent Man Investment of Trust Funds During Inflation," *California Law Review* 39 (1951): 380; *New York Times*, 18 Jan. 1981, F13.

20 John H. Langbein and Richard A. Posner, "Market Funds and Trust-Investment Law," *American Bar Foundation Research Journal* 1 (1976): 1–34; Jeffrey N. Gordon, "The Puzzling Persistence of the Constrained Prudent Man

As a result, every state repealed the prudent man rule by the end of the twentieth century. After nearly two centuries of trying to draw a line between investment and speculation, the task was abandoned as fruitless. "We no longer use speculation as a tool for dealing with trustee investment misadventures because it is considered sloppy, sentimental, and inefficient," one law professor explained. "The reforms imported modern investing theory and practice into trust law." Rather than asking whether the trustee was investing or speculating, the new laws tended instead to ask whether the trustee was advancing the purpose of the trust with skill and diligence. Under this new rule, trusts included more stock than they had before.[21] It was simply too hard to tell where investment stopped and speculation began.

TAXING SPECULATORS

When the federal government began taxing income in 1913, capital gains were not given any special treatment. They were taxed at the same rates as other income. This was a recurring source of complaint from people who owned land and other property that had appreciated for many years and who thus faced very large tax bills when they sold the property. "Under the present law," explained the Senate Finance Committee in 1921, "many sales of farms, mineral properties, and other capital assets have been prevented by the fact that gains and profits earned over a series of years are under the present law taxed as a lump sum." To provide relief to such taxpayers, Congress decided to count as

Rule," *New York University Law Review* 62 (1987): 52–114; Edward C. Halbach Jr., "Trust Investment Law in the Third Restatement," *Real Property, Probate and Trust Journal* 27 (1992): 407–65; Michael T. Johnson, "Speculating on the Efficacy of 'Speculation': An Analysis of the Prudent Person's Slipperiest Term of Art in Light of Modern Portfolio Theory," *Stanford Law Review* 48 (1996): 419–47.

21 Joel C. Dobris, "Speculations on the Idea of 'Speculation' in Trust Investing: An Essay," *Real Property, Probate and Trust Journal* 39 (2004): 453; William P. Wade, "The New California Prudent Investor Rule: A Statutory Interpretive Analysis," *Real Property, Probate and Trust Journal* 20 (1985): 1023; Max M. Schanzenbach and Robert H. Sitkoff, "Did Reform of Prudent Trust Investment Laws Change Trust Portfolio Allocation?," *Journal of Law and Economics* 50 (2007): 681–711.

income only 40 percent of the capital gains realized upon the sale of an asset. The result was to make the tax on capital gains only 40 percent of the tax on ordinary income.[22]

But this change raised a new problem. Many of the taxpayers who would benefit from the reduced rate were not selling the family farm; they were selling shares of corporations, sometimes shares they had purchased but a short time before. Taxing capital gains at a lower rate would be a windfall to speculators. "Is this desirable?" wondered the economist Willford King. "Speculation tends to degenerate into gambling and gambling is generally recognized as an anti-social form of activity." Senator David Walsh of Massachusetts raised the same concern on the floor of the Senate. "Under the proposed amendment and bill a lawyer or any other professional man who derived as a fee from a large case or a merchant who through a substantial increase in sales derived an income of, say, $100,000 per year is taxable upon the full amount of income," Walsh complained. But "the speculator who derives an income of $100,000 a year upon the New York Stock Exchange or in any other manner would be taxable only on 40 per cent of his net income, or $40,000."[23] Why should speculators pay lower taxes than everyone else?

Walsh proposed a solution. "If the benefits of this amendment are limited to cases of the sale of capital assets which have been owned by the taxpayer for a period of three years or more," he suggested, relief would be afforded to those who deserved it, "but the speculator will not be included and will be forced to pay a tax upon his entire net income, the same as every other taxpayer." The idea of making speculators pay the full tax received instant approval from Walsh's colleagues, who quibbled only about how best to achieve that goal. Porter McCumber of North Dakota proposed that the law should require full taxation only of "speculative stocks and securities" and give preferential treatment to all other capital gains. But this idea was shot down by Irvine Lenroot of Wisconsin, who pointed out that it would be very difficult for the

22 S. Rep. No. 275, 67th Cong., 1st Sess. (1921), 12.
23 Willford I. King, "Earned and Unearned Income," *Annals of the American Academy of Political and Social Science* 95 (1921): 258; *Congressional Record* 61 (1921): 6575.

Treasury Department, in collecting the tax, to determine which of a taxpayer's transactions were "speculative" and which were not. The only way to distinguish speculation from investment, Lenroot counseled, was to look to the length of time between purchase and sale, as Walsh had suggested. In the end, Congress agreed on requiring a two-year holding period before a taxpayer could get the advantage of the lower rate.[24]

For the rest of the twentieth century and into the twenty-first, the principle that speculators should be taxed at a higher rate than investors remained a central part of the tax law. Congress tinkered with the details every so often. The two-year holding period was replaced in 1934 with a sliding scale of holding periods, ranging from one year to ten years, with a lower tax rate the longer the time between purchase and sale. In 1938, the sliding scale was replaced by an eighteen-month holding period, which was shortened to six months in 1942 and then lengthened to twelve months in 1976. Tax rates changed even more frequently, and as they did, so did the size of the preference given to investors over speculators. There were recurring changes in the tax treatment of capital losses, in the provisions relating to the sale of homes, and in many technical details that were attended to primarily by tax lawyers and accountants. But the one consistent goal of the capital gains tax, throughout all this change, was that the lower tax rate for capital gains should be available to investors, not to speculators. "Capital gains are as desirable a basis for taxation as any other kind of income," explained the economist R. S. Tucker, "and to the extent that they represent speculative or purely chance income, even more desirable a basis."[25]

24 *Congressional Record* 61 (1921): 6575.
25 James R. Repetti, "The Use of Tax Law to Stabilize the Stock Market: The Efficacy of Holding Period Requirements," *Virginia Tax Review* 8 (1989): 591–637; C. Thomas Paschall, "U.S. Capital Gains Taxes: Arbitrary Holding Periods, Debatable Tax Rates," *Southern California Law Review* 73 (2000): 843–78; Congressional Research Service, *Individual Capital Gains Income: Legislative History* (2006); Van Mayhall, "Capital Gains Taxation—The First One Hundred Years," *Louisiana Law Review* 41 (1980): 81–99; Anita Wells, "Legislative History of the Treatment of Capital Gains Under the Federal Income Tax, 1913–1948," *National Tax Journal* 2 (1949): 12–32; R. S. Tucker, "Government Control of Investments and Speculation," *American Economic Review* 25 (1935): 148.

But taxing speculators more than investors was easier said than done, because of the difficulty of drawing a clear line between speculation and investment. On one side, there were repeated calls to lengthen the required holding period on the ground that the existing period was so short that it permitted speculators to get the advantage of the lower rates, and there were frequent arguments for raising the rates on short-term capital gains on the ground that higher rates were needed to deter speculation. On the other side, there were repeated calls to shorten the period and lower the rates, or even to exempt capital gains from taxation completely, so as not to discourage investment.[26] The age-old debate over the distinction between investment and speculation had become a debate over the capital gains tax.

In early 1945, for example, Federal Reserve Chair Marriner Eccles proposed a sharp increase in the short-term capital gains rate, to 90 percent, and a lengthening of the holding period from six months to two years, to tame wartime inflation. His proposal was aimed at "speculation—not investment," Eccles explained. It would "discourage all such speculative transactions, whether in homes, farms, stocks, or commodities, and whether based upon credit or cash—and would do so without interference with normal, non-speculative transactions." Eccles's proposal aroused a storm of criticism. Taxing speculation would not just be an ineffective way of reducing inflation, charged the economist Aaron Sakolski. It would also "stop progress," because "without speculation, would there be progress of any kind?" *Barron's*, a business newspaper, compared Eccles's plan to a tax that had been imposed in Nazi Germany.[27] Eccles's proposal was shelved.

Alongside these recurring political battles ran a long-standing debate over a more fundamental question: was the distinction between short-term and long-term holdings a sensible way to divide speculators from investors? "There is nothing in accounting, in economics, or in fiscal policy which justifies the distinction of speculation and investment on

26 *Atlanta Constitution*, 1 May 1929, 8; *New York Times*, 20 Jan. 1938, 1; 4 Jan. 1931, N20; *Wall Street Journal*, 24 June 1931, 8; *Chicago Daily Tribune*, 18 Oct. 1935, 39; *Daily Boston Globe*, 27 Nov. 1936, 14; *Wall Street Journal*, 21 Mar. 1942, 3.

27 *Commercial and Financial Chronicle*, 1 Mar. 1945, 963; 8 Mar. 1945, 1061; 1 Mar. 1945, 929, 943; *Barron's*, 26 Mar. 1945, 5.

the basis of time," testified Elisha Friedman, an economist at New York University, before the House Ways and Means Committee. "There is no justification for segregating short-term from long-term gains." On this view, the tax law had adopted an utterly arbitrary distinction, because the line between short-term and long-term holdings had no correspondence with the line between speculators and investors. Stanley Surrey, who shuttled between Harvard Law School and the Treasury Department throughout the mid-twentieth century, agreed that the distinction between short-term and long-term holdings "leaves some strange results." In the long-term category were a heterogeneous collection of market participants—"the professional speculator whose purchases and sales are substantial and frequent but involve more than a six months' holding period, the large investor who is constantly perfecting his portfolio through changes in its composition, the modest investor who occasionally changes his portfolio, and the amateur speculator who takes a chance now and then." As Surrey saw it, "we are thus left with a congressional feeling that speculation and investment are different matters, but with no statutory differentiation between the two except as respects the in-and-out, daily traders."[28]

Others argued that even if speculators *intended* to hold assets for shorter periods than investors did, the unpredictability of market conditions made the actual holding period a poor way of distinguishing between the two groups. When the market was down, as in the early 1930s, stock that had originally been purchased for speculative purposes might be held for years, in the hope that its price might climb back upward. The Chicago tax lawyer Herman Reiling thus complained in 1932 that confining "speculation" to short-term holdings "appears to ignore the facts." And when the market was up, even a person who had purchased with the intent to hold for a long time might be tempted to sell. The Investment Bankers Association accordingly proposed defining as a speculator only "the day-to-day trader," who "makes his

---

Revenue Revision of 1942: Hearings Before the Committee on Ways and Means, House of Representatives, 75th Cong., 2nd Sess. (Washington, D.C.: Government Printing Office, 1942), 1:944; Stanley S. Surrey, "Definitional Problems in Capital Gains Taxation," *Harvard Law Review* 69 (1956): 999–1000.

living by stock transactions." All others, the IBA argued, were investors who deserved the lower rate.[29]

The standard response to such arguments was that the holding period, while no doubt an imperfect way of distinguishing speculation from investment, was the only feasible way. The economist Robert Murray Haig noted that Weimar Germany had tried to distinguish speculative from investment income on the basis of the taxpayer's intent; if he intended to speculate, he was a speculator. But this effort proved impractical. "It led to vagueness, to debates between administrators and taxpayers, and to litigation," Haig recalled. After a few years, Germany gave up. "In place of the vague test of 'intent' in the mind of the taxpayer, appeared the definite test of the length of the time-period covered by the transaction," Haig explained. In Germany, as in the United States, "a speculation is a short-term transaction and an investment a long-term venture." The short-term/long-term distinction sometimes produced anomalous results, acknowledged the New York tax lawyer Peter Miller, but "the necessities of administration explain this anomaly." Speculators differ from investors "only in state of mind and not in easily recognizable overt behavior. If 'the devil himself knoweth not the thought of man,' the Commissioner of Internal Revenue could hardly be expected to."[30]

There was little doubt, in any event, that the distinction between short-term and long-term holdings mapped onto a widely held, if not fully theorized, distinction in the public mind between speculators and investors. When congressional committees tinkered with the length of the holding period, they repeatedly explained that the holding period's purpose was "separating, in a practical way, speculative transactions from investment transactions" (as a 1938 House report put it), or to serve as "a sufficient deterrent to the speculator as contrasted with the legitimate investor" (in the words of a 1942 Senate report). "The underlying concept," declared a 1976 report of Congress's Joint

29 Herman T. Reiling, "Stock Transactions and the Income Tax," *Tax Magazine* 10 (1932): 207; *Los Angeles Times*, 28 Nov. 1941, 29.
30 *Wall Street Journal*, 8 Apr. 1937, 4; Peter Miller, "The 'Capital Asset' Concept: A Critique of Capital Gains Taxation: I," *Yale Law Journal* 59 (1950): 843.

Committee on Taxation, "is that a person who holds an asset for only a short time is primarily interested in obtaining quick gains from short-term market fluctuations, which is a distinctive speculative activity. In contrast, the person who holds an asset for a long time probably is interested fundamentally in the income from his investment and in the long-term appreciation value." All transactions involved an element of investment and an element of speculation, conceded William Healy, a federal judge in Idaho. But Healy, like many others, nevertheless perceived a difference between the two. "The 'in-and-out' market hanger-on who buys and sells through brokers on margin is a typical example of the pure speculator," he reasoned. "On the other hand, an investor is ordinarily thought to be a person who acquires property for the income it will yield rather than for the profit he hopes to obtain on a resale."[31]

Of course, using the tax code to distinguish between speculation and investment made sense only if there *was* a distinction between speculation and investment, and opinion on that question was no more settled than it had ever been. Beardsley Ruml, chairman of the Macy's department store company, thought "the discussion is somewhat confused by the use of the term speculation. It seems to me, as an example, that at Macy's when we buy some women's dresses to sell in six months or six weeks, that is speculation, if we want to use that horrid term. What you have is buying and selling of things," which was the same no matter what name was attached to it. The *Chicago Tribune* agreed that "the dividing line between investment and speculation is often indistinct," because even an ostensible investor hoped one day to sell his investment for more than he had paid. "All investors are interested in the probable price movements of their assets," declared the economist Lawrence Seltzer. "Like professional speculators, they try to take future price movements into account in the prices at which they buy and sell."[32] If investment and speculation were identical, there was

31 H.R. Rep. No. 1860, 75th Cong., 3rd Sess. (1938), 7; S. Rep. No. 1631, 77th Cong., 2nd Sess. (1942), 50; Joint Committee on Taxation, *General Explanation of the Tax Reform Act of 1976* (Washington, D.C.: Government Printing Office, 1976), 426; *United States v. Chinook Inv. Co.*, 136 F.2d 984, 985 (9th Cir. 1943).

32 *Capital Gains Taxation* (New York: Tax Institute, 1946), 87–88; *Chicago Daily Tribune*, 17 Nov. 1946, A11; Lawrence H. Seltzer, *The Nature and Tax Treatment*

no reason to use the capital gains tax to encourage one and discourage the other.

And even if speculation could be distinguished from investment, there was always a considerable body of opinion that the two should be treated identically, because speculation was just as good. In the 1950s, *Life* magazine was willing to concede that speculation differed from investment, because "speculation is putting the desire for enhancement ahead of the desire for generally predictable returns—for growth, rather than dividends. It is the difference between buying Ford stock in 1903 and buying Standard Oil, whose success was already established; or between buying a uranium stock today and buying G.M." But *Life* insisted that speculation and investment should both be encouraged. "People who are willing and able to take such risks enable new industries to get born, and in that sense speculation is a social good," the magazine reasoned. "In a very real sense, America grew great on speculation."[33]

The use of the capital gains tax to encourage investment but discourage speculation was also attacked on technical grounds, from both directions. In the early years of the capital gains tax, critics charged that differential tax rates had little influence on the conduct of either investors or speculators, who had more important things to worry about. "The operations of such individuals are . . . relatively insensitive to capital gains tax provisions," Treasury staff concluded in 1937. "It must be emphasized that tax factors operate in practice among a welter of other considerations, and that, by reason of this fact, they are commonly robbed of a great deal of their force." When the Twentieth Century Fund studied the tax system at approximately the same time, it likewise concluded that tax rates were unlikely to affect decisions to buy or sell securities, decisions taxpayers would base solely on their expectations as to future prices. If capital gains taxes did not affect the conduct of speculators or investors, it would be pointless to fiddle with rates as a means of deterring the former or encouraging the latter. The Treasury could focus instead on raising revenue, a goal

of Capital Gains and Losses (New York: National Bureau of Economic Research, 1951), 67.

33 "The Market and Its 'Friends,'" *Life*, 21 Mar. 1955, 46.

that stood in tension with that of discouraging speculation, because the more that speculation was discouraged, the less revenue a tax on speculation would raise.[34]

In later years, however, critics of the distinction between long-term and short-term profits charged precisely the opposite—that the distinction had too great an effect on the conduct of speculators and investors. In 1948, a security analyst in New York named Goldie Stone interviewed a small sample of brokers, accountants, and bankers to find out how the capital gains tax affected the buying and selling of securities. One obvious strategy, she noted, was not to sell securities on which there were gains until the expiration of the six-month holding period, but to sell all securities on which there were losses before the period expired, so that the short-term losses could offset any short-term gains. Aside from that simple practice, Stone found that sophisticated taxpayers engaged in several other "highly complicated and devious methods" of manipulating the short-term/long-term distinction to their advantage. One technique was to use short sales to convert a short-term gain into a long-term gain without fear of loss. The owner of the stock would sell the stock short, wait for the six-month period to pass, and then cover the short sale with his own stock. He would get the same gain as if he had sold the stock earlier, but now it was long-term gain rather than short-term gain. The same goal could also be accomplished by buying put options, which would allow the owner of the stock to lock in a gain but defer it until after six months had passed. A second technique, the mirror image of the first, was to take advantage of a short-term loss without having to lose one's position in a stock. The owner of the stock would sell it short, purchase additional stock, and then a month later cover the short sale with his original stock. He would have a short-term loss, but he would still own as much of the stock as before. The same goal could also be accomplished with call options, which would allow

34 "Tax Treatment of Capital Gains and Losses" (staff memo, Division of Tax Research, Treasury Department, 1937), section V.A.2-3, http://www.taxhistory.org/Civilization/Documents/Surveys/hst23731/23731-1.htm; Twentieth Century Fund, *Facing the Tax Problem: A Survey of Taxation in the United States and a Program for the Future* (New York: Twentieth Century Fund, 1937), 190; *New York Times*, 16 Feb. 1938, 20.

him to sell the stock and buy it back at the same price thirty days later. And this was just the beginning of a long list of clever transactions savvy taxpayers engaged in, transactions with no purpose other than taking advantage of the distinction between short-term and long-term capital gains. "The dominant result of these interviews," Stone concluded, "appears to be that tax-saving manipulations are restricted to a fairly limited group of large stockholders with ample cash reserves who trade in substantial blocks of securities. This type of individual has, in addition, sufficient time to discover the many available devices and sufficient money to employ expert advice to inform him of these possibilities."[35]

One of those expert advisors was M. Francis Bravman, a tax lawyer in New York and the chair of the American Bar Association's committee on income taxation. Bravman admitted that the structure of the capital gains tax "places a very high premium on the use of devices to transmute ordinary income into capital gains, or capital losses into ordinary deductions, or short-term gains into long-term gains." A great deal of time, money, and intelligence was devoted to gaming the system, because "this approach to the taxation of capital gains has resulted in a complicated federal income tax law, containing very tempting incentives for taxpayers to reduce their taxes."[36] If speculators could use tricks to make themselves look like investors at tax time, there was no point in trying to treat the two groups differently.

But all this criticism, from all these directions, had no discernible effect on the apparently widespread belief that speculators should be taxed more heavily than investors. Unlike the law of trusts, which abandoned as futile the effort to distinguish investment from speculation, the tax law continues to draw a line between the capital gains of investors and those of speculators.

---

35 Goldie Stone, "How the Capital Gains Tax Affects Buying and Selling Securities," *Taxes* 26 (1948): 1041–48.
36 M. Francis Bravman, "Integration of Taxes on Capital Gains and Income," *Virginia Law Review* 37 (1951): 527–28.

THE ACTIVITIES OF A CASINO

Wartime brings new taxes, as the government needs to finance new expenditures. The Spanish-American War was no exception. In 1898, Congress imposed a wide range of new taxes, including an estate tax and taxes on tobacco, flour, cosmetics, and many other items. One of the new taxes was a tax on stock transactions. It was very small, only 1 cent per $100 of stock. The purpose of all these taxes was "to raise moneys for the support of the government," as the Supreme Court explained.[37] The stock transfer tax was no more intended to deter stock trading than the cosmetics tax was intended to deter the use of cosmetics or the estate tax was intended to deter dying. There was a war on, and the government needed the money.

The federal stock transfer tax was repealed when the war was over. But the idea lingered on. In 1905, when the state of New York faced a looming budget deficit, New York imposed a tax of 2 cents on each $100 of stock sold. The purpose was again to raise money, but as one economics journal observed, "the tax probably falls in the main upon the purchasers [of stock], but this means very often the speculative buyers," who engaged in the most frequent transactions. "The burden upon the investing public is slight," the journal concluded, drawing a distinction between speculators who traded frequently and investors who traded only rarely. The *New York Times* agreed that the tax would be felt primarily by "large speculators whose daily purchases much exceed 1,000 shares." The federal government resumed taxing stock transfers in 1914, with the start of World War I. Both governments would continue to impose small taxes on stock transfers for a long time. The federal tax remained in effect until 1966, and New York's until 1981.[38]

The stock market crash of 1929 prompted several calls for a much stiffer transaction tax, intended not to raise revenue but to suppress

37 Steven A. Bank, Kirk J. Stark, and Joseph J. Thorndike, *War and Taxes* (Washington, D.C.: Urban Institute Press, 2008); 30 Stat. 448–70 (1898); *Nicol v. Ames*, 173 U.S. 509, 516 (1899).

38 "Changes in the Tax Laws of New York State in 1905," *Quarterly Journal of Economics* 20 (1905): 153; *New York Times*, 22 Apr. 1905, 10; Joseph J. Thorndike, "Speculation and Taxation: Time for a Transaction Tax?" (2008), Tax History Project Article Archive, http://www.taxhistory.org.

speculation. "This terrible calamity occurred because we had no legislation to prevent speculation," averred Representative Jed Johnson of Oklahoma, who proposed taxing stock and commodity futures trades at rates high enough that "the exchanges would be virtually put out of business." The idea received considerable circulation among economists when John Maynard Keynes suggested a milder version of it in his widely read *General Theory of Employment, Interest, and Money*. Keynes drew a distinction between speculation, which he defined as "forecasting the psychology of the market," and enterprise, defined as "forecasting the prospective yield of assets over their whole life." This distinction was very much like the short-term/long-term line drawn at the time by American lawyers for purposes of trust law and the capital gains tax. As Keynes saw it, the predominance of speculation over enterprise in the 1920s had been one of the causes of the rise and then fall of the market. "Speculators may do no harm as bubbles on a steady stream of enterprise," Keynes explained. "But the position is serious when enterprise becomes the bubble on a whirlpool of speculation. When the capital development of a country becomes a by-product of the activities of a casino, the job is likely to be ill-done." One possible solution, Keynes suggested, was to raise the tax rate on stock transactions to reduce their frequency. "The introduction of a substantial Government transfer tax on all transactions might prove the most serviceable reform available," he concluded, "with a view to mitigating the predominance of speculation over enterprise in the United States."[39]

The idea of a transfer tax to dampen speculation re-emerged among economists in the 1970s, when the liberalization of foreign exchange markets allowed traders to move quickly from one currency to another, to a degree that seemed to threaten the ability of national governments to set their own monetary policy. "How can some national monetary autonomy be preserved?" worried the economist James Tobin. "Some sand has to be thrown into the well-greased channels of the Eurodollar market." Tobin's solution was "an internationally agreed uniform tax,

39 *Congressional Record* 78 (1934): 8097–98; John Maynard Keynes, *The General Theory of Employment, Interest, and Money* (New York: Harcourt, Brace and Co., 1936), 158–60.

say 1%, on all spot conversions of one currency into another."[40] The idea was soon widely known as a "Tobin tax"—a tax intended to reduce the number of transactions in a market thought to be too active, by making the transactions substantially more expensive to carry out.

In the late 1980s, after a brief period of extraordinary volatility in stock markets all over the world, including the largest one-day decline in the history of the US market, several leading economists proposed a similar tax on stock speculation. Joseph Stiglitz urged a tax "to discourage short-term speculative trading," which he contended was the cause of a wasteful arms race in which competing speculators made "excessive expenditures on gathering information and on financial innovation." In Stiglitz's view, "resources devoted to gambling—and to short-term speculation in the stock market—could be devoted to more productive uses." Lawrence Summers agreed that "the efficiency benefits of curbing speculation are likely to exceed any costs of reduced liquidity or increased costs of capital that come from taxing transactions more heavily." The Treasury Department contemplated proposing such a tax. Members of Congress introduced narrower versions of a transaction tax. A bill called the Excessive Churning and Speculation Act of 1989, introduced by the two senators from Kansas, would have imposed a 10 percent tax on the gains of pension funds from the sale of assets held for thirty days or less. Another bill introduced a few months later would have barred pension funds from selling assets held for less than three months. None of these proposed taxes was ever imposed, but the idea of a tax to discourage stock speculation lingered on, to be debated every few years by lawyers and economists.[41]

---

40 James Tobin, *The New Economics One Decade Older* (Princeton, N.J.: Princeton University Press, 1974), 88–89; see also James Tobin, "A Proposal for International Monetary Reform," *Eastern Economic Journal* 4 (1978): 153–59.

41 Joseph E. Stiglitz, "Using Tax Policy to Curb Speculative Short-Term Trading," *Journal of Financial Services Research* 3 (1989): 102–3, 109; Lawrence H. Summers and Victoria P. Summers, "When Financial Markets Work Too Well: A Cautious Case for a Securities Transaction Tax," *Journal of Financial Services Research* 3 (1989): 263; Donald W. Kiefer, "The Security Transactions Tax: An Overview of the Issues," *Tax Notes* 48 (1990): 885; Joint Committee on Taxation, *Tax Treatment of Short-Term Trading* (Washington, D.C.: Government Printing Office, 1990), 8; Scott W. MacCormack, "A Critique of the Reemerging Securities Transfer Excise Tax," *Tax Lawyer* 44 (1991): 927–41; G. William Schwert and

In the early 2010s, amid growing concern about the detrimental effects of high-frequency trading, attention turned once again to the possibility of a transfer tax. High-frequency traders pushed short-term speculation to its physical limits, buying and selling the same asset within microseconds, to earn minuscule profits per trade on a very high volume of trades. Critics suggested that a tiny transfer tax per trade, as small as three hundredths of 1 percent, would be enough to deter high-frequency trading without causing much reduction in ordinary trading at conventional time scales.[42]

The argument against a transfer tax has always been that a tax is a blunt instrument that will discourage the good transactions along with the bad. Opponents of a tax on high-frequency trading argued that by making trading more expensive, the tax would reduce the earnings of ordinary investors in mutual funds, because even if the investors themselves do not trade regularly, the funds do. Opponents also contended that the tax would fall heavily on market makers, who would compensate by widening their bid-ask spreads, a result that would likewise harm ordinary investors.[43]

High-frequency trading was a new phenomenon, but it raised a perennial dilemma: how to deter speculation without also deterring investment. And that question rested in turn on a more fundamental question: was it even possible to tell the two apart?

Paul J. Seguin, "Securities Transaction Taxes: An Overview of Costs, Benefits and Unresolved Questions," *Financial Analysts Journal* 49 (1993): 27–35; Lynn A. Stout, "Are Stock Markets Costly Casinos? Disagreement, Market Failure, and Securities Regulation," *Virginia Law Review* 81 (1995): 699–702; Paul G. Mahoney, "Is There a Cure for 'Excessive' Trading?," *Virginia Law Review* 81 (1995): 727–36; Anna Pomeranets and Daniel Weaver, "Security Transaction Taxes and Market Quality" (2013), http://ssrn.com/abstract=1980185.

42 Lee Sheppard, "A Tax to Kill High Frequency Trading," *Forbes*, 16 Oct. 2012; *New York Times*, 8 Apr. 2014, B1.

43 Charles M. Jones, "What Do We Know About High-Frequency Trading?" (2013), http://ssrn.com/abstract=2236201.

9

Deregulation and Crisis?

"TIME TO MAN UP and regulate these guys correctly," complained John Scollin Jr., of Winter Springs, Florida. "Somalian pirates have a better sense of ethics and meth-addled winos are more trustworthy than these guys." Scollin was referring to the speculators he held responsible for the financial crisis of 2007–08. He was hardly alone in his certainty that the crisis had been caused by deregulation, which had allowed banks and other financial intermediaries to engage in dangerously speculative transactions. "I couldn't be more angry over how my government allowed regulations to become so lax," fumed Charles Yeargen of Beckley, West Virginia. Nathaniel Powell of Los Angeles agreed. "It's unfortunate that our congress, especially [House Speaker Nancy] Pelosi, is spineless. Stop the gambling!" Powell urged. Barbara Coulson of Marshall, North Carolina, observed that the government had lost sight of an old truth—"the awful consequences of risky trading." The only conceivable explanation for why the government had allowed so much speculation to take place, suggested Louis Spain Jr., of Lakewood, Washington, was that the federal employees nominally responsible for overseeing the markets were actually "domestic terrorists working secretly for the Taliban." The speculators themselves were far worse, worried Jerry Lujan of Albuquerque: "The Wall Street Leaches and Banking Parasites are today's equivalent of the MONEY CHANGERS Jesus was so upset about," Lujan warned. "They are THE ANTI-CHRIST!!" Thomas Tague of Burien, Washington, had a simple solution to all this speculation. "Stop it now," he lectured federal officials. "Do your regulatory jobs. Pass and enforce laws that put the American people first, not banks and corporations."[1]

These critics of the government were not experts. They were ordinary citizens with strong opinions on financial regulation. As their comments suggest, the financial crisis focused more public attention on speculation than at any time since the Great Depression. Critiques of speculation carried an even sharper edge this time, however, because of the widely shared view that overspeculation was a direct result of the deregulation of the financial markets. When *Time* magazine listed the "25 people to blame for the financial crisis," the list included Bill Clinton, whom *Time* held responsible for "financial deregulation, which in many ways set the stage for the excesses of recent years"; George W. Bush, who "embraced a governing philosophy of deregulation"; and Senator Phil Gramm, "Washington's most prominent and outspoken champion of financial deregulation." It was a charge leveled over and over again: overspeculation had once been contained by laws prohibiting the most risky transactions, but those safeguards had been rashly removed, and now we were all suffering the consequences. "Welcome to the Third World!" smirked the law professor Rosa Brooks. "Policies of irresponsible government deregulation" had produced "an energy crisis, a housing crisis, a credit crisis and a financial market crisis, all at once, and accompanied (and partly caused) by impressive levels of corruption and speculation."[2]

Critics saw deregulation as the triumph of ideology over common sense. "The meltdown of the financial industry across the spectrum is due to the failed economics of Milton Friedman–style, unstructured capitalism," insisted one newspaper columnist who had seen his retirement account lose a third of its value. "Deregulation gives those

---

1 Comments 1373, 1338, 1379, 1358, 1378, 1380, and 1372 on Financial Stability Oversight Council Notice 2010-0002, *Public Input for the Study Regarding the Implementation of the Prohibitions on Proprietary Trading and Certain Relationships with Hedge Funds and Private Equity Funds* (Nov. 2010), available at http://www .regulations.gov.

2 "25 People to Blame for the Financial Crisis," *Time*, 11 Feb. 2009; Rosa Brooks, "An Intervention Strategy for the U.S. Economic Mess," *L.A. Times*, 18 Sept. 2008.

opportunists a fast track to quick riches," he reasoned, and "the result is the worst financial crisis in history." A member of the Missouri state legislature declared that because the New Deal regulatory structure had been dismantled "at the behest of Wall Street and some academics . . ., the door was open for commercial banks, securities houses and insurers to engage in risky speculative investments." Even the United Nations opined that "blind faith in the efficiency of deregulated financial markets" had "licensed profligacy through speculative finance." The government-appointed Financial Crisis Inquiry Commission, tasked to explain what had happened, concluded that "the sentries were not at their posts, in no small part due to the widely accepted faith in the self-correcting nature of the markets." The commission lamented that "more than 30 years of deregulation . . . had stripped away key safeguards, which could have helped avoid catastrophe."[3]

Some critics focused their venom on particular measures. The law professor Lynn Stout blamed the Commodity Futures Modernization Act of 2000, which in her view caused a "sudden and wholesale removal of centuries-old legal constraints on speculative trading." The financial columnist James Rickards thought "the financial crisis might not have happened at all but for the 1999 repeal of the Glass-Steagall law that separated commercial and investment banking." The economist Joseph Stiglitz also pointed the finger at the repeal of the Glass-Steagall Act, which in his view gave rise to "a demand for the kind of high returns that could be obtained only through high leverage and big risk-taking." As the subtitle of one popular account of the crisis put it, "Washington's wise men" had "turned America's future over to Wall Street."[4]

3 James Murr, "Financial Markets Must Be Regulated," *Santa Maria Times*, 9 Jan. 2009; Jeanne Kirkton, "Financial Security Is National Security," *St. Louis Post-Dispatch*, 8 July 2011; United Nations Conference on Trade and Development, *The Global Economic Crisis: Systemic Failures and Multilateral Remedies* (New York and Geneva: United Nations, 2009), iii; *The Financial Crisis Inquiry Report* (Washington, D.C.: Government Printing Office, 2011), xviii.

4 Lynn A. Stout, "Derivatives and the Legal Origin of the 2008 Credit Crisis," *Harvard Business Law Review* 1 (2011): 4; James Rickards, "Repeal of Glass-Steagall Caused the Financial Crisis," *U.S. News & World Report*, 27 Aug. 2012; Joseph E. Stiglitz, *Freefall: America, Free Markets, and the Sinking of the World Economy* (New York: W. W. Norton, 2010), 163; Michael Hirsh, *Capital*

Was it all true? What exactly had been deregulated, and why? And what were the links between deregulation, speculation, and the financial crisis? Did deregulation give rise to unsafe levels of speculation? If so, was speculation a cause of the crisis? Had we really forgotten the lessons painfully learned in earlier depressions?

BADLY BURNED

The idea of deregulating financial markets did not become a serious possibility until the 1990s, by which time several other markets had already undergone substantial and high-profile programs of deregulation. Most of these programs yielded a similar pattern—greater competition in the relevant industry, yielding enormous savings for consumers and a correspondingly precarious position for producers and their employees.

Perhaps the most conspicuous case was the airline industry. Before 1978, airfares and route changes had to be approved by a federal agency called the Civil Aeronautics Board. The airlines were largely insulated from price competition, so airfares were high and the airlines competed instead to offer in-flight perks like food and drinks. Stephen Breyer, who was counsel to the Senate Judiciary Committee in the 1970s, recalled that when the committee held hearings about airline deregulation, one of Senator Ted Kennedy's constituents asked, " 'Senator, why are you holding hearings about airlines? I've never been able to fly.' Kennedy replied: 'That's why I'm holding the hearings.' " The move toward deregulation began during the Ford administration and gained momentum in 1977, when President Carter appointed the economist Alfred Kahn as chair of the Civil Aeronautics Board. In the Airline Deregulation Act of 1978, Congress ended the regulation of fares and route changes. The airline industry was opened to competition.[5]

Offense: How Washington's Wise Men Turned America's Future Over to Wall Street (Hoboken, N.J.: John Wiley & Sons, 2010).

5 Stephen G. Breyer, "Airline Deregulation, Revisited," *Bloomberg Businessweek*, 20 Jan. 2011; Anthony E. Brown, *The Politics of Airline Deregulation* (Knoxville: University of Tennessee Press, 1987).

The results were not surprising. Consumers were the net beneficiaries from competition, producers the net losers. Airfares declined dramatically, adjusted for inflation, which brought air travel within the reach of millions of moderate-income passengers. This influx of new price-conscious customers would itself cause some new problems, including crowded airports and crowded planes, but there is little doubt that on balance, deregulation increased consumer welfare. Not so for the welfare of producers. Some airlines, unable to compete in the new marketplace, went out of business. The surviving airlines had to cut costs, which led to a decline in the wages of airline employees. But the point of deregulation was to benefit consumers by forcing the airlines to compete. From consumers' point of view, the deregulation of the airlines was a tremendous success.[6]

Similar events took place, with similar results, in several other markets in ensuing years. Until 1980, trucking rates were set by "rate bureaus" composed of trucking firms and overseen by the Interstate Commerce Commission. The Motor Carrier Act of 1980 brought price competition to trucking. "The purpose of the legislation is clear," declared President Jimmy Carter in his signing statement. "Protective and wasteful regulations are to be replaced wherever possible by competition and the discipline of the free market. These changes will work to the benefit of all consumers." They did just that. Trucking prices declined steadily over the ensuing decade. Gains to consumers were losses to trucking firms and to truck drivers, whose wages underwent a corresponding decline.[7] But that was precisely the purpose of deregulation—to subject producers to price competition, for the benefit of consumers.

6 Steven Morrison and Clifford Winston, *The Economic Effects of Airline Deregulation* (Washington, D.C.: Brookings Institution, 1986); Elizabeth E. Bailey, David R. Graham, and Daniel P. Kaplan, *Deregulating the Airlines* (Cambridge, Mass.: MIT Press, 1985); Thomas Gale More, "U.S. Airline Deregulation: Its Effects on Passengers, Capital, and Labor," *Journal of Law & Economics* 29 (1986): 1–28.

7 John Richard Felton and Dale G. Anderson, eds., *Regulation and Deregulation of the Motor Carrier Industry* (Ames: Iowa State University Press, 1989); Dorothy Robyn, *Braking the Special Interests: Trucking Deregulation and the Politics of Policy Reform* (Chicago: University of Chicago Press, 1987); Carter's signing statement at http://www.presidency.ucsb.edu/ws/?pid=44689; Veiko Parming, *Competition and Productivity in the U.S. Trucking Industry Since Deregulation* (Cambridge,

The railroad industry was also deregulated, in the Staggers Rail Act of 1980. Price competition among railroads benefited consumers by reducing the cost of shipping goods by rail. Some railroad lines went out of business because they were unable to compete, and the surviving railroads paid lower wages than they had before. Markets in telephone service and natural gas were also opened to price competition during this period, with broadly similar results.[8]

The lesson seemed to be that elementary economics was exactly right. Regulatory schemes dating back to the 1930s insulated producers from competition. Deregulation forced these firms to compete on price, which made life more difficult for the firms and their employees, but which yielded enormous benefits for consumers. Finance was one more heavily regulated industry, also dating back to the 1930s. The consumers of finance were investors on one side and enterprises seeking investment on the other; the producers were the banks, the stock exchanges, and the various other intermediaries between the two. The experience of deregulation in the last quarter of the twentieth century suggested that here, too, deregulation could facilitate competition among producers and thus gains for consumers.

The period was one in which economic conditions were unusually conducive to this view. Between the early 1980s and the late 2000s, the volatility of economic activity declined quite sharply. Virtually every aggregate measure—output, employment, inflation—became much more stable than it had ever been. The business cycle seemed to have nearly disappeared. By 2002, economists were speaking of a "Great Moderation" that was taking place, not just in the United States but throughout the industrialized world. The "problem of depression prevention has been solved," declared the Nobel Prize winner Robert

Mass.: MIT Press, 2013); Michael H. Belzer, *Sweatshops on Wheels: Winners and Losers in Trucking Deregulation* (New York: Oxford University Press, 2000).

8 Clifford Winston, *The Success of the Staggers Rail Act of 1980*, AEI-Brookings Joint Center for Regulatory Studies Publication 05-24 (2005); Ernst R. Berndt et al., "Cost Effects of Mergers and Deregulation in the U.S. Rail Industry," *Journal of Productivity Analysis* 4 (1993): 127–44; Clifford Winston, "U.S. Industry Adjustment to Economic Deregulation," *Journal of Economic Perspectives* 12 (1998): 89–110; James Peoples, "Deregulation and the Labor Market," *Journal of Economic Perspectives* 12 (1998): 111–30.

Lucas. Ben Bernanke, then one of the governors of the Federal Reserve System, was only slightly less triumphant. He cited "the increased depth and sophistication of financial markets, deregulation in many industries, the shift away from manufacturing toward services, and increased openness to trade and international capital flows," along with "better monetary policy," as causes of what appeared to be a permanently stable economy.[9]

One persistent (although persistently disputed) rationale for limiting speculation had always been that speculators amplified the business cycle—that they made the highs even higher and the lows even lower. But if the business cycle was no longer such a serious problem, this rationale was no longer as important. The Great Moderation thus contributed to an intellectual climate receptive to deregulating financial markets, by weakening one of the traditional arguments for regulation. As the federal judge Richard Posner observed in his autopsy of the crisis, deregulation "was a government failure abetted by the political and ideological commitments of mainstream economists, who overlooked the possibility that the financial markets seemed robust because regulation had prevented previous financial crises."[10]

The intellectual climate of the late twentieth century was also influenced by a view of financial markets called the efficient market hypothesis. Here we need to be careful, because there is a misunderstanding of the efficient market hypothesis that pervades much of the post–financial crisis critique of deregulation and that

9 Steven J. Davis, "Interpreting the Great Moderation: Changes in the Volatility of Economic Activity at the Macro and Micro Levels," *Journal of Economic Perspectives* 22 (2008): 155–80; James H. Stock and Mark W. Watson, "Has the Business Cycle Changed and Why?," in *NBER Macroeconomics Annual 2002,* ed. Mark Gertler and Kenneth Rogoff (Cambridge, Mass.: MIT Press, 2003), 162; Peter M. Summers, "What Caused the Great Moderation? Some Cross-Country Evidence," *Federal Reserve Bank of Kansas City Economic Review: Third Quarter 2005,* 5–32; Robert E. Lucas Jr., "Macroeconomic Priorities," *American Economic Review* 93 (2003): 1; Ben S. Bernanke, "The Great Moderation" (remarks at the meeting of the Eastern Economic Association, 2004), http://www.federalreserve.gov/BOARDDOCS/SPEECHES/ 2004/20040220/default.htm.

10 Richard A. Posner, *A Failure of Capitalism: The Crisis of '08 and the Descent Into Depression* (Cambridge, Mass.: Harvard University Press, 2009), 260.

ascribes too much direct causal force to the EMH.[11] In correcting this mistake, however, it would be equally wrong to deny any connection between the EMH and one's view as to the propriety of regulation. The point that deserves emphasis is that this connection was more diffuse and perhaps even more emotional than is usually acknowledged.

The efficient market hypothesis simply states that the prices in a capital market (such as a stock market) fully reflect all available relevant information. The implication is that investing in stocks chosen by so-called experts will be no more profitable than investing in stocks chosen at random. The EMH was a staple of the academic literature by the early 1970s. Since then it has been criticized, defended, and restated in various forms, but in all versions it is an empirical claim about how quickly new information affects the prices of securities.[12] The EMH is not a normative claim that markets are good or that regulation is bad.

This point was sometimes lost in the aftermath of the financial crisis, when critics blamed the efficient market hypothesis for causing regulators to fall asleep at the wheel. "The upside of the current Great Recession is that it could drive a stake through the heart of the academic nostrum known as the efficient-market hypothesis," thundered the journalist Roger Lowenstein. "The mistaken faith in markets turned regulators into fawning groupies." The investor Jeremy Grantham insisted that the efficient market hypothesis "left our economic and government establishment sitting by confidently, even as a lethally dangerous combination of asset bubbles, lax controls, pernicious incentives and wickedly complicated instruments led to our current plight."[13] This sort of criticism is misdirected, if taken literally. The efficient market hypothesis has no necessary relationship to

---

11 For a forceful expression of this view, see Ray Ball, "The Global Financial Crisis and the Efficient Market Hypothesis: What Have We Learned?," *Journal of Applied Corporate Finance* 21, no. 4 (2009): 8–16.

12 Eugene F. Fama, "Efficient Capital Markets: A Review of Theory and Empirical Work," *Journal of Finance* 25 (1970): 383–417; Burton G. Malkiel, "The Efficient Market Hypothesis and Its Critics," *Journal of Economic Perspectives* 17 (2003): 59–82.

13 Roger Lowenstein, "Book Review: 'The Myth of the Rational Market,'" *Washington Post*, 7 June 2009; Joe Nocera, "Poking Holes in a Theory on Markets," *New York Times*, 6 June 2009.

the appropriate level of regulation. One can believe that stock prices incorporate all available information and simultaneously believe that certain transactions should not be allowed, for any of the reasons conventionally offered for prohibiting transactions. For example, an adherent of the EMH can still favor limits on speculating with borrowed money, on the ground that highly leveraged transactions are too risky, whether for individual speculators or for the financial system as a whole. To call the market "efficient" is merely to say that stock prices cannot be predicted; the term does not imply that whatever we observe in the market must be good.

On the other hand, there is a less direct relationship between the efficient market hypothesis and one's attitude toward financial regulation, one that may have facilitated deregulation. The EMH implies that if investors have no way of knowing whether prices are too high or too low, neither do regulators. There is no way to identify a bubble while it is occurring, or even afterward—the best one can say is that prices at the peak reflected the information available at the peak, and prices at the trough reflected the information available at the trough. When it comes to prices, regulators are no wiser than investors. A person accustomed to thinking of markets in this way can easily grow skeptical that regulators will be any wiser than investors when it comes to other matters, like whether investors have taken on too much risk, or whether investors fully understand the securities they are buying. Attitudes toward regulation are based on moods or general feelings as much as on careful analyses of the pros and cons of particular regulatory programs. This point obviously should not be taken too far. There were booms and crashes, and arguments for and against regulation, long before anyone thought of the efficient market hypothesis. The EMH did not *cause* the financial crisis or even any of the legal developments that preceded it. But the EMH may have helped to propagate a mood that was conducive to deregulation.

There was considerable weakening, at the same time, in Americans' traditional moral disapproval of gambling. In the 1970s, casino gambling was lawful only in Nevada, but by the end of the century there were casinos in nearly half the states and on many Indian reservations as well. At midcentury there were no state-run lotteries, but by the century's end almost every state ran a lottery. Denunciations of speculative financial transactions as gambling carried significant weight when gambling was generally considered a social evil, but they gradually lost their force as gambling was reconceived as a respectable activity.

Toward the end of the twentieth century, then, the intellectual climate was just right for financial deregulation. Meanwhile, the financial markets were rapidly expanding, particularly markets for derivatives, which increased the political support for deregulation.

The idea of a derivative was already centuries old. A derivative is simply an asset whose value is derived from the value of some other asset. An option to buy a share of stock is a derivative, for example; its value is determined in part by the value of the stock. The commodity futures bought and sold on boards of trade beginning in the middle of the nineteenth century were derivatives whose value depended in part on the value of the underlying bushels of wheat and corn. But if the concept of derivatives was not new, the particular *kinds* of derivatives were. In the late twentieth century, banks invented all sorts of derivative contracts that would have been impractical to trade before computers became standard equipment. The notional value of the derivatives market more than doubled between 1995 and 2001, more than doubled again between 2001 and 2004, and then more than doubled again between 2004 and 2007. More than $500 trillion of derivative contracts were outstanding by June 2007. Notional values are misleading, because they bear no necessary relationship to the values of any real assets or potential losses, but there is little doubt that the derivatives market was growing much faster than the real economy. By the end of 2007, when the notional value of the derivatives market was nearing $600 trillion, the combined worldwide value of all publicly traded stocks was less than $70 trillion.[14]

The new derivatives flourished in part because they facilitated the hedging of risks that had previously been difficult or impossible to hedge. Older derivatives like commodity futures had allowed farmers and other participants in the grain trade to protect themselves against

---

14 These figures come from the triennial reports published by the Bank for International Settlements. They are available at the bank's website, http://www .bis.org.

the risk that prices would change between one time period and another. The new derivatives allowed companies to hedge all sorts of other risks, like changes in currency exchange rates, changes in interest rates, or even bad weather. For example, a firm that had to make investments in the present in one currency but expected future revenue in a different currency could enter into a derivative contract that would allow it to remove the risk of loss from an adverse change in the exchange rate between the two currencies, by paying a counterparty to absorb that risk. A firm with obligations to pay debt at a variable interest rate but with expected income at a fixed rate could enter into a derivative contract that would allow it, in effect, to convert its variable interest to fixed interest, by swapping debt obligations with a counterparty willing to absorb the risk of adverse changes in the variable interest rate. Unlike the older, simpler derivatives, which had been standard contracts traded on exchanges, the new derivatives tended to be custom tailored to the needs of each individual purchaser and were thus not traded on exchanges. But they served the same hedging purpose as the older derivatives, by allowing parties to transfer risk, for a price, to those willing to bear it.

And, as with the older derivatives, the hedgers were only part of the market. It would be quite a coincidence if a firm wishing to hedge a particular risk could find another firm that simultaneously wished to hedge an equal and opposite risk, so the hedger's counterparty in these transactions was normally not a hedger but a speculator—someone willing to take on risk in the expectation of making a profit. And many transactions involved no hedgers at all, but rather speculators on both sides, who simply had different expectations of what the future would bring.[15] The new derivatives, like the old, thus opened up new methods of speculation.

As always, with new methods of speculation came new ways of making or losing large sums of money very quickly. Startling stories of massive losses from trading in derivatives, sometimes incurred by

---

15 Sergey Chernenko and Michael Faulkender, "The Two Sides of Derivatives Usage: Hedging and Speculating with Interest Rate Swaps," *Journal of Financial and Quantitative Analysis* 46 (2011): 1727–54.

seemingly sophisticated institutions, were recurring features in news reports throughout the 1990s.[16]

In 1994, for example, Procter & Gamble announced that it had lost $157 million in interest rate swaps. The *New York Times* wondered: "What is a soap company doing in the swap market speculating with hundreds of millions of dollars?" For many years, Procter & Gamble, like most large international companies, had used swaps to hedge against changes in exchange rates and interest rates. But in late 1993 and early 1994, Procter & Gamble agreed to two atypically large and complex contracts with Bankers Trust, in which Procter & Gamble would pay a floating interest rate to Bankers Trust in exchange for receiving a fixed interest rate from Bankers Trust. These contracts proved disastrous to Procter & Gamble when interest rates rose. The Procter & Gamble officers who were responsible for these deals apparently did not understand their full consequences, and indeed Procter & Gamble sued Bankers Trust on the theory that Bankers Trust had misled Procter & Gamble about the transactions. "Derivatives like these are dangerous and we were badly burned," Procter & Gamble's chairman told the press. "We won't let that happen again."[17]

Later that year, Orange County, California, declared bankruptcy after losing $1.65 billion from leveraged investments in derivatives with payoffs that varied inversely with interest rates. County Treasurer Robert Citron had been re-elected for more than twenty years, because he consistently earned higher returns than his counterparts in other municipalities. As it turned out, the secret of his ostensible success was that he was taking more risks than his counterparts, and when interest rates rose, the Orange County Investment Pool lost big. The elected officials who could have inquired into Citron's strategy, before it was too late, appear to have lacked the financial knowledge to understand it. It is not entirely clear whether Citron himself fully understood the

---

16 Laurent L. Jacque, *Global Derivative Debacles: From Theory to Malpractice* (Singapore: World Scientific, 2010).

17 Lawrence Malkin, "Procter & Gamble's Tale of Derivatives Woe," *New York Times*, 14 Apr. 1994; *Procter & Gamble Co. v. Bankers Trust Co.*, 925 F. Supp. 1270, 1276–77 (S.D. Ohio 1996).

risk of his investments—it was later discovered that he relied on an astrologer and a psychic to foretell the course of interest rates.[18]

Even more astonishing was the demise of Barings Bank the following year, when one of its traders in Singapore managed to lose $1.3 billion before his supervisors noticed. Barings was as well established as a bank could be. It was founded in 1762. It was the underwriter for the Louisiana Purchase. But a single employee in his twenties brought the bank to an end by speculating in derivatives linked to the Nikkei 225 stock index. When the Kobe earthquake of January 1995 caused Japanese stock prices to plummet, Barings was wiped out.[19]

Perhaps most surprising of all was the fate of Long Term Capital Management, a hedge fund run by some of the most sophisticated investors in the world. LTCM's partners included two Nobel Prize–winning economists, some former faculty members at Harvard Business School, and several veterans of the investment bank Salomon Brothers. LTCM began by engaging in nearly riskless arbitrage, but when such opportunities grew scarce the fund shifted to riskier transactions. After the Asian financial crisis of 1997 and the Russian financial crisis of 1998, LTCM lost more than $4 billion. The Federal Reserve Bank of New York organized a bailout by the fund's main creditors, to prevent other firms from failing as well.[20]

These losses seemed enormous at the time, but much larger losses would accompany the financial crisis of 2007–08. The government's bailout of the insurance company AIG, for example, totaled $182 billion, much of which AIG lost by investing indirectly but heavily in real estate, through the purchase of mortgage-backed securities and the sale of credit default swaps (effectively insurance against defaults) on securities backed largely by mortgages.[21]

---

18 Mark Baldassare, *When Government Fails: The Orange County Bankruptcy* (Berkeley: University of California Press, 1998).

19 *Report of the Board of Banking Supervision Inquiry Into the Circumstances of the Collapse of Barings* (London: HMSO, 1995).

20 Roger Lowenstein, *When Genius Failed: The Rise and Fall of Long Term Capital Management* (New York: Random House, 2000).

21 Robert McDonald and Anna Paulson, "AIG in Hindsight," *Journal of Economic Perspectives* 29, no. 2 (2015): 81–106.

The new derivatives were extraordinarily useful, because they allowed parties to hedge against risks that had previously been unhedgeable. But they were also extraordinarily dangerous, because, just like the old derivatives, they opened up forms of speculation in which even the most sophisticated investors could lose everything.

This was not a new dilemma. For two centuries Americans had argued about this tension between the positive and negative aspects of speculation. The law had shifted this way and that, in a collective effort to limit the dangers of speculation without destroying its benefits. The new derivatives markets of the late twentieth and early twenty-first centuries gave rise to the most recent installment of this debate, particularly after the market crashed in 2007–08. Had deregulation contributed to the crisis by permitting methods of speculation that would have been prohibited in an earlier era?

A WIDE RANGE OF FINANCIAL ACTIVITIES

The most conspicuous example of financial deregulation, and the one perhaps most often cited as a cause of the crisis, was the Gramm-Leach-Bliley Act of 1999.[22] The very first sentence of the law declared that it was repealing the Glass-Steagall Act of 1933, which barred commercial banks from entering the securities business. Back in 1933, the purpose of separating commercial banks from investment banks had been to prevent banks from speculating with their depositors' funds. But the wall between commercial and investment banking was knocked down with bipartisan support in Congress. "The Gramm-Leach-Bliley Act makes the most important legislative changes to the structure of the U.S. financial system since the 1930s," declared President Bill Clinton in his signing statement. "Financial services firms will be authorized to conduct a wide range of financial activities, allowing them freedom to innovate in the new economy."[23]

---

22 See, e.g., Joseph Karl Grant, "What the Financial Services Industry Puts Together Let No Person Put Asunder: How the Gramm-Leach-Bliley Act Contributed to the 2008–2009 American Capital Markets Crisis," *Albany Law Review* 73 (2010): 371–420.

23 Clinton's signing statement at http://www.presidency.ucsb.edu/ws/?pid=56922.

The Gramm-Leach-Bliley Act was a product of long-term intellectual and institutional changes. For many years, the economists who studied the issue most closely had concluded that, contrary to what was widely believed in the 1930s, the commercial banks' securities affiliates had in fact not contributed to the stock market crash of 1929 or the long depression that followed. Using statistical tools that had not been available in 1933, the economists argued that separating commercial from investment banks had been a costly mistake all along.[24]

Meanwhile, after decades of regulatory changes, the supposed barrier between commercial and investment banking had already become quite flimsy. On one side of the wall, the higher interest rates of the mid-twentieth century made commercial bank deposits unattractive from the customer's point of view, which led institutions that were not formally commercial banks to offer higher-return substitutes for bank accounts. On the other side, commercial banks repeatedly sought to re-enter the lucrative securities business. As early as 1957, the Comptroller of the Currency ruled that commercial banks could offer profit-making brokerage services for their customers. By the 1980s, the Federal Deposit Insurance Corporation and the Federal Reserve allowed commercial banks, with some restrictions, to underwrite securities. Such regulatory interpretations of the Glass-Steagall Act were by and large upheld by the courts when they were challenged. By 1999, the Gramm-Leach-Bliley

---

24 George J. Benston, *The Separation of Commercial and Investment Banking: The Glass-Steagall Act Revisited and Reconsidered* (New York: Oxford University Press, 1990); Eugene Nelson White, "Before the Glass-Steagall Act: An Analysis of the Investment Banking Activities of National Banks," *Explorations in Economic History* 23 (1986): 33–55; Randall S. Kroszner and Raghuram G. Rajan, "Is the Glass-Steagall Act Justified? A Study of the U.S. Experience with Universal Banking Before 1933," *American Economic Review* 84 (1994): 810–32; Carlos D. Ramirez, "Did Glass-Steagall Increase the Cost of External Finance for Corporate Investment? Evidence from Bank and Insurance Company Affiliations," *Journal of Economic History* 59 (1999): 372–96; Carlos D. Ramirez and J. Bradford DeLong, "Understanding America's Hesitant Steps Toward Financial Capitalism: Politics, the Depression, and the Separation of Commercial and Investment Banking," *Public Choice* 106 (2001): 93–116; Carlos D. Ramirez, "Did Banks' Security Affiliates Add Value? Evidence From the Commercial Banking Industry During the 1920s," *Journal of Money, Credit and Banking* 34 (2002): 393–411.

Act was ratifying changes that had already taken place more than it was actually making any change. "The Glass-Steagall Act was already a dead letter when Gramm-Leach-Bliley was passed," concluded the law professor Jonathan Macey. "All the Act did was formalize the death."[25]

Back in the early 1930s, much of the motivation for the Glass-Steagall Act had been the cascade of bank failures, many of which contemporaries attributed to speculation. By the late twentieth century, banks still failed, but bank failures had lost their sharp edge because of the advent of deposit insurance. Losses from bank failures were now borne by the banking system generally and by the government rather than by the particular depositors unfortunate enough to have entrusted their funds to a now-insolvent bank. In 1933, bank depositors were keen to keep their money from being sent in risky directions. In 1999, they were no longer as worried.

Because the Gramm-Leach-Bliley Act was the culmination of incremental changes rather than a major change in its own right, it makes sense to ask, not whether the act itself contributed to the financial crisis, but whether the crisis was facilitated by the gradual reblending of commercial and investment banking. The answer is almost certainly no. The Glass-Steagall Act would not have prevented any banks from making subprime mortgage loans, investing in mortgage-backed securities, or being so highly leveraged that a small drop in the value of their assets would wipe them out. The activities that commercial banks were newly allowed to enter were not the ones that lost them vast sums of money. And many of the financial institutions that lost the

25 Philip A. Wallach, "Competing Institutional Perspectives in the Life of Glass-Steagall," *Studies in American Political Development* 28 (2014): 26–48; Robert E. Lucas Jr., "Glass-Steagall: A Requiem," *American Economic Review: Papers and Proceedings* 103, no. 3 (2013): 45–46; George G. Kaufman and Larry R. Mote, "Glass-Steagall: Repeal by Regulatory and Judicial Reinterpretation," *Banking Law Journal* 107 (1990): 388–421; Donald C. Langevoort, "Statutory Obsolescence and the Judicial Process: The Revisionist Role of the Courts in Federal Banking Regulation," *Michigan Law Review* 85 (1987): 672–733; James R. Barth, R. Dan Brumbaugh Jr., and James A. Wilcox, "The Repeal of Glass-Steagall and the Advent of Broad Banking," *Journal of Economic Perspectives* 14 (2000): 191–204; Jonathan R. Macey, "The Business of Banking: Before and After Gramm-Leach-Bliley," *Journal of Corporation Law* 25 (2000): 692.

most were investment banks and insurance companies, not commercial banks, so the Glass-Steagall Act would not have constrained them. The financial crisis would most likely have looked very similar even if the Glass-Steagall Act had still been in full force.[26]

But if separating the functions of commercial and investment banks would not have prevented the financial crisis, there were many who nevertheless thought it wise for a different reason. The federal government insures the deposits in commercial banks, but there is no analogous insurance for the assets of investment banks. Deposit insurance raises two concerns: that taxpayers will be required to bail out a commercial bank that speculates unsuccessfully with its depositors' money, and that the managers of commercial banks, aware of this safety net, will take undue risks with the depositors' money. Paul Volcker, the former chair of the Federal Reserve, accordingly suggested after the crisis that commercial banks should be barred from the most speculative transactions. The idea quickly became known as the "Volcker Rule" when President Barack Obama referred to it by that name. The Volcker Rule was enacted into law as part of the Dodd-Frank Act of 2010. Commercial banks are now barred from "proprietary trading" and from owning an interest in "a hedge fund or private equity fund."[27] The transactions now off-limits to commercial banks are not exactly congruent with those once proscribed by the Glass-Steagall Act. But the purpose of the two laws is the same—to prevent banks from speculating with the funds entrusted to them by depositors.

A GIANT, GLOBAL, ELECTRONIC PONZI

A less well-known set of changes in the law, culminating in the Commodity Futures Modernization Act of 2000, has a more plausible link to the

---

26 Paul G. Mahoney, *Wasting a Crisis: Why Securities Regulation Fails* (Chicago: University of Chicago Press, 2015), 155–56; Jerry W. Markham, "The Subprime Crisis—A Test Match for the Bankers: Glass-Steagall vs. Gramm-Leach-Bliley," *University of Pennsylvania Journal of Business Law* 12 (2010): 1081–134; Lawrence J. White, "The Gramm-Leach-Bliley Act of 1999: A Bridge Too Far? Or Not Far Enough?," *Suffolk University Law Review* 43 (2010): 937–56.

27 Paul Volcker, "How to Reform Our Financial System," *New York Times*, 31 Jan. 2010; *New York Times*, 23 Jan. 2010, B1; 12 U.S.C. § 1851(a)(1).

financial crisis, although it is not clear that "deregulation" is the right word for these changes, and even here the connection to the financial crisis is uncertain.

In the 1980s, when the new derivatives became commercially significant, transactions in derivatives were still largely governed by the legal framework established in the 1920s, when the main derivatives were options and futures relating to agricultural commodities. The Grain Futures Act of 1922 had been replaced by the Commodity Exchange Act of 1936, but both statutes essentially required derivatives to be traded on organized exchanges approved by the federal government. Many states still had their anti–bucket shop laws on the books, and in principle the common law of every state still rendered unenforceable all off-exchange transactions in which the parties did not actually intend the delivery of a physical commodity. In practice, though, state law largely fell by the wayside after the enactment of the Commodity Exchange Act, which created an administrative agency, the Commodity Exchange Authority (later replaced by the Commodity Futures Trading Commission), charged with overseeing derivative trading nationwide.

At first, the new derivatives of the 1980s occupied an uncertain position within this legal framework.[28] They tended to be tailored to individual circumstances rather than being standardized products, so they were not traded on exchanges. Did that make them unlawful? In swap transactions, for example, parties exchanged future cash flows. "The economic reality of swaps," the CFTC observed, "resembles that of futures contracts." But *were* they futures contracts? If so, they were illegal if they were not traded on an exchange, and they were subject to the full array of CFTC regulation. In 1989, the CFTC determined that swaps were not futures contracts so long as, among other things, their terms were individually tailored and they were entered into "in conjunction with a line of business"—that is, they were limited to hedgers and financial institutions. The CFTC declared that it would

28 This discussion compresses and simplifies an intricate story; for more details, see Philip McBride Johnson and Thomas Lee Hazen, *Derivatives Regulation* (New York: Aspen, 2004), 1:50–85.

not regulate such transactions.[29] In later years the CFTC would issue similar determinations for other new kinds of derivatives.

But that only raised a new question. If the new derivatives were not subject to CFTC regulation, did that mean they were governed by state law instead? Could a state court condemn them as gambling transactions in violation of state anti–bucket shop statutes or the common-law prohibition on contracts without intent to deliver? Congress ended this uncertainty three years later, by declaring that federal law in this area preempted state law. The Futures Trading Practices Act of 1992 provided that derivatives were not subject to "any State or local law that prohibits or regulates gaming or the operation of 'bucket shops.' "[30] The new derivatives had cleared the last legal hurdle.

Some government officials were uncomfortable with allowing unfettered derivatives trading. In 1994, on the same day that Procter & Gamble announced it had lost $157 million in swaps, the House Banking Committee held hearings on the topic. The purchaser of a derivative is "entering into a gamble," worried Representative Henry Gonzalez of Texas, the committee chair. "I picture it as an inverted pyramid where the apex is a basic nominal value and then derived up to this tremendous base are offshoots of all these formidable definitions and forms of derivatives." As Gonzalez saw the new market, participants were not profiting "in the usual financial term of things, but by out and out gambling." He foresaw "the possibility of a giant, global, electronic Ponzi" that one day would come crashing down. The financier George Soros shared Gonzalez's concern. "Some of those instruments appear to be specifically designed to enable institutional investors to take gambles which they would not otherwise be permitted to take," he explained. "For example, some bond funds have invested in synthetic bond issues which carry a tenfold or twentyfold multiple of the normal risk within defined limits. And some other instruments offer exceptional returns because they carry the seeds of a total wipeout." If a meltdown were to occur, Soros noted, "the regulatory authorities may find themselves obliged to step in to preserve the integrity of the system. It is in that

29 "Policy Statement Concerning Swap Transactions," *Federal Register* 54 (1989): 30694.
30 106 Stat. 3590, 3631–32 (1992).

light that the authorities have both the right and an obligation to supervise and regulate derivative instruments."[31]

Within the Clinton administration, the leading voice in favor of regulation was the Washington lawyer Brooksley Born, who was chair of
the CFTC between 1996 and 1999. Born repeatedly urged greater government oversight of the ballooning derivatives market, particularly the
idea of requiring buyers and sellers of derivatives to make disclosures of
their financial positions so their counterparties would be able to evaluate their creditworthiness. "No reporting requirements are imposed
on most OTC derivatives market participants," she observed shortly
after the collapse of Long Term Capital Management, in a speech that
would look quite prescient a decade later. "This lack of basic information about the positions held by OTC derivatives users and about the
nature and extent of their exposures potentially allows OTC derivatives
market participants to take positions that may threaten our regulatory
markets or, indeed, our economy without the knowledge of any federal regulatory authority."[32] But Born's view was not shared by senior
government economic officials, including Treasury Secretary Robert
Rubin and Federal Reserve Chair Alan Greenspan, who believed that
market participants already had every incentive to evaluate their counterparties' creditworthiness. "Individuals who lend money to others,"
Greenspan responded, "have a very important interest in getting that
money back."[33]

Instead, the Clinton administration went in the opposite direction.
The President's Working Group on Financial Markets, made up of
Greenspan, Lawrence Summers (Rubin's successor as Treasury secretary),
William Rainer (Born's successor as CFTC chair), and Arthur Levitt
(the chair of the Securities and Exchange Commission), concluded

---

31 *Risks That Hedge Funds Pose to the Banking System: Hearing Before the Committee
    on Banking, Finance and Urban Affairs* (Washington, D.C.: Government
    Printing Office, 1994), 14, 38.

32 Richard B. Schmitt, "The Born Prophecy," *ABA Journal*, May 2009, 50–55;
    Brooksley Born, "The Lessons of Long-Term Capital Management L.P." (Oct.
    15, 1998), http://www.cftc.gov/opa/speeches/opaborn-37.htm. "OTC" stands
    for "over the counter"—that is, not traded on an exchange.

33 Greenspan quoted in Sebastian Mallaby, *More Money Than God: Hedge Funds
    and the Making of a New Elite* (New York: Penguin, 2010), 245.

in 1999 that all trading of financial derivatives by sophisticated participants like banks and pension funds should be exempt from the regulatory regime that had long applied to the older commodity-based derivatives. Congress implemented this proposal the following year with overwhelming bipartisan support. The Commodity Futures Modernization Act of 2000 provided that financial derivatives were not subject to the requirement of being traded on an exchange and were not otherwise subject to the rules governing the older derivatives.[34]

Whether to call this "deregulation" depends on one's opinion of what the law had been before. There are two plausible ways to tell the story. On one view, ever since the 1920s, the organized exchanges had held a government-mandated monopoly on the trading of derivatives, so that market participants would have some assurance that their counterparties would not default. That monopoly was broken by the Commodity Futures Modernization Act, which allowed derivatives to be traded outside of exchanges, thus removing the protections against default that had wisely been in place for three-quarters of a century. If we tell the story this way, it is a tale of deregulation. On the other view, the system of regulation adopted in the 1920s was for the older agricultural derivatives. When the new financial derivatives began to be traded, there was genuine uncertainty as to whether the old rules should apply to the new circumstances. The Commodity Futures Modernization Act removed this uncertainty by clarifying that only the older derivatives had to be traded on exchanges, thus freeing up sophisticated institutional traders to buy and sell financial derivatives among one another. This was the view taken by the President's Working Group on Financial Markets, who argued that exempting the new derivatives was necessary because "uncertainty arises from concerns under current law as to whether some of these contracts could be construed to be subject to the" Commodity Exchange Act. And it was the view taken by Congress: the title of the relevant section of the Commodity Futures Modernization Act is "Legal Certainty for Excluded Derivative Transactions."[35] If we tell the

34 *Over-the-Counter Derivatives Markets and the Commodity Exchange Act: Report of the President's Working Group on Financial Markets* (Nov. 1999), http://www .treasury.gov/resource-center/fin-mkts/Documents/otcact.pdf; 114 Stat. 2763A (2000), at 377, 404.

35 *Over-the-Counter Derivatives Markets*, 6; 114 Stat. 2763A (2000), at 377.

story this way, "nonregulation" would be a better word than "deregulation," because it was not clear that there was any preexisting law that had been removed.

But it makes little difference what we call it. Either way, there can be little doubt that speculation in the new derivatives was facilitated by exempting them from the rules governing the old derivatives, especially the requirement of being traded on an exchange. Some of the new derivatives were custom tailored to the hedging needs of particular firms and were thus impractical to trade on an exchange. To require such contracts to be traded on an exchange would have been equivalent to prohibiting them. Other derivatives were more amenable to standardization. They could have been traded on an exchange, and indeed after the crisis the Dodd-Frank Act of 2010 directed the CFTC to establish such an exchange, along with a method of clearing transactions modeled on the clearinghouses that had long been used in commodity trading. It is likely that the absence of such requirements before 2010 helped the market grow so quickly.

The resulting increase in speculation may not have *caused* the financial crisis, but it almost certainly contributed to the size of the crisis. There is, of course, no shortage of competing theories as to what caused the crisis. But any plausible explanation of the *magnitude* of the crisis has to take some account of the massive amount of mortgage-backed derivatives held by financial institutions, and the likewise massive amount of credit default swaps linked to the health of those institutions. The root cause of the problem may have been imprudent lending to homebuyers who would be unable to pay back their loans unless housing prices kept rising. No doubt all this lending would have led to a crisis even without speculation in derivatives. There have been similar boom-and-bust cycles for centuries, including in real estate, without the benefit of exotic new financial products.[36] But much of the money available to lend was provided by investors in derivatives backed by these mortgages. Without all this capital coming into the

---

36 Andrew W. Lo, "Reading About the Financial Crisis: A Twenty-One-Book Review," *Journal of Economic Literature* 50 (2012): 151–78; Carmen M. Reinhart and Kenneth S. Rogoff, *This Time Is Different: Eight Centuries of Financial Folly* (Princeton, N.J.: Princeton University Press, 2009).

mortgage market, the lending might well have tapered off sooner, so the crisis might not have been as severe. And when the housing bubble burst, the firms facing insolvency were not just the banks that held mortgage loans. Equally imperiled were a host of other institutions that held derivatives linked to those loans, derivatives that had not existed in previous housing bubbles. Speculation in derivatives thus may have made the crisis more pervasive than it would otherwise have been.

After the crisis, some urged the prohibition of derivatives that are used primarily for speculation (in the sense that they are bought and sold because market participants have different expectations about the future) rather than for some other purpose such as hedging. As the title of one such effort put it, trading in such derivatives was simply "gambling by another name."[37] "Financial products are socially beneficial when they help people insure risks," reasoned one pair of authors, "but when those same products are used for gambling they can instead be socially detrimental." After earlier market downturns, critics had likewise urged that new financial products should be banned. Defenders of the market had always responded by pointing out how difficult it would be to distinguish the harmful transactions from the beneficial ones. The most recent crisis once again elicited these arguments. Would it even be possible for government officials to distinguish trading motivated by hedging from trading motivated by differences in beliefs about the future? Were purely speculative traders necessary to make a market for traders wishing to hedge, in the same way that insurance would be impossible to buy without the existence of insurance companies? Were hedgers actually distinct entities from speculators, or did hedgers

---

37 Timothy E. Lynch, "Gambling by Another Name: The Challenge of Purely Speculative Derivatives," *Stanford Journal of Law, Business & Finance* 17 (2011): 67–130; Saule T. Omarova, "License to Deal: Mandatory Approval of Complex Financial Products," *Washington University Law Review* 90 (2012): 63–140; Eric A. Posner and E. Glen Weyl, "An FDA for Financial Innovation: Applying the Insurable Interest Doctrine to Twenty-First-Century Financial Markets," *Northwestern University Law Review* 107 (2013): 1307–57. For an earlier suggestion along similar lines, see Lynn A. Stout, "Why the Law Hates Speculators: Regulation and Private Ordering in the Market for OTC Derivatives," *Duke Law Journal* 48 (1999): 701–86.

speculate too?[38] Such questions were no easier to answer in the early twenty-first century than they had been in earlier eras.

Among the questions raised by the financial crisis were thus some that Americans had debated for more than two centuries. In the twenty-first century, as in preceding centuries, virtually everyone agreed that investment was necessary and should be encouraged. While gambling had shed some of its moral stigma, virtually everyone agreed that gambling was often harmful and thus that it should be discouraged or even prohibited. As always, speculation lay somewhere in the middle. Before one could form an opinion about how best to regulate speculators, one needed to distinguish between two kinds of risky commercial transactions, the good and the bad. Drawing that line has never been easy, and it has not become any easier today.

---

38 Posner and Weyl, "An FDA for Financial Innovation," 1308; Darrell Duffie, "Challenges to a Policy Treatment of Speculative Trading Motivated by Differences in Beliefs," *Journal of Legal Studies* 43 (2014): S173–82; Ing-Haw Cheng and Wei Xiong, "Why Do Hedgers Trade So Much?," *Journal of Legal Studies* 43 (2014): S183–207.

INDEX